Hopkins collected at Gonzaga

Ruth Seelhammer

LOYOLA UNIVERSITY PRESS
Chicago   60657

MANLEY HOPKINS ROOM

Filiis Ignatii

Gerardi Fratribus

D D D

R S

Foreword

Recently news has come of a Hopkins Society being formed in England to promote the study and appreciation of Hopkins' poetry. It is good news indeed, but it also may give to us former colonials the glow of satisfaction reserved for pioneers. And the remarkable collection at Crosby Library is one of the outstanding evidences of the interest American scholars have taken in Hopkins' work.

During my own work with this collection I learned to appreciate first-hand the advantages of having not only the primary and secondary sources, in various editions, at one's elbow, but the usefulness and broadening suggestiveness of having as well so many of the central and peripheral probable and possible background sources.

This Hopkins collection, under the inspiration and guidance of Crosby Library's learned director and with the cooperation of his friendly and competent staff, has well served the cause of literature. Not only Gonzaga University but the academic and cultural communities of our country have already drawn large profit from it. May it in the years ahead make even greater progress in its aim to serve those concerned with the greatest of the fine arts!

Robert Boyle, S.J.
Marquette University

Preface

Trees, for Gerard Manley Hopkins, were fascinating as subject and as object. Among the numerous references in his journals there are the Spanish chestnut, the ash clusters like grapes, the thickleaved alder, the starrily tasselled elms, the early sycomores (Hopkins' spelling), the tall larches and the two great spreading laurels. There is also reference to the birch, in one instance the leaves. "Birch leaves on a fading tree give three colours, green, white and yellow."

One of the birch doors in Crosby Library at Gonzaga University has on it a sign which reads "Gerard Manley Hopkins." To open this door and to enter the room is to find there the material which occasions this work since this is a listing of the published works of Hopkins and the published and some of the unpublished works about Hopkins in the Gonzaga University Collection of Gerard Manley Hopkins.

The collection, begun before the room existed, was moved into a room of its own in November of 1957 at the time the library which Bing Crosby gave to his Alma Mater was to be formally opened. The first architectural drawings of Crosby Library, at the instigation of Father Clifford Carroll, S.J., Librarian of the University at that time, included space for the Hopkins Room. To him it was a matter not merely of acquiring but also of preserving the material so worthy of protection for future use and admiration.

Among the writers who have themselves published work on Hopkins, the Library staff has been privileged to welcome as visitors to the Hopkins Room the Jesuit Fathers Martin D'Arcy, Robert Boyle, W. A. M. Peters, Gerald F. Lahey and Walter Ong. Not to be forgotten is the late Father William T. Costello, S.J., who was himself a poet. His intimacy with the words of Hopkins would often "flame out" during the years he headed Gonzaga University's English Department to the inspiration of those who were fortunate enough to be within the range of his presence.

The collection originated with Father Anthony Bischoff, S.J., who did research on Hopkins in England and Ireland while gathering material for his Yale University doctoral dissertation of 1952. It has continued to benefit from his favor through the years since then.

Once the collection was housed in suitable space a serious and earnest attempt was made, under Father Carroll's direction, to augment the original material in every possible way. Father Bischoff's continuing interest has been most helpful. In January of 1962 Anna Elizabeth Speyrer, Father Carroll's then Assistant Librarian, finished the preparation of a bibliography of the collection as partial fulfillment of the requirements for the Master of Arts degree at Gonzaga University. There are 911 numbered items in the Speyrer bibliography.

That number of acquisitions has more than tripled in the seven years since that time. This has been accomplished, as a first step, by consulting every potential source of reference to material on Hopkins which has come into the Library. In addition to all the ordinary exhaustive bibliographical checking which would have been done for any Victorian poet, and the checking of each bibliography of each book and thesis on Hopkins that has come into the collection, every book coming into the Library that might have any possible connection was checked for an index reference to Hopkins.

As each new item was discovered, if not already in the Library, an attempt was made to obtain it either in its original or in its facsimile form. The cooperation from the Pacific Northwest Bibliographical Center, under the direction of Mollie Hollreigh, has been outstanding as was that of various libraries over the world. Particularly gratifying was the generous response to requests for permission to copy certain materials which were simply not available in their original state.

Judgment as to whether a work has much or little value has not been the deciding factor for inclusion in this listing. The Japanese proverb to which we have adverted reads "Ko no kusuri wa otsu no doku." If we may say, then, that "the medicine of one is the poison of another," a brief reference from one who understands a significance in Hopkins can be of more overwhelming import than countless paragraphs by another who does not.

One limiting element has been that it is published works, principally, which are included here although theses and dissertations have not been excluded. There are of course manuscript materials and original documents in the collection and others belonging to it which are not available at this time since they have not yet been deposited in the collection itself. In their entirety these are of such scope as to make them, when they do become available, the source of great value in a different way.

The location of material is unessential to a bibliographical listing but the location to a research scholar is everything. The material here listed is of immediate availability. Father Carroll, now Director of Libraries of the University, has taken the kind of interest and provided the means to make this possible. The personal interest shown by his staff, which has gone to great lengths to assist ungrudgingly in the acquisition and compilation, has expressed itself in diverse and at times in unexpected and original ways.

This preface does not celebrate Hopkins for the bibliography as a whole is a celebration, as are the works that lie in the collection, to the man who could not pass a tree without seeing the color of the leaves. The Japanese have an anthology of poetry in twenty volumes, from an early period of their history, called the Manyoshu--"Collection of Ten Thousand Leaves." The registry of these works concerning Hopkins which are housed in Crosby Library is offered with the thought that if the number of listings could triple with such rapidity, ten thousand leaves on the tree of Hopkins scholarship are not at all unthinkable.

Ruth Seelhammer
Crosby Library
Gonzaga University

CONTENTS

ILLUSTRATIONS

I Works by Hopkins

THE WRECK OF THE DEUTSCHLAND.

This great disaster in the North Sea, which was commented upon, as well as the terrible colliery explosions, in our leading article of last week, has continued to engage attention. Our Artist went out to see and sketch the wreck on the Thursday morning, as will appear from one of the Illustrations now given. Another shows the Harwich tug steamer Liverpool, on the Tuesday, lying close alongside the wreck, and the crowding on board to rescue the survivors of the crew and passengers, who had been twenty-eight hours clinging to the wreck. This scene is most correctly as well as vividly delineated by our Artist, who went out in the tug, by permission of Mr. Carrington, its worthy master. There is no life-boat stationed at Harwich, and the want of such provision has been remarked since the late shipwreck, with much regret. It is now to be supplied by the gift of the Earl of Strafford, having been recommended by the Royal National Life-Boat Institution. The conduct of some part of the shore boatmen or "smacks-men," but certainly not of them all, when they got aboard the Deutschland, has also been mentioned with disapproval. Those to whose behaviour we refer showed more alacrity on the Wednesday and Thursday in stripping the saloon and cabins of valuable property than in any other service. Our Artist, having been a witness to this proceeding on the second day named, gives his evidence in the form of a sketch, the perfect veracity of which may be relied upon. The *Times* of Monday last, in a letter from its own reporter, contains ample information on this painful subject. We now add some precise details of the whole sad affair to our brief report of last week.

The Deutschland was a screw steam-ship belonging to the North German Lloyd's Company, and employed on the line from Bremen to New York, touching at Southampton. She was not registered at Lloyd's in London, but was entered in the "Liverpool Underwriters' Book of Iron Vessels." She was of British build, and was launched by Messrs. Caird, of Greenock, in 1866. She was 328 ft. long, 26 deep, and 40 beam. Her engines were two of direct action, of 600-horse power in all. Her registered tonnage was 2690 under deck, 2898 gross, 1971 net. She had five bulkheads—that is to say, she was in six compartments. This ship had eight large boats, of which either two or three were life-boats. The boats thus provided were enough for more than a hundred passengers and a hundred seamen. She is said by the owners' agents to have had on board no less than 1000 life-belts. The 'tween-decks, where the steerage passengers slept, were "roofed" with these appliances, and there was a life-belt at the head of every first and second class passenger's bunk. At Southampton she would have taken on board more passengers and the English mails, which the company has been in the habit of carrying during fourteen years. She had both a Weser pilot and an English Channel pilot on board when she struck; and her master, Captain Brickenstein, had been many years in the service of the company.

The inquiry now commenced should account by some explana-

I Works by Hopkins

1 "Ad Mariam," Stonyhurst Magazine, 5 (February, 1894), 233.

2 The Correspondence of Gerard Manley Hopkins and Richard Watson Dixon, edited by Claude Colleer Abbott. London: Oxford University Press, 1935.

3 The Correspondence of Gerard Manley Hopkins and Richard Watson Dixon, edited by Claude Colleer Abbott. 2nd impression, rev. London: Oxford University Press, 1955. [Title page autographed by editor.]

4 "A Curious Halo," Nature, 27 (November 16, 1882), 53.

5 "Dorothea and Theophilus," Dublin Review, 167 (July, 1920), 45-6.

6 "Early Poems and Extracts from the Notebooks and Papers of Gerard Manley Hopkins," Criterion, 15 (October, 1935), 1-17.

7 "Extracts from Hopkins' 'Journal'," edited by J.G. MacLeod, S.J., Letters and Notices, 28 (April, 1906), 390-401.

8 "Extracts from Hopkins' 'Journal'," edited by J.G. MacLeod, S.J., Letters and Notices, 29 (April, October, 1907), 129-35, 270-81.

9 "Football Barefoot" (Letter to the Editor from 'Gymnosophist,' dated Sept. 17,1888), Stonyhurst Magazine, No. 40 (November, 1888), 236-37. [Reprinted and authenticated as a letter written by Gerard Manley Hopkins in Stonyhurst Magazine, 31 (April, 1953), 168-69.]

10 Further Letters of Gerard Manley Hopkins Including his Correspondence with Coventry Patmore, edited by Claude Colleer Abbott. London: Oxford University Press, 1938.

11 Further Letters of Gerard Manley Hopkins Including his Correspondence with Coventry Patmore, edited by Claude Colleer Abbott. 2nd impression, rev. and enl. London: Oxford University Press, 1956. [Title page autographed by editor.]

12 Further Letters of Gerard Manley Hopkins Including his
    Correspondence with Coventry Patmore, edited by
    Claude Colleer Abbott. rev. page proofs. London:
    Oxford University Press, gatherings dated 12
    October 1955 through 16 August 1956.
13 Further Letters of Gerard Manley Hopkins Including his
    Correspondence with Coventry Patmore, edited by
    Claude Colleer Abbott. 2nd ed., rev. London:
    Oxford University Press, 1956. [Uncorrected proof
    copy.]
14 Gedichte, Schriften, Briefe, translated by Wolfgang and
    Ursula Clemen. Munich: Kosel-Verlag, 1954.
15 "God's Grandeur," Land and Home, 9 (June, 1946), 46.
16 "Heaven Haven," Living Age, 236 (January 10, 1903),
    128.
17 "His Prose (Extracts from Diaries in the possession of
    Father Keating, S.J.)," Dublin Review, 167 (July,
    1920), 58–66.
18 A Hopkins Reader, edited by John Pick. London: Oxford
    University Press, 1953.
19 A Hopkins Reader, edited by John Pick. New York:
    Oxford University Press, 1953.
20 A Hopkins Reader, edited by John Pick. rev. and enl. ed.
    New York: Doubleday & Company, Inc., Image Books,
    1966.
21 "Iesu, Dulcis Memoria," "Odi Profanum Vulgus," and
    "Persicos Odi," translated by Gerard Manley Hopkins,
    America, 77 (September 6, 1947), 633–35.
22 "Iesu Dulcis Memoria," translated by Gerard Manley
    Hopkins, Month, 184 (October, 1947), 182–83.
23 The Journals and Papers of Gerard Manley Hopkins,
    edited by Humphry House, completed by Graham
    Storey. London: Oxford University Press, 1959.
24 The Letters of Gerard Manley Hopkins to Robert Bridges,
    edited by Claude Colleer Abbott. London: Oxford
    University Press, 1935.
25 The Letters of Gerard Manley Hopkins to Robert Bridges,
    edited by Claude Colleer Abbott. 2nd impression, rev.
    London: Oxford University Press, 1955. [Title page
    autographed by editor.]
26 "The May Magnificat," Sheed & Ward's Own Trumpet,
    No. 27 (April–May, 1951), 1. [Reprinted from The
    Mary Book.]
27 "Milton (translated from Dryden)," Stonyhurst Magazine,
    1 (July, 1881), 35.

28 "Il Mistero Dei Magi," l'Illustrazione Italiana (Milan), (June, 1961), 34-7. [Unidentified translation into Italian.]

29 "Nativity Hymn," translated by Ronald Knox, Tablet (London), 168 (December 26, 1936), 897-98.

30 Le Naufrage du Deutschland, translated by Pierre Leyris. Paris: Editions du Seuil, 1964.

31 Il Naufragio del Deutschland: La Fine Dell'Euridice, translated by Augusto Guidi. Brescia: Morcelliana, 1947.

32 "Nondum," Month, 126 (September, 1915), 246.

33 The Note-Books and Papers of Gerard Manley Hopkins, edited by Humphry House. London: Oxford University Press, 1937. [Inscribed by author to D. A. Bischoff. Second edition, 1959, is comprised of The Journals and Papers of Gerard Manley Hopkins, edited by Humphry House, completed by Graham Storey, and The Sermons and Devotional Writings of Gerard Manley Hopkins, edited by Christopher Devlin, S.J.]

34 "O Jesu Vivens in Maria," translated by Gerard Manley Hopkins, Harvester, 11 (1949), 111.

35 "An Old English Rhythm Revived" (Editor's title). Discussions of Poetry: Rhythm and Sound, edited by George Hemphill. Boston: D. C. Heath and Co., 1961, 47-9. [Reprinted from "Author's Preface" to Poems of Gerard Manley Hopkins, edited by Robert Bridges. London: Oxford University Press, 1930, 1-6.]

36 "Out of Captivity," Living Age, 302 (September 13, 1919), 704.

37 "Pages from Hopkins' Journal," Griffin (New York), 2 (July, 1953), 27-9.

38 "The Paraclete," Catholic Worker, 20 (June, 1954), 1. [Sermon excerpt]

39 "Pied Beauty," Good Housekeeping, 134 (May, 1952), 4.

40 "Pied Beauty," Housewife (London), (July, 1951), 51.

41 "Pied Beauty," Scholastic, 47 (November 19, 1945), 15.

42 "Poeme par Gerard Manley Hopkins," translated by Jean Mambrino, Christus Cahiers, No. 3 (July, 1954), 7-15.

43 Poems and Prose of Gerard Manley Hopkins, edited by W. H. Gardner. Melbourne: Penguin Books, 1953.

44 Poems and Prose of Gerard Manley Hopkins, edited by
    W. H. Gardner. Melbourne: Penguin Books, 1953.
    [Final page proofs corrected by W. H. Gardner.
    Inscribed "For Fr. A. Bischoff, S. J., with kind
    regards from W. H. Gardner."]

45 Poems and Prose of Gerard Manley Hopkins, edited by
    W. H. Gardner. Harmondsworth, Middlesex:
    Penguin Books, 1953, reprinted 1954.

46 Poems and Prose of Gerard Manley Hopkins, edited by
    W. H. Gardner. Harmondsworth, Middlesex:
    Penguin Books, 1953, reprinted 1956.

47 Poems and Prose of Gerard Manley Hopkins, edited by
    W. H. Gardner. Baltimore: Penguin Books, 1953,
    reprinted 1966.

48 Poems by Gerard Manley Hopkins and John Keats, read
    by Margaret Rawlings. Phonodisc. London: Argo
    Record Company Limited, n.d. [John Carroll, editor;
    program notes by Harley Usill on slipcase.]

49 Poems of Gerard Manley Hopkins, edited by Robert
    Bridges. London: Humphrey Milford, 1918.

50 Poems of Gerard Manley Hopkins, edited by Robert
    Bridges. 2nd ed. London: Humphrey Milford, Oxford
    University Press, 1930.

51 Poems of Gerard Manley Hopkins, edited by Robert
    Bridges. 2nd ed. London: Humphrey Milford, Oxford
    University Press, 1930. [Inscribed "For Father
    Anthony from Lionel Hopkins, 13 October 1947."]

52 Poems of Gerard Manley Hopkins, edited by Robert
    Bridges. 2nd ed. London: Oxford University Press,
    1930, reprinted in The Oxford Bookshelf, May, 1937.

53 Poems of Gerard Manley Hopkins, edited by Robert
    Bridges. 2nd ed. London: Oxford University Press,
    1930, reprinted July, 1940.

54 Poems of Gerard Manley Hopkins, edited by Robert Bridges.
    2nd ed. London: Oxford University Press, 1930,
    reprinted 1944.

55 Poems of Gerard Manley Hopkins, edited by W. H.
    Gardner. 3rd ed. London: Geoffrey Cumberlege,
    Oxford University Press, 1947. [Uncorrected proof
    copy.]

56 Poems of Gerard Manley Hopkins, edited by W. H.
    Gardner. 3rd ed. New York: Geoffrey Cumberlege,
    Oxford University Press, 1948.

57 Poems of Gerard Manley Hopkins, edited by W. H.
    Gardner. 3rd ed. London: Geoffrey Cumberlege,
    Oxford University Press, 1948, third impression, 1950.
58 Poems of Gerard Manley Hopkins, edited by W. H.
    Gardner. London: Geoffrey Cumberlege, Oxford
    University Press, 1948, fourth impression, 1952.
59 Poems of Gerard Manley Hopkins, edited by W. H.
    Gardner. London: Geoffrey Cumberlege, Oxford
    University Press, 1948, fifth impression, rev., 1956.
60 Poems of Gerard Manley Hopkins, edited by W. H.
    Gardner. London: Geoffrey Cumberlege, Oxford
    University Press, 1948. [Corrected page proofs dated
    4 February 1947 through 23 April 1947. Includes
    corrections typed by W. H. Gardner. Incomplete set.]
61 Poems of Gerard Manley Hopkins, edited by W. H.
    Gardner. 3rd English edition; 1st American edition.
    New York, London: Oxford University Press, 1948,
    third printing, 1950.
62 Poems of Gerard Manley Hopkins, edited by W. H.
    Gardner and N. H. MacKenzie. 4th ed. New York:
    Oxford University Press, 1967.
63 Poems of Gerard Manley Hopkins, edited by W. H.
    Gardner and N. H. MacKenzie. 4th ed. New York:
    Oxford University Press, 1967. [Page proofs
    inscribed by co-editor Norman MacKenzie.]
64 Poems of Gerard Manley Hopkins . Mt. Vernon, New
    York: Peter Pauper Press, [195-?].
65 The Poems of Gerard Manley Hopkins, read by Richard
    Gray. Phonodisc. New York: Spirit Records 1001,
    1965. [Biographical notes by John F. McKinney on
    slipcase. Texts of the 35 poems inserted. Cover
    design from an original sketch of Hopkins.]
66 The Poems of William Blake and Gerard Manley Hopkins,
    read by Robert Speaight. Phonodisc. New Rochelle,
    New York: Spoken Arts, Inc. 814, 1961. [Includes 16
    Hopkins works. Presented by Arthur Luce Klein.
    Cover design by Howard Russo.]
67 Poesie di G. M. Hopkins, translated by Augusto Guidi.
    Collezione Fenice, No. 10, edited by Attilio
    Bertolucci. Parma: Guanda, 1942.
68 Poesie e Prose Scelte dal Diario, dalle Prediche e dalla
    Corrispondenza, translated by Augusto Guidi.
    Collana Fenice, N.S. No. 15, edited by Giacinto
    Spagnoletti. Parma: Guanda, 1965.

69 The Poetry of Gerard Manley Hopkins, read by Cyril Cusack. Phonodisc. New York: Caedmon Publishers TC 1111, [1958]. [Howard O. Sackler, director; program notes by George N. Shuster on slipcase.]

70 Reliquiae: Vers Proses Dessins, translated by Pierre Leyris. Paris: Editions du Seuil, 1957.

71 "The Remarkable Sunsets," Nature, 29 (January 3, 1884), 222-23.

72 "Rosa Mystica," Irish Monthly, 26 (May, 1898), 234-35.

73 "Rosa Mystica," Month, 133 (May, 1919), 339-40. [Reprinted from Irish Monthly, 26 (May, 1898), 234-35.]

74 "St. Thecla: An Unpublished Poem," Month, N.S. 16 (July, 1956), 12-13.

75 "St. Thecla: An Unpublished Poem," Studies, 45 (Summer, 1956), 186-87. [Includes "Editor's Note" initialed R.B.S.]

76 Selected Poems. London: Nonesuch Press, 1954. [Numbers 6 and 120 of 1100 copies printed.]

77 Selected Poems of Gerard Manley Hopkins, edited by James Reeves. The Poetry Bookshelf. Melbourne: W. Heinemann, 1953.

78 Selected Poems of Gerard Manley Hopkins, edited by James Reeves. The Poetry Bookshelf. New York: Macmillan, 1957.

79 Selections from the Note-Books of Gerard Manley Hopkins, edited by T. Weiss. The Poets of the Year Series. Norfolk, Connecticut: New Directions, 1937.

80 Selections from the Note-Books of Gerard Manley Hopkins, edited by T. Weiss. The Poets of the Year Series. Norfolk, Connecticut: New Directions, 1945.

81 The Sermons and Devotional Writings of Gerard Manley Hopkins, edited by Christopher Devlin, S.J. London: Oxford University Press, 1959.

82 The Sermons and Devotional Writings of Gerard Manley Hopkins, edited by Christopher Devlin, S.J. London: Oxford University Press, 1959. [Revised page proofs dated 21 July 1958, 24 April, 12 May through 21 July 1958. Complete set.]

83 The Sermons and Devotional Writings of Gerard Manley Hopkins, edited by Christopher Devlin, S.J. London: Oxford University Press, 1959. [Page proofs. First gathering is revision of 21 July 1958. Remaining gatherings dated 24 April, 12 May through 21 July 1958. Incomplete set.]

84 "The Sermons of Gerard Manley Hopkins" Pt. 1 [Sermon on the Paraclete], Tablet (London), 168 (November 14, 1936), 665-68.

85 "The Sermons of Gerard Manley Hopkins" Pt. 2, Tablet (London), 168 (November 21, 1936), 703-04.

86 "The Sermons of Gerard Manley Hopkins" Pt. 3, Tablet (London), 168 (November 28, 1936), 739-40.

87 "The Sermons of Gerard Manley Hopkins" Pt. 4, Tablet (London), 168 (December 5, 1936), 772.

88 "The Sermons of Gerard Manley Hopkins" Pt. 5, Tablet (London), 168 (December 12, 1936), 830-31.

89 "The Sermons of Gerard Manley Hopkins" Pt. 6, Tablet (London), 168 (December 19, 1936), 864-65.

90 "Shadow-Beams in the East at Sunset," Nature, 29 (November 15, 1883), 55.

91 "The Silver Jubilee," "Morning, Midday and Evening Sacrifice," and "At the Wedding March" (Poets' Column), New York Times Book Review, (September 12, 1948), 2.

92 "Simeon the Stileite," Partisan Review, 15 (February, 1948), 150. [Drawing]

93 Some Poems of Gerard Manley Hopkins . London: Michael White, 1945.

94 "The Song of Chaucer's Clerk of Oxenford, 'Angelus ad Virginem'," Month , 44 (January, 1882), 100-111. [Modernization of Chaucer's hymn, published anonymously.]

95 "Songs from Shakspeare, in Latin. No. 1. 'Full fathom five thy father lies'," Irish Monthly, 14 (November, 1886), 628. [Hopkins' translation into Latin, published anonymously.]

96 "Songs from Shakspere in Latin. No. II.--'Come Unto these Yellow Sands'," Irish Monthly, 15 (February, 1887), 92. [Hopkins' translation into Latin, printed over "G.H."]

97 "Spelt from Sibyl's Leaves," Ave Maria, 75 (May 10, 1952), 582.

98 "Spring and Fall," Classical Bulletin, 33 (March, 1957), 33. [First eleven lines only.]

99 "The Superb Images," VVV, 1 (June, 1942), 26. [Opening lines of "The Windhover."]

100 "To him who ever thought of me . . . . ," Pilgrim, 62 (Summer, 1950), 12.

101 "A Trio of Triolets," Stonyhurst Magazine, 1 (March, 1883), 162.

102 "Two Translations by Gerard Manley Hopkins: New English Version of two Odes of Horace," Tablet (London), 190 (September 27, 1947), 199.

103 "An Uncollected Letter of Gerard Manley Hopkins," Dublin Review, 239 (Autumn, 1965), 289-92.

104 "Unpublished Journal of Fr. G. M. Hopkins," Month, N.S. 4 (December, 1950), 375-84. [Extracts]

105 A Vision of the Mermaids. London: Humphrey Milford, Oxford University Press, 1929. [Numbers 3, 78 and 94 of 250 facsimile copies printed. Number 3 inscribed "Arthur Hopkins from Kate and Grace, Oct: 1st 1929-".]

106 "Winter with the Gulf Stream," Once a Week, 8 (February 14, 1863), 210.

II Association Items

107 Abbott, Claude Colleer. The Sand Castle and Other Poems.
    London: Jonathan Cape, 1946.
108 An Act To Prevent the Assumption of Certain Ecclesiastical
    Titles in Respect of Places in the United Kingdom.
    (1 August 1851). London: Eyre and Spottiswoode, 1851.
109 Addis, William Edward. Christianity and the Roman Empire.
    London: B. C. Hare, 1893.
110 _____ Christianity and the Roman Empire. London:
    Sunday School Association, 1893.
111 _____ Hebrew Religion to the Establishment of Judaism
    under Ezra. Vol. 16: Crown Theological Library.
    London: Williams and Norgate; New York: G. P.
    Putnam's Sons, 1906.
112 _____, ed. The Book of Job and the Book of Ruth. London:
    J. N. Dent & Co.; Philadelphia: J. B. Lippincott Co.,
    1902.
113 _____, trans. The Documents of the Hexateuch. 2 vols.
    London: David Nutt, 1892–1898.
114 Aeschylus. Choephoroi, edited by A. Sidgwick.
    Oxford: Clarendon Press, 1884.
115 _____ The Tragedies of Aeschylus, edited by F. A. Paley.
    4th ed., rev. Bibliotheca Classica. London:
    Whittaker and Co.; George Bell & Sons, 1879.
116 Ainger, Arthur Campbell, comp. Eton in Prose and Verse:
    An Anthology. London: Hodder and Stoughton, 1910.
117 Alden, Edward Cox, comp. Alden's Oxford Guide. 29th
    ed. Oxford: Alden, 1903.
118 Alden, John E., ed. Alden's Oxford Guide. Oxford:
    Alden, 1952.
119 All Saints' Church, London. The Story of the Parish
    Church of All Saints', Knightsbridge. London: The
    Church Council of All Saints', 1949.
120 Allies, Thomas William. The See of St. Peter, the Rock of
    the Church, the Source of Jurisdiction and the Center of
    Unity. Pusey Library Pamphlets. London: Burns &
    Lambert, 1850.

121 Allport, Douglas. <u>Collections</u> <u>Illustrative</u> <u>of</u> the <u>Geology</u>, <u>History</u>, <u>Antiquities</u> and <u>Associations</u> <u>of</u> <u>Camberwell</u>. Camberwell: Printed for the author, 1841.

122 Altick, Richard & William R. Matthews. <u>Guide</u> to <u>Doctoral</u> <u>Dissertations</u> in <u>Victorian</u> <u>Literature</u> <u>1886-1958</u>. Urbana: University of Illinois Press, 1960.

123 Anderdon, W. H., S.J. <u>The</u> <u>Jesuits</u>: <u>A</u> <u>Sermon</u> <u>Preached</u> in the <u>Church</u> <u>of</u> the <u>Holy</u> <u>Name</u>, <u>Manchester</u>, on the <u>Second</u> <u>Sunday</u> <u>in</u> <u>Advent</u>, <u>1880</u>. London: Burns & Oates, 1881.

124 Andrews, A.B. de T. <u>A</u> <u>Guide</u> to <u>All</u> <u>Saints</u>'. London: All Saints', Margaret Street, 1953.

125 Andrews, William, ed. <u>Bygone</u> <u>Essex</u>. London: Simpkin, Marshall, Hamilton, Kent, & Co., 1892.

126 <u>Arabian</u> <u>Nights</u>' <u>Entertainments</u>, translated by Edward William Lane. 3 vols. London: Charles Knight & Co., 1840-1841.

127 Armstrong, Walter. <u>The</u> <u>Art</u> <u>of</u> <u>William</u> <u>Quiller</u> <u>Orchardson</u>. London: Seeley and Co., Limited; New York: Macmillan and Co., 1895.

128 Arnold, Matthew. <u>Letters</u> <u>of</u> <u>Matthew</u> <u>Arnold</u> <u>1848-1888</u>. 2 vols. London: Macmillan and Co., 1895.

129 Arnold, Thomas. <u>A</u> <u>Manual</u> <u>of</u> <u>English</u> <u>Literature</u>. 5th ed., rev. London: Longmans, Green and Co., 1885.

130 _____ <u>A</u> <u>Manual</u> <u>of</u> <u>English</u> <u>Literature</u>. 6th ed., rev. London: Longmans, Green and Co., 1888.

131 _____ <u>Passages</u> <u>in</u> <u>a</u> <u>Wandering</u> <u>Life</u>. London: Edward Arnold, 1900.

132 Atkins, Frank. <u>The</u> <u>Story</u> <u>of</u> <u>St</u>. <u>Peter's</u> <u>Parish</u> <u>Church</u>, <u>Bournemouth</u>. 6th ed. Gloucester, England: British Publishing Company, n.d.

133 <u>Bacon's</u> <u>Map</u> <u>of</u> the <u>Environs</u> <u>of</u> <u>Dublin</u>. London: Bacon, n.d.

134 Baedeker, Karl. <u>London</u> <u>and</u> <u>its</u> <u>Environs</u>. 5th ed., rev. London: Dulau and Co., 1885.

135 _____ <u>London</u> <u>and</u> <u>its</u> <u>Environs</u>. 20th ed., rev. London: George Allen & Unwin, 1951.

136 Baines, Frederick Ebenezer, ed. <u>Records</u> <u>of</u> <u>the</u> <u>Manor</u>, <u>Parish</u>, <u>and</u> <u>Borough</u> <u>of</u> <u>Hampstead</u>, <u>in</u> <u>the</u> <u>County</u> <u>of</u> <u>London</u>, <u>to</u> <u>December</u> <u>31st</u>, <u>1889</u>. London: Richard Clay and Sons, Limited, 1890.

137 Balsdon, Dacre. <u>Oxford</u> <u>Life</u>. London: Eyre & Spottiswoode, 1957.

138 Balston, Thomas. <u>Dr</u>. <u>Balston</u> at <u>Eton</u>. London: Macmillan & Co., Ltd, 1952.

139 Bampton, Joseph M., S.J. Funeral Words on Fr. Bernard
    Vaughan, S.J., and Tercentenary Address on St. Ignatius
    of Loyola and St. Francis Xavier. London: Sands & Co.,
    1922.
140 _____ The National Mission of Repentance and Hope and
    Faith in Christ. Sermon preached on October 29, 1916 at
    Farm Street Church, London. London: Burns & Oates,
    1916.
141 _____ Out of the Abundance of the Heart. Sermon preached
    on November 17, 1918 at Farm Street Church, London.
    London: Burns & Oates, Ltd., 1918.
142 _____ The Secret of Saint Francis. Address on the Seventh
    Centenary of St. Francis of Assisi, October, 1926.
    London: Burns, Oates & Washbourne Ltd, 1926.
143 Barber, Thomas. Barber's Picturesque Illustrations of the
    Isle of Wight. London: Simpkin & Marshall, 1834.
144 Barnes, William. Poems of Rural Life in the Dorset
    Dialect. Second Collection. 2nd ed. London: John
    Russell Smith, 1863.
145 Barratt, Thomas J. The Annals of Hampstead. 3 vols.
    London: Adam and Charles Black, 1912.
146 Barraud, Clement William, S.J. Lays of the Knights.
    London: Longmans, Green and Co., 1898.
147 Basset, Bernard, S.J. Farm Street. London: Douglas
    Organ, 1948.
148 Beaumont College. Windsor, England. The History of St.
    Stanislaus College Beaumont: A Record of Fifty Years,
    1861-1911. Beaumont: The 'Beaumont Review' Office,
    1911.
149 Bede, Cuthbert. The Adventures of Mr. Verdant Green.
    London: James Blackwood, 1857.
150 Bell, Harold Idris and C. C. Bell. Welsh Poems of the
    Twentieth Century in English Verse. Wrexham, England:
    Hughes & Son, 1925.
151 Bellasis, Edward. The Money Jar of Plautus. London:
    Kegan Paul, Trench and Co., 1885.
152 _____ The New Terence at Edgbaston. 3rd issue. London:
    Kegan Paul, Trench and Co., 1885.
153 Belloc, Hilaire. Advice. London: Curwen Press, 1960.
154 Benham, William. The Tower of London. London: Seeley
    and Co. Limited; New York: E. P. Dutton & Co., 1906.
155 Bennett, Frank. Chester Cathedral. Chester, England:
    Phillipson and Golder Ltd., n.d.
156 Benson, Arthur Christopher. Walter Pater. English Men of
    Letters Series. London: Macmillan & Co., Ltd., 1906.

157 Bergk, Theodore. Poetae Lyrici Graeci. 3 vols. 4th ed.
Leipzig: B. G. Teubner, 1878-1882.

158 Bibliographies of Modern Authors. No. 1. Robert Bridges.
London: Leslie Chaundy & Co., 1921.

159 Bicknell, W. Illustrated London or a Series of Views in
the British Metropolis and its Vicinity. London: E. T.
Bain, 1847.

160 Bird, James. The Geography of the Port of London.
London: Hutchinson University Library, 1957.

161 Bischoff, D. Anthony, S.J. St. Aloysius: The First
Eighty Years 1875-1955. Oxford: University Press,
1955.

162 Blackmore, Richard Doddridge. Springhaven. A Tale of
the Great War. 3 vols. Sampson Low, Marston,
Searle & Rivington, 1887.

163 Bloom, Ursula. Victorian Vinaigrette. London:
Hutchinson, 1956.

164 Bolton, Geoffrey Douglas. Presenting Britain. London:
Oliver and Boyd, 1957.

165 Boltz, Cecil Leonard. Crown to Mend: A Letter on Poetry.
London: Hamish Hamilton, 1945.

166 Bonomi, Joseph. Nineveh and its Palaces. The
Discoveries of Botta and Layard, Applied to the
Elucidation of Holy Writ. 2nd ed., rev. London:
Ingram, Cooke & Co., 1853.

167 Bosanquet, Bernard. Bernard Bosanquet and his Friends:
Letters Illustrating the Sources and the Development of
his Philosophical Opinions, edited by J. H. Muirhead.
London: George Allen & Unwin, 1935.

168 Bosanquet, Helen. Bernard Bosanquet: A Short Account of
his Life. London: Macmillan & Co., 1924.

169 Boulton, William B. The Amusements of Old London. 2
vols. London: John C. Nimmo, 1901.

170 Bowen, Elizabeth. Anthony Trollope: A New Judgement.
New York: Oxford University Press, 1946.

171 Bowra, Cecil Maurice. Edith Sitwell. Monaco: Lyre-
bird Press, 1947.

172 Bradbrook, Muriel Clara. T. S. Eliot. rev. ed.
Bibliographical Series of Supplements to 'British Book
News'. London: Longmans, Green & Co., Ltd., 1951.

173 Bradley, Arthur Granville. Highways and Byways in
North Wales. London: Macmillan & Co., 1898.

174 Bradley, Henry. The Collected Papers of Henry Bradley
with a Memoir by Robert Bridges. Oxford: Clarendon
Press, 1928.

175 Bradley, Henry and Robert Bridges. On the Terms Briton, British, Britisher. S.P.E. Tract No. 14. Oxford: Clarendon Press, 1923, 2-17.

176 Braye, [Alfred]. Fewness of my Days: A Life in Two Centuries. London: Sands & Co., 1927.

177 _____ Poems: A Selection from the Works of Lord Braye. new ed. London: Robert Washbourne, 1887.

178 _____, ed. The Position of the Catholic Church in England and Wales During the Last Two Centuries: Retrospect and Forecast. London: Burns & Oates; New York: Catholic Publications Society, 1892.

179 Bremond, Henri. Prayer & Poetry: A Contribution to Poetical Theory, translated by Algar Thorold. London: Burns Oates & Washbourne Ltd., 1927.

180 Brewer, Robert Frederick. Orthometry: The Art of Versification and the Technicalities of Poetry. new and rev. ed. Edinburgh: John Grant, 1928.

181 Bridges, John A. Idylls of a Lost Village. London: Macmillan and Co., 1889.

182 _____ In a Village. London: Elkin Mathews, 1898.

183 _____ Reminiscences of a Country Politician. London: T. Werner Laurie, 1906.

184 Bridges, Robert Seymour. Achilles in Scyros: A Drama in a Mixed Manner. London: Edward Bumpus, 1890.

185 _____ Achilles in Scyros. London: Geo. Bell & Sons, 1892.

186 _____ Achilles in Scyros. G. Bell & Sons, Ltd., 1913.

187 _____ An Address to the Swindon Branch of the Workers' Educational Assn. Given on October 28, 1916. Oxford: Clarendon Press, 1916.

188 _____ Augustan Books of Modern Poetry. London: Ernest Benn, n.d.

189 _____ Britannia Victrix. London: Oxford University Press, 1918.

190 _____ "A Case of Thickening of the Cranial Bones in an Infant due to Congenital Syphilis," Transactions of the Clinical Society of London, 12 (1879), 140-42.

191 _____ The Christian Captives. London: Edward Bumpus, 1890.

192 _____ Collected Essays Papers &c. of Robert Bridges. 30 pts. in 10 vols. London: Oxford University Press, Humphrey Milford, 1927-1936.

193 _____ Correspondence of Robert Bridges and Henry Bradley 1900-1923. Oxford: Clarendon Press, 1940.

194 _____ Demeter: A Mask. Oxford: Clarendon Press, 1905.

17

195 _____ Demeter: A Mask. Lyrics and Incidental Music by
W. H. Hadow. Oxford: Clarendon Press, 1905.
196 _____ The Dialectal Words in Blunden's Poems. S.P.E.
Tract No. 5. Oxford: Clarendon Press, 1921, 23-32.
197 _____ Eden: An Oratorio. Set to music by C. V. Stanford.
London: Geo Bell & Sons, Novello Ewer and Co., 1891.
198 _____ Eight Plays. Nero, parts 1 & 2. Palicio. Ulysses.
Captives. Achilles. Humours. Feast of Bacchus.
London: G. Bell & Sons, 1885-1894.
199 _____ English Handwriting, Continued from Tract XXIII.
S.P.E. Tract No. 28. Oxford: Clarendon Press, 1927.
200 _____ Eros & Psyche. London: George Bell and Sons,
1885.
201 _____ Eros & Psyche. London: George Bell and Sons,
1894.
202 _____ Eros and Psyche, with wood-cuts from designs by
Edward Burne-Jones. Newtown, Mont. Wales:
Gregynog Press, 1935.
203 _____ The Feast of Bacchus. London: George Bell & Sons
and J. & E. Bumpus, 1894.
204 _____ The Growth of Love. Oxford: H. Daniel, 1890.
[Number 76 of 100 copies printed.]
205 _____ The Growth of Love. Portland, Maine: Thomas B.
Mosher, 1894. [Number 184 of 400 copies printed.]
206 _____ The Growth of Love. Portland, Maine: Thomas B.
Mosher, 1894. [Number 230 of 400 copies printed.]
207 _____ The Humours of the Court. Covent Garden: George
Bell & Sons; Holborn Bars: J. & E. Bumpus, n.d.
208 _____ The Humours of the Court: A Comedy and Other
Poems. New York: Macmillan and Co.; London: G.
Bell and Sons, 1893. [Inscription in Bridges' hand on
verso of half-title page.]
209 _____ The Influence of the Audience: Considerations
Preliminary to the Psychological Analysis of
Shakespeare's Characters. Garden City, New York: One
hundred copies printed for Stanley Morison at the Press
of Doubleday, Page & Co., 1926.
210 _____ Lord Kitchener. London: One of 20 copies
privately printed by Clement Shorter, 1916.
211 _____ The Message of One of England's Greatest Poets to
a Printer and Printers, Especially Those Who Possess
Love of Craft. London: George W. Jones, 1931.

212 _____ The Message of One of England's Greatest Poets to a Printer and Printers, Especially Those Who Possess Love of Craft. London: George W. Jones, 1931. [Number 176 of 250 copies printed.]

213 _____ Milton's Prosody. Oxford: Clarendon Press, 1893. [Number 106 of 250 copies printed.]

214 _____ Milton's Prosody. Oxford: Clarendon Press, 1894.

215 _____ Milton's Prosody with a Chapter on Accentual Verse and Notes. Oxford: Clarendon Press, 1921.

216 _____ Milton's Prosody with a Chapter on Accentual Verse and Notes. Oxford: Clarendon Press, 1965.

217 _____ and William Johnson Stone. Milton's Prosody by Robert Bridges & Classical Metres in English Verse by William Johnson Stone. Oxford: Henry Frowde, 1901. [Inscribed "Robert Bridges."]

218 _____ The Necessity of Poetry. Oxford: Clarendon Press, 1918.

219 _____ Nero. Part 1. The First Part of the Reign of Nero, Comprising the Murder of Britannicus to the Death of Agrippina. London: George Bell & Sons and J. and E. Bumpus, 1885.

220 _____ Nero. Part 2. From the Death of Burrus to the Death of Seneca. Comprising the Conspiracy of Piso. London: George Bell & Sons and J. and E. Bumpus, n.d.

221 _____ New Verse Written in 1921. Oxford: Clarendon Press, 1925.

222 _____ Now in Wintry Delights. Oxford: Daniel Press, 1903.

223 _____ October and Other Poems. London: William Heinemann, 1920. [Number 32 of 65 copies printed, inscribed "Robert Bridges."]

224 _____ October and Other Poems. London: Humphrey Milford, Oxford University Press, n.d.

225 _____ "Ode on the Tercentenary Commemoration of Shakespeare." n.p. [Dated 1916 in what appears to be Bridges' hand.]

226 _____ Ode for the Bicentenary Commemoration of Henry Purcell, With Other Poems and a Preface on the Musical Setting of Poetry. London: Elkin Mathews, 1896.

227 _____ On English Homophones. S.P.E. Tract No. 11. Oxford: Clarendon Press, 1919.

228 _____ "On Receiving 'Trivia' from the Author." Stanford Dingley: Mill House Press, 1930.

229 _____ Palicio. London: Edward Bumpus, 1890.

230 _____ Pictorial, Picturesque, Romantic, Grotesque, Classical. S.P.E. Tract No. 15. Oxford: Clarendon Press, 1923, 15-21.

231 _____ Poems. London: Edward Bumpus, 1879.

232 _____ Poetical Works of Robert Bridges. 6 vols. London: Smith, Elder & Co., 1898-1905.

233 _____ Poetical Works of Robert Bridges. 6 vols. Oxford: Clarendon Press, [1929-1930].

234 _____ Poetical Works of Robert Bridges Excluding the Eight Dramas. London: Henry Frowde, Oxford University Press, 1912.

235 _____ Poetry. London: British Broadcasting Corporation, 1929.

236 _____ Prometheus the Firegiver. London: George Bell and Sons, 1884.

237 _____ "Pronunciation of Clothes, &c.," S.P.E. Tract No. 30. Oxford: Clarendon Press, 1928, 305-09.

238 _____ The Return of Ulysses. London: Edward Bumpus, 1890.

239 _____ "Reviews and Miscellaneous Notes," S.P.E. Tract No. 22. Oxford: Clarendon Press, 1925, 55-65.

240 _____ Selected Poems. 4th impression. London: Faber and Faber, 1943.

241 _____ The Shorter Poems of Robert Bridges. Book V. London: Geo. Bell & Sons, 1894.

242 _____ Shorter Poems of Robert Bridges. 5 parts. Oxford: Daniel, 1894.

243 _____ The Shorter Poems of Robert Bridges. London: Geo. Bell & Sons; Oxford: Horace Hart, 1899.

244 _____ The Shorter Poems of Robert Bridges. London: Geo. Bell & Sons; Oxford: Horace Hart, 1910.

245 _____ The Shorter Poems of Robert Bridges. enl. ed., 2nd impression. Oxford: Clarendon Press; London: Humphrey Milford, 1931.

246 _____ The Shorter Poems of Robert Bridges. enl. ed., 3rd impression. Oxford: Clarendon Press; London: Geoffrey Cumberlege, 1946.

247 _____ The Small Hymn-Book: The Word-Book of the Yattendon Hymnal. Oxford: B. H. Blackwell; London: Simpkin, Marshall, Hamilton, Kent, & Co., 1899. [Inscribed "Robert Bridges."]

248 _____ The Society's Work. S.P.E. Tract No. 21. Oxford: Clarendon Press, 1925.

249 _____ Sonnet XLIV of Michelangelo Buonarroti Translated
for Andrew Lang by Robert Bridges with His Accompanying
Epistle Thereunto. n.p., 1912.
250 _____ The Tapestry: Poems by Robert Bridges. London:
Privately printed, 1925. [150 copies printed.]
251 _____ The Testament of Beauty: A Poem in Four Books.
Oxford: Clarendon Press, 1929. [Number 221 of 250
copies printed.]
252 _____ The Testament of Beauty: A Poem in Four Books.
Oxford: Clarendon Press, 1929. [Number 25 of 250
copies printed, inscribed "Robert Bridges." Bookplate
"Ex Libris Eric Gill, T.O.S.D., Pigotts near Speen,
Buckinghamshire."]
253 _____ The Testament of Beauty: A Poem in Four Books.
Oxford: Clarendon Press; London: Humphrey Milford,
1929.
254 _____ The Testament of Beauty: A Poem in Four Books.
New York: Oxford University Press, 1929.
255 _____ The Testament of Beauty: A Poem in Four Books.
Oxford: Clarendon Press, 1930.
256 _____ The Testament of Beauty: A Poem in Four Books.
Oxford: Clarendon Press; London: Humphrey Milford,
1945.
257 _____ Three Friends: Memoirs of Digby Mackworth Dolben,
Richard Watson Dixon, Henry Bradley. London: Humphrey
Milford, Oxford University Press, 1932.
258 _____ Three Friends: Memoirs of Digby Mackworth Dolben,
Richard Watson Dixon, Henry Bradley. London: Humphrey
Milford, Oxford University Press, 1938.
259 _____ A Tract on the Present State of English Pronunciation.
First published 1910 in Essays and Studies by members
of the English Association, collected by A. C. Bradley.
Oxford: Clarendon Press, 1913.
260 _____ XXI Letters: A Correspondence Between Robert
Bridges and R. C. Trevelyan on New Verse and The
Testament of Beauty. Stanford Dingley, near Reading:
Mill House Press, 1955.
261 _____ Verses Written for Mrs. Daniel. Oxford: Clarendon
Press, 1932. [Number 52 of 300 copies printed.]
262 _____ Yattendon Hymns. Oxford: Horace Hart, University
Press; London: Henry Frowde, 1897.
263 _____, comp. The Chilswell Book of English Poetry.
London: Longmans, Green & Company, 1924.

264 _____, ed. The B.B.C.'s Recommendations for Pronounc-
        ing Doubtful Words. S.P.E. Tract No. 32. Oxford:
        Clarendon Press, 1929.
265 _____, ed. Chants for the Psalter, Yattendon. Oxford:
        Clarendon Press, 1897.
266 _____, ed. Hymns from the Yattendon Hymnal. Oxford:
        Henry Daniel, 1899. [Number 79 of 150 copies printed.]
267 _____, ed. Hymns from the Yattendon Hymnal. Oxford:
        Henry Daniel, 1899. [Number 99 of 150 copies printed.]
268 _____, ed. Hymns: The Yattendon 4-part Hymns. Part 1.
        Oxford: Horace Hart, Clarendon Press, 1895. [Number 7
        of 50 copies printed in large size folio, inscribed
        "Robert Bridges."]
269 _____, ed. Hymns: The Yattendon 4-part Hymns. Part 1.
        Oxford: Horace Hart, Clarendon Press, 1895.
270 _____, ed. Hymns: The Yattendon Hymnal. Part 3.
        Oxford: Horace Hart; London: Henry Frowde, 1898.
271 _____ and H. Ellis Wooldridge, eds. Hymns: The
        Yattendon Hymnal. Part 4. Oxford: Horace Hart, 1899.
272 _____ and H. Ellis Wooldridge, eds. Hymns: The
        Yattendon Hymnal. Oxford: Horace Hart, Oxford
        University Press, 1899. [Inscribed "To Sydney C.
        Cockerell from Robert Bridges August 11, 1913 Chilswell.]
273 _____ and H. Ellis Wooldridge, eds. Hymns: The
        Yattendon Hymnal. London: Humphrey Milford, Oxford
        University Press; Oxford: Basil Blackwell, 1920.
274 _____ and Monica Bridges. (Matthew Barnes, pseud.)
        "What is Pure French," S.P.E. Tract No. 8. Oxford:
        Clarendon Press, 1922, 3-10.
275 _____ and Monica Bridges. (Matthew Barnes, pseud.)
        "Words from the French," S.P.E. Tract No. 30. Oxford:
        Clarendon Press, 1928, 298-305.
276 "Bridges (Robert-Seymour)." Larousse Mensuel, No. 282
        (August, 1930), 466-67.
277 Brimley, George. Essays, edited by William George
        Clark. 2nd ed. Cambridge: Macmillan and Co., 1860.
278 Briscoe, John Fetherstonhaugh and H. F. B. Mackay with a
        foreword by Viscount Halifax. A Tractarian at Work: A
        Memoir of Dean Randall. 2nd impression. London: A. R.
        Mowbray & Co. Ltd.; Milwaukee: Morehouse Publishing
        Co., 1932.
279 British Museum. Department of Greek and Roman
        Antiquities. A Guide to the Department of Greek and
        Roman Antiquities. 6th ed. London: William Clowes &
        Sons, Limited, 1928.

280 Brown, Thomas Edward. Letters of Thomas Edward Brown, edited by Sydney T. Irwin. 4th ed. Liverpool: University Press, 1952.

281 _____ Poems of T. E. Brown. Introductory Memoir by Sir Arthur Quiller-Couch. 2 vols. Liverpool: University Press, 1952.

282 Browne, Henry, S.J. Our Renaissance: Essays on the Reform and Revival of Classical Studies. New York: Longmans, Green & Co., 1917.

283 Bryant, Arthur. Pageant of England (1840-1940). New York: Harper & Brothers, 1941. [Published in England under the title of English Saga (1840-1940).]

284 Bryce, James. Studies in Contemporary Biography. London: Macmillan and Co., Limited, 1903.

285 Buckler, William Earl, ed. Prose of the Victorian Period. Boston: Houghton Mifflin Company, 1958.

286 Buckton, A. Through Human Eyes: Poems. Oxford: Daniel, 1901.

287 Bullen, Arthur Henry, ed. Lyrics from the Song-books of the Elizabethan Age. London: John C. Nimmo, 1887. [Number 136 of 500 copies printed, inscribed "Gertrude F. M. Hopkins, Christmas 1886."]

288 _____, ed. More Lyrics from the Song-Books of the Elizabethan Age. London: John C. Nimmo, 1888. [Number 127 of 750 copies printed, inscribed "Gertrude F. M. Hopkins, Christmas 1887, From K. H."]

289 Burdett, Osbert. "Coventry Patmore," Dublin Review, 165 (October, 1919), 245-260.

290 Burne-Jones, Georgiana (MacDonald). Memorials of Edward Burne-Jones, 1833-1898. 2 vols. London: Macmillan and Co., Limited, 1904.

291 Burns, George, S.J. Brother Daniel Shields, S.J.: A Memoir. Roehampton: Manresa Press, 1947.

292 Bussey, George Moir, ed. Fables, Original and Selected: by the most Esteemed European and Oriental Authors, illustrated by J. J. Grandville. London: Thomas Kelly, 1840.

293 C. P. Hastings, Lewes, Rye and the Sussex Marches. London: George Bell and Sons, 1887. [Reprinted from St. James's Gazette.]

294 Caine, T. Hall. Recollections of Dante Gabriel Rossetti. London: Elliot Stock, 1882.

295 _____, ed. Sonnets of Three Centuries: A Selection. London: Elliot Stock, 1882. [Number 33 of 50 copies printed.]

296 Calverley, Charles Stuart. The Complete Works of C. S. Calverley. London: George Bell and Sons, 1901.

297 Cambridge University, King's College Chapel. King's College Chapel: A General Description. n.p., n.d.

298 _____ King's College Chapel: Some Opinions, 1564-1947. n.p., n.d.

299 _____ King's College Chapel: The Great Windows. n.p., n.d.

300 Cameron, J. M. John Henry Newman. Bibliographical Series of Supplements to 'British Book News' on Writers and Their Work. London: Longmans, Green & Co., 1956.

301 Campbell, Roy. The Collected Poems of Roy Campbell. London: Bodley Head, 1955.

302 "Cardinal Newman and the Society of Jesus." Paper read at St. Beuno's Essay Society, February 21, 1891.

303 Carlingford, Chichester Samuel Parkinson-Fortescue. ' . . . and Mr. Fortescue': A Selection from the Diaries from 1851 to 1862 of Chichester Fortescue, Lord Carlingford, K. P., edited by Osbert Wyndham Hewett. London: J. Murray, 1958.

304 Case, Thomas. Letters to 'The Times' 1884-1922, edited by R. B. Mowat. Oxford: John Johnson at the University Press, 1927.

305 Cash, J. Allan and A. F. Kersting. The English Countryside in Colour. London: B. T. Batsford, Ltd., 1957.

306 Casson, Hugh. An Introduction to Victorian Architecture. New York: Pellegrini & Cudahy, 1948.

307 Catalogus Provinciae Angliae Societatis Jesu. Roehampton: 1869-1871, 1873-1874, 1876-1878, 1886-1890.

308 A Catholic Barrister (pseud.). The New Departure in Catholic Liberal Education. London: Burns and Oates, 1878.

309 Catholic Church. The Rite of Conferring Orders, translated with annotations from The Roman Pontifical. Roehampton: Manresa Press, 1886.

310 Catholic Poor-School Committee, London. The Thirty-Seventh Annual Report of the Catholic Poor-School Committee. London: Catholic Poor-School Committee, 1884.

311 Catholic Truth Society, London. The First Report. London: Catholic Truth Society, 1869.

312 Cecil, David. Walter Pater: The Scholar-Artist. The Rede
Lecture, delivered in the University of Cambridge, 19
May 1955. Cambridge, England: The Syndics of the
Cambridge University Press, 1955.
313 Cellier, Francois & Cunningham Bridgeman. Gilbert,
Sullivan and D'Oyly Carte: Reminiscences of the Savoy
and the Savoyards. London: Sir Isaac Pitman & Sons,
Ltd., 1914.
314 Century of English Cathedral Divines. Pusey Library
Pamphlet. London: Roake and Varty, n.d.
315 Chandler, Henry William. A Practical Introduction to
Greek Accentuation. Oxford: University Press, 1862.
316 Charteris, Evan Edward. The Life and Letters of Sir
Edmund Gosse. London: William Heinemann Ltd, 1931.
317 Chester, England. The Visitors' Chester Guide. Chester:
W. H. Evans, Sons & Co. Ltd., n.d.
318 Chichester, Charles Raleigh. Schools. London: Burns &
Oates; Dublin: James Duffy & Sons, 1882.
319 The Christian Year: Thoughts in Verse for the Sundays and
Holydays Throughout the Year. 54th ed. Oxford: John
Henry and James Parker, 1858.
320 Church of the Immaculate Conception, London. Farm Street
Church Yearbook 1954. n.p., n.d.
321 _____ Photographs. London: Photographic Tourists'
Association, n.d.
322 _____ A Short Guide to Farm Street Church. London:
Salesian Press, n.d.
323 Clare, James, S.J. The Science of Spiritual Life According
to the Spiritual Exercises. London: Art and Book
Company, 1896.
324 Clark, Andrew, ed. The Colleges of Oxford: Their History
and Traditions. London: Methuen & Co., 1891.
325 Clarke, Charles Phillip Stewart. The Oxford Movement and
After. London: A. R. Mowbray & Co., Ltd., 1932.
326 Clarke, Marcus Andrew Hislop. For the Term of his
Natural Life. London: Macmillan and Co., Limited,
1912.
327 _____ Holiday Peak and Other Tales. Melbourne: George
Robertson, 1873.
328 _____ Stories of Australia in the Early Days. 2nd ed.
London: Hutchinson & Co., 1897.
329 _____ 'Twixt Shadow and Shine. 2nd ed. London:
George Robertson and Company, 1893.
330 Clarke, Richard Frederick, S.J. A Personal Visit to
Distressed Ireland. London: Burns & Oates, 1883.

331 Clifford, Sigerson. Travelling Tinkers. Dublin: Dolmen Press, 1951.

332 Clongowes Wood College. Naas, Co. Kildare. Prospectus of Clongowes Wood College. (Conducted by the Jesuit Fathers.) n.p., n.d.

333 Cockton, Henry. The Life and Adventures of Valentine Vox the Ventriloquist. London: George Routledge & Sons, [1840].

334 Coleridge, Mary Elizabeth. Gathered Leaves from the Prose of Mary E. Coleridge with a Memoir by Edith Sichel. London: Constable and Company, 1910.

335 _____ Non Sequitur. London: James Nisbet & Co., Ltd., 1890.

336 Collins, Wilkie. The Haunted Hotel: A Mystery of Modern Venice to which is added My Lady's Money. London: Chatto & Windus, 1878.

337 Comerford, M. Collections Relating to the Dioceses of Kildare and Leighlin. 3 vols. Dublin: James Duffy and Sons, 1883-1886.

338 Conquest, Robert. Poems. London: Macmillan & Co. Ltd, 1955.

339 _____, ed. New Lines: An Anthology. London: Macmillan & Co., Ltd., 1956.

340 Corcoran, Timothy, S.J. The Clongowes Record 1814 to 1932 with Introductory Chapters on Irish Jesuit Educators 1564 to 1813. Dublin: Browne and Nolan Limited, 1932.

341 Courtney, Janet Elizabeth (Hogarth). The Making of an Editor: W. L. Courtney 1850-1928. London: Macmillan and Co., Limited, 1930.

342 Cox, George Valentine. Recollections of Oxford. London: Macmillan and Co., 1868.

343 Crawley, Richard. In Memoriam: Letters and Poems of Richard Crawley. London: Gresham Press, n.d.

344 Creighton, Louise (von Gehn). Life and Letters of Mandell Creighton Sometime Bishop of London. 2 vols. London: Longmans, Green, and Co., 1905.

345 Crusading for Christ: Centenary Brochure, Christ Church, West Croydon 1852-1952. n.p., n.d.

346 Curran, C. P. Newman House and University Church. Dublin: University College, n.d.

347 Curtis, John, S.J. The Way of Religious Perfection in the Spiritual Exercises of St. Ignatius of Loyola. 3rd ed. Dublin: M. H. Gill & Son, 1885.

348 Dale, Amy Marjorie. The Lyric Metres of Greek Drama. Cambridge, England: University Press, 1948.

349 The Daniel Press. Memorials of C. H. O. Daniel with a Bibliography of the Press, 1845-1919. Oxford: Daniel Press, 1921.

350 Daryush, Elizabeth (Bridges). "Robert Bridges: His Work on the English Language." S.P.E. Tract No. 35. Oxford: Clarendon Press, 1931, 503-13.

351 _____ Selected Poems, selected and with a foreword by Yvor Winters. New York: Swallow Press, 1948.

352 Davie, Donald. Articulate Energy: An Inquiry into the Syntax of English Poetry. London: Routledge & Kegan Paul, 1955.

353 Davies, Edward. Celtic Researches, on the Origin, Traditions & Language of the Ancient Britons; with some Introductory Sketches, on Primitive Society. London: J. Barfield for the Author, 1804.

354 Davis, Henry William Carless. Balliol College. University of Oxford College Histories. London: F. E. Robinson and Co., 1899.

355 Day-Lewis, Cecil. Collected Poems. London: Jonathan Cape with the Hogarth Press, 1954.

356 _____ A Hope for Poetry (Reprint with a Postscript). 4th ed. Oxford: Basil Blackwell, 1939.

357 _____ and John Lehmann, eds. The Chatto Book of Modern Poetry 1915-1955. London: Chatto & Windus, 1956.

358 Deane, Anthony Charles. Time Remembered. London: Faber and Faber Limited, 1945.

359 "Death of Frederick Lucas" (Reprint), The Cork Examiner, (October 26, 1855).

360 Declaration of the Catholic Bishops, the Vicars Apostolic and their Coadjutors in Great Britain. Pusey Library Pamphlet. London: Keating and Brown, 1826.

361 Delaney, William, S.J. Irish University Education: A Plea for Fair Play. Dublin: Browne. & Nolan. Limited, 1904.

362 De Lara, Isidore. The Garden of Sleep: A Summer Song, words by Clement Scott. London: Chappell, n.d.

363 _____ The Garden of Sleep: Waltz on the Popular Song 'Garden of Sleep' and Other Melodies. London: Chappell, n.d.

364 De Morgan, Augustus. A Budget of Paradoxes. London: Longmans, Green, and Co., 1872.

365 Denison, George Anthony. Paper Delivered in the Registry of the Diocese of Bath and Wells, September 30, 1856. Pusey Library Pamphlet. London: Masters, 1856.

366 Devlin, Christopher, S.J. The Psychology of Duns Scotus.
  Aquinas Paper No. 15. Oxford: Blackfriars, 1950.
367 Devon and Cornwall in Colour: A Collection of Colour
  Photographs, introductory text and notes on the
  illustrations by Jane Tregarthen. London: B. T.
  Batsford Ltd, 1957.
368 Dicey, Albert Vern. Why England Maintains the Union: A
  Popular Rendering of "England's Case Against Home
  Rule." London: John Murray, 1887.
369 Dickinson, Patric. The Scale of Things: Poems. London:
  Chatto & Windus, 1955.
370 The Dictionary of National Biography 1922-1930, edited by
  J. R. H. Weaver. London: Humphrey Milford, Oxford
  University Press, 1937.
371 Disher, Maurice Willson. Victorian Song from Dive to
  Drawing Room. London: Phoenix House Ltd, 1955.
372 Ditchfield, Peter Hampson, ed. Memorials of Old
  Oxfordshire. London: Bemrose and Sons, Limited, 1903.
373 Dixon, Richard Watson. History of the Church of England
  from the Abolition of the Roman Jurisdiction. 6 vols.
  London: Smith, Elder, 1878-1902.
374 _____ The Last Poems of Richard Watson Dixon, selected
  and edited by Robert Bridges. London: Henry Frowde,
  1905.
375 _____ Lyrical Poems. ("Dedicated to the Reverend Gerard
  Hopkins, by the Author.") Oxford: H. Daniel, 1887.
  [Microfilm]
376 _____ Mano: A Poetical History. London: George
  Routledge & Sons, 1883.
377 _____ Mano: A Poetical History. 2nd ed. London:
  George Routledge & Sons, Limited, 1891.
378 _____ Poems, memoir by Robert Bridges. London: Smith,
  Elder & Co., 1909.
379 _____ Songs and Odes. Elkin Mathews' Shilling Garland.
  London: Elkin Mathews, 1896.
380 The Doctrine of the Catholic Church in England on the
  Holy Eucharist. Pusey Library Pamphlet. Oxford:
  Parker; London: Rivington, 1841.
381 Dodgson, Charles Lutwidge. (Lewis Carroll, pseud.) The
  Diaries of Lewis Carroll. 2 vols., edited by Roger
  Lancelyn Green. London: Cassell & Company Ltd,
  1953.
382 Dolben, Digby Mackworth. The Poems of Digby Mackworth
  Dolben, edited with a memoir by Robert Bridges. London:
  Henry Frowde, Oxford University Press, 1911.

383 Dore, Gustave and Blanchard Jerrold. London: A Pilgrimage. London: Grant & Co., 1872.

384 Dowden, Edward. New Studies in Literature. London: Kegan Paul, Trench, Trubner & Co., Ltd., 1895.

385 Doyle, Richard. The Foreign Tour of Messrs Brown Jones and Robinson. London: George Routledge and Sons, Limited, 1904.

386 Dublin. University. A Handbook to Trinity College. Dublin: Hodges, Figgis, & Co., 1929.

387 _____ The National University Handbook 1908-1932. Dublin: The Senate, National University of Ireland, 1932.

388 _____ The National University of Ireland: Summary of Progress for the Seven Years 1932-1939. A Supplemental Issue to the University Handbook of 1932. Dublin: The Senate, National University of Ireland, 1939.

389 Dugdale, Giles. William Barnes of Dorset. London: Cassell & Company Ltd., 1953.

390 An Echo of the Passion of Our Lord Jesus Christ. Extract from a letter found in an old Chateau in France and translated from the Latin by a Priest; it was afterwards preserved in a Convent. Attributed to Claudia Procula, wife of Pontius Pilate. n.d.

391 Edinburgh. The National Museum of Antiquities of Scotland. A Short Guide to Scottish Antiquities. Edinburgh: His Majesty's Stationery Office, 1949.

392 Edlin, Herbert Leeson. British Plants and their Uses. London: B. T. Batsford Ltd., 1951.

393 Elliott-Binns, Leonard Elliott. Religion in the Victorian Era. London: Lutterworth Press, 1964.

394 Ellis, Henry. The Elgin and Phigaleian Marbles of the Classical Ages, in the British Museum. 2 vols. London: M. A. Nattali, 1846.

395 _____ The Townley Gallery of Classic Sculpture, in the British Museum. London: M. A. Nattali, 1846.

396 Elton, Oliver. Robert Bridges and 'The Testament of Beauty'. English Association Pamphlet No. 83. London: Humphrey Milford, Oxford University Press, 1932.

397 Empson, William. Collected Poems. London: Chatto and Windus, 1955.

398 Engels, Friedrich. The Condition of the Working Class in England, translated and edited by W. O. Henderson and W. H. Chaloner. Oxford: Basil Blackwell, 1958.

399 England's New Cardinal: Rome and Westminster 1946.
Sussex: Ditchling Press, n.d.
400 Essays Mainly on the Nineteenth Century Presented to
Sir Humphrey Milford. London: Geoffrey Cumberlege,
Oxford University Press, 1948.
401 Fairbrother, William Henry. The Philosophy of Thomas
Hill Green. London: Methuen & Co., 1896.
402 Farm Street Church Year Book 1954. London: St. John's
Publishing Co. Ltd., n.d.
403 "Father John Gerard. (In Memoriam.)," Month, 121
(January, 1913), 1-7.
404 "Father Joseph William Amherst," n.p., n.d.
405 "Father Reginald Colley," n.p., n.d.
406 Fathers of the Society of Jesus, comp. A Page of Irish
History: Story of University College, Dublin 1883-1909.
Dublin: Talbot Press, 1930, 72-3, 101, 104-06, 117,
194.
407 "Feestnummer Aangeboden Aan Prof. Dr. Aurelius Pompen
O.F.M. Op Zijn Zestigsten Verjaardag 15 Mei 1939,"
Tijdschrift voor Taal en Letteren (Amsterdam), (April,
1939), [Entire issue]
408 Ferguson, Samuel. Poems of Sir Samuel Ferguson. Dublin:
Talbot Press, Ltd.; London: T. Fisher Unwin, Ltd.,
[1918].
409 Fisher's Drawing Room Scrap-Book with Poetical Illustrations by L. E. L. (Letitia Elizabeth Landon). 2nd ed.
London: Fisher, Son & Co., 1839.
410 Fitzgerald, Percy Hetherington. Father Gallwey: A Sketch
with some Early Letters. London: Burns and Oates,
1906.
411 _____ Stonyhurst Memories; or, Six Years at School.
London: Richard Bentley & Son, 1895.
412 Fletcher, Charles Robert Leslie. A Handy Guide to Oxford.
rev. ed. reprinted. London: Humphrey Milford, Oxford
University Press, 1934.
413 Fraser, Maxwell. Oxford--in Pictures. Oxford: Thames
Valley Art Productions, n.d.
414 Frith, William Powell. A Victorian Canvas: The Memoirs
of W. P. Frith, R.A., edited by Nevile Wallis.
London: Geoffrey Bles, 1957.
415 Fry, Katharine. History of the Parishes of East and West
Ham, edited and revised by G. Pagenstecher. London:
Aug. Siegle, 1888.
416 Furniss, Harry. The Confessions of a Caricaturist. 2 vols.
London: T. Fisher Unwin, 1901.

417 _____ Unpublished letters.
418 Gallwey, Peter, S.J. In Memoriam. Funeral Words by
　　　Father Gallwey, S.J. over the Remains of Charles Weld,
　　　in the Chapel of Chideock Manor, February 3, 1885.
　　　London: Burns and Oates, 1885.
419 Gardner, William Henry. "The Achievement of Coventry
　　　Patmore--I," Month, N.S. 7 (February, 1952), 89-98.
420 _____ "The Achievement of Coventry Patmore--II," Month,
　　　N.S. 7 (April, 1952), 220-30.
421 The Garland of Rachel by Divers Kindly Hands. Portland,
　　　Maine: Thomas B. Mosher, 1902.
422 Gathorne-Hardy, Alfred Erskine. Autumns in Argyleshire
　　　with Rod and Gun. new ed. London: Longmans, Green
　　　and Co., 1901.
423 Gavin, Michael, S.J. Requiescat in Pace. A Discourse
　　　Delivered at the Requiem Mass for Father Gallwey, S.J.
　　　in Farm Street Church, September 27, 1906. London:
　　　Burns and Oates (Limited), 1906.
424 Gerard, John, S.J. Centenary Record: Stonyhurst College:
　　　Its Life Beyond the Seas, 1592-1794 and on English Soil,
　　　1794-1894. Belfast: Marcus Ward & Co., Limited,
　　　1894.
425 Gernsheim, Helmut. Masterpieces of Victorian Photography.
　　　London: Phaidon Press, 1951.
426 Gibson, Alexander Craig. The Folk-Speech of Cumberland
　　　and Some Districts Adjacent. London: Bemrose & Sons;
　　　Carlisle: G. & T. Coward, 1880.
427 Gibson, Strickland. Some Oxford Libraries. London:
　　　Humphrey Milford, Oxford University Press, 1914.
428 Gibson, William Sidney. The Prize Essay on the History
　　　and Antiquities of Highgate. London: Smith, Elder, and
　　　Co., 1842.
429 Gill, Eric. Autobiography. London: Right Book Club, 1944.
430 Gillig, Charles A. New Guide to London and Important
　　　Suburban Districts. London: Gillig's United States
　　　Exchange; Chicago: Rand, McNally & Co., 1885.
431 Gilman, Alexander William. The Gillmans of Highgate with
　　　Letters from Samuel Taylor Coleridge, &C. London:
　　　Eliot Stock, 1895.
432 Glasgow Art Gallery and Museum. Catalogue Descriptive
　　　and Historical of the Pictures in the Glasgow Art Gallery
　　　and Museum, Kelvingrove, compiled by James Paton.
　　　spec. ed. Glasgow: Robert Anderson, 1908.

433 A Glossary of Terms used in Grecian, Roman, Italian, and Gothic Architecture. 3 vols. 3rd ed. enl. Oxford: John Henry Parker; London: Charles Tilt, 1840-1841.

434 Gordon, George Stuart. The Lives of Authors. London: Chatto and Windus, 1950.

435 _____ Robert Bridges. Rede Lecture, 1931. Cambridge, England: University Press, 1946.

436 Gorman, William James Gordon. Converts to Rome Since the Tractarian Movement to May, 1899. 4th ed., rev. and enl. London: Swan Sonnenschein & Co., Lim., 1899, 115.

437 Gosse, Edmund William. Books on the Table. London: William Heinemann, 1921.

438 _____ From Shakespeare to Pope. Cambridge, England: University Press, 1885.

439 _____ More Books on the Table. New York: Charles Scribner's Sons, 1923.

440 _____ Portraits and Sketches. New York: Charles Scribner's Sons, 1912.

441 _____ The Secret of Narcisse: A Romance. London: William Heinemann, 1892. [Inscribed "Coventry Patmore."]

442 Grant, George M. Ocean to Ocean: Sandford Fleming's Expedition through Canada in 1872. London: Sampson Low, Marston, Low, & Searle, 1873.

443 Graves, Robert. The Crowning Privilege. London: Cassell & Company Ltd, 1955.

444 Great Britain. Arts Council. Welsh Committee. David Jones: An Exhibition of Paintings, Drawings and Engravings. Pwyllgor Cymreig: Cyngor Celfyddyd Prydain Fawr, 1954.

445 Great Shipwrecks. A Record of Perils and Disasters at Sea.--1544 to 1877. [By W. H. D. Adams]. London: Thomas Nelson and Sons, [1877].

446 Green, Thomas Hill. Prolegomena to Ethics, edited by A. C. Bradley. 3rd ed. Oxford: Clarendon Press, 1890.

447 _____ Works of Thomas Hill Green, edited by R. L. Nettleship. 3 vols. 2nd ed. London: Longmans, Green, and Co., 1889-1890.

448 Grigson, Geoffrey and Charles Harvard Gibbs-Smith, eds. "Discoverer of Vitamins." [Hopkins, Sir Frederick Gowland]. People: A Volume of the Good, Bad, Great & Eccentric who Illustrate the Admirable Diversity of Man. Vol. 1: People, Places and Things. London: Grosvenor Press, 1954, 196-197.

449 Grindor, Leopold Hartley. Lancashire: Brief Historical and Descriptive Notes. London: Seeley and Co., Limited, 1892.

450 Guerard, Albert Joseph. Robert Bridges: A Study of Traditionalism in Poetry. Cambridge, Massachusetts: Harvard University Press, 1942.

451 Gwynn, Stephen Lucius. A Holiday in Connemara. London: Methuen & Co., 1909.

452 The Habits of Good Society: A Handbook of Etiquette for Ladies and Gentlemen. London: James Hogg & Sons, [1859].

453 Hahn, Emily, Charles Roetter and Harford Thomas. Meet the British. London: Newman Neame Limited, 1953.

454 Hake, Thomas Gordon. The Poems of Thomas Gordon Hake. London: Elkin Mathews and John Lane; Chicago: Stone and Kimball, 1894.

455 Hall, Samuel Carter. The Book of Gems: The Modern Poets and Artists of Great Britain. London: Whittaker and Co., 1838.

456 Hall, William Winslow. English Poesy: An Induction. London: J. M. Dent & Sons, Ltd., 1911.

457 Hampstead, England. Hampstead Scientific Society. Hampstead Heath: Its Geology and Natural History. London: T. Fisher Unwin, 1913.

458 A Hand-Book for Visitors to Oxford. Oxford: John Henry Parker, 1847.

459 Hare, Augustus J. C. In My Solitary Life: Being an Abridgement of the Last Three Volumes of The Story of My Life, edited by Malcolm Barnes. London: George Allen & Unwin Ltd, 1953.

460 _____ The Years with Mother: Being an Abridgement of the First Three Volumes of The Story of My Life, edited by Malcolm Barnes. London: George Allen & Unwin Ltd, 1952.

461 Harland, John, ed. Ballads & Songs of Lancashire Ancient and Modern. 2nd ed. London: George Routledge and Sons and L. C. Gent, 1875.

462 Harper, Thomas, S.J. Memoir of Father James Harris, S.J. Roehampton: Manresa Press, 1884.

463 Haslemere, England. "The Garth" Haslemere, Surrey, For Sale by Auction at the White Horse Hotel, High Street, Haslemere, Surrey, on Thursday, 4th September, 1952, at 3 o'clock, Precisely (Unless previously sold by Private Treaty). n.p., n.d. [Sales Catalog]

464 _____. Haslemere Urban District Council. Guide to
Haslemere,, Hindhead and the Surrounding Country.
Haslemere: Harry J. R. Oliver, 1947-1948.
465 _____ Guide to Haslemere and Hindhead (The Switzerland
of Surrey) and the Surrounding Country. Surrey: Harry
J. R. Oliver, n.d.
466 Haslemere (Parish), England. A Short History of the Church
of St. Bartholomew and St. Christopher in the Parish of
Haslemere. Gloucester: British Publishing Company
Limited, n.d.
467 Hawkes, Jacquetta. "Gowland Hopkins and Scientific
Imagination," Listener, 43 (February 2, 1950), 191-92.
468 Hayes, Louis M. Reminiscences of Manchester and some
of its Local Surroundings from the Year 1840. London:
Sherratt & Hughes, 1905.
469 Hearn, Lafcadio. Pre-Raphaelite and Other Poets:
Lectures by Lafcadio Hearn , edited by John Erskine.
New York: Dodd, Mead and Company, 1922.
470 Henley, William Ernest. A Century of Artists: A Memorial
of the Glasgow International Exhibition 1888. Glasgow:
James MacLehose & Sons, 1889.
471 Henson, Herbert Hensley. Retrospect of an Unimportant
Life. 3 vols. London: Oxford University Press, 1942.
472 _____, ed. A Memoir of the Right Honourable Sir William
Anson. Oxford: Clarendon Press, 1920.
473 Hewitson, Anthony. Stonyhurst College, Present and Past:
Its History, Discipline, Treasures, and Curiosities.
2nd ed., rev. and enl. Preston: "Chronicle" Office,
1878.
474 Hints Offered to Young Masters in the Colleges of the
English Province, S.J. rev. ed. Clitheroe: Parkinson
& Blacow, 1898.
475 Hobhouse, Christopher. 1851 and the Crystal Palace.
rev. ed. London: John Murray, 1950.
476 Hogan, Edmund Ignatius, S.J. Ibernia Ignatiana Seu
Ibernorum Societatis Iesu Patrum Monumenta. Vol. 1.
Dublin: Excudebat Societas Typographica Dubliniensis,
1880.
477 Holland, Henry Scott. Memoir and Letters, edited by
Stephen Paget. London: John Murray, 1921.
478 Holmes, Charles John and C. H. Collins Baker. The
Making of the National Gallery 1824-1924. London:
National Gallery, 1924.
479 Homer. The Iliad of Homer. 2 vols. English notes by
F. A. Paley. London: Whittaker and Co., 1866.

480 The Odyssey of Homer, translated by J. G. Cordery. London: Methuen & Co., 1897.
481 Hone, Joseph Maunsell. The Life of George Moore. London: Victor Gollancz Ltd, 1936.
482 Hope-Scott, James Robert. Memoirs of James Robert Hope-Scott, edited by Robert Ornsby. 2 vols. London: John Murray, 1884.
483 _____ Sancta Mater, Istud Agas, Crucifixi fige Plagas, Cordi meo Valide. n.p., n.d.
484 Hopkins and Biochemistry 1861-1947: Papers concerning Sir Frederick Gowland Hopkins, O.M., P.R.S., with a Selection of his Addresses and a Bibliography of his Publications, edited by Joseph Needham and Ernest Baldwin. Cambridge, England: W. Heffer and Sons Limited, 1949.
485 Hopkins, Gerard. The Friend of Antaeus: A Comedy of Fantastic People. New York: E. P. Dutton & Company, 1928.
486 _____ Seeing's Believing: Variations on a Theme. London: Victor Gollancz Ltd, 1928.
487 _____ Something Attempted. London: Victor Gollancz Ltd, 1929.
488 _____ An Unknown Quantity. London: Chatto & Windus, 1922. [Inscribed "For Mother and Father with all love from Gerry."]
489 _____ An Unknown Quantity. New York: E. P. Dutton & Company, 1923.
490 _____, ed. The Battle of the Books. London: Allan Wingate, 1947.
491 Hopkins, Lionel Charles. The Guide to Kuan Hua: A Translation of the "Kuan Hua Chih Nan" with an Essay on Tone and Accent in Pekinese and a Glossary of Phrases. Shanghai: Kelly & Walsh, Limited, 1900.
492 Hopkins, Manley. Hawaii: The Past, Present, and Future of its Island-Kingdom. London: Longman, Green, Longman, and Roberts, 1862.
493 _____ Hawaii: The Past, Present, and Future of its Island-Kingdom. 2nd ed., rev. and continued. London: Longmans, Green, and Co., 1866.
494 _____ Spicilegium Poeticum: A Gathering of Verses. London: Leadenhall Press, Ltd, [1892].
495 Horizon (London). The Golden Horizon, edited by Cyril Connolly. London: Weidenfeld & Nicolson Limited, 1953.

496 Hotten, John Camden. The Piccadilly Annual of Entertaining Literature Restrospective and Contemporary. London: John Camden Hotten, 1870.

497 House, Humphrey. Aristotle's Poetics: A Course of Eight Lectures. rev. ed. London: Rupert Hart-Davis, 1956.

498 How I Managed and Improved My Estate. London: George Bell and Sons, 1886. [Reprinted from Saint James's Gazette.]

499 Howitt, William. The Northern Heights of London or Historical Associations of Hampstead, Highgate, Muswell Hill, Hornsey, and Islington. London: Longmans, Green, and Co., 1869.

500 Hugel, Anatole Andreas von. Charles von Hugel, April 25, 1795--June 2, 1870. Cambridge, England: Privately printed, 1903.

501 Hughes, Mabel L. Violet. Everyman's Testament of Beauty: A Study in 'The Testament of Beauty' of Robert Bridges. London: Student Christian Movement Press, 1932.

502 Hughes, Mary Vivian (Thomas). A London Family 1870-1900: A Trilogy. London: Geoffrey Cumberlege, Oxford University Press, 1946.

503 Hughes Clarke, Arthur William. Monumental Inscriptions in the Church and Churchyard of St. Mary's, Wimbledon. London: Mitchell Hughes and Clarke, 1934.

504 Humphrey, William, S.J. "Conscience" (Reprint), Month, 72 (April, 1893), 501-18.

505 _____ "Human Responsibility" (Reprint), Month, 72 (February, 1893), 229-55.

506 _____ The Unity and Continuity of the Church: A Sermon. London: Burns & Oates, Limited, 1891.

507 Hunt, John. Religious Thought in England in the Nineteenth Century. London: Gibbings & Co., Limited, 1896.

508 Hunter Blair, David Oswald. Flying Leaves. London: Heath Cranton Limited, [1923].

509 _____ In Victorian Days and other Papers. London: Longmans, Green and Co., 1939.

510 _____ More Memories and Musings. London: Burns Oates & Washbourne Ltd., 1931.

511 Huntly House Museum: History, Architectural Features, and Guide. Leith: Edinburgh Public Libraries and Museums Committee, 1953.

512 Igdrasil: Journal of the Ruskin Reading Guild. A Magazine of Literature, Art, and Social Philosophy. 1 (January to September, 1890).

513 The Illustrated Exhibitor, A Tribute to the World's Industrial
    Jubilee. Nos. 1-30, June 7--December 27, 1851.
    London: John Cassell, 1851.
514 Inman, Henry Turner. Near Oxford, revised by J. E.
    Alden. 6th ed. Oxford: Alden & Co. Ltd., 1946.
515 _____ Near Oxford, revised by J. E. Alden. 7th ed.
    Oxford: Alden & Co. Ltd., 1948.
516 Ireland in Colour: A Collection of Forty Colour Photographs,
    introductory text and notes on the illustrations by W. R.
    Rodgers. London: B. T. Batsford Ltd, 1957.
517 The Irish Catholic Directory and Almanac for 1895. Dublin:
    James Duffy and Co., Ltd., n.d.
518 The Irish Catholic Directory and Almanac for 1897. Dublin:
    James Duffy and Co., Ltd., n.d.
519 The Irish Catholic Directory and Almanac for 1898. Dublin:
    James Duffy and Co., Ltd., n.d.
520 The Isle of Wight in a Series of Views Printed in Oil
    Colours. London: T. Nelson and Sons, n.d.
521 Jacks, Laurence Pearsall. From Authority to Freedom: The
    Spiritual Pilgrimage of Charles Hargrove. London:
    Williams & Norgate, 1920.
522 Jebb, Richard Claverhouse. Homer: An Introduction to the
    Iliad and the Odyssey. 2nd ed. Glasgow: James
    Maclehose and Sons, 1887.
523 Jesuits. General Examination, Summary of Bulls, Triduum
    Letters. Roehampton: Manresa Press, 1883.
524 Jesuits. Irish Province. Catalogus Provinciae Hiberniae
    Societatis Jesu. Dublin: Brown and Nolan, 1884.
525 _____ The Irish Jesuit Directory and Year Book 1954.
    Dublin: "Irish Messenger" Office, n.d.
526 Johnson, Edgar. Charles Dickens: His Tragedy and
    Triumph. New York: Simon and Schuster, 1952.
527 Johnson, Lionel. Selected Poems. London: Burns Oates &
    Washbourne Ltd., 1934.
528 Johnston, John Octavius. Life and Letters of Henry Parry
    Liddon. London: Longmans, Green, and Co., 1904.
529 Jones, David. David Jones: An Exhibition of Paintings,
    Drawings and Engravings. 2nd ed. Cardiff, Wales:
    Arts Council of Great Britain, Welsh Committee, 1954.
530 Jowett, Benjamin. Letters of Benjamin Jowett, M.A.,
    Master of Balliol College, Oxford, edited by Evelyn
    Abbott and Lewis Campbell. London: John Murray, 1899.
531 _____ The Life and Letters of Benjamin Jowett, M. A.,
    Master of Balliol College, Oxford. 2 vols. 3rd ed.
    London: John Murray, 1897.

37

532 Keats, John. Odes Sonnets & Lyrics of John Keats.
Oxford: Daniel, 1895.

533 Kelshall, T. M. Robert Bridges: (Poet Laureate). London:
Robert Scott, [1924].

534 Kennedy, J. The Manor and Parish Church of Hampstead
and its Vicars. London: S. Mayle, 1906.

535 Kent, William. London for the Literary Pilgrim. London:
Rockliff, 1949.

536 Kilbracken, Arthur Godley. Reminiscences of Lord
Kilbracken. London: Macmillan and Co., Limited, 1931.

537 Kilburn, Edmund E. Catholic Emancipation and the Second
Spring: A Century's Record from 1829 to 1929. London:
Burns Oates & Washbourne Ltd., 1929.

538 _____ A Walk Round the Church of the London Oratory.
7th ed. London: Sands & Co., n.d.

539 Knight, Charles, ed. London. 6 vols. in 3. London:
Henry G. Bohn, 1851.

540 _____, ed. Old England: A Pictorial Museum of Regal,
Ecclesiastical, Municipal, Baronial, and Popular
Antiquities. 2 vols. London: James Sangster and Co.,
n.d.

541 Knight, William. Wordsworthiana: A Selection from Papers
read to The Wordsworth Society. London: Macmillan &
Co., 1889.

542 Koch, Edward. The Parish Church of Saint John, Hampstead.
London: Society for Promoting Christian Knowledge, 1928.

543 LaDriere, J. Craig. "The Comparative Method in the Study
of Prosody," Proceedings of the Second Congress of the
International Comparative Literature Association. Vol. I.
Chapel Hill, 1959, 160-75.

544 Lamalle, Edmund, S.J. "Bibliographia de Historia
Societatis Iesu" (Reprint), Archivum Historicum
Societatis Iesu, 17 (1948), 226-85.

545 Lancelot, John Bennett. Francis James Chavasse: Bishop
of Liverpool. Oxford: Basil Blackwell, 1929.

546 Lataste, Marie, Sister, R.S.C.J. Letters and Writings of
Marie Lataste, translated by E. H. Thompson. 3 vols.
2nd ed. London: Burns & Oates, 1893-1894.

547 La Tour du Pin, Patrice de. The Dedicated Life in Poetry
and the Correspondence of Laurent de Cayeux,
translated by G. S. Fraser. Changing World Series.
London: Harvill Press, 1948.

548 Laver, James. English Costume of the Nineteenth Century.
London: Adam & Charles Black, 1950.

549 _____, comp. Victorian Vista. London: Hulton Press, 1954.

550 Layard, Austen Henry. Discoveries in the Ruins of Nineveh
    and Babylon. London: John Murray, 1853.
551 _____ Nineveh and Its Remains. 2 vols. London: John
    Murray, 1849.
552 Lear, Edward. Nonsense Songs, Stories, Botany, and
    Alphabets. London: Robert John Bush, 1871.
553 Lee, Frederick George. Historical Sketches of the
    Reformation. London: Griffith, Farran, Okeden &
    Welsh, [1878].
554 Leo XIII, Pope. Letter Apostolic Concerning Anglican
    Orders. London: Catholic Truth Society, 1896.
555 Liddell, Adolphus George Charles. Notes from the Life of
    an Ordinary Mortal: Being a Record of Things Done,
    Seen and Heard at School, College, and in the World
    During the Latter Half of the 19th Century. New York:
    E. P. Dutton and Company, 1911.
556 Liddon, Henry Parry. The Divinity of Our Lord and Saviour
    Jesus Christ: Eight Lectures Preached Before the
    University of Oxford in the Year 1866. London:
    Rivingtons, 1869.
557 _____ Life of Edward Bouverie Pusey, edited by J. O.
    Johnston and Robert J. Wilson. 4 vols. 3rd ed. London:
    Longmans, Green, and Co., 1893.
558 _____ Sermons Preached Before the University of Oxford
    Chiefly During the Years 1863-1865. 2nd ed. London:
    Rivingtons; Oxford: James Parker and Co., 1866.
559 Lillie, Handley William Russell, S.J. Father John Driscoll,
    S.J.: A Memoir. Roehampton: Manresa Press, 1947.
560 Lindsay, Donald and E. S. Washington. A Portrait of
    Britain Between the Exhibitions 1851-1951. Oxford:
    Clarendon Press, 1952.
561 Linton, William James. Threescore and Ten Years 1820 to
    1890: Recollections. New York: Charles Scribner's
    Sons, 1894.
562 Little, Vilma G. The Sacrifice of Praise: An Introduction
    to the Meaning and Use of the Divine Office. London:
    Longmans, Green and Co, 1957.
563 Lloyd's Register of British & Foreign Shipping. Annals of
    Lloyd's Register: Being a Sketch of the Origin,
    Constitution, and Progress of Lloyd's Register of British
    & Foreign Shipping. London: Wyman and Sons, 1884.
564 Lockhard, John Gilbert. The Story: All Saints, Margaret
    Street. London: All Saints, Margaret Street, 1950.
565 Loftie, William John. A History of London. 2 vols. 2nd
    ed., rev. and enl. London: Edward Stanford, 1884.

566 London. Brief Guide to the National Museums and
Galleries of London: London: H. M. Stationery Office,
1935.

567 Loyola, Ignacio de, Saint. Exercitia Spiritualia S. P.
Ignatii de Loyola cum Versione Litterali ex Autographo
Hispanico, Notis Illustrata Addita Appendice de Ratione
Meditandi. Editio Parisiensis Prima, Juxta Romanam
Editionem Quintam. Lutetiae Parisiorum: Typis V.
Goupy et Sociorum, 1865.

568 Lucas, Frederick. Reasons for Becoming a Roman Catholic;
Addressed to The Society of Friends. London: Charles
Dolman, 1839.

569 Lucas, Herbert W., S.J. The Road to Reunion: Two
Lectures Delivered in St. Winefride's Church, St.
Asaph, on June 24th and 26th, 1896. Cardiff: St.
Teilo's Catholic Historical Society of Wales, 1896.

570 Mackail, John William. James Leigh Strachan-Davidson
Master of Balliol: A Memoir. Oxford: Clarendon Press,
1925.

571 _____ The Life of William Morris. 2 vols. London:
Longmans, Green and Co, 1899.

572 McKay, George Leslie. A Bibliography of Robert Bridges.
New York: Columbia University Press; London: Oxford
University Press, 1933.

573 Mackenzie, Faith Compton. William Cory: A Biography
with a Selection of Poems, some Unpublished, Others
from 'Ionica,' and a List of Cory's Works. London:
Constable, 1950.

574 Mackinnon, Alan Murray. The Oxford Amateurs: A Short
History of Theatricals at the University. London:
Chapman and Hall, Ltd., 1910.

575 MacNeice, Louis. Modern Poetry: A Personal Essay.
London: Oxford University Press, 1938.

576 Macqueen-Pope, W. Twenty Shillings in the Pound.
London: Hutchinson & Co. Ltd, 1951.

577 Magnus, Laurie. Herbert Warren of Magdalen: President
and Friend 1853-1930. London: John Murray, 1932.

578 Mallock, William Hurrell. The New Republic: Or
Culture, Faith, and Philosophy in an English Country
House. new ed. London: Chatto & Windus, 1900.

579 Mangan, Francis Joseph, S.J. "The Province During the
War" (Reprint), Letters and Notices, 55 (January,
1947), 18-26.

580 Manning, Henry Edward, Cardinal. The Present Crisis of
The Holy See Tested by Prophecy: Four Lectures.
London: Burns & Lambert, 1861.
581 _____ The Preservation of Unendowed Canonries. Pusey
Library Pamphlet. London: Rivingtons, 1840.
582 Margrie, William, comp. The Poets of Peckham: A
Collection of Democratic Poems and Pieces Mainly
About South London. London: W. Margrie, n.d.
583 Mariale Novum: A Series of Sonnets on the Titles of Our
Lady's Litany by Members of the Society of Jesus.
London: Longmans, Green, & Co., 1907.
584 Markby, A. Wilkinson, ed. A Short Guide to St. Peter's
Church Dorchester. rev. ed. Dorchester: Longmans
(Dorchester) Ltd., 1953.
585 Martindale, Cyril Charles, S.J. Bernard Vaughan, S.J.
London: Longmans, Green and Co., 1923.
586 _____ Catholics in Oxford: Being a Sketch of their
Struggles and Fortunes from the Martyrdom of Edmund
Campion in 1581 down to the Present Day in
Commemoration of the Jubilee of the Parish Church of
St. Aloysius. Oxford: Basil Blackwell, 1925.
587 Masefield, John. "Poetry and Perfection," Saturday
Review, 35 (March 12, 1952), 9-11, 41.
588 Mason, Frederick B. Gibb's Illustrated Guide to St.
Alban's Abbey. St. Alban's: Gibbs & Bamforth, 1876.
589 Mateaux, Clara L. Rambles Round London Town. London:
Cassell & Company, Limited, n.d.
590 Maxwell, Anna. Hampstead: Its Historic Houses, Its
Literary and Artistic Associations. London: James
Clarke & Co.; Hampstead: James Hewetson & Son, n.d.
591 Maxwell-Scott, Mary Monica. Henry Schomberg Kerr:
Sailor and Jesuit. London: Longmans, Green, and Co.,
1901.
592 Mee, Arthur, ed. Oxfordshire: County of Imperishable
Fame. London: Hodder and Stoughton Limited, 1948.
593 Merchant Taylors' School Register 1851-1920, edited by
E. P. Hart. London: Adlard and Son and West Newman,
Limited, 1923.
594 Meynell, Alice Christiana (Thompson). The Second Person
Singular and other Essays. London: Humphrey Milford,
Oxford University Press, 1922.
595 Meynell, Wilfrid. Benjamin Disraeli: An Unconventional
Biography. 2 vols. Vol. 1 is 2nd ed. London:
Hutchinson & Co., 1904.

596 Meyrick, Frederick. Memories of Life at Oxford, and
Experiences in Italy, Greece, Turkey, Germany, Spain,
and Elsewhere. London: John Murray, 1905.

597 Middleton, John Henry. Ancient Rome in 1885. Edinburgh:
Adam and Charles Black, 1885.

598 _____ The Remains of Ancient Rome. 2 vols. London:
Adam and Charles Black, 1892.

599 Middleton, Robert Dudley. Newman & Bloxam: An Oxford
Friendship. London: Geoffrey Cumberlege, Oxford
University Press, 1947.

600 Mill, John Stuart. An Examination of Sir William Hamilton's
Philosophy and of the Principal Philosophical Questions
Discussed in his Writings. 4th ed. London: Longmans,
Green, Reader, and Dyer, 1872.

601 Millais, John Guille. The Life and Letters of Sir John
Everett Millais, President of the Royal Academy.
2 vols. London: Methuen & Co., 1899.

602 Milton, John. The Poetical Works of John Milton,
edited by Egerton Brydges. new ed. London: William
Tegg & Co., 1853.

603 Minchin, Humphrey Cotton, ed. The Legion Book. London:
Cassell and Company Ltd., 1929.

604 Miniatures of the Life of Our Lady: From the Collection of
Medieval Manuscripts in the Baden State Library,
Karlsruhe, West Germany, notes by Dr. Franz Schmitt.
Westminster, Maryland: Newman Press, 1960.

605 "Minor Queries Answered: Selion," Notes and Queries,
First Series, 4 (October 4, 1851), 258.

606 Minot, Laurence. The Poems of Laurence Minot, edited by
Joseph Hall. 2nd ed. Clarendon Press Series. Oxford:
Clarendon Press, 1897.

607 Mitchell, Rosamund Joscelyne and Mary Dorothy Rose Leys.
A History of London Life. London: Longmans, Green
and Co, 1958.

608 Molesworth, William Nassau. The History of the Reform
Bill of 1832. London: Chapman and Hall; Manchester:
Ireland and Co., 1865.

609 Monro, Margaret Theodora. Blessed Margaret Clitherow.
New York: Longmans, Green and Co., 1947.

610 Morrah, Herbert Arthur. The Oxford Union 1823-1923.
London: Cassell & Company, Ltd, 1923.

611 Morris, John, S.J. "Jesuits and Seculars in the Reign of
Elizabeth" (Reprint), Dublin Review, 23 (April, 1890),
243-55.

612 _____ Daily Duties: An Instruction for Novices of the
Society. Roehampton: Manresa Press, 1889.
613 _____ Journals Kept During Times of Retreat, edited by
J. H. Pollen, S.J. 2nd ed. London: Burns and Oates,
Limited; New York: Benziger Brothers, 1896.
614 _____ Meditation: An Instruction for Novices. Roehampton:
Manresa Press, 1885.
615 Morton, William Cuthbert. The Language of Anatomy,
edited by Robert Bridges. S.P.E. Tract No. 9. Oxford:
Clarendon Press, 1922.
616 Mount St. Mary's College, Sheffield, England. Centenary
Record 1842-1942. n.p., n.d.
617 _____ Mount St. Mary's College, Spinkhill . . . via
Sheffield: Barlborough Hall School (Preparatory).
Sheffield: Sir W. C. Leng & Co., Ltd., 1939.
618 Mozley, Thomas. Reminiscences Chiefly of Oriel College
and the Oxford Movement. 2 vols. London: Longmans,
Green, and Co., 1882.
619 Myers, Frederic William H. Fragments of Prose & Poetry,
edited by Eveleen Myers. London: Longmans, Green,
and Co., 1904.
620 National Book League, London. Victorian Fiction: An
Exhibition of Original Editions at 7 Albermarle Street,
London, January to February 1947, arranged by John
Carter with the Collaboration of Michael Sadleir.
London: Cambridge University Press, 1947.
621 Nettleship, Richard Lewis. Memoir of Thomas Hill Green.
London: Longmans, Green, and Co., 1906.
622 _____ Philosophical Remains of Richard Lewis Nettleship,
edited by A. C. Bradley. 2nd ed. London: Macmillan
and Co., Limited, 1901.
623 A New Pocket Companion for Oxford: Or, Guide Through
the University. new ed. Oxford: Printed for J. Cooke,
1813.
624 Newbolt, Henry John. The Later Life and Letters of Sir
Henry Newbolt, edited by Margaret Newbolt. London:
Faber and Faber Limited, 1942.
625 _____ My World as in my Time: Memoirs of Sir Henry
Newbolt 1862-1932. London: Faber and Faber Limited,
1932.
626 Newman, John Henry. An Essay in Aid of a Grammar of
Assent. London: Burns, Oates, & Co., 1870.
627 _____ A Letter Addressed to His Grace the Duke of Norfolk
on Occasion of Mr. Gladstone's Recent Expostulation.
London: B. M. Pickering, 1875.

628 _____ Letters of John Henry Newman, edited by Derek
     Stanford and Muriel Spark. London: Peter Owen
     Limited, 1957.
629 Newton, Douglas. Catholic London. London: Robert Hale
     Limited, 1950.
630 Nichols, Beverley. 25: Being a Young Man's Candid
     Recollections of his Elders and Betters. London:
     Jonathan Cape, 1931.
631 Northcote, J. Spencer. A Pilgrimage to La Salette.
     Pusey Library Pamphlet. London: Burns and Lambert,
     1852.
632 Noyes, Alfred. The Wine-Press: A Tale of War. Edinburgh:
     William Blackwood and Sons, 1913. [Bookplate printed
     "W. R. Innes Hopkins."]
633 Noyes, Hugh, comp. The Isle of Wight Bedside Anthology.
     Bognor Regis: Arundel Press, 1951.
634 Nute, Grace Lee. "Voyageurs' Artist," Beaver, 278
     (June, 1947), 32-7.
635 Odds and Ends. 2 vols. Edinburgh: Edmonston and
     Douglas, 1866-1867.
636 Ogilvie, John, ed. The Imperial Dictionary, English,
     Technological, and Scientific; Adapted to the Present
     State of Literature, Science, and Art. 2 vols. Glasgow:
     Blackie and Son, 1851.
637 _____, ed. A Supplement to the Imperial Dictionary.
     Glasgow: Blackie and Son, 1862.
638 Ogilvie, Vivian. The English Public School. London:
     B. T. Batsford Ltd, 1957.
639 The Old Public School-Boys' Who's Who Series: Eton.
     London: St. James's Press, 1933.
640 Oliphant, Margaret (Wilson). Annals of a Publishing
     House: William Blackwood and His Sons, Their
     Magazine and Friends. 3 vols. Edinburgh: William
     Blackwood and Sons, 1897-1898.
641 Oliver, Edward James. Coventry Patmore. London: Sheed
     and Ward, 1956.
642 O'Meara, Kathleen (Grace Ramsay, pseud.) Thomas Grant:
     First Bishop of Southwark. London: Smith, Elder, &
     Co., 1874.
643 Omond, Thomas Stewart. A Study of Metre. London:
     Alexander Moring Ltd. 1920.
644 "On Robert Bridges," Periodical, 31 (Winter, 1955-1956),
     144-47.

645 O'Riordan, Michael. Catholicity and Progress in Ireland.
2nd ed. London: Kegan Paul, Trench, Trubner & Co.,
Ltd.; St. Louis: B. Herder, 1905.
646 Otis, William Bradley and Morriss H. Needleman, eds.
An Outline-History of English Literature. 2 vols. V. 1,
4th ed. V. 2, 2nd ed. New York: Barnes & Noble,
Inc., 1954.
647 Ouseley, Frederick Arthur Gore. A Treatise on Counterpoint,
Canon and Fugue Based Upon That of Cherubini.
Clarendon Press Series. Oxford: Clarendon Press, 1869.
648 Oxford City Council. Oxford Official Handbook. Oxford:
Alden & Co., Ltd., n.d.
649 Oxford Society for Promoting the Study of Gothic Architecture. A Guide to the Architectural Antiquities in the
Neighbourhood of Oxford. Oxford: John Henry Parker,
1846.
650 Oxfordshire, England. Heythrop Hall. Photographs taken
by Fr. de Zulueta & Fr. Tritart [?] at Heythrop Hall on
May 24, 1923.
651 Page, Frederick. Patmore: A Study in Poetry. London:
Humphrey Milford, Oxford University Press, 1933.
652 Pagenstecher, Dr. History of East & West Ham. 3rd ed.
Stratford: Wilson & Whitworth, Ltd., 1909.
653 Pantasaph Monastery. Holywell, Wales. The History of
Pantasaph. new and rev. ed. Nottingham: Turner's
Catholic Press, n.d. [Site of Well of St. Winefride.]
654 Paravicini, Frances de. Early History of Balliol College.
London: Kegan Paul, Trench, Trubner, & Co., Ltd.,
1891.
655 Parker, John Henry. An Introduction to the Study of Gothic
Architecture. 6th ed. Oxford: Parker and Co., 1881.
656 Parkhurst, C. A. A Simple History of India. rev. ed.
Calcutta: Macmillan and Co., Limited, 1948.
657 Parry, Thomas. A History of Welsh Literature, translated
by H. Idris Bell. Oxford: Clarendon Press, 1955.
658 Pater, Walter Horatio. Appreciations with an Essay on
Style. London: Macmillan and Co., Limited, 1898.
659 _____ Gaston de Latour: An Unfinished Romance. London:
Macmillan and Co., Limited, 1920.
660 _____ Greek Studies: A Series of Essays. London:
Macmillan and Co., Limited, 1922.
661 _____ Imaginary Portraits. London: Macmillan and Co.,
1887.
662 _____ Marius the Epicurean: His Sensations and Ideas.
2 vols. London: Macmillan and Co., Limited, 1902.

663 _____ Miscellaneous Studies: A Series of Essays. London: Macmillan and Co., Limited, 1900.

664 _____ The Renaissance: Studies in Art and Poetry. 2nd ed. London: Macmillan and Co., 1877.

665 Paterson, Daniel. Paterson's Roads; Being an Entirely Original and Accurate Description of all the Direct and Principal Cross Roads in England and Wales, with Part of the Roads of Scotland. London: Rees, Orme, Brown, Green, and Longman; etc., [1826].

666 Patmore, Coventry Kersey Dighton. The Angel in the House: The Betrothal. London: John W. Parker and Son, 1854.

667 _____ The Angel in the House. Book II. The Espousals. London: John W. Parker and Son, 1856.

668 _____ The Angel in the House. 2 vols. London: Macmillan and Co., 1863.

669 _____ The Angel in the House. Book I, II. 3rd ed. London: John W. Parker and Son, 1860.

670 _____ The Angel in the House. 4th ed. London: Macmillan and Co., 1866.

671 _____ The Angel in the House. 5th ed. London: George Bell and Sons, n.d.

672 _____ The Angel in the House. 6th ed. London: George Bell and Son, 1885.

673 _____ The Angel in the House. London: George Bell and Son, 1905.

674 _____ The Angel in the House. London: G. Bell and Sons, Ltd., 1920.

675 _____ Faithful For Ever. London: John W. Parker and Son, 1860.

676 _____ Florilegium Amantis, edited by Richard Garnett. London: George Bell & Sons, [1879].

677 _____ Odes. Boston: Boston College, 1936.

678 _____ Poems. 2 vols. 3rd collective ed. London: George Bell and Son, 1887.

679 _____ Poems. 2 vols. 4th collective ed. London: George Bell and Son, 1890.

680 _____ Poems. 2 vols. 9th collective ed. London: George Bell and Sons, 1906.

681 _____ Poems. London: George Bell and Sons, 1909.

682 _____ Poems. London: G. Bell and Sons, Ltd., 1915.

683 _____ Poems. London: G. Bell and Sons, Ltd., 1921.

684 _____ The Poems of Coventry Patmore, edited by Frederick Page. London: Geoffrey Cumberlege, Oxford University Press, 1949.

685 _____ Principle in Art Etc. new ed. London: George Bell
and Sons, 1898.

686 _____ Principle in Art, Religio Poetae and Other Essays.
London: Duckworth & Co., 1913.

687 _____ Religio Poetae Etc. London: George Bell and Sons,
1893.

688 _____ The Rod, the Root and the Flower, edited by Derek
Patmore. London: Grey Walls Press, 1950.

689 _____ Selected Verse. London: Burns Oates &
Washbourne, 1934.

690 _____ A Selection of Poems by Coventry Patmore,
edited by Derek Patmore. London: Grey Walls Press,
1948.

691 _____ The Unknown Eros. I.-XLVI. London: George Bell
and Sons, 1878.

692 _____ The Victories of Love. London: Macmillan and Co.,
1863.

693 Patmore, Derek. The Life and Times of Coventry Patmore.
London: Constable and Company Ltd, 1949.

694 _____ The Life and Times of Coventry Patmore. New York:
Oxford University Press, 1949.

695 _____ Portrait of My Family. London: Cassell & Co.,
Ltd., 1935.

696 Paul, Charles Kegan. Memories. London: Kegan Paul,
Trench, Trubner & Co. Ltd, 1899.

697 Payn, James. By Proxy. 2 vols. London: Chatto and
Windus, 1878. [With twelve illustrations by Arthur
Hopkins.]

698 Pearl, Cyril. The Girl with the Swansdown Seat.
Indianapolis: Bobbs-Merrill Company, Inc., 1955.

699 The Penguin Book of Contemporary Verse, edited by
Kenneth Allott. Melbourne: Penguin Books, 1953.

700 Perrin, Noel. "Answers to Poets' Questions," New
Yorker, 41 (June 26, 1966), 23.

701 Petre, William. Catholic Systems of School Discipline:
Being Part II of the 'Position and Prospects of Liberal
Education'. London: Burns and Oates, 1878.

702 _____ The Position and Prospects of Catholic Liberal
Education, I. London: Burns and Oates, 1878.

703 Peyre, Henri. Problemes Francais de Demain: Reflexions
a Propos d'un Livre Recent. New York: Moretus Press,
1943.

704 Philip Neri, Saint. The London Oratory 1849-1949.
London: Oratory of St. Philip Neri; The Catholic
Truth Society, 1949.

705 Phillips, Claude. Frederick Walker and his Works.
London: Seeley and Co. Limited; New York: Macmillan
Company, 1897.

706 Phillipson, Wulstan, O.S.B. "Digby Mackworth Dolben,"
Downside Review, 53 (January, 1935), 52-68.

707 Philip's Plan of the Town and Port of Liverpool with
Birkenhead and the Adjoining Cheshire Coast. London:
Philip, n.d.

708 Phythian, John Ernest, comp. Handbook to the Permanent
Collection of the Manchester City Art Gallery.
Manchester: Artistic Printing Co. Ltd., 1910.

709 Picton, James Allanson. Memorials of Liverpool Historical
and Topographical Including a History of the Dock
Estate. 2 vols. 2nd ed. rev. London: Longmans,
Green & Co.; Liverpool: G. G. Walmsley, 1875.

710 Plowden, Robert. A Sermon Preached at the Opening of
the Roman Catholic Chapel, Trenchard Street, Bristol.
Bristol: M. F. Hickey, 1890.

711 Plowman, Max. Bridge into the Future: Letters of Max
Plowman, edited by Dorothy Lloyd Plowman. London:
Andrew Dakers Limited, 1944.

712 Poets at Work: Essays Based on the Modern Poetry
Collection at the Lockwood Memorial Library, Univer-
sity of Buffalo. New York: Harcourt, Brace and
Company, 1948.

713 Pollen, John Hungerford, S.J. "The Conversion of Father
John Morris" (Reprint), Month, 82 (October, 1894),
167-83.

714 _____ "Father John Strassmaier, S.J., Assyriologist"
(Reprint), Month, 135 (February, 1920), 137-44.

715 _____ "In Memoriam: Father Joseph Stevenson, S.J. A
Biographical Sketch, with a list of his published works"
(Reprint), Month, 83 (March-April, 1895), 331-44.

716 _____ The Life and Letters of Father John Morris of the
Society of Jesus. 1826-1893. London: Burns and
Oates, Limited; New York: Benziger Brothers, 1896.

717 _____ "A Memorial of Father John Morris, S.J." (Reprint),
Month, 79 (November, 1893), 467-77.

718 _____ "Relics of Saint Beuno, Being a Study of the Extant
Traces of that Saint" (Reprint), Month, 80 (February,
1894), 235-47.

719 Porter, George, S.J. The Letters of the Late Father George
Porter, S.J., Archbishop of Bombay. London: Burns &
Oates, Limited; New York: Catholic Publication
Society Co., 1891.

720 Practica Quaedam ad Formulam Scribendi, Paradigmata
Informationum et Formulae Variae. Florentiae:
Raphaelis Ricci, 1884.

721 Preston, Joseph Harold. The Story of Hampstead. London:
Staples Press, 1948.

722 Price, J. B. "Robert Bridges," Contemporary Review, 185
(1954), 290-94.

723 Proceedings Against the Archdeacon of Taunton; Grounds
and Principles of Defence, with the Archdeacon's Eight
Propositions. Pusey Library Pamphlet. n.p., 1856.

724 Proctor, Richard Wright. Memorials of Bygone Manchester
with Glimpses of the Environs. Manchester: Palmer and
Howe; London: Simpkin, Marshall, & Co., 1880.

725 _____ Memorials of Manchester Streets. Manchester:
Thomas Sutcliffe, 1874.

726 Pugin, Augustus Welby Northmore. Some Remarks on the
Articles Which have Recently Appeared in the "Rambler,"
Relative to Ecclesiastical Architecture and Decoration.
London: Charles Dolman, 1850.

727 Purcell, William. Onward Christian Soldier: A Life of
Sabine Baring-Gould, Parson, Squire, Novelist,
Antiquary 1834-1924. London: Longmans, Green and
Co, 1957.

728 Pusey, Edward Bouverie. The Church of England a Portion
of Christ's One Holy Catholic Church, and a Means of
Restoring Visible Unity: An Eirenicon, in a Letter to the
Author of "The Christian Year." London: Gilbert and
Rivington, 1865.

729 _____ Spiritual Letters of Edward Bouverie Pusey, edited
by J. O. Johnston and W. C. E. Newbolt. London:
Longmans, Green, and Co., 1898.

730 Putt, Samuel Gorley. Cousins and Strangers. Cambridge,
Massachusetts: Harvard University Press, 1956.

731 Pycroft, James. Oxford Memories: A Retrospect After
Fifty Years. 2 vols. London: Richard Bentley & Son,
1886.

732 Quennell, Marjorie (Courtney) and C. H. B. Quennell. A
History of Everyday Things in England. Vol. 4: The Age
of Production 1851-1948. 4th ed. rev. London: B. T.
Batsford Ltd, 1948.

733 Quennell, Peter. Victorian Panorama: A Survey of Life &
Fashion from Contemporary Photographs. London: B. T.
Batsford Ltd., 1937.

734 Raleigh, Walter Alexander. A Selection from the Letters of Sir Walter Raleigh (1880-1922), edited by Lady Raleigh. London: Methuen & Co. Ltd., 1928. [Introduction by Robert Bridges.]

735 "Recollections of Oxford: A Day with the Christchurch Drag," Once a Week, 2 (January 21, 1860), 77-81.

736 Resesdale, Lord. Observations on the Judgments in the Gorham Case. London: Rivingtons, 1850.

737 Richards, Ivor Armstrong. Speculative Instruments. London: Routledge & Kegan Paul, 1955.

738 Ritchie, Anna Isabella (Thackeray). The Village on the Cliff. 2nd ed. London: Smith, Elder & Co., 1867.

739 Ritchie, James Ewing. East Anglia. Personal Recollections and Historical Associations. 2nd ed., rev. London: Jarrold & Sons, 1893.

740 "Robert Bridges, Poet Laureate," Dial (Chicago), 55 (August 1, 1913), 69-71.

741 Roberts, William. Sir William Beechey, R.A. London: Duckworth and Co.; New York: Charles Scribner's Sons, 1907.

742 Robertson, George Stuart. The Law of Copyright. Oxford: Clarendon Press, 1912.

743 Rogers, James Edwin Thorold. Education in Oxford: Its Method, its Aids, and its Rewards. London: Smith, Elder and Co., 1861.

744 Rolfe, Frederick William (Frederick Baron Corvo, pseud.). Letters to Grant Richards by Frederick Baron Corvo. London: Peacock Press, 1952.

745 "Roman Vignettes" (Reprint), Month, 175 (January, 1940), 57-64.

746 Roper, Harold, S.J. Farm Street Church: Short History and Guide. London: Salesian Press, n.d.

747 Roscoe, Thomas. Wanderings and Excursions in North Wales. London: Charles Tilt, and Simpkin and Co.; Birmingham: Wrightson and Webb, [1836].

748 Rossetti, Christina Georgina. New Poems, edited by William Michael Rossetti. London: Macmillan and Co., 1896.

749 _____ A Pageant and Other Poems. London: Macmillan and Co., 1881.

750 _____ The Prince's Progress and Other Poems. London: Macmillan and Co., 1866.

751 Rothenstein, William. Men and Memories: Recollections of William Rothenstein. 2 vols. V. 1, 1872-1900; V. 2, 1900-1922. London: Faber & Faber Ltd., 1931, 1934.

752 _____ Twelve Portraits. London: Faber & Faber Limited, 1929.

753 _____ Twenty-Four Portraits with Critical Appreciations by Various Hands. London: George Allen & Unwin Ltd., 1920.

754 Rottmann, Alexander. London Catholic Churches: A Historical & Artistic Record. London: Sands & Co., 1926.

755 Routh, Harold Victor. Towards the Twentieth Century: Essays in the Spiritual History of the Nineteenth. New York: Macmillan Company; Cambridge, England: University Press, 1937.

756 Rowse, Alfred Leslie. The English Spirit: Essays in History and Literature. New York: Macmillan Company, 1946.

757 Royal Society of Painters in Water Colours. London. The Old Water-Colour Society's Club 1928-1929, edited by Randall Davies. Vol. 6. London: The Society, 1929. [Arthur Hopkins listed as member, p. 81.]

758 Russell, George William Erskine. Dr. Pusey. Leaders of the Church 1800-1900 Series. London: A. R. Mowbray & Co. Limited, 1907.

759 _____ Portraits of the Seventies. London: T. Fisher Unwin, Ltd., 1916.

760 Ryder, Henry Ignatius Dudley. Poems, Original and Translated. Dublin: M. H. Gill and Son, 1882.

761 St. Aloysius Church. Oxford, England. Twelve Photographs. n.d.

762 St. Beuno's College. Wales. Chronological Tables from the Time of Christ to the Present Day. Asaph, Wales: St. Beuno's College, 1897.

763 St. Francis Xavier's Church. Dublin. Upper Gardiner Street. Twelve Photographs. n.d.

764 St. Thomas's Church. Canterbury. Burgate Street. Church Year Book, 1948/49. Ramsgate: Graham Cumming, Ltd., n.d.

765 Saintsbury, George Edward Bateman. A History of Nineteenth Century Literature (1780-1900). London: Macmillan and Co., Limited, 1901.

766 _____ A Last Scrap Book. London: Macmillan and Co., Limited, 1924.

767 _____ The Later Nineteenth Century. Vol. 12: Periods of European Literature. Edinburgh: William Blackwood and Sons, 1907.

768 _____ A Scrap Book. London: Macmillan and Co.,
Limited, 1922.
769 _____ A Second Scrap Book. London: Macmillan and Co.,
Limited, 1923.
770 Sala, George Augustus Henry. Gaslight and Daylight, with
some London Scenes they Shine Upon. new ed. London:
Tinsley Brothers, 1872.
771 Salford, England. (Diocese). Official Handbook of
Celebrations for Catholic Emancipation Centenary
1829-1929, Diocese of Salford. Manchester: Service
Guild, 1929.
772 Salter, Herbert Edward, ed. The Oxford Deeds of Balliol
College. Oxford: Privately printed by Horace Hart at
the University Press, 1913.
773 Sansom, Clive. The Witnesses and Other Poems. London:
Methuen & Co. Ltd, 1956.
774 Sayce, Archibald Henry. The Ancient Empires of the East.
London: Macmillan and Co., 1884.
775 Scarfe, Francis. Auden and After: The Liberation of Poetry
1930-1941. London: George Routledge & Sons Ltd.,
1947.
776 Scherer, Edmond Henri Adolphe. Essays on English
Literature, translated by George Saintsbury. London:
Sampson Low, Marston & Company, 1891.
777 Schorer, Mark, Josephine Miles and Gordon McKenzie,
eds. Criticism: The Foundations of Modern Literary
Judgment. New York: Harcourt, Brace and Company,
1948.
778 Scott, Dixon. Liverpool, painted by J. Hamilton Hay.
London: Adam and Charles Black, 1907.
779 Scrope, Simon Thomas. The Past, Present, and Future of
Ireland. A paper read before the Northallerton Liberal
Club, May 21st, 1887. Northallerton: J. Vasey, 1887.
780 Sephton, John. A Handbook of Lancashire Place-Names.
Liverpool: Henry Young & Sons, 1913.
781 Sherwood, William Edward. Oxford Yesterday: Memoirs of
Oxford Seventy Years Ago. Oxford: Basil Blackwell,
1927.
782 The Shotover Papers, or, Echoes from Oxford. Vol. 1,
Nos. 1-13; February 23, 1874--February 9, 1875.
Oxford: J. Vincent, 1874-1875.
783 Simpson, Richard. Edmund Campion: A Biography.
London: Williams and Norgate, 1867.
784 Skelton, Robin. The Poetic Pattern. London: Routledge
and Kegan Paul, 1956.

52

785 Smalley, T., S.J. <u>Brother William Shaw, S.J.: A Memoir</u>.
    Roehampton: Manresa Press, 1947.
786 Smith, Arthur Lionel. <u>Reminiscences of Jowett</u>. Reprinted
    from 'The Blue Book.' Letchworth: Arden Press, n.d.
787 Smith, James and Horace Smith. <u>Rejected Addresses: or,
    The New Theatrum Poetarum</u>. new ed. London: John
    Murray, 1879.
788 Smith, Logan Pearsall. "Robert Bridges: Recollections."
    S.P.E. Tract No. 35. Oxford: Clarendon Press, 1931,
    481-502.
789 Smith, Charles Nowell. <u>Notes on 'The Testament of
    Beauty</u>.' London: Humphrey Milford, Oxford University
    Press, 1931.
790 Smith, William, ed. <u>A Dictionary of Greek and Roman
    Biography and Mythology</u>. 3 vols. London: John
    Murray, 1880.
791 Smyth, Herbert Weir. <u>Greek Grammar</u>, revised by Gordon
    M. Messing. Cambridge, Massachusetts: Harvard
    University Press, 1956.
792 Society for Pure English. S.P.E. Tracts. Nos. 1-22,
    24-5, 28-38, 41-50, 53, 56, 58-65.
793 "Some Further Notes on our Late Editor" [Father Gerard]
    (Reprint), <u>Month</u>, 121 (February, 1913), 113-28.
794 <u>The Song of Roland</u>, translated by John O'Hagan. 2nd ed.
    London: Kegan Paul, Trench & Co., 1883.
795 Sophocles. <u>The Oedipus Tyrannus</u>, edited by R. C. Jebb.
    Cambridge, England: Cambridge University Press, 1885.
796 _____ <u>The Plays and Fragments</u>. Part I: <u>The Oedipus
    Tyrannus</u>, edited by R. C. Jebb. Cambridge, England:
    Cambridge University Press, 1883.
797 _____ <u>The Plays and Fragments</u>. Part I: <u>The Oedipus
    Tyrannus</u>, edited by R. C. Jebb. 2nd ed. Cambridge,
    England: Cambridge University Press, 1887.
798 Sotheby & Co. <u>Catalogue of Nineteenth Century and
    Modern First Editions, Presentation Copies, Autograph
    Letters and Literary Manuscripts</u>. London: Sotheby &
    Co., 1966. Items 115-16, 675-99.
799 Sparrow, John Hanbury Angus. <u>Robert Bridges</u>. Biblio-
    graphical Series of Supplements to 'British Book News'
    on Writers and their Work, No. 147. London: Longmans,
    Green & Co., 1962.
800 Spender, Stephen. <u>Collected Poems 1928-1953</u>. London:
    Faber and Faber, 1955.

801 _____, Elizabeth Jennings and Dannie Abse, eds. New
    Poems 1956. 5th P.E.N. Anthology. London: Michael
    Joseph, 1956.
802 The Spirit of Praise: A Collection of Hymns Old and New.
    London: F. Warne and Co.; New York: Scribner,
    Welford & Co., n.d.
803 Sprigg, Christopher St. John. (Christopher Caudwell,
    pseud.) Illusion and Reality: A Study of the Sources of
    Poetry. London: Lawrence & Wishart, 1947.
804 Squire, John Collings. "Robert Bridges's Lyrical Poems,"
    London Mercury, 1 (April, 1920), 708-17.
805 Stanford, Derek. Dylan Thomas: A Literary Study. London:
    Neville Spearman, 1954.
806 _____ The Freedom of Poetry: Studies in Contemporary
    Verse. London: Falcon Press Limited, 1947.
807 Stanley, Arthur Penrhyn. The Life and Correspondence of
    Thomas Arnold, D.D. 6th ed. London: B. Fellowes,
    1846.
808 Stapleton, Mary Helen Alicia (Dolman). A History of the
    Post-Reformation Catholic Missions in Oxfordshire with
    an Account of the Families Connected with Them.
    London: Henry Frowde, 1906. [Hopkins family, p. 235]
809 Stenning, Ernest Henry. Isle of Man. The County Books
    Series. London: Robert Hale Limited, 1950.
810 Sterne, Laurence. A Sentimental Journey Through France
    and Italy. London: Williams and Norgate, 1910.
    [Number 389 of 500 copies printed. Illustrated by
    Everard Hopkins. Inscribed "Everard Hopkins."]
811 _____ A Sentimental Journey Through France and Italy.
    New York: G. P. Putnam's Sons, 1910. [Illustrated by
    Everard Hopkins.]
812 Steuart, Robert Henry Joseph, S.J. The Last Lap,
    September 28th--November 11th, 1918. n.p., n.d.
813 Stonyhurst College, England. Memorials of Stonyhurst
    College. London: Burns and Oates, 1881.
814 _____ A Stonyhurst Handbook for Visitors and Others.
    Stonyhurst: Stonyhurst College, n.d.
815 _____ Stonyhurst Lists 1794-1886. Stonyhurst:
    Stonyhurst Magazine Office, 1886.
816 _____ Stonyhurst Magazine: Centenary Number. No. 76
    (September, 1894).
817 _____ Views of Stonyhurst College. Derby: Bemrose &
    Sons Ltd., 1931.

818 Stonyhurst College. England. Observatory. Results of
    Geophysical and Solar Observations, 1937. Blackburn:
    Thomas Briggs Ltd., n.d.
819 Stuart, Charles Douglas and A. J. Park. The Variety Stage:
    A History of the Music Halls from the Earliest Period to
    the Present Time. London: T. Fisher Unwin, 1895.
820 Sturgeon, Mary C. Studies of Contemporary Poets.
    London: George G. Harrap & Company, 1916.
821 Swanton, Ernest William Brockton, ed., aided by P.
    Woods. Bygone Haslemere. London: West, Newman
    & Co., 1914.
822 Symonds, John Addington. Sketches and Studies in Italy.
    London: Smith, Elder, & Co., 1879.
823 Talbot, M. D. The Supremacy and Jurisdiction of the
    Roman Pontiffs . . . . by Verax (pseud.), a Catholic
    Layman. Pusey Library Pamphlet. London: Jones,
    1843.
824 Taylor, Geoffrey. The Victorian Flower Garden. London:
    Skeffington, 1952.
825 Taylor, Tom. Leicester Square: Its Associations and its
    Worthies. London: Bickers and Son, 1874.
826 Tepe, G. Bernardo, S.J. Institutiones Theologicae
    in Usum Scholarum. 4 vols. Paris: P. Lethielleux,
    1894-1896.
827 Thomas, Dylan. Adventures in the Skin Trade. London:
    Putnam, 1955.
828 _____ Collected Poems 1934-1952. London: J. M. Dent
    & Sons Ltd, 1953.
829 _____ Deaths and Entrances: Poems. London: J. M.
    Dent & Sons Ltd, 1954.
830 _____ The Doctor and the Devils. London: J. M. Dent &
    Sons Ltd, 1953.
831 _____ 18 Poems. London: Fortune Press, 1934.
832 _____ Portrait of the Artist as a Young Dog. Guild Books
    No. 250. London: J. M. Dent & Sons Ltd, 1948.
833 _____ A Prospect of the Sea and Other Stories and Prose
    Writings, edited by Daniel Jones. London: J. M. Dent
    & Sons Ltd, 1955.
834 _____ Quite Early One Morning: Broadcasts. London:
    J. M. Dent & Sons Ltd, 1954.
835 _____ Twenty-Six Poems. London: J. M. Dent & Sons,
    Ltd, 1949. [Number 27 of 150 copies printed,
    inscribed "Dylan Thomas."]

836 _____ Under Milk Wood: A Play for Voices, preface and
     musical settings by Daniel Jones. London: J. M. Dent
     & Sons Ltd, 1954.
837 Thomas, Edward. Walter Pater: A Critical Study. London:
     Martin Secker, 1913.
838 Thomas a Kempis. The Imitation of Christ, translated by
     Leo Sherley-Price. Melbourne: Penguin Books, 1954.
839 Thompson, Edward John. Robert Bridges 1844-1930.
     London: Oxford University Press, 1944.
840 _____ Robert Bridges 1844-1930. London: Oxford Univer-
     sity Press, 1945.
841 Thornbury, George Walter and Edward Walford. Old and
     New London: A Narrative of its History, its People,
     and its Places. 6 vols. (Vols. 1-2 by Thornbury; Vols.
     3-6 by Walford.) London: Cassell, Petter, & Galpin,
     n.d.
842 Thorpe, James Ernest, ed. Milton Criticism: Selections
     from Four Centuries. New York: Rinehart & Company,
     Inc., 1950.
843 Timbs, John. Walks and Talks about London. London:
     Lockwood & Co., 1865.
844 The Times. London. Catholicism To-Day: Letters to the
     Editor Reprinted from The Times with a Special Article
     and a Leading Article. London: Times Publishing
     Company, Limited, 1949.
845 Tollemache, Lionel Arthur. Benjamin Jowett: Master of
     Balliol. 2nd ed. London: Edward Arnold, n.d.
846 Tracts for the Times. Nos. 1-90, 1833-1841. 6 vols.
     London: J. G. F. & J. Rivington; Oxford: J. H.
     Parker, 1840.
847 Tracts for the Times. Nos. 1-46. (Includes Records of
     the Church, Nos. 1-18.) Vol. 1, 1833-1834. new ed.
     London: J. G. & F. Rivington; Oxford: J. H. Parker,
     1838.
848 Treece, Henry. Dylan Thomas: 'Dog Among the Fairies.'
     2nd ed. rev. and reset. London: Ernest Benn Limited,
     1956.
849 Trench, George F. The Land Question: Are the Landlords
     Worth Preserving? or Forty Years' Management of an
     Irish Estate. Dublin: Hodges, Figgis, & Co.; London:
     William Ridgway, 1881.
850 Trench, Richard Chenevix. On the Study of Words. 4th
     ed., rev. London: John W. Parker and Son, 1853.
851 _____ On the Study of Words. 17th ed., rev. London:
     Macmillan and Co., 1878.

852 Trevelyan, Janet Penrose. The Life of Mrs. Humphry Ward. London: Constable and Company Ltd., 1923.

853 Triebner, T. F. A Letter to the Very Revd. J. W. Kirwan D.D., on some Variations from the more Ancient Liturgies of the Church in the form Prescribed in the Canon of the Mass for the Consecration of the Most Holy Eucharist. Pusey Library Pamphlet. London: W. Spooner, 1844.

854 Tristam, Henry. Cardinal Newman and the Church of the Birmingham Oratory: A History and a Guide. Gloucester: British Publishing Company Ltd., 1934.

855 Tuckwell, William. Reminiscences of Oxford. London: Cassell and Company, Limited, 1900.

856 Turner, Vincent, S. J. Father Francis Woodlock, S.J. 1871-1940. Roehampton: Manresa Press, 1947.

857 Turner, Walter James, ed. Impressions of English Literature. Britain in Pictures Series. London: Collins, 1944.

858 Upham, Thomas Cogsell. Life, Religious Opinions and Experience of Madame de la Mothe Guyon: Together with some Account of the Personal History and Religious Opinions of Fenelon, Archbishop of Cambray. 2nd ed. London: Sampson Low, Son, and Co.; Edinburgh: Thomas Constable and Co., 1856.

859 Vance, John Gabriel and J. W. Fortescue. Adrian Fortescue: A Memoir. London: Burns, Oates & Washbourne Ltd, 1924.

860 Vassall-Phillips, Oliver Rodie. After Fifty Years. London: Sheed & Ward, 1928.

861 Vaughan, Charles Edwyn. The Influence of English Poetry upon the Romantic Revival on the Continent. Warton Lecture on English Poetry IV, delivered October 29, 1913. London: Humphrey Milford, Oxford University Press, n.d.

862 Walford, Edward. Greater London: A Narrative of its History, its People, and its Places. 2 vols. London: Cassell & Company, Limited, n.d.

863 _____ Pleasant Days in Pleasant Places. 3rd ed. London: W. H. Allen & Co., 1885.

864 Walford, Lucy Bethia (Colquhon). Memories of Victorian London. London: Edward Arnold, 1912.

865 Walker, William Sidney. Corpus Poetarum Latinorum. London: George Bell & Sons, 1878.

866 Wallis, John Eyre Winstanley. Whalley Abbey: A Short Sketch of its History and Buildings. London: Society for Promoting Christian Knowledge, 1923.

867 Walsh, William Joseph. The Irish University Question:
The Catholic Case. Dublin: Browne and Nolan,
Limited, 1897.

868 Ward, Maisie. Young Mr. Newman. London: Sheed and
Ward, 1948.

869 Ward, Mary Augusta (Arnold). A Writer's Recollections,
by Mrs. Humphry Ward. London: W. Collins Sons &
Co. Ltd., 1918.

870 Warren, Alba H. English Poetic Theory 1825-1865.
Princeton Studies in English, No. 29. Princeton, New
Jersey: Princeton University Press, 1950.

871 Warren, Thomas Herbert. Robert Bridges, Poet Laureate:
Readings from his Poems. A Public Lecture Delivered
in the Examination Schools on November 8, 1913.
Oxford: Clarendon Press, 1913.

872 Warwick Castle: A Brief Account of the Earls of Warwick,
Together with a Description of the Castle and some of
the more Notable Works of Art Therein. Warwick:
Warwick Castle Estate Office, 1954.

873 Watkin, Dom Aelred. "Digby Mackworth Dolben and the
Catholic Church: Some Fresh Evidence," Dublin
Review, 225 (Third Quarter, 1951), 65-70.

874 Weale, William Henry James. Gerard David: Painter and
Illuminator. London: Seeley and Co., limited; New
York: Macmillan and Co., 1895.

875 Weld, Alfred, S.J. Mission of the Zambesi. Part 2.
London: Burns and Oates; Dublin: M. H. Gill and
Son, n.d.

876 Westminster Cathedral Chronicle. Westminster, England.
England's New Cardinal, Rome and Westminster, 1946.
Westminster: The Cathedral Chronicle, 1946.

877 Westminster, England. The City of Westminster Official
Guide. 4th ed. London: Ed. J. Burrow and Co. Ltd.,
1937.

878 Westrup, J. A. "A Great English Song-Writer," Listener,
30 (July 22, 1943), 109.

879 Wheelwright, Philip. Metaphor & Reality. Bloomington:
Indiana University Press, 1962.

880 Whitaker, Thomas Dunham. An History of the Original
Parish of Whalley, and Honor of Clitheroe, in the
Counties of Lancaster and York. 3rd ed., rev. and
enl. London: Nichols, Son, and Bentley, 1818.

881 White, Charles. Country Walks. First Series. London:
London Transport, 1936.

882 _____ Country Walks. Second Series. London: London
Transport, 1936.

883 White, George. Memoir of His Eminence Cardinal
Wiseman, with Portrait and Autograph. 2nd ed. London:
Richardson and Son, 1865.

884 White, Terence Hanbury. Farewell Victoria. London:
Jonathan Cape, 1960.

885 Williams, Charles. Poetry at Present. Oxford: Clarendon
Press, 1931.

886 Williams, Gwyn. An Introduction to Welsh Poetry from the
Beginnings to the Sixteenth Century. London: Faber and
Faber Limited, 1953.

887 _____, trans. The Rent That's Due to Love: A Selection of
Welsh Poems. London: Editions Poetry London Ltd.,
1950.

888 Winters, Yvor. "Robert Bridges and Elizabeth Daryush,"
American Review, 8 (January, 1937), 353-67.

889 The Wonderful Story of London, edited by B. Webster
Smith. 3rd ed. London: Odhams Press, 1956.

890 Wood, Alexander. Ecclesiastical Antiquities of London
and its Suburbs. London: Burns and Oates, 1874.

891 Wood, John George. The Illustrated Natural History. 3
vols. London: George Routledge and Sons, 1865-1875.

892 Woodruff, Douglas. The Tichborne Claimant: A Victorian
Mystery. London: Hollis & Carter, 1957.

893 Wright, Elizabeth Cox. Metaphor Sound and Meaning in
Bridges' 'The Testament of Beauty.' Philadelphia:
University of Pennsylvania Press; London: Geoffrey
Cumberlege, Oxford University Press, 1951.

894 Wright, Elizabeth Mary (Lea). The Life of Joseph Wright.
2 vols. London: Humphrey Milford, Oxford University
Press, 1932.

895 Wright, Thomas (1810-1877). A History of Caricature &
Grotesque in Literature and Art. London: Virtue
Brothers & Co., 1865.

896 Wright, Thomas (1859-1936). The Life of Walter Pater.
2 vols. London: Everett & Co., 1907.

897 Wyatt-Edgell, Alfred. Amadeus and Other Poems. London:
Smith, Elder, & Co., 1873.

898 Yates, Edmund Hodgson. Fifty Years of London Life:
Memoirs of a Man of the World. New York: Harper &
Brothers, 1885.

899 Young, Francis Brett. Robert Bridges: A Critical Study.
London: Martin Secker, 1914.

900 Zulueta, Francis M. de, S.J. <u>Hymns</u> <u>for</u> <u>Easter-Time</u> <u>and</u>
    <u>Corpus</u> <u>Christi</u>. Glory be to God Series III.
    Roehampton: Manresa Press, 1934.
901 _____ <u>Hymns</u> <u>for</u> <u>Lent</u>, <u>Retreats</u>, <u>and</u> <u>Missions</u>. Glory be
    to God Series II. Roehampton: Manresa Press,
    1933-1934.

III Writings on Hopkins

902 Abbott, Claude Colleer. "Further Letters of G. M. Hopkins" (Letter to the Editor), Times Literary Supplement, (February 1, 1957), 65.

903 _____ "Gerard Manley Hopkins" (Letter to the Editor), Times Literary Supplement, (March 13, 1937), 188.

904 _____ "Gerard Manley Hopkins: A Letter and Drafts of Early Poems," Durham University Journal, 32 (January, 1940), 65-73.

905 _____ "Gerard Manley Hopkins: Letters," Notes and Queries, 172 (March 20, 1937), 210.

906 _____ Review of Gerard Manley Hopkins: Priest and Poet, by John Pick. Review of English Studies, 19 (July, 1943), 311-13.

907 _____ "Letters of Gerard Manley Hopkins" (Letter to the Editor), Times Literary Supplement, (March 21, 1935), 176.

908 _____ "The Letters of Gerard Manley Hopkins" (Letter to the Editor), Times Literary Supplement, (October 29, 1954), 696.

909 _____ "The Listener's Book Chronicle." Review of Robert Bridges and Gerard Hopkins 1863-1889: A Literary Friendship, by Jean-Georges Ritz. Listener, 63 (June 23, 1960), 1107-08.

910 _____ "Priest and Poet." Review of Gerard Manley Hopkins: Sermons and Devotional Writings, edited by Christopher Devlin and Journals and Papers, edited by Humphry House and Graham Storey. Listener, 61 (March 12, 1959), 476, 479.

911 _____, ed. Anonymous Review of Further Letters of Gerard Manley Hopkins. New Yorker, 14 (June 25, 1938), 59.

912 _____, ed. Anonymous Review of Further Letters of Gerard Manley Hopkins. Quarterly Review, 295 (July, 1957), 363-64.

913 _____, ed. "Gerard Hopkins." Anonymous Review of The Letters of Gerard Manley Hopkins to Robert Bridges and The Correspondence of Gerard Manley Hopkins and Richard Watson Dixon. Times Literary Supplement, (January 31, 1935), 59.

914 _____, ed. "Gerard Manley Hopkins." Anonymous
     Review of Further Letters of Gerard Manley Hopkins.
     Tablet (London), 171 (May 21, 1938), 666-67.
915 _____, ed. "Gerard Manley Hopkins: A Mind Entirely
     Religious." Anonymous Review of Further Letters of
     Gerard Manley Hopkins. Times Literary Supplement,
     (May 7, 1938), 312.
916 _____, ed. "Hopkins to his Family." Anonymous Review
     of Further Letters of Gerard Manley Hopkins. Times
     Literary Supplement, (December 21, 1956), 763.
917 _____, ed. "Letters of Gerard Hopkins Published."
     Anonymous Review of The Letters of Gerard Manley
     Hopkins to Robert Bridges and The Correspondence of
     Gerard Hopkins and Richard Watson Dixon. Republican
     (Springfield, Massachusetts), (February 24, 1935), 7.
918 _____, ed. Anonymous Review of The Letters of Gerard
     Manley Hopkins to Robert Bridges and The Correspond-
     ence of Gerard Manley Hopkins with R. W. Dixon.
     Life and Letters, 11 (February, 1935), 613-15.
919 _____, ed. "Of Poetry and Poets." Anonymous Review of
     Letters of Gerard Manley Hopkins to Robert Bridges
     and The Correspondence of Gerard Manley Hopkins and
     Richard Watson Dixon, new ed. America, 93 (August
     20, 1955), 496.
920 Abbott, William Henry. "The Image of Time in the Poetry
     of Gerard Manley Hopkins." M.A. thesis, Louisiana
     State University, 1965.
921 Abel, Darrel. "A Biography of Gerard M. Hopkins."
     Review of Gerard Manley Hopkins: A Life, by Eleanor
     Ruggles. South Atlantic Quarterly, 42 (October, 1944),
     415-17.
922 Abraham, John. "The Hopkins Aesthetic" Parts I and II,
     Continuum, 1 (Spring, Autumn, 1963), 32-9, 355-60.
923 Abraham, John August. "Hopkins and Scotus: An Analogy
     between Inscape and Individuation." Ph.D.,
     University of Wisconsin, 1959.
924 Abrams, Meyer Howard. Literature and Belief. English
     Institute Essays. New York: Columbia University
     Press, 1958, 47-8.
925 Adams, Juliette Rose Marie. "The Theory of Language in
     the Poetics of Gerard Manley Hopkins." M.A.
     thesis, University of Toronto, 1963.
926 Agnew, Francis Henry. "The Prosodic Theory of Gerard
     Manley Hopkins and the Philosophy of Duns Scotus."
     M.A. thesis, De Paul University, 1964.

927 Akey, John. "Liturgical Imagery in the Poetry of Gerard Manley Hopkins, Thomas Merton, and Robert Lowell." M.A. thesis, University of Vermont, 1950.

928 Aldington, Richard, ed. The Viking Book of Poetry of the English-Speaking World. New York: Viking Press, 1941, xx-xxi, 1059-62.

929 Alexander, Calvert, S.J. The Catholic Literary Revival. Milwaukee: Bruce Publishing Company, 1935.

930 Allen, Louis. Review of Further Letters of Gerard Manley Hopkins. Durham University Journal, N.S. 18 (June, 1957), 136-37.

931 Allen, Trevor. "Poets as Human Beings," John O'London's Weekly, (September 17, 1948), 435.

932 Allison, Alexander W. "Hopkins' 'I Wake and Feel the Fell of Dark'," Explicator, 17 (May, 1959), 54.

933 Alonso, Damaso. Poesia Espanola: Ensayo de Metodas y Limites Estilisticos. Biblioteca Romanica Hispanica. II. Estudios y Ensayos Vol. 1. 2nd ed. Madrid: Gredos, 1952, 77, 266.

934 _____ "Seis Poemas de Hopkins." Poetas Espanoles Contemporaneos. Biblioteca Romanica Hispanica. II. Estudios y Ensayos Vol. 6. Madrid: Gredos, 1952, 403-22. [Reprinted from "Ensayos Hispano-Ingleses." Homenaje a Walter Starkie. Barcelona: Janes, 15-32.]

935 _____ "Seis Poemas de Hopkins," Trivium (Monterey, Mexico), (January, 1949), 10-17.

936 Altenbernd, Lynn and Leslie Lisle Lewis. Introduction to Literature: Poems. New York: Macmillan Company, 1963, 396-99. [2nd ed., 1969, 349-52.]

937 Altick, Richard D. "Four Victorian Poets and an Exploding Island," Victorian Studies, 3 (March, 1960), 249-60.

938 Ames, Ruth. Review of Further Letters of Gerard Manley Hopkins. Catholic World, 185 (May, 1957), 155.

939 _____ Review of A Hopkins Reader. Catholic World, 177 (August, 1953), 397-98.

940 Amis, Kingsley. "Communication and the Victorian Poet," Essays in Criticism, 4 (October, 1954), 386-99.

941 Anderson, Mary Ann. "Fruit of Silence," Mundelein College Review, 14 (May, 1944), 249-54.

942 Anderson, Walter J. "'The Golden Echo': Religion in the Life and Poetry of Gerard Manley Hopkins." M.A. thesis, Trinity College, 1955.

943 Andreach, Robert J. "Proof in the Putting." Anonymous Review of Studies in Structure. Times Literary Supplement, (August 5, 1965), 680.

944 _____ "The Spiritual Life in Hopkins, Joyce, Eliot and Hart Crane." Ph.D., New York University, 1963.

945 _____ Studies in Structure: The Stages of the Spiritual Life in Four Modern Authors. New York: Fordham University Press, 1964.

946 Angus, Ann Margaret. "Gerard Manley Hopkins," Canadian Poetry, 3 (June, 1938), 9-14.

947 Antonini, Giacomo. "Poesia inglese e americana," Nazione (Florence), (August 14, 1959).

948 "Apollo Society Recital," Times (London), (February 12, 1952).

949 Applejoy, Petronius. "Hopkins Sets a Poetic Signpost," Catholic World, 151 (May, 1940), 184-90.

950 Aprahamian, Felix. "New Spice at the Spa," Sunday Times (London), (July 20, 1958).

951 Armstrong, Robert. "Lifting the Veil," Review of Further Letters of Gerard Manley Hopkins. Poetry Review, 48 (April-June, 1957), 109-10.

952 Armstrong, Thomas. "G. M. Hopkins as a Musician," Oxford Mail (Oxford, England), (December 16, 1957).

953 Arnheim, Rudolf. Poets at Work. New York: Harcourt, Brace & Company, 1948, 33, 58, 91.

954 Arns, Karl. "Sprache und Literatur." Review of "Germanisches Formgefuhl bei Gerard Manley Hopkins," by Georg Karp. Anglia Beiblatt, 52 (1941), 167-69.

955 Aronowitz, Herbert. "The Relationship of the Spiritual Exercises of St. Ignatius to the Poetry of Gerard Manley Hopkins as Evidenced in 'The Wreck of the Deutschland'." B.A. thesis, Rutgers University, 1957.

956 Ash, Lee and Denis Lorenz, comps. Subject Collections. New York: R. R. Bowker Company, 1967, 502.

957 Ashburner, Phoebe. Review of Gerard Manley Hopkins: Priest and Poet, by John Pick. Adelphi, 19 (September, 1943), 127-28.

958 Assad, Thomas J. "A Closer Look at Hopkins' '(Carrion Comfort)'," Tulane Studies in English, 9 (1959), 91-102.

959 _____ "Hopkins' 'The Windhover'," Tulane Studies in English, 11 (1961), 87-95.

960 A [staldi], M [aria] L [uisa]. "Hopkins, Gerard Manley." Dizionario Letterario Bompiani Degli Autori. Vol. 2. Milan: Valentino Bompiani, 1957, 273-74.

961 Astel, Arnfrid. "Ingestalt und Inkfraft bei Gerard Manley Hopkins," Neue Deutsche Hefte (Gutersloh), 93 (May-June, 1963), 48-66.

962 Auden, Wystan Hugh. Review of Gerard Manley Hopkins,
      by E. E. Phare. Criterion, 13 (April, 1934), 497-500.
963 _____ "A Knight of the Infinite." Review of Gerard Manley
      Hopkins: A Life, by Eleanor Ruggles. New Republic,
      111 (August 21, 1944), 223-24. [Reprinted in Literary
      Opinion in America, edited by Morton Dauwen Zabel,
      as "Makers of Modern Poetry: A Knight of the Infinite
      (Gerard Manley Hopkins)." 2nd ed. New York: Harper,
      1951, 253-55.]
964 August, Eugene R. "Hopkins' Dangerous Fire," Victorian
      Poetry, 1 (January, 1963), 72-4.
965 _____ "Notes, Documents, and Critical Comment: The
      Growth of 'The Windhover'," PMLA, 82 (October, 1967),
      465-68.
966 _____ "Word Inscapes: A Study of the Poetic Vocabulary
      of Gerard Manley Hopkins." Ph.D., University of
      Pittsburgh, 1964.
967 "Aus dem Konzertsaal: Kammermusik," Musica
      (Kassel-Wilhelmshoehe, Germany), 14 (December, 1960),
      827.
968 "The Axe and the Stone: A Note on Poetry and Criticism"
      (Editorial), Blue Guitar, 1 (Fall, 1953), unpaginated.
969 Ayers, Robert W. "Hopkins' 'The Windhover': A Further
      Simplification," Modern Language Notes, 71 (December,
      1956), 577-84.
970 Backscheider, Paula. "The Revelation of God to Gerard
      Manley Hopkins as Expressed in his Mature, Complete
      Poems." M.A. thesis, Southern Connecticut State
      College, 1967.
971 Baily, Bertha. "Remembering Gerard Manley Hopkins"
      (Letter to the Editor), Listener, 57 (February 14, 1957),
      275.
972 Baird, Sister Mary Julian, R.S.M. "Blake, Hopkins and
      Thomas Merton," Catholic World, 183 (April, 1956),
      46-9.
973 Baker, Carlos. "The Poetry of Gerard Manley Hopkins."
      Review of Gerard Manley Hopkins, Priest and Poet, by
      John Pick. New York Times Book Review, (June 13,
      1943), 10.
974 Baker, James V. "The Lark in English Poetry," Prairie
      Schooner, 24 (Spring, 1950), 70-9.
975 Baker, Joseph E., ed. The Reinterpretation of Victorian
      Literature. Princeton: Princeton University Press, 1950.

976 Baker, William E. Syntax in English Poetry 1870-1930.
Perspectives in Criticism No. 18. Berkeley: University
of California Press, 1967.

977 Baldi, Sergio. "Cattolicesimo e Poesia nel 'Naufragio del
Deutschland'," Frontespizio (Rome), 11 (1939), 154-64.

978 _____ Gerard Manley Hopkins. Brescia, Italy:
Morcelliana, 1941.

979 _____ "Nota su una Traduzione da Hopkins," Letteratura
(Florence), 4 (1942-1943), 111-13.

980 _____ "Risposta di S. Baldi" (Correspondence), Anglica:
Rivista di Studi Inglesi e Americani (Florence), 1
(October, 1946), 211-12.

981 Balthasar, Hans Urs von. "Hopkins." Herrlichkeit: Eine
Theologische Asthetik, II. Einsiedeln: Johannes Verlag,
1962, 717-66.

982 Barber, Samuel. "A Nun Takes the Veil: Heaven-Haven."
Op. 13, No. 1: Four Songs for Voice and Piano. New
York: G. Schirmer, Inc., 1941. [Musical Setting]

983 Bardacke, Theodore Joseph. "Gerard Manley Hopkins."
M.A. thesis, Syracuse University, 1940.

984 Barker, George. "To Father Gerard Manley Hopkins, S.J."
(Poem). Collected Poems 1930-1955. London: Faber
and Faber, 1957, 174-75.

985 Barnes, Roslyn Tennie. "Gerard Manley Hopkins and
Pierre Teilhard de Chardin: A Formation of Mysticism
for a Scientific Age." M.A. thesis, University of
Iowa, 1962.

986 Barnes, T. R. English Verse: Voice and Movement from
Wyatt to Yeats. Cambridge: University Press, 1967.

987 Baron, Ronald. "Traduciendo a Hopkins," Criterio
(Buenos Aires), 23 (December 21, 1950), 1005-10.

988 Barrett, Alfred, S.J. "As the Air we Breathe," Ave Maria,
N.S. 31 (March 8, 1930), 289-91.

989 _____ "Critics, Communists, and Gerard Manley Hopkins,"
America, 56 (October 31, 1936), 90-1.

990 _____ "Image Makers and Image Breakers," Spirit, 7
(July, 1940), 84-7.

991 _____ "The Tradition of Wit." Return to Poetry, edited by
John G. Brunini, et. al. New York: Declan X. McMullen
Company, 1947, 76-80. [Reprinted from Spirit, January,
1936.]

992 Barry, John. "Gerard Manley Hopkins," Salesianum, 38
(April, 1943), 55-6.

993 Bartlett, John. Familiar Quotations, edited by Christopher
Morley and Louella D. Everett. 11th ed. Boston:
Little, Brown and Company, 1940, 672-73.

994 Bartlett, Phyllis Brooks. Poems in Process. New York:
Oxford University Press, 1951.

995 Barton, John M. T. "Odd Priest Out," Times Literary
Supplement, (October 20, 1966), 959.

996 Barton, Mary. "Rare Books and Other Bibliographical
Resources in Baltimore Libraries," Papers of the
Bibliographical Society of America, 55 (First Quarter,
1961), 1-16.

997 Basil, Sister M., O.S.F. "Gerard Manley Hopkins,"
Burnished Gold (College of St. Francis, Joliet, Illinois),
1 (1936), 62-7.

998 Bateman, David. "A Poet's Notebook." Review of The
Journals and Papers of Gerard Manley Hopkins and
The Sermons and Devotional Writings of Gerard Manley
Hopkins. Western Mail (Cardiff, Wales), (February 14,
1959).

999 Bates, Ronald. "Downdolphinry," University of Toronto
Quarterly, 36 (April, 1967), 229-36.

1000 _____ "Hopkins' Ember Poems: A Liturgical Source,"
Renascence, 17 (Fall, 1964), 32-7.

1001 _____ " 'The Windhover'," Victorian Poetry, 2 (Winter,
1964), 63-4.

1002 Bateson, Frederick W. English Poetry and the English
Language. 2nd ed. New York: Russell & Russell,
1961, 118-20.

1003 Batho, Edith Clara and Bonamy Dobree. The Victorians
and After. Vol. 4: Introductions to English Literature.
New York: Robert M. McBride and Company, 1938.

1004 Baugh, Albert Croll, ed. A Literary History of England.
2nd ed. New York: Appleton-Century-Crofts, 1967,
1536-38.

1005 Baum, Paull F. "Sprung Rhythm," PMLA, (September,
1959), 418-25.

1006 Beach, Joseph Warren. The Concept of Nature in
Nineteenth-Century English Poetry. New York: Pageant
Book Co., 1956, 556.

1007 Beauregard, David Napoleon. "The Aesthetic Theory of
Gerard Manley Hopkins." M.A. thesis, Ohio State
University, 1960.

1008 Bedirian, George L. "Spelt from Sibyl's Leaves: A Study
in Dichotomies." M.A. thesis, University of
Massachusetts, 1967.

1009 Beeching, Henry Charles, ed. A Book of Christmas Verse.
London: Methuen and Company, 1895.
1010 _____, ed. Lyra Sacra: A Book of Religious Verse.
London: Methuen & Co., 1895.
1011 _____, ed. Anonymous Review of Lyra Sacra: A Book of
Religious Verse. Irish Monthly, 31 (July, 1903),
413-14.
1012 _____, ed. A Paradise of English Poetry. 2 vols.
London: Percival & Co, 1893.
1013 Behn, Irene. "Gerard Manley Hopkins," Stimmen Der
Zeit, 145 (December, 1949), 172-78.
1014 _____ "Gerard Manley Hopkins und seine Dichtung,"
Hochland (Munich), 32 (May, 1935), 148-69.
1015 Bell, Sister Ann Charles, S.N.D. "Gerard Manley
Hopkins and the Mystical Life." M.A. thesis,
Villanova University, 1959.
1016 Bell, David. "The Problem of Translation." Dafydd ap
Gwilym: Fifty Poems, edited by David Bell and H.
Idris Bell. London: The Honourable Society of
Cymmrodorion, 1942, 75-103. [Also in Y Cymmrodor,
48 (May, 1942), 63-103.]
1017 Beloof, Robert Lawrence. The Performing Voice in
Literature. Boston: Little, Brown and Company, 1966.
1018 Bender, Robert M. and Charles Squier, eds. The Sonnet:
A Comprehensive Anthology of British and American
Sonnets from the Renaissance to the Present. New
York: Washington Square Press, Inc., 1965, 14,
387-92.
1019 Bender, Todd K. Gerard Manley Hopkins: The Classical
Background and Critical Reception of his Work.
Baltimore: Johns Hopkins Press, 1966.
1020 _____ "Hopkins' 'God's Grandeur'," Explicator, 21
(March, 1963), 55.
1021 _____ "Some Derivative Elements in the Poetry of Gerard
Manley Hopkins." Ph.D., Stanford University, 1962.
1022 Benet, William Rose. "Centenary" (Poem), Saturday
Review, 27 (September 2, 1944), 28.
1023 _____ "Round About Parnassus," Saturday Review, 10
(February 24, 1934), 508.
1024 Benham, Allen R. "A Biography by Eleanor Ruggles."
Review of Gerard Manley Hopkins: A Life, by Eleanor
Ruggles. Interim, 1 (Winter, 1945), 42-4.
1025 Bennett, Joan. Four Metaphysical Poets. Cambridge,
England: University Press, 1934, 66-7.

1026 Bennett, Victor. (Letter to the Editor), G. K.'s Weekly, 22 (October 24, 1935), 70.

1027 Bensen, Alice R. "Problems of Poetic Diction in Twentieth-Century Criticism," PMLA, 60 (March, 1945), 271-86.

1028 "Bequest to University Library in Return for Books Borrowed," Aberdeen Press and Journal, (March 16, 1949).

1029 Berchmans, Sister Louise, S.N.D. "Superb? Absurd?" (Correspondence), America, 56 (February 6, 1937), 425.

1030 Berg, Sister Mary Gretchen, O.S.F. The Prosodic Structure of Robert Bridges' "Neo-Miltonic Syllabics." Washington, D. C.: Catholic University of America Press, 1962. [Ph.D., Catholic University of America, 1962.]

1031 Bergonzi, Bernard. "The English Catholics: Forward from 'The Chesterbelloc'," Encounter (London), (January, 1965), 19-30.

1032 Berkeley, Lennox. "Autumn's Legacy." Op. 58 for High Voice and Pianoforte. Pt. 5: "Hurrahing in Harvest," by Gerard Manley Hopkins. London: J. & W. Chester Ltd, 1963. [Musical Setting]

1033 Bernad, Miguel A., S.J. "Hopkins' 'Pied Beauty': A Note on its Ignatian Inspiration," Essays in Criticism, 12 (April, 1962), 217-20.

1034 Bernard, Ronald. "The Trend in Modern Catholic Poetry," Catholic World, 149 (July, 1939), 430-35.

1035 Bernstein, Melvin Herbert. "Nature and Pessimism in Gerard Manley Hopkins: A Study in the Romantic Agony." M.A. thesis, New York University, 1941.

1036 Berryman, John. Review of Gerard Manley Hopkins: Priest and Poet, by John Pick. Harvard Advocate, 129 (March, 1943), 31-2.

1037 Bertolucci, Attilio. "La Poesia Inglese Contemporanea da Gerard M. Hopkins a Dylan Thomas," Radiocorriere (Rome), (May 1, 1954).

1038 Bethell, S. L. "Gerard Manley Hopkins, Priest and Poet." Review of Immortal Diamond, edited by Norman Weyand, S.J. Church of England Newspaper, (December 9, 1949).

1039 Betocchi, Carlo. "Poesia Inglese," l'Eco di Bergamo, (April 24, 1951).

1040 Bett, Henry. "Poet who Tortured Language." Review of
Gerard Manley Hopkins: A Critical Essay toward the
Understanding of his Poetry, by W. A. M. Peters, S.J.
British Weekly (London), (January 13, 1949).

1041 Bewley, Marius. "Hopkins and his Critics." Review of
Gerard Manley Hopkins: The Man and the Poet, by
K. R. Srinivasa Iyengar and Immortal Diamond, edited
by Norman Weyand, S.J. Partisan Review, 16 (May,
1949), 543-47.

1042 _____ "Some Aspects of Modern American Poetry."
Modern Poetry: Essays in Criticism, edited by John
Hollander. London: Oxford University Press, 1968,
257. [Reprinted from The Complex Fate: Hawthorne,
Henry James and Some Other American Writers, by
Marius Bewley. London: Chatto and Windus, 1952,
159.]

1043 Bhattacherje, M. M. (Mohinimohana Bhattacharya).
"Gerard Manley Hopkins." Pictorial Poetry.
Hoshiarpur, India: Research Bulletin (Arts) of the
University of the Panjab, 1954, 118-46.

1044 Binsse, H. L. "Gerard Manley Hopkins," Saturday
Review, 7 (August 9, 1930), 33-4.

1045 Binyon, Laurence. "Gerard Hopkins and his Influence,"
University of Toronto Quarterly, 8 (April, 1939),
264-70.

1046 _____ Tradition and Reaction in Modern Poetry. English
Association Pamphlet No. 63. London: Oxford
University Press, 1926.

1047 "Bird-Watching," Punch, 212 (June 23, 1947), 4.

1048 Birrell, T. A. Review of Further Letters of Gerard Manley
Hopkins, edited by Claude Colleer Abbott. English
Studies (Amsterdam), 38 (1957), 225-26.

1049 _____ Review of The Journals and Papers of Gerard Manley
Hopkins, edited by Humphry House; The Sermons and
Devotional Writings of Gerard Manley Hopkins, edited
by Christopher Devlin, S.J.; The Shaping Vision of
Gerard Manley Hopkins, by Alan Heuser and Robert
Bridges and Gerard Hopkins 1863-1889, by Jean-Georges
Ritz. English Studies (Amsterdam), 44 (1963), 462-65.

1050 Bischoff, Dolph Anthony, S.J. "Forgotten Hopkins Poem,"
America, 97 (August 3, 1957), 464-65. ['Persephone,'
by Digby Macworth Dolben, erroneously attributed to
Gerard Manley Hopkins, according to note in Father
Bischoff's handwriting.]

1051 _____ Review of Further Letters of Gerard Manley Hopkins, edited by Claude Colleer Abbott. Thought, 32 (Autumn, 1957), 455-57.

1052 _____ "G. Manley Hopkins" (Letter to the Editor), Times Literary Supplement, (February 15, 1947), 91.

1053 _____ "G. Manley Hopkins" (Letter to the Editor), Times Literary Supplement, (April 12, 1947), 171.

1054 _____ "Gerard Manley Hopkins," Victorian Newsletter, 13 (Spring, 1958), 23-4.

1055 _____ "Gerard Manley Hopkins as Literary Critic." Ph.D., Yale University, 1952.

1056 _____ "Hopkins," Jubilee, 3 (May, 1955), 1, 20-9.

1057 _____ "Hopkins Comes Home." Review of Immortal Diamond, edited by Norman Weyand, S.J. America, 21 (April 16, 1949), 86. [Also in Sheed & Ward's Own Trumpet, 20 (September, 1949), 10.]

1058 _____ "Hopkins's Spiritual Diaries" (Letter to the Editor), Times Literary Supplement, (June 7, 1957), 349.

1059 _____ "The Manuscripts of Gerard Manley Hopkins," Thought, 26 (Winter, 1951-1952), 551-80.

1060 _____ "Postscript on Hopkins" (Correspondence), America, 72 (October 14, 1944), 39.

1061 _____ "Tussaud Creation." Review of Gerard Manley Hopkins: A Life, by Eleanor Ruggles. America, 71 (September 2, 1944), 539-40.

1062 Blacam, Aodh de. "Catholics and the Revival of Letters." Review of The Catholic Literary Revival, by Calvert Alexander, S.J. Irish Monthly, 63 (November, 1935), 63, 745-52.

1063 Blackmur, Richard P. "Mature Intelligence of an Artist." Review of Further Letters of Gerard Manley Hopkins, edited by Claude Colleer Abbott. Kenyon Review, 1 (Winter, 1939), 96-9.

1064 _____ "Text and Texture." Review of The Notebooks and Papers of Gerard Manley Hopkins, edited by Humphry House. Virginia Quarterly Review, 13 (Summer, 1937), 449-53.

1065 Blair, Walter and W. K. Chandler. Approaches to Poetry. 2nd ed. New York: Appleton-Century-Crofts, Inc., 1953, 684-85.

1066 Blakiston, J. M. G. "An Unpublished Hopkins Letter," Times Literary Supplement, (September 25, 1948), 548.

1067 Bliss, Geoffrey. "The Hopkins Centenary," Month, 180 (July-August, 1944), 233-40.

1068 _____ "In a Poet's Workshop: I. An Unfinished Poem by G. M. Hopkins," Month, 167 (February, 1936), 160-67.

1069 _____ "In a Poet's Workshop: II. 'The Woodlark' by Gerard Manley Hopkins," Month, 167 (June, 1936), 528-35.

1070 Bloom, Lionel. "The Mystic Pattern in the Poetry of Gerard Manley Hopkins." M.A. thesis, Columbia University, 1963.

1071 Blum, Sister Magdalen Louise, S.C. "The Imagery in the Poetry of Gerard Manley Hopkins." M.A. thesis, University of New Mexico, 1950.

1072 Blume, Bernhard. "Sein und Scheitern: Zur Geschichte Einer Metapher," Germanisch-Romanische Monats-schrift (Heidelberg), N.S. 5 (July, 1959), 277-87.

1073 Boas, Frederick Samuel. "The Nineteenth Century and After," Year's Work in English Studies, 18 (1939), 259-60.

1074 Boase, Frederic. "Hopkins, Rev. Gerard Manley." Modern English Biography. Vol. 1, 2nd impression. New York: Barnes & Noble, 1965.

1075 Bogan, Louise. "The Hidden Stream." Review of Further Letters of Gerard Manley Hopkins, edited by Claude Colleer Abbott. Nation, 147 (July 30, 1938), 111-12.

1076 _____ "The Letters of Gerard Manley Hopkins." Selected Criticism. New York: Noonday Press, 1955, 42-7.

1077 Bolsius, E. "Gerard Manley Hopkins, de Dichter en de Religieus." Review of The Journals and Papers of Gerard Manley Hopkins, edited by Humphry House and The Sermons and Devotional Writings of Gerard Manley Hopkins, edited by Christopher Devlin, S.J. Streven (Amsterdam), 13 (October, 1959), 49-54.

1078 Bolsover, Philip. "Eye for the Future." Review of Gerard Manley Hopkins, by W. H. Gardner. Daily Worker (London), (September 17, 1953).

1079 Bonn, John Louis. "Greco-Roman Verse Theory and Gerard Manley Hopkins." Immortal Diamond, edited by Norman Weyand, S.J. New York: Sheed & Ward, 1949, 73-92.

1080 Bostetter, Edward. "Recent Studies in the Nineteenth Century." Review of Gerard Manley Hopkins: The Classical Background and Critical Reception of his Work, by Todd Bender. Studies in English Literature, 7 (Autumn, 1967), 755-56.

1081 Boulton, Marjorie. The Anatomy of Poetry. London:
Routledge & Kegan Paul Ltd, 1953, 51.
1082 Bowen, C. "Reminiscences of Father Gerard Hopkins,"
Month, 134 (August, 1919), 158-59.
1083 Bowen, Paul. "Music Last Week," Listener (London),
74 (November 4, 1965), 733.
1084 Bowen, Robert O. "Hopkins and Welsh Prosody,"
Renascence, 8 (Winter, 1955), 71-4, 87.
1085 _____ "Scotism in Gerard Manley Hopkins," History of
Ideas Newsletter, 5 (Winter, 1959), 11-4.
1086 Bowra, Cecil Maurice. The Creative Experiment. London:
Macmillan & Company Ltd., 1949, 4-5.
1087 _____ The Heritage of Symbolism. London: Macmillan
and Co., Ltd., 1943, 4, 15, 182.
1088 _____ Poetry & Politics: 1900-1960. Cambridge:
University Press, 1966, 7-9, 12, 140.
1089 Bowyer, John Wilson and John Lee Brooks, eds. The
Victorian Age. New York: Appleton, Century, Crofts,
Inc., 1938, 750-51, 1153-54.
1090 Boyle, Robert R., S.J. "Duns Scotus in the Poetry of
Hopkins." Manuscript copy of paper read at Seventh
Centenary Symposium, "Scotus Speaks Today" held at
Duns Scotus College, Southfield, Michigan, April 21,
22, 23, 1966.
1091 _____ "Footnote on 'The Windhover'," America, 82
(November 5, 1949), 129-30.
1092 _____ "Gerard Manley Hopkins" (Correspondence),
America, 71 (September 30, 1944), 623.
1093 _____ Review of Gerard Manley Hopkins: The Classical
Background and Critical Reception of his Work, by
Todd K. Bender. Journal of English and Germanic
Philology, 66 (October, 1967), 609-13.
1094 _____ Review of Gerard Manley Hopkins: The Classical
Background and Critical Reception of his Work, by
Todd K. Bender. Thought, 42 (Winter, 1967), 624-26.
1095 _____ Review of Gerard Manley Hopkins: A Study of
his Ignatian Spirit, by David A. Downes. Thought, 36
(Spring, 1961), 135-37.
1096 _____ "Hopkins, Gerard Manley." New Catholic
Encyclopedia. Vol. 7. New York: McGraw-Hill Book
Co., 1967, 144-47.
1097 _____ "Hopkins' Imagery: The Thread for the Maze,"
Thought, 25 (Spring, 1960), 57-90.
1098 _____ Metaphor in Hopkins. Chapel Hill: University of
North Carolina Press, 1961.

1099 _____ "The Nature and Function of the Mature Imagery of Gerard Manley Hopkins." Ph.D., Yale University, 1955.

1100 _____ "The Nature of Metaphor," Modern Schoolman, 31 (May, 1954), 257-80.

1101 _____ Review of Studies in Structure, by Robert J. Andreach. James Joyce Quarterly, 3 (Fall, 1965), 77-81.

1102 _____ Review of Studies in Structure, by Robert J. Andreach, Thought, 40 (Winter, 1965), 598-600.

1103 _____ "The Teaching of Hopkins," Jesuit Educational Quarterly, 7 (October, 1944), 91-5.

1104 _____ "The Thought Structure of 'The Wreck of the Deutschland'." Immortal Diamond, edited by Norman Weyand, S.J. New York: Sheed & Ward, 1949, 333-50.

1105 _____ Review of The Wreck of the Deutschland: An Essay and Commentary, by John E. Keating. Journal of English and Germanic Philology, 63 (July, 1964), 536-38.

1106 Bradbrook, Muriel C. Review of Gerard Manley Hopkins, by W. A. M. Peters, S.J. Cambridge Review, (October 16, 1948).

1107 _____ Review of A Hopkins Reader, by John Pick and Selected Poems of Gerard Manley Hopkins, edited by James Reeves. Modern Language Review, 49 (July, 1954), 370.

1108 _____ Review of Robert Bridges and Gerard Hopkins 1863-1889, by Jean-Georges Ritz. Modern Language Review, 57 (1962), 254-55.

1109 Bradbury, Ernest. "Song Cycle of Poems by Gerard Manley Hopkins," Yorkshire Post (Leeds), (July 16, 1958).

1110 Braybrooke, Neville, ed. A Partridge in a Pear Tree: A Celebration for Christmas. Westminster, Maryland: Newman Press, 1960, 189-92.

1111 Bregy, Katherine. "Coventry Patmore," Catholic World, 90 (March, 1910), 803.

1112 _____ "Gerard Hopkins, an Epitaph and an Appreciation," Catholic World, 88 (January, 1909), 433-47.

1113 _____ The Poets' Chantry. London: Herbert & Daniel, 1912.

1114 Bremond, Andre, S.J. "Art and Inspiration in Hopkins," New Verse, No. 14 (April, 1935), 5-12.

1115 _____ "La Poesie Naive et Savante de Gerard Hopkins," Etudes, 221 (October 5, 1934), 23-49.

1116 _____ "Quelques Reflexions sur la Poesie et les Styles
Poetiques a Propos d'une Correspondance," Etudes,
242 (February 5, 1940), 310-17.
1117 Brennan, Joseph Xavier. "Gerard Manley Hopkins:
A Critical Interpretation of his Poetry." M.A. thesis,
Brown University, 1949.
1118 Brennan, Norman Charles. "An Objective Interpretation of
Three Mature Sonnets of Gerard Manley Hopkins."
M.A. thesis, Niagara University, 1962.
1119 Bretelle, Leon. "Gerard Manley Hopkins," Kirche in der
Welt (Munich), 8 (1955), 241-42.
1120 Bridges, Robert Seymour. "Gerard Manley Hopkins."
Robert Bridges and Contemporary Poets. Vol. 8: The
Poets and Poetry of the Century, edited by Alfred Henry
Miles. London: Hutchinson & Co., 1898, 161-70.
1121 _____ "The Late Poet Laureate and Father Gerard Hopkins,"
Carminia, No. 2 (September, 1930), 22.
1122 _____ "The Oddities of Genius." A Collection of Critical
Essays, edited by Geoffrey H. Hartman. Englewood
Cliffs, New Jersey: Prentice-Hall, Inc., 1966, 71-5.
[Originally published as "Preface to Notes" in 1st ed.
of The Poems of Gerard Manley Hopkins.]
1123 _____, ed. "Gerard Hopkins." Anonymous Review of
Poems of Gerard Manley Hopkins. Times Literary
Supplement, (January 10, 1919), 19.
1124 _____, ed. "Gerard Hopkins' Poems." Anonymous Review
of Poems of Gerard Manley Hopkins. Tablet, (April 5,
1919), 420-22.
1125 _____, ed. "Gerard Manley Hopkins." Anonymous Review
of Poems of Gerard Manley Hopkins. Times Literary
Supplement, (January 18, 1952), 58.
1126 _____, ed. "Gerard Manley Hopkins." Anonymous Review
of Poems of Gerard Manley Hopkins and Gerard Manley
Hopkins, by G. F. Lahey, S.J. Times Literary
Supplement, (December 25, 1930), 1099.
1127 _____, ed. Anonymous Review of Poems of Gerard Manley
Hopkins. Booklist, 27 (March, 1931), 322.
1128 _____, ed. Anonymous Review of Poems of Gerard Manley
Hopkins. Dial, No. 66 (May 31, 1919), 572.
1129 _____, ed. Anonymous Review of Poems of Gerard Manley
Hopkins. Glasgow Herald, (January 2, 1919), 3.
1130 _____, ed. Anonymous Review of Poems of Gerard Manley
Hopkins. Methodist Recorder, (May 29, 1919), 9.
1131 _____, ed. Anonymous Review of Poems of Gerard Manley
Hopkins. Nation, 132 (January 28, 1931), 105.

1132 _____, ed. Anonymous Review of Poems of Gerard Manley
Hopkins. Oxford Magazine, 37 (May 23, 1919), 310-11.
1133 _____, ed. "The Prophet Unveiled." Anonymous Review of
The Poems of Gerard Manley Hopkins. New Statesman,
12 (March 15, 1919), 530.
1134 _____, ed. The Spirit of Man: An Anthology. London:
Longmans Green & Co., 1916.
1135 _____, ed. The Spirit of Man: An Anthology. 2nd
impression. London: Longmans Green & Co., 1916.
1136 _____, ed. The Spirit of Man: An Anthology. new
impression. London: Longmans Green & Co., 1927.
1137 _____, ed. The Spirit of Man: An Anthology. new
impression. London: Longmans Green & Co., 1937.
1138 Brinkley, Maxine. "He Gave You Song (On Reading Gerard
Manley Hopkins)" (Poem), College English, 11
(December, 1949), 156.
1139 Brinlee, Robert Washington. "The Religion and Poetic
Theory of Gerard Manley Hopkins." M.A. thesis,
University of Tulsa, 1958.
1140 Brion, Marcel. "Chronique Litteraire: Resurrections."
Review of Le Poete Gerard Manley Hopkins, S.J.: Sa
Vie et Son Oeuvre, by Jean-Georges Ritz and Le
Naufrage du Deutschland par Gerard Manley Hopkins,
translated by Pierre Leyris. Concours Medical (Paris),
(September 19, 1964), 5209-12.
1141 Britton, John, S.J. " 'Pied Beauty' and the Glory of God,"
Renascence, 11 (Winter, 1959), 72-5.
1142 Broadbent, John Barclay. Poetic Love. London: Chatto
& Windus, 1964, 4, 68, 90-1, 99-104, 125-28,
302-03.
1143 Brockington, Alfred Allen. Mysticism and Poetry on a
Basis of Experience. London: Chapman & Hall Ltd.,
1934, 101-07, 110, 130, 150, 197.
1144 Brooke, Jocelyn. "Silver Age," Time and Tide, 32 (July 7,
1951), 646.
1145 Brooke-Rose, Christine. A Grammar of Metaphor. London:
Secker & Warburg, 1965. [Partially reprinted in Essays
on the Language of Literature, edited by Seymour
Chatman and Samuel R. Levin. Boston: Houghton
Mifflin Company, 1967, 197-208.]
1146 _____ "La Syntaxe et le Symbolisme dans la Poesie de
Hopkins," Europe (Paris), 25 (July, 1947), 30-9.
1147 Brooks, Cleanth. "Gerard Manley Hopkins" (Editor's
Note), Kenyon Review, 6 (Summer, 1944), 321.

1148 _____ Modern Poetry and the Tradition. Chapel Hill: University of North Carolina Press, 1939, 241.

1149 _____ The Well Wrought Urn: Studies in the Structure of Poetry. New York: Reynal & Hitchcock, 1947, 210.

1150 _____ and Robert Penn Warren. Understanding Poetry: An Anthology for College Students. 3rd ed. rev. New York: Henry Holt & Company, 1957, 522-23.

1151 _____, John Thibaut Purser and Robert Penn Warren, eds. An Approach to Literature. 3rd ed. New York: Appleton-Century-Crofts, Inc., 1952, 316, 361.

1152 Brooks, Edna Belle. Review of Immortal Diamond, edited by Norman Weyand, S.J. Clarke College Labarum (Dubuque, Iowa), 41 (Summer, 1949), 277-78.

1153 Brophy, James. "The Noble Brute: Medieval Nuance in 'The Windhover'," Modern Language Notes, 76 (December, 1961), 673-74.

1154 Brophy, James D., Jr. "The Early Poems of Gerard Manley Hopkins and their Place in Hopkins Criticism." M.A. thesis, Columbia University, 1950.

1155 Brown, Alec. "Gerard Hopkins and Associative Form," Dublin Magazine, N.S. 3 (April, 1928), 6-20.

1156 Brown, Edward K. Victorian Poetry. New York: Thomas Nelson & Sons, 1942, xix-xx, xliii-xlv, 732-35,901-02.

1157 Brown, Sister Margaret Eugene, C.S.J. "Gerard Manley Hopkins: Literary Critic." M.A. thesis, Saint John's University, 1945.

1158 Brown, Marie Patricia. "The Sensuous Concept of Nature in G. M. Hopkins' Poetic Images." M.A. thesis, Georgetown University, 1964.

1159 Brown, Stephen, S.J. "A Catholic Approach to English Literature," Irish Ecclesiastical Review, 64 (December, 1944), 368-77.

1160 _____ "Some Notes on Modern Poetry, Irish Rosary (Dublin), (June, 1961), 137-44.

1161 Brown, T. J. "English Literary Autographs XXXIX: Gerard Manley Hopkins, 1844-1889," Book Collector, 10 (Autumn, 1961), 320-21.

1162 Browne, Wynyard. "Introduction to Hopkins." Review of The Poetry of Gerard Manley Hopkins, by E. E. Phare. Bookman (London), 85 (Christmas, 1933), 228-29.

1163 Buckley, Jerome H. "The Fourth Dimension of Victorianism," Victorian Newsletter, 21 (Spring, 1952), 1-4.

1164 _____ "General Materials." The Victorian Poets, edited by Frederic E. Faverty. Cambridge: Harvard University Press, 1956, 2, 4.

1165 _____ Victorian Poets and Prose Writers. Goldentree
Bibliographies. New York: Appleton-Century-Crofts,
1966.

1166 _____ The Victorian Temper: A Study in Literary Culture.
Cambridge, Massachusetts: Harvard University Press,
1951, 205.

1167 Buckley, Vincent. Poetry and Morality: Studies on the
Criticism of Matthew Arnold, T. S. Eliot and F. R.
Leavis. London: Chatto & Windus, 1961, 145, 155-56,
171-73, 186-87, 229.

1168 Buggy, Sister James Marita, I.H.M. "Growth of the
Literary Reputation of Gerard Manley Hopkins." M.A.
thesis, Villanova University, 1959.

1169 Bullough, Geoffrey. Mirror of Minds: Changing Psychological Beliefs in English Poetry. Toronto: University
of Toronto Press, 1962, 182-83.

1170 _____ "Poetry." Anonymous Review of The Trend of
Modern Poetry, by Geoffrey Bullough and Gerard Manley
Hopkins: A Study of Poetic Idiosyncracy in Relation to
Poetic Tradition, by W. H. Gardner. Sunday News of
India (Bombay), (July 3, 1949).

1171 _____ The Trend of Modern Poetry. 3rd ed., rev. and
enl. Edinburgh: Oliver and Boyd, 1949, 15, 20, 24-6,
131, 202, 209, 218.

1172 Bungert, Hans. Review of The Journals and Papers of
Gerard Manley Hopkins, edited by Humphry House.
Archiv fur das Studium der Neueren Sprachen (Brunswick),
201 (1964), 221-22.

1173 Burckhardt, Sigurd. "The Poet as Fool and Priest," ELH,
23 (1956), 279-98.

1174 _____ "Poetry and the Language of Communion." Hopkins:
A Collection of Critical Essays, edited by Geoffrey
H. Hartman. Englewood Cliffs, New Jersey: Prentice-
Hall Inc., 1966, 160-67. [Originally published as
"Poetry, Language and the Condition of Man,"
Centennial Review, 4 (Winter, 1960).]

1175 Burdett, Osbert. "The Letters of Gerard Manley Hopkins."
Review of The Letters of Gerard Manley Hopkins to
Robert Bridges, edited by Claude Colleer Abbott and
The Correspondence of Gerard Manley Hopkins and
Richard Watson Dixon, edited by Claude Colleer
Abbott. Nineteenth Century and After, 117 (February,
1935), 234-41.

1176 Burgess, Anthony. "The Democracy of Prejudice,"
Encounter, 29 (August, 1967), 71-6.

1177 _____ "Hopkins Pickings." Review of The Poems of
Gerard Manley Hopkins, edited by W. H. Gardner and
N. H. MacKenzie and Hopkins: Selections, edited by
Graham Storey. Times Literary Supplement, (October
5, 1967), 937.

1178 Burgum, Edwin Berry. "Three English Radical Poets."
Proletarian Literature in the United States, by Granville
Hicks. New York: International Publishers, 1937,
330-39.

1179 Burke, Francis, S.J. "The Muse Called Grace," Measure:
The Journal of the Gerard Manley Hopkins Society, 1
(Christmas, 1932), 27-31.

1180 _____ "Poetic Reality," Measure: The Journal of the
Gerard Manley Hopkins Poetry Society, 1 (Easter, 1933),
30-6.

1181 Burke, Kenneth. Philosophy of Literary Form: Studies in
Symbolic Action. 2nd ed. Baton Rouge: Louisiana
State University Press, 1967, 10, 48, 52, 375.

1182 _____ and Stanley Romaine Hopper. "Mysticism as a
Solution to the Poet's Dilemma, Part I." Spiritual
Problems in Contemporary Literature, edited by Stanley
Romaine Hopper. New York: Harper & Brothers, 1957,
98-103.

1183 Burke, Molly M. "Gerard Manley Hopkins," Commonweal,
12 (September 10, 1930), 459-60.

1184 Burke, Sister Pauline, S.S.J. "The Wreck of the
Deutschland." M.A. thesis, Boston College, 1944.

1185 Burns, Chester A., S.J. "Gerard Manley Hopkins, Poet of
Ascetic and Aesthetic Conflict." Immortal Diamond,
edited by Norman Weyand, S.J. New York: Sheed &
Ward, 1949, 175-91.

1186 Burnshaw, Stanley. "The Three Revolutions of Modern
Poetry." Varieties of Literary Experience, edited by
Stanley Burnshaw. New York: New York University
Press, 1962, 150-51. [Also in Sewanee Review, 70
(Spring, 1962), 431-32.]

1187 Burr, Carol. "Compound Epithets in the Poetry of Gerard
Manley Hopkins." M.A. thesis, Columbia University,
1967.

1188 Burton, James Rector. "The Metrical Theory of Gerard
Manley Hopkins." M.A. thesis, University of Texas,
1939.

1189 Busby, Christopher. "Time's Andromeda." Review of
The Journals and Papers of Gerard Manley Hopkins,
edited by Humphry House and The Sermons and
Devotional Writings of Gerard Manley Hopkins, edited
by Christopher Devlin, S.J. Dublin Review, 233
(Summer, 1959), 183-90.
1190 Bush, Douglas. English Poetry: The Main Currents from
Chaucer to the Present. New York: Oxford University
Press, 1963, 78, 93, 175-76, 183-85, 195.
1191 _____ Mythology and the Romantic Tradition. Harvard
Studies in English, Vol. 18. Cambridge, Massachusetts:
Harvard University Press, 1937, 276-78, 296-97, 343,
394, 412-13, 436, 440, 530.
1192 Byles, Mary. Review of Gerard Manley Hopkins: A Life,
by Eleanor Ruggles. Catholic World, 160 (November,
1944), 184.
1193 Byrne, Virginia Carmel. "The Creator and the Maker in
the Aesthetics of Gerard Manley Hopkins," McNeese
Review, 14 (1963), 60-73.
1194 _____ "Inscape in the Aesthetic Theory and Poetic
Practice of Gerard Manley Hopkins." M.A. thesis,
College of the Holy Names (Oakland, California),
1960.
1195 C. B. "Reminiscences of Father Gerard Hopkins," Month,
134 (August, 1919), 158-59.
1196 C. T. Review of Gerard Manley Hopkins: Priest and Poet,
by John Pick. Poetry Review, 34 (January-February,
1943), 33-5.
1197 Cabau, Jacques. "Ce Masochisme qu'on Appelle la Grace."
Review of Le Naufrage du Deutschland, translated by
Pierre Leyris. l'Express (Paris), (March 26, 1964).
1198 Caine, Hall. "Gerard Hopkins" (Letter to the Editor),
New Statesman, 9 (June 23, 1917), 277.
1199 Cairns, Huntington, ed. The Limits of Art. New York:
Pantheon Books, 1947, 1335-37.
1200 Caliri, Flavia M. "Gerard Manley Hopkins, S.J.: A
Poet for the Twentieth Century--his Inspiration,"
Ethos, 12 (Spring, 1939), 71-5.
1201 Callahan, Virginia Woods. Review of Gerard Manley
Hopkins: A Critical Essay towards the Understanding
of his Poetry, by W. A. M. Peters, S.J. Books on
Trial, 7 (March, 1949), 258.
1202 Campbell, Roy. "Inscape of Skytehawks on the Cookhouse
Roof (In Homage to Gerard Manley Hopkins)" (Poem),
Nine, 3 (April, 1952), 272.

1203 Campbell, Sister M. Mary, S.C.M.M. "The Silent Sonnet: Hopkins' 'Shepherd's Brow'," Renascence, 15 (Spring, 1963), 133-42.

1204 Campbell, Vivian, ed. A Christmas Anthology of Poetry and Painting. New York: The Woman's Press, 1947, 47.

1205 Capellanus. "Windhover" (Letter to the Editor), America, 70 (February 12, 1944), 531.

1206 Carey, Charles M. Review of Gerard Manley Hopkins: Priest and Poet, by John Pick. Ave Maria, (July 10, 1943), 58.

1207 Carlson, Sister Marian Raphael, S.H.N. "Gerard Manley Hopkins and his Critics." Ph.D., Loyola University (Chicago), 1946.

1208 Carpenter, Maurice. Review of The Correspondence of Gerard Manley Hopkins and Richard Watson Dixon, edited by Claude Colleer Abbott and The Letters of Gerard Manley Hopkins to Robert Bridges, edited by Claude Colleer Abbott. Poetry Review, 26 (1935), 166.

1209 Carroll, Martin C., S.J. "Gerard Manley Hopkins and the Society of Jesus," Immortal Diamond, edited by Norman Weyand, S.J. New York: Sheed & Ward, 1949, 3-50.

1210 Carroll, Patrick J., C.S.C. "The Editor's Page . . ." Ave Maria, 75 (May 10, 1952), 582.

1211 Carver, George, Sister M. Eleanore and Katherine Bregy, eds. The Stream of English Literature. New York: Heath & Co., 1930, 351.

1212 Cary-Elwes, Columba, O.S.B. Review of Robert Bridges and Gerard Hopkins 1863-1889, by Jean-Georges Ritz. Critic, 19 (December 1960-January 1961), 57.

1213 [Casalandra], Sister M. Estelle, O.P. "The Blessed Virgin compared to the Air we Breathe," Rosary, 94 (November, 1943), 16, 30.

1214 _____ "The Tragedy of Gerard Manley Hopkins," Rosary, 95 (May, 1944), 21-4.

1215 Cascio, Joseph E., Jr. "Gerard Manley Hopkins and the Arts of Literary Criticism, Painting, and Music." M.A. thesis, St. John's University, 1959.

1216 Cassidy, Lawrence P. "Gerard Manley Hopkins' Ideas on Beauty and Truth as shown in his Poems and Letters." M.A. thesis, DePaul University, 1955.

1217 Castelli, Alberto. "Il Naufragio del Deutschland," Scrittori Inglesi Contemporanei. Messina: Casa Editrice Giuseppe Principato, 1939, 7-29.

1218 Caster, Sister Mary Cassilda, S.S.N.D. "Elements of
     Mysticism in Hopkins." M.A. thesis, DePaul
     University, 1932.
1219 "A Catholic Poet" (Editorial), Commonweal, 13 (November
     12, 1930), 32-3.
1220 Cattaui, Georges. "Gerard Manley Hopkins," Schweizer
     Rundschau (Einsiedeln), 44 (1944), 370-76.
1221 _____ "Gerard Manley Hopkins et 'l'Inspect' des Choses."
     Review of Le Naufrage du Deutschland, translated by
     Pierre Leyris; Le Poete Gerard Manley Hopkins, by
     Jean-Georges Ritz and Gerard Manley Hopkins: A Study
     of Poetic Idiosyncrasy, by W. H. Gardner. Critique
     (Paris), 21 (November, 1965), 935-49.
1222 _____ "Gerard Manley Hopkins ou un Nouveau Lyrisme
     Baroque." Trois Poetes: Hopkins, Yeats, Eliot. Paris:
     Egloff, 1947, 11-44.
1223 _____ "Note sur Gerard Manley Hopkins" (with French
     translation of "The Leaden Echo and the Golden Echo"),
     Yggdrasill (Paris), 1 (March 25, 1937), 15-6.
1224 Caudwell, Hugo. The Creative Impulse in Writing and
     Painting. London: Macmillan and Co., Ltd., 1951.
1225 Caulfield, Jeanne. "Gerard Manley Hopkins, S.J.: A
     Poet for the Twentieth Century--his Life," Ethos, 12
     (Spring, 1939), 75-8.
1226 Cazamian, Louis. Review of The Letters of Gerard Manley
     Hopkins to Robert Bridges, edited by Claude Colleer
     Abbott and The Correspondence of Gerard Manley
     Hopkins and Richard Watson Dixon, edited by Claude
     Colleer Abbott. Revue Anglo-Americaine, 13 (April,
     1936), 349-50.
1227 Cecil, Lord David. The Oxford Book of Christian Verse.
     Oxford: Clarendon Press, 1940, xi-xxxiii, 492-503.
1228 Chaigne, Louis, comp. La Litterature Catholique a
     l'Etranger. Paris: Editions Alsatia, 1947, 140-45.
1229 "Challenge to Voice and Piano," Times (London),
     (November 16, 1963).
1230 Chamberlain, Charles Martin, III. "Hopkins' Rejection of
     Estheticism." Ph.D., University of Colorado, 1966.
1231 Chamberlain, Robert L. "George MacDonald's 'A
     Manchester Poem' and Hopkin's [sic] 'God's Grandeur',"
     Personalist, 44 (Autumn, 1963), 518-27.
1232 Chambers, W. and R., eds. "Gerard Manley Hopkins."
     Chamber's Cyclopaedia of English Literature. Vol. 3.
     London: W. and R. Chambers, 1938, 713.

1233 Champneys, Basil. Memoirs and Correspondence of
      Coventry Patmore. 2 vols. London: George Bell &
      Sons, 1900. Vol. 1: 175, 318; Vol. 2: 40, 246-49,
      345-55.
1234 Chapin, Elsa and Russell Thomas. A New Approach to
      Poetry. Chicago: University of Chicago Press, 1929,
      96.
1235 Charboneau, Damian M., O.S.M. "Gerald [sic] Manley
      Hopkins: Poet Laureate of Mary and May," Our Lady's
      Digest, 8 (May, 1953), 40-3. [Condensed from
      Magnificat, May, 1952.]
1236 Chard, Leslie F. "Once More into 'The Windhover',"
      English Language Notes, 2 (June, 1965), 282-85.
1237 Charlesworth, Barbara. Dark Passages: The Decadent
      Consciousness in Victorian Literature. Madison:
      University of Wisconsin Press, 1965, 44.
1238 Charney, Maurice. "A Bibliographical Study of Hopkins
      Criticism, 1918-1949," Thought, 25 (June, 1950),
      297-326.
1239 Chase, John W. "The Poet Unlocked." Review of
      Immortal Diamond, edited by Norman Weyand, S.J.
      New York Times Book Review, (September 18, 1949), 12.
1240 Chavez, Fray Angelico. "To Gerard Manley Hopkins
      (Accused of Exaggerated Mariolatry)" (Poem), Spirit, 7
      (July, 1940), 74.
1241 Chevigny, Bell Gale. "Instress and Devotion in the Poetry
      of Gerard Manley Hopkins," Victorian Studies, 9
      (December, 1965), 141-53. [Reprinted in Victorian
      Literature: Selected Essays, edited by Robert O.
      Preyer, 225-40.]
1242 Chew, Samuel C. "Letters of Hopkins and Bradford."
      Review of The Letters of Gerard Manley Hopkins to
      Robert Bridges; The Correspondence of Gerard Manley
      Hopkins and Richard Watson Dixon, edited by Claude
      Colleer Abbott and The Letters of Gamaliel Bradford,
      edited by Van Wyck Brooks. Yale Review, 25 (Autumn,
      1935), 209-12.
1243 _____ The Nineteenth Century and After: A Literary History
      of England, edited by Albert C. Baugh. New York:
      Appleton-Century-Crofts, 1948, 1536-38.
1244 Chiari, Joseph. Realism and Imagination. London: Barrie
      and Rockliff, 1960, 64-5, 82, 105, 122, 144.
1245 _____ Symbolisme from Poe to Mallarme: The Growth of a
      Myth. London: Rockliff, 1956, 8, 41, 53-4, 79, 124,
      171.

1246 Chrestien, Michel. "Gerard Manley Hopkins," Carrefour (Paris), (April 2, 1958).

1247 Christy, Arthur and Henry W. Wells. World Literature. New York: American Book Company, 1947, 187, 1066.

1248 Churchill, R. C. "Gerard Hopkins--A Christian Socialist," London Tribune, (June 10, 1944), 15.

1249 Ciardi, John. Review of recording Poems of Gerard Manley Hopkins, read by Richard Gray. Saturday Review, 49 (February 12, 1966), 49.

1250 Clancy, L. J. "The Poetry of Thomas W. Shapcott," Meanjin Quarterly, 25 (June, 1967), 182-87.

1251 Clark, Eleanor Grace. Review of Immortal Diamond, edited by Norman Weyand, S.J. Catholic World, 171 (April, 1949), 78-9.

1252 Clark, L. D. Review of Gerard Manley Hopkins: A Study of his Ignatian Spirit, by David Anthony Downes. Arizona Quarterly, 16 (1960), 282-83.

1253 Clark, Robert Boykin, S.J. "Hopkins's 'The Shepherd's Brow'," Victorian Newsletter, 28 (Fall, 1965), 16-8.

1254 Clarke, Austin. "The American Muse." Review of A Little Treasury of Modern Poetry: English and American, edited by Oscar Williams; Selected Poems, by John Crowe Ransom and Poems, 1920-1945. A Selection, by Allen Tate. Irish Times (Dublin), (June 26, 1948).

1255 _____ "Apollo's Men." Review of Immortal Diamond, edited by Norman Weyand, S.J.; The Poems of Coventry Patmore, edited by Frederick Page; Rilke: Man and Poet, by Nora Wydenbruck; The Buried Self: A Background to the Poems of Matthew Arnold 1848-1851, by Isobel MacDonald; A Life of John Keats, by Dorothy Hewlett and Byron: Selections from the Poetry, Letters and Journal, edited by Peter Quennell. Irish Times (Dublin), (December 24, 1949).

1256 _____ "Art and State." Review of Why Do I Write? An Exchange of Views Between Elizabeth Bowen, Graham Greene and V. S. Pritchett and Poems of Gerard Manley Hopkins, by W. H. Gardner, 3rd ed., rev. and enl. Irish Times (Dublin), (January 8, 1949).

1257 _____ "Critics' Circle." Review of English Literature Between the Wars, by B. Ifor Evans; Gerard Manley Hopkins: A Critical Essay Towards the Understanding of his Poetry, by W. A. M. Peters, S.J.; Portrait of William Morris, by Esther Meynell and Byron, by C. E. Vulliamy. Irish Times (Dublin), (June 12, 1948).

1258 _____ "The Devil in the House." Review of The Life and Times of Coventry Patmore, by Derek Patmore and Gerard Manley Hopkins (1844-1889): A Study of Poetic Idiosyncrasy in Relation to Poetic Tradition. Vol. 2, by W. H. Gardner. Irish Times (Dublin), (July 23, 1949).

1259 _____ "Father Hopkins and James Joyce." Review of The Poetry of Gerard Manley Hopkins: A Survey and Commentary, by E. E. Phare and James Joyce by Louis Golding. Observer (London), (November 26, 1933), 9.

1260 _____ "The Great Unread." Review of Dryden: Poetry, Prose and Plays, edited by Douglas Grant and The Common Pursuit, by F. R. Leavis. Irish Times (Dublin), (February 9, 1952).

1261 _____ "No Pudding for Poets." Review of A Hopkins Reader, edited by John Pick. Irish Times (Dublin), (August 22, 1953).

1262 _____ "Poet and Priest." Review of Gerard Manley Hopkins: A Life, by Eleanor Ruggles. Irish Times (Dublin), (February 28, 1948), 4.

1263 _____ "Recapitulation." Review of Poems and Prose of Gerard Manley Hopkins, edited by W. H. Gardner. Irish Times (Dublin), (November, 1953).

1264 Clarke, Egerton. "Gerard Hopkins, Jesuit." Review of Letters of Gerard Manley Hopkins to Robert Bridges and R. W. Dixon, edited by Claude Colleer Abbott; Gerard Manley Hopkins, by G. F. Lahey, S.J.; Poems of Gerard Manley Hopkins, edited by Robert Bridges and The Mind and Poetry of Gerard Manley Hopkins, S.J., by Bernard Kelly. Dublin Review, 198 (January, 1936), 127-41.

1265 Cleary, Helen Kae. "In His Own Image: A Study of Hopkins' Poetic Treatment of Man." M.A. thesis, Cornell University, 1962. [Microfilm]

1266 Clemen, Ursula. "Neue Ausgaben der Werke von G. M. Hopkins," Anglia, 80 (1962), 220-23.

1267 _____ Review of Robert Bridges and Gerard Hopkins 1863-1889. A Literary Friendship, by Jean-Georges Ritz and A Poet Hidden. The Life of Richard Watson Dixon, by James Sambrook. Anglia, 83 (1965), 114-18.

1268 Clemen, Wolfgang. "Die Tagebucher des Gerard Manley Hopkins," Merkur (Stuttgart), 3 (January, 1949), 571-84.

1269 _____ "Die Tagebucher des Gerard Manley Hopkins," Schweizer Rundschau (Einsiedeln), 49 (July, 1949), 248-59.

1270 Clines, Gerald Patrick. "Gerard Manley Hopkins' Ascetic-Aesthetic Conflict." B.A. thesis, University of Santa Clara, 1953.

1271 Coanda, Richard. "Hopkins and Donne: 'Mystic' and Metaphysical," Renascence, 9 (Summer, 1956), 180-87.

1272 Coblentz, Catherine Cate. "A Catholic Poet Comes into his Own," Ave Maria, N.S. 33 (February 7, 1931), 161-63.

1273 Cochrane, Josephine M. "Gerard Manley Hopkins: His Conception of Catholicism." M.A. thesis, New York University, 1938.

1274 Cock, Albert A. Review of The Poetry of Gerard Manley Hopkins. A Survey and Commentary, by E. E. Phare. Wessex, 3 (1934), 95-7.

1275 _____ "Robert Bridges' Testament of Beauty with some References to Gerard Manley Hopkins." France-Grande Bretagne (Paris), (April, 1937), 92-6.

1276 Cocking, J. M. "Duns Scotus and Hopkins" (Letter to the Editor), Times Literary Supplement, (July 31, 1948), 429.

1277 Cockshut, A. O. J. "Father Hopkins." Review of Further Letters of G. M. Hopkins, edited by Claude Colleer Abbott, 2nd ed. Manchester Guardian, (January 1, 1957), 3.

1278 _____ "A Lonely Vision." Review of Further Letters of G. M. Hopkins, edited by Claude Colleer Abbott, 2nd ed. Tablet (London), 208 (December 8, 1956), 500, 502.

1279 Coffin, Charles Monroe. The Major Poets: English and American. New York: Harcourt, Brace and Co., 1954.

1280 Cohen, Edward H. "A Bibliography Including the Published Works of Gerard Manley Hopkins and Criticism of the Works of Gerard Manley Hopkins." Ph.D., University of New Mexico, 1967.

1281 _____ "A Comprehensive Hopkins Bibliography: 1863-1918," Bulletin of Bibliography, 25 (September, 1967), 79-81.

1282 Cohen, J. M. "The Road not Taken: A Study in the Poetry of Robert Bridges," Cambridge Journal, 4 (June, 1950), 555-64.

1283 Cohen, Selma Jeanne. "Hopkins' 'As Kingfishers Catch Fire'," Modern Language Quarterly, 11 (June, 1950), 197-204.

1284 _____ "The Poems of Gerard Manley Hopkins in Relation to his Religious Thought." Ph.D., University of Chicago, 1946.

1285 _____ "The Poetic Theory of Gerard Manley Hopkins," Philological Quarterly, 26 (January, 1947), 1-20.

1286 Colavecchio, Barbara Marie. "The Dominant Symbols in Gerard Manley Hopkins' 'The Wreck of the Deutschland'." M.A. thesis, University of Rhode Island, 1963.

1287 Cole, David Bruce. " 'Charged with the Grandeur of God': God's Majesty, as Expressed in the Poetry of Gerard Manley Hopkins." Honors essay, Harvard University, 1955.

1288 College Survey of English Literature, edited by B. J. Whiting, et. al. Vol. 2. New York: Harcourt, Brace and Co., 1948, 382, 878-81, 951, 953, 1137.

1289 Colligan, Geraldine. "The Mysticism of Hopkins," Ave Maria, N.S. 58 (November 6, 1943), 591-93.

1290 Collins, James. "Philosophical Themes in G. M. Hopkins," Thought, 22 (March, 1947), 67-106.

1291 Collins, Winston Lee. "Tennyson and Hopkins: Intellectual and Poetic Affinities." M.A. thesis, University of Toronto, 1963.

1292 Colson, Ted Donald. "An Analysis of Selected Poems of Gerard Manley Hopkins for Oral Interpretation and a Study of his Poetic Theories." Ph.D., University of Oklahoma, 1964.

1293 Colum, Mary M. "Poets and their Problems," Forum, (June, 1935), 343-47.

1294 Combecher, Hans. "Drei Victorianische Gedichte," Neueren Sprachen (Marburg), (1964), 257-67.

1295 Concilio, Peter F. "Gerard Manley Hopkins' 'The Wreck of the Deutschland' and the Sonata-Allegro: A Comparative Study." M.A. thesis, Niagara University, 1966.

1296 Conlay, Iris. "Hopkins: Priest Because Poet." Review of Gerard Manley Hopkins: Priest and Poet, by John Pick. Catholic Herald (London), (October 16, 1942), 3.

1297 Conley, John. "Hopkins Enshrined." Review of Poems of Gerard Manley Hopkins, edited by W. H. Gardner; Gerard Manley Hopkins, by W. H. Gardner; Gerard Manley Hopkins, by K. R. Srinivasa Iyengar; Gerard Manley Hopkins, by W. A. M. Peters, S.J. and Immortal Diamond, edited by Norman Weyand, S.J. Poetry, 74 (August, 1949), 292-300.

1298 Conlon, Michael J. "A Bibliography of the Writings and Ana of Gerard Manley Hopkins from January 1, 1947 to January 1, 1958." M.A. thesis, University of Kentucky, 1961.

1299   Conlon, Sister M. Brendan. "The Fire Image in the Poetry
       of Gerard Manley Hopkins." M.A. Thesis, Creighton
       University, 1956.
1300   Connolly, Francis X. "Poetry and Politics." Return to
       Poetry, edited by John G. Brunini, et al. New York:
       Declan X McMullen Company, 1947, 127-31.
       [Reprinted from Spirit, May, 1935.]
1301   _____ "Reaffirmations of Poetic Values," Spirit, 13
       (May, 1946), 52-7.
1302   _____ The Types of Literature. New York: Harcourt,
       Brace & World, Inc., 1955.
1303   Connor, Sister Juanita Maria, S.S.J. "The Relationship
       of Gerard Manley Hopkins and his Life of Consecra-
       tion." M.A. thesis, Villanova University, 1957.
1304   Consolata, Sister Mary. "A Theme Song for the Marian
       Year," America, 90 (February 6, 1954), 480-82.
1305   Coogan, Marjorie D. "Dare-Gale Skylark," Fonthill
       Dial (College of Mount St. Vincent, New York), 19
       (June, 1938), 12-9.
1306   _____ "Inscape and Instress: Further Analogies with
       Scotus," PMLA, 65 (March, 1950), 66-74.
1307   _____ "The Nature Poetry of Gerard Manley Hopkins,
       S.J." M.A. thesis, Catholic University of America,
       1939.
1308   Cook, Albert. The Classic Line: A Study in Epic Poetry.
       Bloomington: Indiana University Press, 1966, 9, 277.
1309   _____ Prisms: Studies in Modern Literature.
       Bloomington: Indiana University Press, 1967.
1310   Coombes, H. Literature and Criticism. London: Chatto
       and Windus, 1953.
1311   _____ Literature and Criticism. Baltimore: Penguin
       Books, 1963.
1312   Cooney, Mother Madeleine Sophie. "A Study of Tone
       Color in the Poetry of Gerard Manley Hopkins, S.J."
       M.A. thesis, Marquette University, 1941.
1313   Cooper, Charles W. Preface to Poetry. New York:
       Harcourt, Brace and Co., 1946, 618, 676-78.
1314   Copleston, Frederick C., W. H. Gardner and Christopher
       Devlin. "Correspondence" (Letters to the Editor),
       Month, N.S. 4 (September, 1950), 208, 211-15.
1315   Corke, Hilary. "Hopkins" (Letter to the Editor),
       Encounter, 13 (July, 1959), 86-7.

1316 _____ "A Housecarl in Loyola's Menie." Review of The
        Journals and Papers of Gerard Manley Hopkins, edited
        by Humphry House and The Sermons and Devotional
        Writings of Gerard Manley Hopkins, edited by
        Christopher Devlin, S.J. Encounter, 12 (May, 1959),
        63-7.
1317 Corr, Gerard M., O.S.M. "Our Lady's Praise in Gerard
        Manley Hopkins," Clergy Review, N.S. 33 (May,
        1950), 289-94.
1318 Corrado da Alatri, O.F.M. "Nel Primo Centenario della
        Nascita di G. M. Hopkins: Poeta Gesuita Cantore di
        Duns Scotus," l'Italia Francescana (Rome), 19 (1944),
        132-48.
1319 Costello, William Thomas, S.J. " 'The Windhover' --A
        Penultimate Opinion." Unpublished paper, n.d.
1320 Couldrey, Oswald. "Hopkinsiana" (Letter to the Editor),
        Times Literary Supplement, (September 24, 1954), 609.
1321 Coursen, Herbert R., Jr. "The Bright Wings and the
        Enormous Dark: Gerard Manley Hopkins," Discourse,
        3 (Summer, 1961), 193-206.
1322 Courtney, Sister Therese, S.N.D. "Hopkins' 'Spelt from
        Sibyl's Leaves'," Explicator, 17 (April, 1959), 45.
1323 Cowley, Malcolm. "Resurrection of a Poet." Review of
        Poems of Gerard Manley Hopkins, edited by Robert
        Bridges; A Vision of the Mermaids, by Gerard Manley
        Hopkins and Gerard Manley Hopkins, by G. F. Lahey,
        S.J. New York Herald Tribune Books, (March 8, 1931),
        1, 6.
1324 Cox, Dorothy Scarborough. "The Mind of Gerard Manley
        Hopkins." M.A. thesis, University of Texas, 1940.
1325 Cox, R. G. "Hopkins and Patmore." Review of Further
        Letters of Gerard Manley Hopkins, edited by Claude
        Colleer Abbott. Scrutiny, 7 (September, 1938), 217-18.
1326 _____ Review of The Notebooks and Papers of Gerard
        Manley Hopkins, edited by Humphry House. Scrutiny
        5 (March, 1937), 455-56.
1327 Cranny, Titus, S.A. "Father Gerard Manley Hopkins:
        Poet of the King," Magnificat, 80 (September, 1947),
        251-58.
1328 Crawford, John. "Hopkins said: 'Irishmen are no Poets'."
        Review of A Hopkins Reader, edited by John Pick.
        Irish Press (Dublin), (June 27, 1953).
1329 Crehan, J. H. "More Light on Gerard Hopkins," Month,
        N.S. 10 (October, 1953), 205-14.

1330 _____ "Poetry and Religious Life: The Case of Gerard
Manley Hopkins, S.J." Month, 166 (December, 1935),
493-503.

1331 "Critical Approaches." Review of The Fine Art of Reading,
by David Cecil; Preliminary Essays, by John Wain and
Craft and Character in Modern Fiction, by Morton
Dauwen Zabel. Times Literary Supplement, (September
13, 1957), 546.

1332 Croce, Benedetto. "Un Gesuita Inglese Poeta. Gerard
Manley Hopkins," Critica (Naples), 35 (March, 1937),
81-100.

1333 _____ "Giansenisti e Gesuiti: Pagine di Restif de la
Bretonne e di G. M. Hopkins," Critica (Bari), 42
(1944), 95-8.

1334 Crompton, Louis. Review of The Disappearance of God:
Five Nineteenth-Century Writers, by J. Hillis Miller.
College English, 25 (May, 1964), 634.

1335 Cronin, Anthony. "Self-Mortifier." Review of The Journals
and Papers of Gerard Manley Hopkins, edited by Humphry
House and The Sermons and Devotional Writings of
Gerard Manley Hopkins, edited by Christopher Devlin,
S.J. Sunday Times (London), (February 15, 1959).

1336 Crowley, Austin. "Gerard Hopkins (An Appreciation),"
Boston College Stylus, 38 (January, 1925), 239-41.

1337 Cruise, Edward. "Development of the Religious Orders."
The English Catholics 1850-1950, edited by George
Andrew Beck. London: Burns Oates, 1950, 456-57.

1338 Cruse, Amy. After the Victorians. London: George Allen
and Unwin, Ltd., 1938, 157.

1339 Culler, A. Dwight. "Among the Victorians." Review of
The Disappearance of God: Five Nineteenth-Century
Writers, by J. Hillis Miller. Yale Review, 53 (March,
1964), 440-43.

1340 Cunningham, Margaret. "Hopkins and Prosody," Spheres
(Mount St. Agnes College, Baltimore, Maryland),
(Spring, 1948), 10-13.

1341 Cunningham, Maureen Michaela. "The Poetry of Gerard
Manley Hopkins, S.J." M.A. thesis, University of
Washington, 1955.

1342 Curran, John Patrick. " 'Inscape' and 'Instress' as Related
Principles in the Theory and Practice of Gerard Manley
Hopkins." M.A. thesis, New York University, 1954.

1343 Currier, Isabel. "Research on Life, Poetry of Gerard
Manley Hopkins." Review of Gerard Manley Hopkins,
by Eleanor Ruggles, Boston Traveler, (August 2, 1944).

1344 D. H. "Hopkins Poems as Song Cycle: Cheltenham
      Music," Daily Telegraph (London), (July 15, 1958).
1345 D. L. K. "A Poet Reinstated." Review of Gerard Manley
      Hopkins: Priest and Poet, by John Pick. Month, 178
      (November-December, 1942), 493-94.
1346 D. W. "Gerard Manley Hopkins." Review of Gerard
      Manley Hopkins: A Study of Poetic Idiosyncrasy in
      Relation to Poetic Tradition. Vol. 1. Tablet (London),
      (January 13, 1945), 22.
1347 D'Agostino, Nemi. "Due Formazioni: Hopkins e Joyce,"
      Fiera Letteraria (Rome), (November 28, 1954).
1348 Daiches, David. Critical Approaches to Literature.
      Englewood Cliffs, New Jersey: Prentice-Hall, Inc.,
      1956, 312, 315, 322, 356.
1349 _____ A Critical History of English Literature. 2 vols.
      New York: Ronald Press, 1960. Vol. 1: 325; Vol. 2:
      877, 1032, 1041-48, 1116, 1125, 1127.
1350 _____ "Gerard Manley Hopkins and the Modern Poets."
      New Literary Values: Studies in Modern Literature.
      Edinburgh: Oliver and Boyd, 1936, 23-51.
1351 _____ "Literary Values." Anonymous Review of New
      Literary Values. Times Literary Supplement,
      (January 31, 1935), 59.
1352 _____ The Present Age: After 1920. Vol. 5: Introductions
      to English Literature, edited by Bonamy Dobree. London:
      Cresset Press, 1962.
1353 _____ A Study of Literature. Ithaca: Cornell University
      Press, 1948, 42, 136, 146, 159, 166, 167, 226.
1354 _____ "Thomas Hardy--A. E. Housman--Gerard Manley
      Hopkins." Poetry and the Modern World. Chicago:
      University of Chicago Press, 1940, 17-37.
1355 _____ and William Charvet, eds. Poems in English. New
      York: Ronald Press, 1950, 563-65.
1356 Daly, James J., S.J. "Conscience Among the Books,"
      America, 66 (October 25, 1941), 73-4.
1357 _____ "Father Hopkins and the Society." The Jesuit in
      Focus. Milwaukee: Bruce, 1940, 189-94.
1358 _____ "Father Hopkins and the Society of Jesus" (Editorial
      Survey), Thought, 13 (March, 1938), 9-13.
1359 _____ "One Way of Getting a Catholic Literature,"
      Thought, 14 (December, 1939), 537-38.
1360 D'Angelo, Frank Joseph. " 'The Wreck of the Deutschland'
      and the Pastoral Tradition." M.A. thesis, Tulane
      University, 1963.

1361 Daniels, Earl. The Art of Reading Poetry. New York:
Rinehart & Company, Inc., 1953, 242-43.

1362 Darby, Harold S. "A Jesuit Poet--Gerard Manley Hopkins,"
London Quarterly and Holborn Review, 168 (April, 1943),
110-22.

1363 D'Arcy, Martin Cyril, S.J. "Gerard Manley Hopkins,"
Tablet (London), 183 (June 24, 1944), 308.

1364 _____ Review of Gerard Manley Hopkins, 1844-1889; A
Centenary Commemmoration. Vol. 1. Month, 181
(January-February, 1945), 67-9.

1365 _____ "Gerard Manley Hopkins, S.J." Archivum
Historicum Societatis Iesu, 1 (1932), 118-22.

1366 _____ "Gerard Manley Hopkins." Great Catholics,
edited by Claude Williamson, O.S.C. London:
Nicholson and Watson, 1938, 438-46. New York:
Macmillan and Company, 1939, 358-66.

1367 _____ The Mind and Heart of Love. New York: Henry
Holt and Company, 1947. [Inscribed "Martin C. D'Arcy,
S.J."]

1368 _____ The Mind and Heart of Love. 2nd ed. rev. London:
Faber and Faber Limited, 1954. [Inscribed "In great
gratitude for a real friend with Mind and Heart, Martin
C. D'Arcy, S.J."]

1369 _____ "A Note on Gerard Hopkins," Month, N.S. 11
(February, 1954), 113-15.

1370 _____ "Religion Today," Spiritual Life, 13 (Fall, 1967),
148-52.

1371 Davenport, John. "Mrs. Spark's Roses." Review of The
Girls of Slender Means, by Muriel Spark. Observer
(London), (September 22, 1963).

1372 Davie, Donald. "Christopher Fry" (Letter to the Editor),
World Review (London), (September, 1952).

1373 _____ "Hopkins, The Decadent Critic," Cambridge Journal,
4 (September, 1951), 725-39.

1374 _____ Purity of Diction in English Verse. London: Chatto
and Windus, 1952, 5, 26, 160-82.

1375 _____ Purity of Diction in English Verse. Reissued with
postscript. London: Routledge & Kegan Paul, 1967.

1376 _____ "Two Analogies for Poetry," Listener, 67 (April 5,
1962), 598-99.

1377 Davies, A. Talfan. "William Barnes, Gerard Manley
Hopkins, Dylan Thomas. The Influence of Welsh Prosody
on Modern English Poetry." Proceedings of the IIIrd
Congress of the International Comparative Literature
Association. The Hague: Mouton & Co., 1962, 90-122.

1378 Davies, Laurence H. "The Bethlehem Star" (Carol Introit--Unison), words by Gerard Manley Hopkins. University Carol Book: A Collection of Basque, French, Dutch, German, English Folk-Carols, Lullabies and Noels. Book 12: Christmas. Brighton: E. H. Freeman Ltd., 1955, 6-7. [Musical setting]

1379 Davies, Phillips George. "A Discovery of Death," CEA Critic (Skidmore College, Saratoga Springs, N. Y.), 27 (May, 1965), 7-8.

1380 _____ "The Return of the Gogynfeirdd," Poet and Critic, 2 (Spring, 1966), 39-45.

1381 Davies, S. J. "Gerard Manley Hopkins" (Letter to the Editor), Guardian, (August 25, 1944), 291.

1382 _____ "Gerard Manley Hopkins: 'To What Serves Mortal Beauty?' " (Letter to the Editor), Guardian, (August 4, 1944), 269-70.

1383 Davis, Peter. "N Y Philharmonic's Anniversary," Times (London), (December 23, 1967).

1384 Day Lewis, Cecil. "Gerard Manley Hopkins: Poet and Jesuit." Review of The Note-Books and Papers of Gerard Manley Hopkins, edited by Humphry House. Left Review, 3 (April, 1937), 172-75.

1385 _____ "A Hope for Poetry, III." Collected Poems 1929-1933 & A Hope for Poetry. New York: Random House, 1935, 167-76.

1386 _____ The Poetic Image. New York: Oxford University Press, 1947, 24, 67, 125-28.

1387 _____ "Records of a Great Poet." Review of The Letters of Gerard Manley Hopkins to Robert Bridges and The Correspondence of Gerard Manley Hopkins and Richard Watson Dixon, edited by Claude Colleer Abbott. New Republic, 83 (May 22, 1935), 52.

1388 _____ "Some Influences on Modern Poetry," Listener, 49 (January 29, 1953), 185-87.

1389 _____ "What is Modern Poetry," Listener, 49 (January 22, 1953), 147-49.

1390 Deferrari, Roy J., ed. "Gerard Manley Hopkins, S.J." Appreciation through Reading. Chicago: Wm. H. Sadlier, 1942, 537-38.

1391 De Graaff, Robert Mark. "Scotism in the Poetry of Gerard Manley Hopkins: A Study in Analogical Relationships." M.A. thesis, Miami University, 1966.

1392 Delahunty, Kenneth R. "Guilt and the Grail: Hopkins, Poet in the Active Voice: Wakefield, Mon Frere." M.A. thesis, Pennsylvania State University, 1965.

1393 Delaney, Sister Anne Cyril, S.N.D. (Mary Genevieve). "The Christocentricity of Gerard Manley Hopkins." M.A. thesis, Boston College, 1945.

1394 Delaney, Joan. " 'The Blessed Virgin compared to the Air we Breathe': An Interpretation." Clarke College Labarum (Dubuque, Iowa), 41 (Summer, 1949), 201-14.

1395 DeLargy, Peggy. "Hopkins and Prose," Spheres (Mount St. Agnes College, Baltimore, Maryland), (Spring, 1948), 7-9.

1396 _____ and Margaret Cunningham. "Hopkins and Analysis: 'Pied Beauty'," Spheres (Mount St. Agnes College, Baltimore, Maryland), (Spring, 1948), 5-6.

1397 DeLaura, David J. Review of Victorian Portraits: Hopkins and Pater, by David A. Downes. Victorian Studies, 9 (March, 1966), 282-83.

1398 De Luca, Giuseppe. "Note e Rassegne," Nuova Antologia (Florence, Rome), 7th series, 12 (April 16, 1934), 635-38.

1399 Demarest, Donald. Review of Immortal Diamond, edited by Norman Weyand, S.J. Catholic Worker, 16 (June, 1949), 8.

1400 _____ Review of Immortal Diamond, edited by Norman Weyand, S.J. Commonweal, 50 (April 29, 1949), 74.

1401 Dent, Alan. "The Milk of Paradise." Review of recording, "Poetry of Gerard Manley Hopkins," read by Cyril Cusack. John O'London's Weekly, (August 2, 1962).

1402 Derrick, Mildred E. " 'To What Serves Mortal Beauty?': Hopkins' Conception of Nature and Man in Relation to God." M.A. thesis, Vanderbilt University, 1967.

1403 De Selincourt, Basil. "Complete Dedication: Letters of Gerard Manley Hopkins." Review of The Letters of Gerard Manley Hopkins to Robert Bridges and The Correspondence of Gerard Manley Hopkins and Richard Watson Dixon, edited by Claude Colleer Abbott. Observer (London),(January 20, 1935), 5.

1404 _____ "Gerard Manley Hopkins. Sidelights and Memories." Review of The Note-Books and Papers of Gerard Manley Hopkins, edited by Humphry House. Observer (London), (January 24, 1937), 5.

1405 de Souza, Frederick J., S.J. "Gerard Manley Hopkins. A Closer Look at the Terrible Sonnets." M.A. thesis, Columbia University, 1963.

1406 Deutsch, Babette. "The Forged Feature." Poetry in Our Time. New York: Henry Holt & Co., 1952, 286-311.

1407 _____ "Fortune's Football." Review of Gerard Manley Hopkins: A Life, by Eleanor Ruggles. Nation, 159 (October 7, 1944), 415-17.

1408 _____ "Gerard Manley Hopkins." Review of The Poetry of Gerard Manley Hopkins: A Survey and Commentary, by E. E. Phare. New York Herald Tribune Books, (January 28, 1934), 2.

1409 _____ "Gerard Manley Hopkins, Poet and Pioneer." Review of The Letters of Gerard Manley Hopkins, 2 vols., edited by Claude Colleer Abbott. New York Herald Tribune Books, 11 (March 17, 1935), 1-2.

1410 _____ "Glimpses of a Rare Spirit." Review of Further Letters of Gerard Manley Hopkins, edited by Claude Colleer Abbott. New York Herald Tribune Books, 14 (August 21, 1938), 12.

1411 _____ "Insight and Inscape." Review of Gerard Manley Hopkins: A Critical Essay Towards the Understanding of his Poetry, by W. A. M. Peters. New York Herald Tribune Weekly Book Review, (January 2, 1949), 11.

1412 _____ "A Priest's View of a Poet." Review of Gerard Manley Hopkins, Priest and Poet, by John Pick. Nation, 157 (August 28, 1943), 247.

1413 _____ "Scholar, Priest and Poet." Review of The Note-Books and Papers of Gerard Manley Hopkins, edited by Humphry House. New York Herald Tribune Books, 13 (May 16, 1937), 21.

1414 _____ "Studies of a Poet's Poet." Review of Gerard Manley Hopkins, by the Kenyon Critics. New York Herald Tribune Weekly Book Review, 22 (March 17, 1946), 12.

1415 _____ This Modern Poetry. New York: W. W. Norton & Co., Inc., 1935.

1416 Dever, Joseph. "Gerard Manley Tuncks!" Stylus, 54 (March, 1941), 5-16.

1417 _____ "Poet of Beauty," Today (Chicago), 4 (February, 1951), 18.

1418 Devlin, Christopher, S.J. "Correspondence" (Letter to the Editor), Month, N.S. 4 (September, 1950), 213-15.

1419 _____ "An Essay on Scotus," Month, 182 (November-December, 1946), 456-66.

1420 _____ "The Heart in Hiding." Review of Further Letters of Gerard Manley Hopkins, edited by Claude Colleer Abbott, 2nd ed., rev. and enl. Month, N.S. 17 (May, 1957), 332-33.

1421 _____ "Hopkins and Duns Scotus," New Verse, No. 14 (April, 1935), 12-7.

1422 _____ "Hopkins and Tradition." Review of Gerard Manley Hopkins, by the Kenyon Critics. Month, N.S. 4 (August, 1950), 141.

1423 _____ "The Ignatian Inspiration of Gerard Hopkins," Blackfriars, 16 (December, 1935), 887-90.

1424 _____ "The Image and the Word--I," Month, N.S. 3 (February, 1950), 114-27.

1425 _____ "The Image and the Word--II," Month, N.S. 3 (March, 1950), 191-202.

1426 _____ "In the Living Tradition," Review of Immortal Diamond, edited by Norman Weyand, S.J. Catholic Herald (London), (December 2, 1949), 6.

1427 _____ "Nature in Hopkins." Review of Gerard Manley Hopkins, by Geoffrey Grigson. New Statesman and Nation, (March 26, 1955), 447.

1428 _____ "Time's Eunuch," Month, N.S. 1 (May, 1949), 303-12.

1429 _____, ed. "Aspects of Hopkins's Genius." Anonymous Review of The Journals and Papers of Gerard Manley Hopkins, edited by Humphry House and The Sermons and Devotional Writings of Gerard Manley Hopkins, edited by Christopher Devlin, S.J. Scotsman (Edinburgh), (March 26, 1959).

1430 _____, ed. "Rare Ill'Broker'd Talent." Anonymous Review of The Journals and Papers, edited by Humphry House and The Sermons and Devotional Writings, edited by Christopher Devlin, S.J. Times Literary Supplement, (September 25, 1959), 544.

1431 Dicus, Sister Mary Vivian. "An Analysis of the Literary Importance of Gerard Manley Hopkins." M.A. thesis, University of Wichita, 1937.

1432 "Did not Live to See his Work in Print: Oxford Tribute to G. M. Hopkins," Oxford Mail, (August 23, 1951).

1433 "Difficult Poetry" (Editorial), Times Literary Supplement, (June 24, 1955), 349.

1434 Dilligan, Robert. "The Influence of John Keats on Gerard Manley Hopkins." M.A. thesis, Columbia University, 1964.

1435 Digges, Sister Mary Laurentia. Gerard Manley Hopkins' Sonnets of Desolation: An Analysis of Meaning. Washington, D.C. Catholic University of America Press, 1937. [Microcards]

1436 Dimnet, Ernest. "Father Hopkins: The Poet Jesuit,"
        Pylon, 3 (April, 1936), 11-2.
1437 Dinnage, Paul. "Two Victorians." Review of The Rod,
        The Root, and The Flower, by Coventry Patmore and
        Browning: Poetry and Prose, selected by Simon
        Nowell-Smith. Spectator (London), (March 30, 1951).
1438 Dobree, Bonamy. The Broken Cistern: The Clark Lectures
        1952-1953. London: Cohen & West Ltd, 1954, 5-6,
        109-10.
1439 _____ Review of Gerard Manley Hopkins, by W. H.
        Gardner. Universities Quarterly (London), (May, 1954).
1440 _____ "The Hopkins Letters." Review of The Letters of
        Gerard Manley Hopkins to Robert Bridges and The
        Correspondence of Gerard Manley Hopkins and Richard
        Watson Dixon, edited by Claude Colleer Abbott.
        Spectator (London), 154 (January 11, 1935), 53.
1441 _____ "The Hopkins Papers." Review of The Note-Books
        and Papers of Gerard Manley Hopkins, edited by
        Humphry House. Spectator (London), 158 (March 12,
        1937), 479-80.
1442 _____ "More Hopkins Letters." Review of Further Letters
        of Gerard Manley Hopkins, edited by Claude Colleer
        Abbott. Spectator (London), 160 (May 13, 1938), 880.
1443 Dobson, Dennis. Review of Gerard Manley Hopkins, by
        the Kenyon Critics. Listener, 43 (April 13, 1950), 664.
1444 Doherty, Francis. "A Note on 'Spelt from Sibyl's Leaves',"
        Essays in Criticism, 14 (October, 1964), 428-32.
1445 Doherty, Kevin F., S.J. "Vergil and Gerard Manley
        Hopkins," Folia, 7 (1953), 30-41.
1446 Doherty, Paul C. "Hopkins 'Spring and Fall: To a Young
        Child'," Victorian Poetry, 5 (Summer, 1967), 140-43.
1447 Dohmann, Sister Ottilia, S.C.C. "The Poetic Mind of
        Gerard Manley Hopkins, S.J." Ph.D., Fordham
        University, 1936.
1448 "Donne and Hopkins," Poetry Review, 24 (1933), 464-65.
1449 Donoghue, Denis. "The Bird as Symbol: Hopkins's
        Windhover," Studies, 44 (Autumn, 1955), 291-99.
1450 _____ "In the Scene of Being," Hudson Review, 14
        (Summer, 1961), 232-46.
1451 _____ "Technique in Hopkins," Studies, 44 (Winter,
        1955), 446-56.
1452 Donovan, Mary. "Gerard Manley Hopkins S.J.: A Poet
        for the Twentieth Century--His Message," Ethos, 12
        (Spring, 1939), 78-81.

1453 Donovan, Mother Mary Inez. "The Aesthetics of Gerard
Manley Hopkins, S.J." M.A. thesis, University of
Detroit, 1957.

1454 Doubleday, Neal Frank. Studies in Poetry: An Introduction
to the Critical Reading of Poems. New York: Harper &
Brothers, 1949, 360-64.

1455 Downes, David Anthony. Gerard Manley Hopkins: A Study
of his Ignatian Spirit. Manuscript copy. [Inscribed
"To: Fr. D. A. Bischoff . . . David A. Downes."]

1456 _____ Gerard Manley Hopkins: A Study of his Ignatian
Spirit. London: Vision Press Limited, 1960.
[Inscribed "To: Father D. A. Bischoff, S.J., . . .
David A. Downes"]

1457 _____ "Hopkins and Thomism," Victorian Poetry, 3
(Autumn, 1965), 270-72.

1458 _____ "The Hopkins Enigma," Thought, 36 (Winter,
1961), 573-94.

1459 _____ Review of Studies in Structure, by Robert J.
Andreach. Renascence, 18 (Spring, 1966), 161-63.

1460 _____ Victorian Portraits: Hopkins and Pater. New York:
Bookman Associates, Inc., 1965.

1461 _____ Anonymous Review of Victorian Portraits: Hopkins
and Pater. Choice, 2 (July-August, 1965), 296.

1462 Downey, Harris. "Gerard Hopkins: A Study of Influences,"
Southern Review, 1 (1936), 837-45.

1463 _____ "Gerard Manley Hopkins." Review of The Letters
of Gerard Manley Hopkins, 2 vols., edited by Claude
Colleer Abbott. Virginia Quarterly Review, 11 (July,
1935), 458-61.

1464 _____ "A Pioneer of Poetry." Review of The Poetry of
Gerard Manley Hopkins, by E. E. Phare. Commonweal,
19 (April 13, 1934), 667-68.

1465 _____ "A Poem Not Understood," Virginia Quarterly
Review, 11 (October, 1935), 506-17. [Windhover]

1466 Doyle, Francis G., S.J. "A Note on Hopkins's Windhover,"
Studies, 45 (Spring, 1956), 88-91.

1467 Doyle, Louis F., S.J. "D-Day for Ariel," America, 80
(December 18, 1948), 293-95.

1468 _____ "In the Valley of the Shadow of Hopkins," Catholic
World, 169 (May, 1949), 102-08.

1469 _____ "To M'sieu Jourdain," America, 79 (September 18,
1948), 541-43.

1470 Doyle-Curran, Mary. "A Commentary on the Poetry of
Gerard Manley Hopkins." Ph.D., University of Iowa,
1946.

1471 Drake, Robert. "The Harrowing Evangel of Flannery
       O'Connor," Christian Century, 81 (September 30,
       1964), 1200-02.
1472 Drake, Walter. (Letter to the Editor). Poetry Review,
       39 (October, 1948), 377-78.
1473 Drew, David. "New Music at York," New Statesman
       (London), (July 8, 1966).
1474 Drew, Elizabeth. Discovering Poetry. New York: W. W.
       Norton & Company, Inc., 1961.
1475 _____ with John L. Sweeney. Directions in Modern Poetry.
       New York: Gordian Press, 1967.
1476 Driscoll, John P., S.J. "Hopkins' 'Spring,' line 2, and
       'Spring and Fall: To a Young Child,' line 2,"
       Explicator, 24 (November, 1965), 26.
1477 Driskell, Leon V. "The Progressive Structure of 'The
       Windhover'," Renascence, 19 (Fall, 1966), 30-6.
1478 Dubliner. (Letter to the Editor). New Statesman (London),
       9 (June 23, 1917), 277.
1479 Duffy, John, C.SS.R. Review of Gerard Manley Hopkins,
       by the Kenyon Critics. Spirit, 13 (July, 1946), 88-91.
1480 _____ "Individualism in Poetry." Return to Poetry, edited
       by John G. Brunini, et al. New York: Declan X.
       McMullen Company, 1947, 31-43. [Reprinted from
       Panel Discussion Paper, Second Congress, Catholic
       Poetry Society of America. Hunter College, 1946.]
1481 _____ A Philosophy of Poetry. Washington: Catholic
       University of America Press, 1945, x-xi, 148-49,
       202-07, 215.
1482 _____ "The Place of the Beautiful." Return to Poetry,
       edited by John G. Brunini, et al. New York: Declan X.
       McMullen Company, 1947, 29-33. [Reprinted from
       Spirit, November, 1941.]
1483 _____ "Poetry: A Fusion of Many Factors." Return to
       Poetry, edited by John G. Brunini, et al. New York:
       Declan X. McMullen Company, 1947, 213-17.
       [Reprinted from Spirit, March, 1943.]
1484 Dumbleton, William Albert. "The Literary Relationship of
       Robert Bridges to Gerard Manley Hopkins, 1889-1930."
       Ph.D., University of Pennsylvania, 1966.
1485 Durant, Albert A., O.S.A. "The Concept of God in the
       Poetry of Gerard Manley Hopkins." M.A. thesis,
       Catholic University of America, 1937.
1486 Durao, Paulo. "A Poesia de G. M. Hopkins," Broteria
       (Lisbon), 58 (March, 1954), 294-309.

1487 _____ "Os Exercicios Espirituais na Poesia de G. M. Hopkins," Broteria (Lisbon), 61 (December, 1955), 520-31.

1488 Durr, Robert A. "Hopkins' 'No Worst, There is None'," Explicator, 11 (November, 1952), 11.

1489 Durrell, Lawrence. Key to Modern Poetry. Calcutta: Rupa & Co., 1961, 128, 149-61.

1490 Durrwachter, Carol J. "John Donne and Gerard Manley Hopkins: A Comparison." M.A. thesis, Pennsylvania State University, 1966.

1491 E. O. "The Poet Hopkins." Review of Poems of Gerard Manley Hopkins, edited by Robert Bridges; Gerard Manley Hopkins, by G. F. Lahey, S.J. and A Vision of the Mermaids, by Gerard Manley Hopkins. Tablet (London), (December 6, 1930), 767-68.

1492 E. S. P. "Hopkins: Priest, Poet." Review of Gerard Manley Hopkins, Priest and Poet, by John Pick. Springfield Republican (Springfield, Massachusetts), (April 29, 1943), 8.

1493 Eberhart, Richard. " 'Heavenly-Mindedness'." Review of Gerard Manley Hopkins, Priest and Poet, by John Pick. Poetry, 62 (September, 1943), 347-50.

1494 _____ "Will and Psyche in Poetry." The Moment of Poetry, edited by Don Cameron Allen. Baltimore: Johns Hopkins Press, 1962, 63.

1495 _____ and Selden Rodman, eds. War and the Poet: An Anthology of Poetry Expressing Man's Attitudes to War from Ancient Times to the Present. New York: Devin-Adair Company, 1945, x-xi, xiii-xiv, 115-16, 221.

1496 Editorial. Measure: The Journal of the Gerard Manley Hopkins Poetry Society, 1 (Christmas, 1932), 4.

1497 Editorial. Psyche (London), 16 (1936), 5-50.

1498 Edridge, Ray. Review of Poems of Gerard Manley Hopkins, edited by W. H. Gardner, 3rd ed. Downside Review, 67 (April, 1949), 231-32.

1499 Edwards, Hugh. "Postscript." Photographs/Algimantas Kezys, S.J., by Algimantas Kezys, S.J. Chicago: Loyola University Press, 1966, n.p.

1500 Ehmann, Benedict. "Father Gerard M. Hopkins, S.J." Catholic Courier (Rochester, New York), (October 12, 1944), 15.

1501 _____ " 'Limber Liquid Youth'," Catholic Courier (Rochester, New York), (October 26, 1944), 15.

1502 _____ "The Poetry of Father Hopkins," Catholic Courier (Rochester, New York), (October 19, 1944), 15.

1503 Eisenbraun, Meredith Visnow. "A Study of Gerard Manley Hopkins' Sonnets with Reference to his own Commentary and to the Formative Influences in his Life." M.A. thesis, University of South Dakota, 1955.

1504 Eleanor, Mother Mary, S.H.C.J. "The Debate of the Body and the Soul," Renascence, 12 (Summer, 1960), 192-97.

1505 _____ "Hopkins' 'Windhover' and Southwell's Hawk," Renascence, 15 (Fall, 1962), 21-2, 27.

1506 Eliot, Thomas Stearns. After Strange Gods. New York: Harcourt, Brace & Co., 1934, 51-3.

1507 _____ On Poetry and Poets. London: Faber and Faber Ltd., 1957, 33, 51.

1508 _____ What is a Classic? An Address Delivered Before the Virgil Society on the 16th of October 1944. London: Faber and Faber Limited, 1945, 29.

1509 Elkins, Bill James. "Hopkins' Terrible Sonnets: A Study of Poetic Progression." Ph.D., Ohio University, 1967.

1510 Ellart, Gerald, S.J. "Catholic Cult and Culture," Catholic Mind, 32 (February 8, 1934), 41-53.

1511 Elliott, Brian. "Gerard Hopkins and Marcus Clarke," Southerly (Sydney), 8 (1947), 218-27.

1512 Ellman, Richard. "Yeats and Hopkins." Anonymous Review of Yeats: The Man and the Masks, by Richard Ellman and Immortal Diamond, edited by Norman Weyand, S.J. Scotsman (Edinburgh), (December 22, 1949).

1513 _____ Yeats: The Man and the Masks. New York: Macmillan Company, 1948, 49.

1514 Ellrodt, Robert. "Grandeur et Misere de Gerard Manley Hopkins," Cahiers du Sud (Paris), 33 (1951), 272-89.

1515 Elton, Oliver. The English Muse. London: Bell & Son, 1933, 399-400.

1516 Elvin, Lionel. Introduction to the Study of Literature. Vol. 1. London: Sylvan Press, 1949, 17-8, 204-17.

1517 Emerson, Dorothy. "Gerard Manley Hopkins," Scholastic, 26 (May 25, 1935), 10.

1518 Empson, William. "Hopkinsiana" (Letter to the Editor), Times Literary Supplement, (October 1, 1954), 625.

1519 _____ "Hopkinsiana" (Letter to the Editor), Times Literary Supplement, (October 29, 1954), 689.

1520 _____ Milton's God. London: Chatto and Windus, 1961, 231-32.

1521 _____ Seven Types of Ambiguity. 2nd ed., rev. London: Chatto and Windus, 1947.

1522 _____ " 'The Windhover' " (Letter to the Editor), Times
Literary Supplement, (May 20, 1955), 269.

1523 Engle, Monroe. "Gerard Manley Hopkins: Inscapist
Poet." B.A. thesis, Harvard University, 1942.

1524 Engle, Paul. "Biography of Poet Reveals his Personality's
Richness." Review of Gerard Manley Hopkins, A Life,
by Eleanor Ruggles. Chicago Tribune Book Supplement,
(July 30, 1944).

1525 "English Poetry: Miss Mary Mather to Give Talk," South
China Morning Post (Hong Kong), (January 24, 1950).

1526 Enright, Dennis Joseph. "Herbert Read's Study of Poetry."
Review of Form in Modern Poetry, by Herbert Read.
Egyptian Gazette (Cairo), (December 5, 1949).

1527 Epstein, David. "Four Songs." A Cycle for soprano, solo
French horn and string orchestra. New York: Mercury
Music Corporation, 1964. [Musical setting. Contents:
"Cuckoo," "Strike, Churl," and "Spring and Fall," by
Gerard Manley Hopkins and "To Sleep," by John Keats.]

1528 Etman, Nol. "Haunting Rhythm," Tijdschrift Voor Taal en
Letteren (Amsterdam), 27 (April, 1939), 94-101.

1529 Evans, Benjamin Ifor. "Gerard Manley Hopkins." English
Poetry in the Later Nineteenth Century. London:
Methuen, 1933, 268-85.

1530 _____ "G.M. Hopkins." Review of A Hopkins Reader,
edited by John Pick. Birmingham Post, (June 23, 1953).

1531 _____ "Letters." Review of Further Letters of Gerard
Manley Hopkins, edited by Claude Colleer Abbott.
Manchester Guardian, (June 24, 1938), 7.

1532 _____ "On Books and People." Review of The Desire and
Pursuit of the Whole, by Frederick Rolfe and A Hopkins
Reader, by John Pick. Truth (London), (June 5, 1953),
689.

1533 _____ "A Poet's Notebook." Review of The Note-Books
and Papers of Gerard Manley Hopkins, edited by
Humphry House. Manchester Guardian, (February 5,
1937), 7.

1534 _____ "Towards the Twentieth Century: Gerard Manley
Hopkins and T. S. Eliot." Tradition and Romanticism:
Studies in English Poetry from Chaucer to W. B. Yeats.
Hamden, Connecticut: Archon Books, 1964, 159,
185-200.

1535 _____, comp. "Gerard Manley Hopkins (1844-1889)."
The Cambridge Bibliography of English Literature,
edited by Frederick W. Bateson. Vol. 3: 1800-1900.
New York: Macmillan Company, 1941, 325-26.

1536 Evans, Illtud, O.P. "Fine, Dull, Beautiful." Review of
      The Journals and Papers of Gerard Manley Hopkins,
      edited by Humphry House and The Sermons and Devo-
      tional Writings of Gerard Manley Hopkins, edited by
      Christopher Devlin, S.J. Blackfriars, 40 (June, 1959),
      270-73.
1537 Evans, Marjorie R., comp. An Anthology of Victorian
      Verse. London: Methuen & Co. Ltd., 1949.
1538 Evans, Richard X. "The Poetry of Gerard Manley Hopkins,"
      Measure: The Journal of the Gerard Manley Hopkins
      Poetry Society, 1 (Easter, 1933), 25-9.
1539 Evarts, Prescott, Jr. "Inscape and Symbol in the Poetry of
      Gerard Manley Hopkins." M.A. thesis, Columbia
      University, 1962.
1540 Evelyn, Sister Mary, R.S.M. "Hopkins and Theology,"
      Spheres (Mount St. Agnes College, Baltimore, Maryland),
      (Spring, 1948), 22-4.
1541 Every, George, S.S.M. "The Two Vocations." Review of
      Gerard Manley Hopkins: A Study of Poetic Idiosyncrasy
      in Relation to Poetic Tradition, by W. H. Gardner and
      Immortal Diamond, edited by Norman Weyand, S.J.
      Poetry (London), (May, 1950), 22-4.
1542 Fabbretti, Nazareno. "Buona Tristezza di Newman,"
      l'Italia (Milan), (October 24, 1950).
1543 Fairbrother, Nan. An English Year. New York: Alfred A.
      Knopf, 1954, 20-1, 23, 46, 71-3, 76, 81, 186, 206,
      230.
1544 Fairchild, Hoxie Neale. Religious Trends in English
      Poetry. Vol. IV: 1830-1880. New York: Columbia
      University Press, 1957, vii, 287, 321-22.
1545 _____ Religious Trends in English Poetry. Vol. V:
      1880-1920. New York: Columbia University Press,
      1962, 60-95.
1546 Fairley, Barker. "Charles Doughty and Modern Poetry."
      London Mercury, 32 (June, 1935), 128-37.
1547 _____ "A Survey and Commentary." Review of The Poetry
      of Gerard Manley Hopkins, by E. E. Phare. Canadian
      Forum, 14 (February, 1934), 186-87.
1548 Farrell, Fran. "Father Bischoff: Hopkins Expert, Journalist,
      Composer, Painter, Teacher," Spectator (Seattle Univer-
      sity, Seattle, Washington), (February 26, 1959).
1549 Farrell, Melvin Lloyd. "The Significance of Christ in the
      Poetry of Gerard Manley Hopkins." M.A. thesis,
      University of Washington, 1956.

1550 Farren, Robert (Roibeard O. Farachain). The Course of
     Irish Verse in English. New York: Sheed and Ward,
     1947, 150-69.
1551 "Fr. G. M. Hopkins in National Portrait Gallery," Letters
     and Notices, 68 (March, 1963), 5.
1552 "Father G. M. Hopkins, S.J., Communist" (Editorial
     Comment), Month, 158 (December, 1936), 487-88.
1553 "Father Gerard Hopkins" (Obituary), Letters and Notices,
     99 (March, 1890), 173-79.
1554 "Father Gerard Hopkins: I. His Poetry," by Frederick
     Page. II. "Dorothea and Theophilus," by Gerard
     Hopkins. III. "His Character," by Plures. IV.
     "His Prose (Extracts from his Diaries)," by Gerard
     Hopkins. Dublin Review, 167 (July-September, 1920),
     40-66.
1555 "Father Gerard Manley Hopkins, S.J.," Aloysian (Parish
     Magazine of St. Aloysius, Glasgow), 258 (September,
     1947), 204-05.
1556 Fausset, Hugh I'Anson. "Gerard Hopkins: A Centenary
     Tribute" and "The Conflict of Priest and Poet in
     Hopkins." Poets and Pundits: Essays and Addresses.
     London: Jonathan Cape, 1947, 96-103, 104-13.
1557 _____ "Poetic Tradition." Review of Gerard Manley
     Hopkins (1844-1889): A Study of Poetic Idiosyncrasy in
     Relation to Poetic Tradition, by W. H. Gardner. Vol. 2.
     Manchester Guardian, (May 31, 1949), 4.
1558 _____ "Gerard Hopkins." Review of Gerard Manley
     Hopkins, by W. A. M. Peters, S.J. Manchester
     Guardian, (April 13, 1948).
1559 _____ "Hopkins Reader." Review of A Hopkins Reader,
     edited by John Pick. Manchester Guardian, (June 16,
     1953).
1560 _____ "The Poet Hopkins." Review of Gerard Manley
     Hopkins (1844-1889): A Study of Poetic Idiosyncrasy in
     Relation to Poetic Tradition, Vol. 2. Times of Ceylon
     (Colombo), (September 11, 1949). [Also as "Poetic
     Tradition" in Manchester Guardian, (May 31, 1949).]
1561 _____ "Priest and Poet." Review of Gerard Manley
     Hopkins, Priest and Poet, by John Pick. Manchester
     Guardian, (October 7, 1942), 3.
1562 Feeney, Leonard, S.J. "By Way of a Summary of Sorts,"
     America, 63 (May 4, 1940), 104.
1563 _____ "Father Hopkins and Professor Abbott," America,
     56 (October 24, 1936), 68-9.

1564 _____ "Father Hopkins' Mystic Songs" (Poem), America, 23 (May 1, 1920), 41. [Also in In Towns and Little Towns: A Book of Poems, by Leonard Feeney, S.J. New York: America Press, 1927, 108.]

1565 _____ "A Further Comment," America, 56 (January 23, 1937), 380.

1566 _____ "Hopkins Without Comment." Review of The Note-Books and Papers of Gerard Manley Hopkins, edited by Humphry House. America, 57 (April 17, 1937), 45-6.

1567 _____ "Literature." Review of The Note-Books and Papers of Gerard Manley Hopkins, edited by Humphry House. America, 58 (December 4, 1937), ii, section 2.

1568 _____ "Oddity and Obscurity in Hopkins," From the Housetops, 1 (December, 1946), 24-9.

1569 _____ "Poetry: To be or to Mean." Return to Poetry, edited by John G. Brunini, et al. New York: Declan X. McMullen Company, 1947, 123-25. [Reprinted from Spirit, July, 1937.]

1570 Feeney, Thomas B., S.J. "Gerard Manley Hopkins, S.J., Priest and Poet" (Radio address), Pilot (Boston), 108 (July 3, 1937), 1, 6.

1571 Fike, Francis George, Jr. "The Influence of John Ruskin upon the Aesthetic Theory and Practice of Gerard Manley Hopkins." Ph.D., Stanford University, 1963.

1572 Finlay, Ida. "Gerard Manley Hopkins--Poet and Priest," Cornhill Magazine, 159 (April, 1939), 467-78.

1573 Fiore, Amadeus, O.F.M. "Hopkins' Relation to the Deutschland Nuns," Renascence, 18 (Autumn, 1965), 45-8.

1574 Fish, Helen Dean, ed. The Boy's Book of Verse. New York: J. B. Lippincott Company, 1951, 247.

1575 Fisher, Phil J. "Three Poetic Minds." Review of Gerard Manley Hopkins, by W. H. Gardner. Vol. 2. Methodist Recorder (December 15, 1949).

1576 Fitts, Dudley. "A Poet's Letters." Review of Further Letters of Gerard Manley Hopkins Including his Correspondence with Coventry Patmore, edited by Claude Colleer Abbott. Saturday Review, 18 (July 9, 1938), 15.

1577 Fitzgerald, R. "Generations of Leaves," Perspectives (New York), No. 8 (1954), 75-8.

1578 Fitzpatrick, A. M., S.T.D. "Life as a Jesuit Didn't Stifle Hopkins' Poetry," Catholic Universe Bulletin (Cleveland, Ohio), (April 15, 1949), 7.

1579 Flanner, Hildegarde (Mrs. Frederick Monhoff). Review of
The Poems of Gerard Manley Hopkins, edited by Robert
Bridges; A Vision of the Mermaids, by Gerard Manley
Hopkins, S. J. and Gerard Manley Hopkins, by G. F.
Lahey, S. J. New Republic, 65 (February 4, 1931),
331-32.

1580 _____ "Stations of the Cross." Review of The Note-Books
and Papers of Gerard Manley Hopkins, edited by
Humphry House. New Republic, 90 (March 31, 1937),
243.

1581 Fleisher, Frederic. "Gerald [sic] Manley Hopkins."
Review of A Hopkins Reader, edited by John Pick and
Poems and Prose of Gerard Manley Hopkins, edited by
W. H. Gardner. Sydsvenska Dagbladet (Malmo),
(December 23, 1953).

1582 Fleming, Lenore Marie Moe. "The Influence of Duns
Scotus on Gerard Manley Hopkins." M.A. thesis,
Loyola University (Chicago), 1954.

1583 Fletcher, John Gould. "Gerard Manley Hopkins--Priest or
Poet?" Review of The Letters of Gerard Manley Hopkins
to Robert Bridges and The Correspondence of Gerard
Manley Hopkins and Richard Watson Dixon, edited by
Claude Colleer Abbott. American Review, 6 (January,
1936), 331-46.

1584 Flinn, Sean, O.F.M. "Scotus and Hopkins: Christian
Metaphysics and Poetic Creativity," Duns Scotus
Philosophical Association Annual Report, 26 (1962),
50-94.

1585 Flower, Desmond. "St. Martin's Summer, and a Winter of
Mars." The Pursuit of Poetry. London: Cassell & Co.,
1939, 248-56, 270.

1586 Foote, Timothy Gilson. "To What Serves Mortal Agony?
A Study of Hopkins' 'The Wreck of the Deutschland' in
Relation to 'Lycidas,' and an Analysis of the 'Terrible
Sonnets' in Relation to The Spiritual Exercises of St.
Ignatius of Loyola; the whole Being Related Generally
to Milton." B.A. thesis, Harvard University, 1949.

1587 Foote, Timothy Gilson (Edward Grey, pseud.) " 'The
Wreck of the Deutschland': An Elegy." Bowdoin prize
entry for dissertations in English, Harvard University,
1949.

1588 Ford, Boris, ed. From Dickens to Hardy. Vol. 6: Pelican
Guide to English Literature. Baltimore, Maryland:
Penguin Books, 1964.

1589 Forster, Leonard. Review of Gerard Manley Hopkins: A
      Critical Essay towards the Understanding of his Poetry,
      by W. A. M. Peters, S.J. English Studies (Amsterdam),
      30 (February, 1949), 18-20.
1590 _____ Review of The Note-Books and Papers of Gerard
      Manley Hopkins, edited by Humphry House. English
      Studies (Amsterdam), 19 (October, 1937), 236-39.
1591 Forte, Felix. "Omaggio a Hopkins," l'Avvenire d'Italia
      (Bologna), (November 20, 1949).
1592 Fowlie, Wallace. The Clown's Grail: A Study of Love in
      its Literary Expression. London: Dennis Dobson,
      1948, 128, 130, 136-37, 153.
1593 Frankenberg, Lloyd. "Immediacy and Simultaneity."
      Pleasure Dome. Boston: Houghton Mifflin Co., 1949,
      11-2, 153, 173, 264.
1594 _____ (Letter to the Editor), New York Times Book Review,
      (November 10, 1957), 34.
1595 _____ "Meaning in Modern Poetry," Saturday Review, 29
      (March 23, 1946), 5-6, 56-7.
1596 Franz, Louis Joseph. "The Concept of the 'Mystical Body
      of Christ' in Selected Poems by Gerard Manley Hopkins."
      Ph.D., University of Southern California, 1966.
1597 Fraser, George Sutherland. "Books in General." Review
      of Selected Poems of Gerard Manley Hopkins, edited by
      James Reeves; A Hopkins Reader, edited by John Pick;
      Poetical Works of Robert Bridges; and Poems and Prose
      of Gerard Manley Hopkins, edited by W. H. Gardner.
      New Statesman (London), 46 (October 10, 1953), 424-25.
1598 _____ Dylan Thomas. Bibliographical Series of Supple-
      ments to 'British Book News' on Writers and their Work,
      No. 90. London: Longmans, Green & Co., 1960, 24.
1599 _____ The Modern Writer and his World: Continuity and
      Innovation in Twentieth-Century English Literature.
      3rd ed. New York: Frederick A. Praeger, 1965, 33,
      139, 191, 282, 294-98, 372.
1600 Fraser, Ronald. "The Windhover Again," Downside
      Review, 85 (January, 1967), 71-3.
1601 Fraunces, John Manning, S.J. "The Meaning and Use of
      Inscape." M.A. thesis, Loyola University (Chicago),
      1940.
1602 Frazier, Alexander. "The Prosody of Gerard Manley
      Hopkins." M.A. thesis, University of Arizona, 1933.
1603 Freeman, Beatrice D. "The Literary Reputation of Gerard
      Manley Hopkins." M.A. thesis, Columbia University,
      1949.

1604 Freeman, James C. "Immortal Diamond: Gerard Manley
     Hopkins. A Review-Article," Journal of Bible and
     Religion, 18 (1950), 42-4.
1605 Friar, Kimon and John Malcolm Brinnin, eds. "Gerard
     Manley Hopkins." Modern Poetry: American and
     British. New York: Appleton-Century-Crofts, Inc.,
     1951, 14-22, 501-04.
1606 Friend-Pereira, F. J. "Gerard Manley Hopkins." Review
     of The Note-Books and Papers of Gerard Manley
     Hopkins, edited by Humphry House. New Review
     (Calcutta), 6 (November, 1937), 473-75.
1607 Frye, Northrop. The Anatomy of Criticism. Princeton,
     New Jersey: Princeton University Press, 1957, 154,
     263, 272, 293-94, 297.
1608 _____ "Introduction: Lexis and Melos." Sound and
     Poetry. English Institute Essays 1956. New York:
     Columbia University Press, 1963, xx, xxi.
1609 _____ "Towards Defining an Age of Sensibility."
     Eighteenth-Century English Literature, edited by
     James L. Clifford. New York: Oxford University
     Press, 1959, 313.
1610 Fuger, Wilhelm. "Gerard Manley Hopkins am Werk:
     Zum Entstehungsprozess von 'The Starlight Night',"
     Neueren Sprachen (Marburg), 66 (September, 1967),
     428-39.
1611 Fulweiler, Howard W. "Gerard Manley Hopkins and the
     'Stanching, Quenching Ocean of a Motionable Mind',"
     Victorian Newsletter, 30 (Fall, 1966), 6-13.
1612 _____ "Mermen and Mermaids: A Note on an 'Alien
     Vision' in the Poetry of Tennyson, Arnold, and
     Hopkins," Victorian Newsletter, 23 (Spring, 1963),
     16-7.
1613 Furness, Clifton Joseph. Review of Gerard Manley
     Hopkins, by Eleanor Ruggles. Atlantic Monthly, 174
     (October, 1944), 131-33.
1614 Fuson, Benjamin Willis. Review of Hopkins: A Collection
     of Critical Essays, edited by Geoffrey Hartman.
     Library Journal, 91 (April 1, 1966), 1898.
1615 Fussell, Paul, Jr. "A Note on 'The Windhover'," Modern
     Language Notes, 64 (April, 1949), 271.
1616 _____ Poetic Meter and Poetic Form: Studies in Language
     and Literature. New York: Random House, 1967, 71-3,
     131-35.

1617 Fussl, Karl Heinz. "Concerto Rapsodico," words by Gerard Manley Hopkins. Wien: Universal Editions, 1964. [Musical Setting]

1618 Futrell, John Carroll, S.J. "Gerard Manley Hopkins and God's 'Poem of Beauty'," Catholic World, 174 (February, 1952), 352-58.

1619 Fyfe, Jean. "The Poets" (Letter to the Editor), British Weekly (London), (July 13, 1950).

1620 G. S. Review of Immortal Diamond, edited by Norman Weyand, S.J. San Francisco Chronicle (This World Supplement), (September 11, 1949), 23.

1621 Gallagher, Donald A. "The Originality of Gerard Manley Hopkins," Fleur de Lis (St. Louis University), 34 (March, 1935), 34-44.

1622 Gallo, Ernest Anthony. "Gerard Manley Hopkins: Linguistic Innovator." M.A. thesis, New York University, 1957.

1623 Gannon, P. J., S.J. "To Gerard Manley Hopkins" (Poem), Irish Independent (Dublin), (June 11, 1949).

1624 Gappa, Richard John. "A Critical Evaluation of 'The Windhover: To Christ Our Lord' and its Criticism." M.A. thesis, University of Colorado, 1963.

1625 Gardiner, Harold C. "Key to Genius." Review of Gerard Manley Hopkins: Priest and Poet, by John Pick. America, 69 (July 24, 1943), 439.

1626 _____ "Poetry, Criticism, Memoirs and Shorter Fiction." Review of Gerard Manley Hopkins: A Study of Poetic Idiosyncrasy in Relation to Poetic Tradition, by W. H. Gardner and Poems, edited by W. H. Gardner. America, 80 (November 13, 1948), xxx, section 2.

1627 Gardner, Edith. "Why Converts Write," Burnished Gold (College of St. Francis, Joliet, Illinois), 1 (1936), 73-5.

1628 Gardner, Ralph. "Two Jesuits," Modern Churchman (London), 42 (December, 1952), 350-59.

1629 Gardner, William Henry. "The Achievement of Coventry Patmore. I. The Early Poems. II. The Prose and Later Poems," Month, N.S. 7 (February, April, 1952), 89-98, 220-30.

1630 _____ "Anvil-Ding and Tongue that Told. I. The Early Journals and Papers of Gerard Manley Hopkins. II. The Sermons and Devotional Writings of Gerard Manley Hopkins," Month, N.S. 25 (January, February, 1961), 34-47, 82-95.

1631 _____ "Biography." Anonymous Review of Gerard Manley Hopkins. Calcutta Statesman, (September 4, 1949).

111

1632 _____ "Bridges's Debt to Hopkins" (Letter to the Editor),
Times Literary Supplement, (August 18, 1961), 549.

1633 _____ "Correspondence" (Letter to the Editor), Month,
N.S. 4 (September, 1950), 210-13.

1634 _____ "Facets of Hopkins." Review of Immortal Diamond,
edited by Norman Weyand, S.J. Month, N.S. 3 (March,
1950), 217-21.

1635 _____ "G. M. Hopkins" (Letter to the Editor), Times
Literary Supplement, (September 7, 1962), 673.

1636 _____ "G. M. Hopkins" (Letter to the Editor), Times
Literary Supplement, (August 3, 1967), 707.

1637 _____ "Gerard Manley Hopkins." Review of Gerard Manley
Hopkins: The Man and the Poet, by K. R. Srinivasa
Iyengar. Month, N.S. 1 (April, 1949), 282-85.

1638 _____ "Gerard Manley Hopkins" (Extract from Introduction
to Poems of Gerard Manley Hopkins, 3rd ed.),
Periodical, 27 (Autumn, 1947), 107-10.

1639 _____ "Gerard Manley Hopkins (1844-1889)." The
Cambridge Bibliography of English Literature, edited by
George Watson. Vol. 5 (Supplement: A.D. 600-1900).
Cambridge, England: University Press, 1957, 600-04.

1640 _____ Gerard Manley Hopkins (1844-1889): A Study of
Poetic Idiosyncrasy in Relation to Poetic Tradition.
2 vols. London: Martin Secker & Warburg, 1944, 1949.
[V. 1 "A Centenary Commemoration." Inscribed by
author.]

1641 _____ Gerard Manley Hopkins (1844-1889): A Study of
Poetic Idiosyncrasy in Relation to Poetic Tradition.
Vol. 1. 2nd ed. rev. London: Martin Secker &
Warburg, 1948.

1642 _____ Gerard Manley Hopkins (1844-1889): A Study of
Poetic Idiosyncrasy in Relation to Poetic Tradition.
Vol. 1. 2nd ed. New Haven: Yale University Press,
1948.

1643 _____ Gerard Manley Hopkins (1844-1889): A Study of
Poetic Idiosyncrasy in Relation to Poetic Tradition.
Vol. 2. London: Martin Secker & Warburg, 1948.
[Printed as manuscript; author's corrections.
Inscribed by author.]

1644 _____ Gerard Manley Hopkins (1844-1889): A Study of
Poetic Idiosyncracy in Relation to Poetic Tradition.
London: Oxford University Press, 1966. [Reprinted:
Vol. 1 from 2nd ed., rev., 1948; Vol. 2 from 1st ed.,
1949.]

1645 _____ Anonymous Review of <u>Gerard</u> <u>Manley</u> <u>Hopkins</u>
(<u>1844-1889</u>): <u>A</u> <u>Study</u> <u>of</u> <u>Poetic</u> <u>Idiosyncrasy</u> <u>in</u> <u>Relation</u>
<u>to</u> <u>Poetic</u> <u>Tradition</u>. Vol. 2. <u>Listener</u>, 42 (July 14,
1949), 77.

1646 _____ Anonymous Review of <u>Gerard</u> <u>Manley</u> <u>Hopkins</u>
(<u>1844-1889</u>): <u>A</u> <u>Study</u> <u>of</u> <u>Poetic</u> <u>Idiosyncrasy</u> <u>in</u> <u>Relation</u>
<u>to</u> <u>Poetic</u> <u>Tradition</u>. <u>New</u> <u>Yorker</u>, 24 (October 2, 1948),
102.

1647 _____ Anonymous Review of <u>Gerard</u> <u>Manley</u> <u>Hopkins</u>
(<u>1844-1889</u>): <u>A</u> <u>Study</u> <u>of</u> <u>Poetic</u> <u>Idiosyncrasy</u> <u>in</u> <u>Relation</u>
<u>to</u> <u>Poetic</u> <u>Tradition</u>. Vol. 2. <u>New</u> <u>Yorker</u>, 25 (February
18, 1950), 90-1.

1648 _____ "G. Manley Hopkins as a Cywyddwr," <u>Transactions</u>
<u>of</u> <u>the</u> <u>Honorable</u> <u>Society</u> <u>of</u> <u>Cymmrodorion</u> (London),
(1940), 184-88.

1649 _____ "Hopkins and Newman" (Letter to the Editor),
<u>Times</u> <u>Literary</u> <u>Supplement</u>, (September 15, 1966), 868.

1650 _____ "Hopkins's Harvest-Home." Review of <u>A</u> <u>Hopkins</u>
<u>Reader</u>, edited by John Pick and <u>Selected</u> <u>Poems</u> <u>of</u>
<u>Gerard</u> <u>Manley</u> <u>Hopkins</u>, edited by James Reeves.
<u>Month</u>, N.S. 10 (November, 1953), 304-08.

1651 _____ "Hopkins's 'Spiritual Diaries' " (Letter to the
Editor), <u>Times</u> <u>Literary</u> <u>Supplement</u>, (March 29, 1957),
193.

1652 _____ "The Listener's Book Chronicle." Anonymous
Review of <u>Gerard</u> <u>Manley</u> <u>Hopkins</u> (<u>1844-1889</u>): <u>A</u> <u>Study</u>
<u>of</u> <u>Poetic</u> <u>Idiosyncrasy</u> <u>in</u> <u>Relation</u> <u>to</u> <u>Poetic</u> <u>Tradition</u>.
<u>Listener</u>, 32 (December 21, 1944), 693-94.

1653 _____ "The Listener's Book Chronicle." Anonymous
Review of <u>Gerard</u> <u>Manley</u> <u>Hopkins</u> (<u>1844-1889</u>): <u>A</u> <u>Study</u>
<u>of</u> <u>Poetic</u> <u>Idiosyncrasy</u> <u>in</u> <u>Relation</u> <u>to</u> <u>Poetic</u> <u>Tradition</u>.
Vol. 2. <u>Listener</u>, 42 (July 14, 1949), 77.

1654 _____ Review of <u>Metaphor</u> <u>in</u> <u>Hopkins</u>, by Robert Boyle.
<u>Modern</u> <u>Language</u> <u>Review</u>, 57 (October, 1962), 600-01.

1655 _____ "A Note on Hopkins and Duns Scotus," <u>Scrutiny</u>,
5 (June, 1936), 61-70.

1656 _____ "Poetry." Anonymous Review of <u>The</u> <u>Trend</u> <u>of</u>
<u>Modern</u> <u>Poetry</u>, by Geoffrey Bullough and <u>Gerard</u>
<u>Manley</u> <u>Hopkins</u>: <u>A</u> <u>Study</u> <u>of</u> <u>Poetic</u> <u>Idiosyncracy</u> <u>in</u>
<u>Relation</u> <u>to</u> <u>Poetic</u> <u>Tradition</u>, by W. H. Gardner. Vol.
2. <u>Sunday</u> <u>News</u> <u>of</u> <u>India</u> (Bombay), (July 3, 1949).

1657 _____ "Rare Masterly Beauties." Anonymous Review of
<u>Gerard</u> <u>Manley</u> <u>Hopkins</u>, 1844-1889. Vol. 2. <u>Times</u>
<u>Literary</u> <u>Supplement</u>, (September 23, 1949), 616.

1658 _____ "The Religious Problem in G. M. Hopkins,"
Scrutiny, 6 (June, 1937), 32-42. [Reprinted in
Critiques and Essays in Criticism 1920-1948, edited by
Robert Wooster Stallman. New York: Ronald Press
Company, 1949, 346-57.]

1659 _____ "Response to G. M. Hopkins: Study in Variations."
Anonymous Review of Gerard Manley Hopkins (1844-1889)
A Study of Poetic Idiosyncrasy in Relation to Poetic
Tradition. Times Literary Supplement, (November 11,
1944), 550.

1660 _____ Review of The Shaping Spirit of Gerard Manley
Hopkins, by Alan Heuser. Modern Language Review,
54 (July, 1959), 424-25.

1661 _____ "The 'Windhover' " (Letter to the Editor), Times
Literary Supplement, (June 24, 1955), 349.

1662 _____ " 'The Wreck of the Deutschland'," Essays and
Studies, 21 (1936), 124-52.

1663 _____ "Book Index." Anonymous Review of Poems of
Gerard Manley Hopkins, 3rd ed. Guardian (London),
(September 3, 1948).

1664 _____, ed. "Hopkins and Habington." Anonymous Review
of Poems of Gerard Manley Hopkins, edited by W. H.
Gardner; The Poems of William Habington, edited by
Kenneth Allott and John Keats, edited by Richard Church.
Scotsman (Edinburgh), (October 28, 1948).

1665 _____, ed. Anonymous Review of Poems of Gerard Manley
Hopkins. Books on Trial, 7 (March, 1949), 258.

1666 _____, ed. Anonymous Review of Poetry and Prose of
Gerard Manley Hopkins. Listener, 50 (October 1,
1953), 557.

1667 _____, ed. "Vocation and Inspiration." Anonymous
Review of Gerard Manley Hopkins: A Selection of
his Poems and Prose. Times Literary Supplement,
(November 13, 1953), 730. [Title above is that given
on cover. Title on title page is Poems and Prose of
Gerard Manley Hopkins.]

1668 Garlick, Raymond. "The Endless Breviary: Aspects of the
Work of Dylan Thomas," Month, 11 (March, 1954),
143-53.

1669 Garvey, Mother Eugenia Marie, O.S.U. "Gerard Manley
Hopkins, S.J.: His Criticism of the Major Writers in
English Literature." M.A. thesis, Fordham University,
1951.

1670 Gavin, Sister Rosemarie Julie, S.N.D. "Hopkins' 'The
Candle Indoors'," Explicator, 20 (February, 1962), 50.

114

1671 Gay, Robert Malcolm, comp. The College Book of Verse 1250-1925. Boston: Houghton Mifflin Company, 1927, 552.

1672 Geldart, Edmund Martin (Nitram Tradleg, pseud.) A Son of Belial: Autobiographical Sketches. London: Trubner & Co., 1882, 156, 167-69.

1673 Gerard, Albert. "Duns Scot et G. M. Hopkins," Revue des Langues Vivantes (Brussels), 12 (1946), 35-8.

1674 "Gerard Manley Hopkins," Tablet (London), 168 (November 14, 1936), 665.

1675 "Gerard Manley Hopkins" (Editorial), Times Literary Supplement, (June 10, 1944), 283.

1676 Gerken, John Diedrich, S.J. "The Date and Sequence of the 'Terrible Sonnets' of Gerard M. Hopkins, S.J." M.A. thesis, Loyola University (Chicago), 1953.

1677 Gerlach, Erika. "Gerard M. Hopkins, S.J. Zum 65. Todestag Gerard M. Hopkins' am 8. Juni 1954." Weltstimmen (Stuttgart), 23 (June, 1954), 271-76.

1678 _____ "Gerard Manley Hopkins: Zur Deutschen Auswahl aus Seinem Gesamtwerk," Weltstimmen (Stuttgart), 24 (June, 1955), 260-62.

1679 Ghiselin, Brewster. "Paeonic Measures in English Verse," Modern Language Notes, 57 (May, 1942), 336-41.

1680 _____ "Reading Sprung Rhythms," Poetry, 17 (May, 1947), 86-93.

1681 Gibson, Frances. "The Influence of Welsh Prosody on the Poetry of Hopkins," Xavier University Studies, 6 (February, 1967), 21-8.

1682 Gibson, Walker. Review of Metaphor in Hopkins, by Robert Boyle. Victorian Studies, 5 (June, 1962), 353.

1683 _____ "Sound and Sense in G. M. Hopkins," Modern Language Notes, 73 (February, 1958), 95-100.

1684 Gibson, William M. "Hopkins' 'To R. B.'," Explicator, 6 (November, 1947), 12.

1685 Gilkes, Martin. "Gerard Manley Hopkins, Pioneer." A Key to Modern English Poetry. London: Blackie & Son, Limited, 1938, 20-39.

1686 _____ "Gerard Manley Hopkins, Pioneer." A Key to Modern English Poetry. 2nd ed. London: Blackie & Son, Limited, 1948, 20-39.

1687 Gill, Brendan. "The Current Cinema: Honorable Failure," New Yorker, 43 (December 30, 1967), 48-50.

1688 Gillet, Eric. Review of Further Letters of Gerard Manley Hopkins, edited by Claude Colleer Abbott. National and English Review, 148 (February, 1957), 87.

1689 _____ Review of Journals and Papers of Gerard Manley Hopkins, edited by Humphry House. National and English Review, 152 (April, 1959), 150.

1690 _____ Review of Life of Gerard Manley Hopkins, [sic] edited by John Pick. National and English Review, 141 (July, 1953), 50.

1691 Gilman, William Henry. "Gerard Manley Hopkins: The Man." M.A. thesis, George Washington University, 1943.

1692 Ginneken, Jac. Van, S.J. "Barbarous in Beauty," Onze Taaltuin (Rotterdam), 5 (July, 1936), 65-73.

1693 Giovannini, Giovanni. "A Literal Gloss of Hopkins' 'The Windhover'." Linguistic and Literary Studies in Honor of H. A. Hatzfeld. Washington, D. C.: Catholic University of America Press, 1964, 203-12.

1694 Giovannini, Margaret. "Hopkins' 'The Caged Skylark'," Explicator, 14 (March, 1956), 35.

1695 _____ "Hopkins' 'God's Grandeur'," Explicator, 24 (December, 1966), 36.

1696 Gleeson, William F. Review of Immortal Diamond, edited by Norman Weyand, S.J. Thought, 25 (September, 1950), 528-30.

1697 _____ Review of The Prosodic Theory of Gerard Manley Hopkins. (A Dissertation), by Sister Marcella Marie Holloway. Thought, 23 (June, 1948), 342-43.

1698 Gleeson, William F., Jr. "Gerard Manley Hopkins and the Society of Jesus." M.A. thesis, Columbia University, 1950.

1699 Gold, Raymond. Poetry and Prose of Gerard Manley Hopkins. Notes on Chosen English Texts, edited by Norman T. Carrington. Bath, Somerset: James Brodie Ltd., 1966.

1700 Goldhurst, Richard. "Translation: sine qua non, Bowra and Hopkins," Classical Journal, 50 (October, 1954), 5-11.

1701 Gomme, A. H. "The Function of Criticism" (Letter to the Editor), Times Literary Supplement, (April 13, 1962), 249.

1702 Gomme, Andor. "A Note on Two Hopkins Sonnets," Essays in Criticism, 14 (July, 1964), 327-31.

1703 Goodin, George. "Man and Nature in Hopkins' 'Ribblesdale'," Notes & Queries, N.S. 6 (December, 1959), 453-54.

1704 Gordon, David. "Ex Voto G M H" (Poem), Tablet (London), 173 (January 14, 1939), 54.

1705 _____ "From Hopkins, Poet to Patmore, Poet." Review of
Further Letters of Gerard Manley Hopkins, edited by
Claude Colleer Abbott. America, 59 (September 17,
1938), 573-74.

1706 _____ "The Prose of Gerard Manley Hopkins," America,
59 (July 16, 1938), 355-56.

1707 _____ "Superb? Absurd?" (Correspondence), America,
56 (February 6, 1937), 425.

1708 Gordon, George Stuart. "Gerard Manley Hopkins and
Robert Bridges." The Discipline of Letters. Oxford:
Clarendon Press, 1946, 168-84.

1709 Gorini, A. "Poeti Inglesi in Italia da Milton a Eliot,"
Osservatore Romano, (April 21, 1950).

1710 Gorman, Patrick, C.S.B. "The Attitude to Nature and the
External World of Gerard Manley Hopkins." M.A.
thesis, University of Toronto, 1950.

1711 Gosse, Edmund. Coventry Patmore. London: Hodder &
Stoughton, 1905, 168-69.

1712 Goudge, Elizabeth. "Poems of Peace." Anonymous
Review of The Book of Peace. Irish News (Belfast),
(December 16, 1967).

1713 Grace, William J. Review of Gerard Manley Hopkins, by
W. H. Gardner. Books on Trial, 7 (March, 1949), 258.

1714 Grady, Thomas J. "A Great Poet." Review of Gerard
Manley Hopkins, by the Kenyon Critics. Books on
Trial, 5 (July-August, 1946), 61.

1715 _____ Review of Immortal Diamond, edited by Norman
Weyand, S.J. New World (Chicago), 57 (April 8,
1949), 15.

1716 _____ "The Poetic Principles of Gerard Manley Hopkins."
M.A. thesis, Loyola University (Chicago), 1944.

1717 _____ "Windhover's Meaning," America, 70 (January 29,
1944), 465-66.

1718 _____ "Poetry and Prose of Gerard Hopkins." Review of
A Hopkins Reader, edited by John Pick. Books on Trial,
11 (June, 1953), 333.

1719 Graham, Aelred. "The Contemplative Approach." Review
of The Forsaken Fountain, by Rosalind Murray. Tablet
(London), (May 8, 1948), 289-90.

1720 Graham, Cuthbert. Review of The Shaping Vision of Gerard
Manley Hopkins, by Alan Heuser. Aberdeen University
Review, 38 (1959), 63-4.

1721 Granger, Edith. "Author Index." Index to Poetry. 5th ed.
rev. and enl. New York: Columbia University Press,
1962, 1762-63.

1722 Graves, Robert. The Common Asphodel: Collected Essays on Poetry, 1922-1949. London: Hamish Hamilton, 1949, 99-101.

1723 _____ "Gerard Manley Hopkins" (Letter to the Editor), Times Literary Supplement, (April 29, 1955), 209.

1724 _____ The White Goddess. New York: Creative Age Press, 1948, 352-53.

1725 Graves, William L. "Gerard Manley Hopkins as Composer: An Interpretive Postscript," Victorian Poetry, 1 (April, 1963), 146-55.

1726 Grebanier, Bernard David. "Gerard Manley Hopkins." English Literature and its Backgrounds. New York: Dryden Press, 1949, 1239-42.

1727 _____ and Seymour Reiter. Introduction to Imaginative Literature. New York: Thomas Y. Crowell, 1960, 217-18, 467-69.

1728 Green, John M., Jr. "Gerard Manley Hopkins: The Inseer as Nature Poet," Juggler of Notre Dame, (Winter, 1953), 38-46.

1729 Greene, Marjorie. "Immortal Diamond," Ethos (Emmanuel College, Boston), 16 (June, 1943), 127-32.

1730 Greene, Sister Moira, S.C.N. "The Poetic Theory of Gerard Manley Hopkins and its Relation to his own Work." M.A. thesis, University of Notre Dame, 1947.

1731 Gregory, Horace. "A Biography of Gerard Hopkins." Review of Gerard Manley Hopkins: A Life, by Eleanor Ruggles. New York Herald Tribune Weekly Book Review, 20 (August 6, 1944), 5.

1732 _____ "Gerard Manley Hopkins." Review of The Note-Books and Papers of Gerard Manley Hopkins, edited by Humphry House and Further Letters of Gerard Manley Hopkins, edited by Claude Colleer Abbott. Yale Review, 28 (December, 1938), 415-18.

1733 _____ "Living Poet, Deadly Critic." Review of Gerard Manley Hopkins: A Study of Poetic Idiosyncrasy in Relation to Poetic Tradition, by W. H. Gardner. Saturday Review, 28 (March 24, 1945), 38-9.

1734 _____ "The Touch of Timelessness." Review of A Hopkins Reader, edited by John Pick. New York Times Book Review, (August 2, 1953), 5.

1735 Greiner, Brother Francis J., S.J. "Hopkins' 'The Habit of Perfection'," Explicator, 21 (November, 1962), 19.

1736 _____ "Hopkins' 'The Windhover' Viewed as a Nature Poem," Renascence, 15 (Winter, 1963), 68-75, 95.

1737 Grennen, Joseph E. "Grammar as Thaumaturgy: Hopkins' 'Heraclitean Fire'," Renascence, 15 (Summer, 1963), 208-11.

1738 Gribben, J. C. "Hopkins, 'Immortal Diamond' in an Appropriate Setting," Cincinnati Enquirer, (April 30, 1949), 6.

1739 Grierson, Herbert John Clifford and J. C. Smith. "Twentieth Century Poetry: Between the Wars, 1919-1939." A Critical History of English Poetry. New York: Oxford University Press, 1944, 548-69.

1740 _____ and J. C. Smith. "Twentieth Century Poetry: Between the Wars, 1919-1939." A Critical History of English Poetry. New York: Oxford University Press, 1946.

1741 Griffin, Sister Mary Ignatia, B.V.M. "Gerard Manley Hopkins' 'That Nature is a Heraclitean Fire and of the Comfort of the Resurrection' - An Analysis of Meaning." M.A. thesis, Catholic University of America, 1950.

1742 Griffith, LL. Wyn. "The Welsh Influence," New Verse, No. 14 (April, 1935), 27-9.

1743 Grigson, Geoffrey. The Arts Today. London: John Lane, The Bodley Head, 1935, 53.

1744 _____ "1. Blood or Bran." "2. Hopkins and Hopkinese," New Verse, No. 14 (April, 1935), 21-6.

1745 _____ "English Drawing through Three Centuries," Listener, 53 (May 19, 1955), 884-86.

1746 _____ "Gerard Hopkins: The Genius who saw Corn like a Lion's Mane." Review of The Notebooks and Papers of Gerard Manley Hopkins, edited by Humphry House. Morning Post (London), (January 26, 1937).

1747 _____ Gerard Manley Hopkins. Bibliographical Series of Supplements to 'British Book News' on Writers and their Work, No. 59. London: Longmans, Green & Co., 1955.

1748 _____ "The Old and the New Botany," Country Life, (January 6, 1950).

1749 _____ "A Poet of Surprise." Review of Poems of Gerard Manley Hopkins, edited by Robert Bridges. 2nd ed. Saturday Review (London), 151 (February 14, 1931), 237-38.

1750 _____ "Poet to be Read with the Ears." Review of Poems of Gerard Manley Hopkins, edited by W. H. Gardner and N. H. Mackenzie. Country Life, 142 (August 3, 1967), 286-87.

1751 _____ Anonymous Review of Writers and their Work, No.
59. Langues Modernes (Paris), (1955), 465-66.

1752 _____, comp. English Drawing from Samuel Cooper to
Gwen John. London: Thames and Hudson, 1955.

1753 _____, comp. The English Year from Diaries and Letters.
London: Oxford University Press, 1967.

1754 _____, comp. The Victorians: An Anthology. London:
Routledge & Kegan Paul Ltd., 1950.

1755 _____ and Charles Harvard Gibbs-Smith, eds. " 'I took
him for a natural'." [Hopkins, Gerard Manley]
People: A Volume of the Good, Bad, Great & Eccentric
who Illustrate the Admirable Diversity of Man. Vol. 1:
People, Places and Things. London: Grosvenor Press,
1954, 197.

1756 Grilo, J. Monteiro. "O Rev. Gerard Manley Hopkins, S.J.
Precursor do Modernismo Poetico Ingles," Diario de
Noticias (Lisbon), (October 25, 1955), 7.

1757 Grimsditch, Herbert S. "Gerard Manley Hopkins." British
Authors of the Nineteenth Century, edited by Stanley
Kunitz. New York: H. W. Wilson Co., 1936, 306-08.

1758 Grisewood, Harman. "The Genius of Hopkins." Review of
Gerard Manley Hopkins: 1844-1889, edited by W. H.
Gardner. Vol. 2. Tablet (London), (August 13, 1949),
104.

1759 _____ "Gerard Manley Hopkins, S.J." Review of Poems of
Gerard Manley Hopkins, edited by Charles Williams,
2nd ed. and Gerard Manley Hopkins, by G. F. Lahey,
S.J. Dublin Review, 189 (October, 1931), 213-26.

1760 _____ "Language and Imagery in Hopkins." Review of
Gerard Manley Hopkins, by W. A. M. Peters. Dublin
Review, 221 (Last quarter, 1948), 163-65.

1761 _____ "A New Life of Hopkins." Review of Gerard Manley
Hopkins, by Eleanor Ruggles. Dublin Review, 221
(First quarter, 1948), 168-71.

1762 _____ "A Tribute to Gerard Manley Hopkins." Review of
Immortal Diamond, edited by Norman Weyand, S.J.
Tablet (London), (December 3, 1949), 380-81.

1763 Groom, Bernard. The Diction of Poetry from Spenser to
Bridges. Toronto: University of Toronto Press, 1955,
13, 224, 239, 241, 266-67.

1764 _____. The Formation and Use of Compound Epithets in
English Poetry from 1579. S.P.E. Tract No. 49.
Oxford: Clarendon Press, 1937, 295-322.

1765 Gross, Harvey Seymour. Sound and Form in Modern Poetry:
A Study of Prosody from Thomas Hardy to Robert Lowell.
Ann Arbor: University of Michigan Press, 1965.

1766 Grunne, Dominique de. "Gerard Manley Hopkins."
Ecrivains Celebres III. Paris: Mezanod, 1953, 188-89.

1767 _____ "Technique du Poete: Gerard Manley Hopkins,"
Critique (Paris), 9 (July, 1953), 579-600.

1768 Guardini, Romano. "Aesthetic-Theological Thoughts on
'The Windhover'." Hopkins: A Collection of Critical
Essays, edited by Geoffrey H. Hartman. Englewood
Cliffs, New Jersey: Prentice-Hall, Inc., 1966, 76-9.
[Translated from Aesthetisch-Theologische Gedanken
zu Hopkins' Gedicht 'Der Sturmfalke'." Sprache--
Dichtung--Deutung. Wurzburg: Werkbund Verlag,
1962.]

1769 _____ "Asthetisch-Theologische Gedanken zu Gerard
Manley Hopkins' Sonett 'Der Turmfalke'." Unter-
scheidung und Berwahrung: Festschrift fur Hermann
Kunisch. Berlin: De Gruyter, 1961, 170-74.
[Reprinted in Sprache--Dichtung--Deutung. Wurzburg:
Werkbund Verlag, 1962, 84-90.]

1770 Guhl, Thane. (Letter to the Editor), New York Times Book
Review, (November 10, 1957), 34.

1771 Guidi, Augusto. "Due Schede Anglosassoni: La Poesia di
Hopkins il Pensiero di Coleridge," Fiera Letteraria
(Rome), (May 15, 1955).

1772 _____"Fortuna e Attualita di un Poeta Gesuita Inglese:
Una Portentosa Ricchezza di Immagini nel Linguaggio
'Difficile' di Hopkins," Giornale d'Italia (Rome),
(December 6, 1959).

1773 _____ Review of Gerard Manley Hopkins, by Eleanor
Ruggles. Rivista di Letterature Moderne (Florence),
N.S. 1 (July, 1950), 71.

1774 _____ Review of G. M. Hopkins, The Penguin Poets.
Idea (Rome), (February 28, 1954).

1775 _____ "Introduzione alla Poetica di G. M. Hopkins,"
Letteratura (Florence), 8 (May-June, 1946), 93-102.

1776 _____ "Lettura di G. M. Hopkins," Poesia (Rome),
(January 1, 1945), 158-60.

1777 _____ "Luci e Riflessi nel Linguaggio di G. M. Hopkins."
Review of A Hopkins Reader, edited by John Pick.
Dialoghia (Rome), (December, 1953), 51-7.

1778 _____ "Milton e Hopkins." English Miscellany, 6. Rome:
Edizioni di Storia e Letteratura, 1955, 31-43.

1779 _____ "Persone e cose nella Poesia di G. M. Hopkins,"
Humanitas (Brescia), (September 1, 1946), 934-38.

1780 _____ "Problemi di Interpretazione in G. M. Hopkins"
(Correspondence), Anglica: Rivista di Studi Inglesi
e Americani (Florence), 1 (October, 1946), 208-11.

1781 _____ "Undici Gesuiti Attorno a Hopkins," Fiera
Letteraria (Rome), (March 26, 1950).

1782 _____, trans. Anonymous Review of Il Naufragio del
Deutschland - La Fine dell'Euridice. Civilta Cattolica
(Rome), 99 (September 4, 1948), 529-30.

1783 Guiguet, Jean. Review of Le Poete G. M. Hopkins, S.J.
(1844-1889). Sa Vie et son Oeuvre, by Jean-Georges
Ritz. Anglia (Tubingen), 84 (1966), 248-50.

1784 Guinness, Alec, comp. A Personal Choice. (Phonodisc).
New York: RCA Victor VDM-102, 1965. [Includes "The
Leaden Echo and the Golden Echo." Descriptive notes
by the compiler on slipcase. Peter Dellheim, producer.]

1785 Guiney, Louis Imogen. "Gerard Hopkins: A Recovered
Poet." Review of Poems of Gerard Manley Hopkins,
edited by Robert Bridges. Month, 133 (March, 1919),
205-14.

1786 _____ "A Lost and Recovered Poet." Review of Poems of
Gerard Manley Hopkins, edited by Robert Bridges. Ave
Maria, N.S. 9 (April 5, 1919), 433-35.

1787 Gunter, Gordon O. "To G. M. Hopkins" (Poem), College
English, 22 (December, 1960), 189.

1788 Gutierrez Mora, Jose Manuel. "Diez Sonetos de Hopkins:
A la Memoria de Gerard Manley Hopkins, en el LXXV
Aniversario de su Ordenacion Sacerdotal. 1877--
Temporas de Otono--1952," Abside (Mexico), 16
(July-September, 1952), 305-20.

1789 _____ "Pied Beauty in Spanish." Anonymous Review of
Hopkinsiana. Times Literary Supplement, (August 13,
1954), 509-10.

1790 _____ "Dos Poetas Ingleses: Alfred, Lord Tennyson
1809-1892, Gerard Manley Hopkins 1844-1889." Et
Caetera, 1 (April-June, 1950), supplement, 1-15.

1791 _____ Hopkinsiana: La Vida, La Obra y La Supervivencia
de Gerard Manley Hopkins. Mexico: Aldina, 1952.

1792 Guzie, Tad W., S.J. "Are Modern Poets Morbid?"
Catholic World, 185 (April, 1957), 27-32.

1793 Gwynn, Frederick Landis. "Hopkins' 'The Windhover':
A New Simplification," Modern Language Notes, 66
(June, 1951), 366-70.

1794 _____, Ralph W. Condee and Arthur O. Lewis, Jr., eds.
The Case for Poetry. New York: Prentice-Hall, Inc.,
1954.

1795 Gyllenbaga, Nils. "Jesuiten Contra Diktaren," Expressen
(Stockholm), (April 5, 1950), 4.

1796 _____ "Rakt pa Pound," Expressen (Stockholm), (April 19,
1950).

1797 H. P. C. L. "To G. M. H., S.J." (Poem), Month, 181
(January-February, 1945), 65.

1798 H. S. "The Poet, the Hodder and the River-Bathe,"
Stonyhurst Magazine, 33 (October, 1960), 503-04.

1799 Haas, Charles Eugene. "A Structural Analysis of Selected
Sonnets of Gerard Manley Hopkins." Ph.D., University
of Denver, 1964.

1800 Haas, Rudolf. "Gerard Manley Hopkins: Zwei Gedichte."
Wege zur Englischen Lyrik in Wissenschaft und Unter-
richt: Interpretationen. Heidelberg: Quelle & Meyer,
1962, 130-43.

1801 Haas, Willy. "Pater, Dichter, Philosoph." Review of
Gerard Manley Hopkins: Gedichte, Schriften, Briefe,
translated by Wolfgang and Ursula Clemen. Die
Welt (Hamburg), (September 24, 1955).

1802 Hache, Mother Irene Marie, R.C.E. "The Place of the
Incarnation in the Poetry of Hopkins." M.A. thesis,
Boston College, 1948.

1803 Haddakin, Lilian. Review of Gerard Manley Hopkins: A
Critical Essay towards the Understanding of his Poetry,
by W. A. M. Peters, S.J. and The Prosodic Theory of
Gerard Manley Hopkins, by Marcella Marie Holloway.
Modern Language Review, 43 (October, 1948), 534-35.

1804 Hafley, James. "Hopkins: 'A Little Sickness in the Air',"
Arizona Quarterly, 20 (Fall, 1964), 215-22.

1805 Halleck, Reuben P. "Supplementary List of Modern Authors:
Hopkins, Gerard Manley." The Story of English Literature. New York: American Book Company, 1937, 725.

1806 Hallgarth, Susan A. "A Study of Hopkins' Use of Nature,"
Victorian Poetry, 5 (Summer, 1967), 79-92.

1807 Halsband, Robert. "Belles-Lettres Notes." Review of
Immortal Diamond, edited by Norman Weyand, S.J.
Saturday Review, 32 (April 30, 1949), 12-3.

1808 _____ "A Sprung Cleric." Review of A Hopkins Reader, by
John Pick. Saturday Review, 36 (August 1, 1953), 13.

1809 Hamer, Enid, ed. The English Sonnet: An Anthology. 2nd
ed. London: Methuen & Co., 1936, xxxix, lvii, 139.

1810 Hamilton, Seymour Charles. "The Unified World-Vision of
Gerard Manley Hopkins." M.A. thesis, University of
Toronto, 1963.

1811 Hampden, John, ed. Great Poems from Shakespeare to
Manley Hopkins. London: Pan Books Ltd, 1949.

1812 Hanlon, R. W. Review of Gerard Manley Hopkins--Priest
and Poet, by John Pick. Catholic Book Club Newsletter,
30 (May, 1943), 1, 6.

1813 Hansen-Love, Friedrich. "Der Dichter der Schopfung: Ein
Hinweis auf Gerard Manley Hopkins," Wort und
Wahrheit (Freiburg), 7 (1952), 457-60.

1814 Hanson, W. G. "Gerard Manley Hopkins and Richard
Watson Dixon," London Quarterly and Holborn Review,
(January, 1944), 63-7.

1815 Harding, H. W. "On First Looking into Gerard Manley
Hopkins," Poetry Review, 35 (March-April, 1944),
77-8.

1816 Harding, John Paul. Review of Gerard Manley Hopkins, by
the Kenyon Critics and Selections from the Notebooks of
Gerard Manley Hopkins, edited by T. Weiss. Liturgical
Arts, 15 (February, 1947), 50.

1817 Hardy, John Edward. "After the New Criticism." Review of
The Shaping Vision of Gerard Manley Hopkins, by Alan
Heuser. Yale Review, 48 (Spring, 1959), 410-13.

1818 Harriott, John F. X. "Hopkins the Victorian," Interim
(Manresa College, Roehampton), 2 (Easter Term, 1955),
4-10.

1819 Harris, Lancelot Stephen. The Nature of English Poetry:
An Elementary Survey. London: J. M. Dent and Sons,
Ltd., 1933, 133.

1820 Harrison, Thomas P. "The Birds of Gerard Manley
Hopkins," Studies in Philology, 54 (July, 1957),
448-63.

1821 Harrold, Charles Frederick. Review of Further Letters of
Gerard Manley Hopkins, edited by Claude Colleer
Abbott. Modern Philology, 35 (May, 1938), 440.

1822 _____ Review of Gerard Manley Hopkins: A Life, by
Eleanor Ruggles. Journal of English and Germanic
Philology, 44 (October, 1945), 434-36.

1823 Hart, Lucia Caroline Romberg (McKay). "The Poetry of
Gerard Manley Hopkins." M.A. thesis, University of
Texas, 1965.

1824 Hart, Sister Mary Adorita, B.V.M. "The Christocentric
Theme in Gerard Manley Hopkins' 'The Wreck of the
Deutschland'." Ph.D., Catholic University of America,
1952. [Microcards]

1825 _____ "Hopkins's 'Wings that Spell' in 'The Wreck of the
Deutschland'," Modern Language Notes, 70 (May,
1955), 345-47.

1826 Harting, E. M. "Gerard Hopkins and Digby Dolben,"
Month, 133 (April, 1919), 285-89.

1827 Hartman, Geoffrey H. "The Dialectic of Sense-Perception."
Hopkins: A Collection of Critical Essays, edited by
Geoffrey H. Hartman. Englewood Cliffs, New Jersey:
Prentice-Hall, Inc., 1966, 117-30. [Reprinted from
The Unmediated Vision, 1954, revised and retitled.]

1828 _____ "Individual Poets." Anonymous Review of The
Unmediated Vision: An Interpretation of Wordsworth,
Hopkins, Rilke, and Valery. Times Literary Supplement,
(July 22, 1955), 414.

1829 _____ "Introduction: Poetry and Justification." Hopkins:
A Collection of Critical Essays, edited by Geoffrey H.
Hartman. Englewood Cliffs, New Jersey: Prentice-
Hall, Inc., 1966, 1-15.

1830 _____ "Recent Studies in the Nineteenth Century,"
Studies in English Literature, 6 (Autumn, 1966), 753-82.

1831 _____ Review of Robert Bridges and Gerard Hopkins
(1863-1889): A Literary Friendship, by Jean-Georges
Ritz. Modern Philology, 58 (May, 1961), 290-92.

1832 _____ The Unmediated Vision: An Interpretation of
Wordsworth, Hopkins, Rilke and Valery. New Haven:
Yale University Press; London: Geoffrey Cumberlege,
Oxford University Press, 1954.

1833 _____ The Unmediated Vision: An Interpretation of
Wordsworth, Hopkins, Rilke, and Valery. New York:
Harcourt, Brace and World, Inc., 1966.

1834 _____ Anonymous Review of The Unmediated Vision.
United States Quarterly Book Review, 11 (1955), 207-08.

1835 _____, ed. Hopkins: A Collection of Critical Essays.
Twentieth Century Views Series. Englewood Cliffs,
New Jersey: Prentice-Hall, Inc., 1966.

1836 Harvey, Paul, ed. "Hopkins, Gerard Manley." The
Oxford Companion to English Literature. Oxford:
Clarendon Press, 1934, 381.

1837 Hasley, Louis. Review of A Hopkins Reader, edited by
John Pick. Ave Maria, N.S. 78 (November 7, 1953), 24.

1838 _____ "Poet of Perfection." Review of A Hopkins Reader,
edited by John Pick. Today, 9 (October, 1953), 21.

1839 Hass, Hans-Egon. "Gerard Manley Hopkins," Begegnung
(Cologne), 4 (July, 1949), 209-12.

1840 Hastings, M. D. "More Comments on G. M. Hopkins,"
Poetry Review, 36 (1945), 149-53.

1841 Haugh, Irene. "Gerald [sic] Manley Hopkins," Irish
Monthly, 60 (April, 1932), 220-27.

1842 Hausermann, H. W. "Drei Generationen uber Hopkins,"
Neue Zurcher Zeitung (Zurich), (August 14, 1955).

1843 Haven, Richard. "The Experience of Gerard Manley
Hopkins: A Contextualist Approach to his Poetry."
Honors thesis, Harvard University, 1948.

1844 Hawkes, Jacquetta. "Gowland Hopkins and Scientific
Imagination," Listener, (February 2, 1950), 191-92.

1845 H[ayes], J. J. "Studies in Poetry." Review of Gerard
Manley Hopkins: A Study of Poetic Idiosyncrasy in
Relation to Poetic Tradition, by W. H. Gardner.
Studies, 33 (December, 1944), 558-61.

1846 Hayes, Richard. "So Flagrant a Mortal Ecstasy." Review
of recording, "The Poetry of Gerard Manley Hopkins,"
read by Cyril Cusack. American Record Guide, 25
(June, 1959), 738-39.

1847 Haynes, Renee. "The Jewel of the Just." Review of
Immortal Diamond, edited by Norman Weyand, S.J.
Time and Tide, 31 (March 11, 1950), 234.

1848 Hazo, Samuel John. "An Analysis of 'Inscape' in the
Poetry of Gerard Manley Hopkins." M.A. thesis,
Duquesne University, 1955.

1849 _____ "Belief and the Critic." The Christian Intellectual:
Studies in the Relation of Catholicism to the Human
Sciences, edited by Samuel John Hazo. Pittsburgh,
Pennsylvania: Duquesne University Press; Louvain:
Editions E. Nauwelaerts, 1963, 81-114.

1850 Healy, Sister M. Aquinas, R.S.M. "Milton and Hopkins,"
University of Toronto Quarterly, 22 (October, 1952),
18-25.

1851 Healy, William J. Review of Gerard Manley Hopkins: A
Study of his Ignatian Spirit, by David A. Downes.
America, 102 (March 12, 1960), 712-13.

1852 Heath-Stubbs, John Francis Alexander. The Darkling
Plain: A Study of the Later Fortunes of Romanticism in
English Poetry from George Darley to W. B. Yeats.
London: Eyre & Spottiswoode, 1950.

1853 Heffernan, Miriam Margaret. "Gerard Manley Hopkins as Critic and Theorist of English Literature." M.A. thesis, Columbia University, 1939.

1854 Hemphill, George. Review of Metaphor in Hopkins, by Robert Boyle, S.J. College English, 23 (March, 1962), 514.

1855 Henderson, Philip. The Poet and Society. London: Secker & Warburg, 1939.

1856 Hennecke, Hans. "Ritter der Unendlichkeit und Unbedingtheit." Kritik. Gesammelte Essays zur Modernen Literatur. Gutersloh: Bertelsmann, 1958, 109-15.

1857 Heppenstall, Rayner. "Hopkins, the Jesuit." Review of Immortal Diamond, edited by Norman Weyand, S. J. New Statesman and Nation, N.S. 39 (April 1, 1950), 337-38.

1858 _____ "Too Much Editing." Review of The Journals and Papers of Gerard Manley Hopkins, edited by Humphry House and The Sermons and Devotional Writings of Gerard Manley Hopkins, edited by Christopher Devlin, S.J. Observer (London), (February 15, 1959).

1859 Herring, Mary Lynn. "Gerard Manley Hopkins as a Critic of Poetry." M.A. thesis, University of Tennessee, 1964.

1860 Hess, M. Whitcomb. "Hopkins and the Metaphor in Poetry," Spirit, 30 (March, 1963), 21-4.

1861 Heuser, Edward Alan. "The Development of Aesthetic Cognition in Gerard Manley Hopkins." Ph.D., Harvard University, 1953.

1862 _____ Review of Gerard Manley Hopkins: A Study of his Ignatian Spirit, by David A. Downes. Queen's Quarterly, 67 (Autumn, 1960), 492.

1863 _____ "An Investigation of the Poetic Imagery of Gerard Manley Hopkins." M.A. thesis, McGill University, 1949.

1864 _____ Review of Metaphor in Hopkins, by Robert Boyle, S.J. Queen's Quarterly, 69 (Summer, 1962), 323.

1865 _____ The Shaping Vision of Gerard Manley Hopkins. London: Oxford University Press, 1958.

1866 _____ Anonymous Review of The Shaping Vision of Gerard Manley Hopkins. College English, 21 (November, 1959), 113-14.

1867 _____ "The Wrong Approach?" Anonymous Review of The Shaping Vision of Gerard Manley Hopkins. Times Literary Supplement, (October 17, 1958), 594.

1868 Heywood, Terence. "Gerard Hopkins and Milton" (Letter to the Editor), Poetry Review, 30 (1939), 308.

1869 _____ "Gerard Manley Hopkins: His Literary Ancestry," English, 3 (Spring, 1940), 16-24.

1870 _____ "Hopkins' Ancestry," Parts 1 and 2. Poetry, 54 (July, August, 1939), 209-18, 271-79.

1871 _____ "Hopkins and Bridges on Trees," Poetry Review, 29 (May-June, 1938), 213-18.

1872 _____ "On Approaching Hopkins," Poetry Review, 30 (May-June, 1939), 185-88.

1873 Highet, Gilbert. The Classical Tradition. New York: Oxford University Press, 1949, 32, 254.

1874 _____ Talents and Geniuses: The Pleasures of Appreciation. Toronto: Oxford University Press, 1957, 63-4.

1875 Hill, A. G. "Victoriana with a Difference." Review of The Journals and Papers of Gerard Manley Hopkins, edited by Humphry House and The Sermons and Devotional Writings of Gerard Manley Hopkins, edited by Christopher Devlin, S.J. Essays in Criticism, 10 (April, 1960), 215-19.

1876 Hill, Archibald A. "An Analysis of 'The Windhover': An Experiment in Structural Method," PMLA, 70 (December, 1955), 968-78.

1877 _____ " 'The Windhover' Revisited: Linguistic Analysis of Poetry Reassessed," Texas Studies in Literature and Language, 7 (Winter, 1965), 349-59.

1878 Hill, Francis Anthony. "An Explication of 'Harry Ploughman' by Gerard Manley Hopkins as an Inscape of Cosmological Motion and the Un-moved Mover." M.A. thesis, Tulane University, 1963.

1879 Hines, Leo. "Pindaric Imagery in G. M. Hopkins," Month, N.S. 29 (May, 1963), 294-307.

1880 Hinkson, Katharine (Tynan). The Middle Years. London: Constable & Company Ltd, 1916, 349-50.

1881 Hoecker, Eric L. "Hopkins, Joyce and the Development of the Artist." M.A. thesis, Columbia University, 1950.

1882 Hoffman, Daniel G. and Samuel Hynes, eds. English Literary Criticism: Romantic and Victorian. New York: Appleton-Century-Crofts, 1963, 274-80.

1883 Hoffman, Frederick J. "The Religious Crisis in Modern Literature," Comparative Literature Studies, 3 (1966), 263-72.

1884 Hogan, Aloysius J., S.J. "Father Hopkins' Poetry," America, 18 (February 16, 1918), 477-78.

1885 Hogue, Caroline. (Letter to the Editor), New York Times Book Review, (November 10, 1957), 34.

1886 Hohoff, Curt. "Hopkins, ein Dichter der Schopfung," Hochland (Munich), 47 (1954-1955), 424-31. [Reprinted in Lob der Schopfung und Argernis der Zeit, edited by Karlheinz Smidthus. Fribourg: Herder-Bucherei, 1959, 101-09. Reprinted in Schnittpunkte, Gessammelte Aufsatze. Stuttgart: Deutsche Verlags-Anstalt, 1963, 195-205.]

1887 Hohman, Janet. "Hopkins and History . . . . ," Spheres (Mount St. Agnes College, Baltimore, Maryland), (Spring, 1948), 14-6.

1888 Hollander, John. "Blake and the Metrical Contract." From Sensibility to Romanticism: Essays Presented to Frederick A. Pottle, edited by Frederick Whiley Hilles and Harold Bloom. New York: Oxford University Press, 1965, 300, 304, 309.

1889 _____ "The Metrical Emblem." Essays on the Language of Literature, edited by Seymour Chatman and Samuel R. Levin. Boston: Houghton Mifflin Company, 1967, 115-26. [Reprinted from Kenyon Review, 21 (Spring, 1959), 279-96.]

1890 Holloway, Sister Marcella Marie, C.S.J. "Gerard Manley Hopkins in the Light of Critical Opinion." M.A. thesis, University of Missouri, 1943.

1891 _____ "Hopkins' Sonnet 65 ('No Worst, There is None')," Explicator, 14 (May, 1956), 51.

1892 _____ The Prosodic Theory of Gerard Manley Hopkins. Washington, D. C.: Catholic University of America Press, Inc., 1964.

1893 Holloway, Roberta. "Some Effects of Classical Study in the Work of Hopkins." Ph.D., University of California, 1945.

1894 Holmes, John. "The Essential Soul of an English Poet." Review of The Note-Books and Papers of Gerard M. Hopkins, edited by Humphry House. Boston Evening Transcript, (May 15, 1937), 1.

1895 _____ The Poet's Work. New York: Oxford University Press, 1939.

1896 _____ "Surroundings and Illuminations." The Moment of Poetry, edited by Don Cameron Allen. Baltimore: Johns Hopkins Press, 1962, 8, 15.

1897 _____ "The Unity of Hopkins as Letter Writer and Poet."
Review of Further Letters of Gerard Manley Hopkins,
edited by Claude Colleer Abbott. Boston Evening
Transcript, (August 20, 1938), 1.

1898 Holroyd, Stuart. Emergence from Chaos. Boston:
Houghton Mifflin Company; Cambridge, Massachusetts:
Riverside Press, 1957, 55, 185-86.

1899 Hone, Joseph Maunsell. "Gerard Hopkins," New Statesman, 9 (June 9, 1917), 231-32.

1900 Hookens, W. "Gerard Manley Hopkins," New Review
(Calcutta), 31 (1950), 132-33.

1901 Hope, Felix. "Gerard Manley Hopkins," Irish Ecclesiastical Record, 5th series, 37 (June, 1931), 561-70.

1902 _____ "A Modern Lycidas: Digby Mackworth Dolben:
1848-1867," Month, 170 (July, 1937), 33-40.

1903 Hopkins, Gerard. "Gerard Manley Hopkins" (Letter to the
Editor), Times Literary Supplement, (June 24, 1944),
309.

1904 Hopkins, J. G. E. "Books in the Balance." Review of
Gerard Manley Hopkins: Priest and Poet, by John Pick.
Columbia, 22 (July, 1943), 20.

1905 _____ "On Innovation in Poetry," Spirit, 2 (July, 1935),
87-8.

1906 Hopkins, L[ionel] C[harles]. "Gerard Hopkins's Birthday,"
Times Literary Supplement, (March 14, 1935), 160.

1907 "Hopkins Discoveries," America, 77 (September 6, 1947),
633-35.

1908 Horst, Karl August. "Zugang zu Hopkins," Wort und
Wahrheit (Freiburg), 10 (Summer, 1955), 716-19.

1909 Hough, Graham. "Hopkins and Patmore." Review of
Further Letters of Gerard Manley Hopkins, edited by
Claude Colleer Abbott. 2nd ed. Spectator (London),
196 (December 28, 1956), 36-7.

1910 _____ The Last Romantics. London: Methuen and Co.,
Ltd., 1947, 212-13.

1911 _____ "The Scalpel and the Scales," Listener (London),
48 (August 28, 1952), 340-43.

1912 Houghton, Walter Edwards. The Art of Newman's Apologia.
New Haven: Yale University Press, 1945, 19, 60, 71.

1913 _____ The Victorian Frame of Mind 1830-1870. New
Haven: Yale University Press, 1957, 84, 158-59.

1914 _____ et al., eds. "Gerard Manley Hopkins." Victorian
Poetry and Poetics. Boston: Houghton Mifflin Company,
1959, 661-65.

1915 Houle, Sister Mary John Bosco, B.V.M. "Readings of Two
     Victorian Poems," Iowa English Yearbook, 10, (Fall,
     1965), 50-2. [Hopkins, "The Caged Skylark" and
     Meredith, "The Lark Ascending."]
1916 Hoult, Norah. "Journey to Silence," John O'Londons
     Weekly, (August 19, 1949).
1917 House, Humphry. All in Due Time: The Collected Essays
     and Broadcast Talks. London: Rupert Hart-Davis, 1955.
1918 _____ "Gerard Hopkins's Metres" (Letter to the Editor),
     Times Literary Supplement, (March 2, 1933), 147.
1919 _____ "Gerard Manley Hopkins: Poet-Priest," Listener,
     31 (June 22, 1944), 692-93.
1920 _____ "The Hopkinses," Times Literary Supplement,
     (November 4, 1949), 715.
1921 _____ "Manley Hopkins--An Interpretation." Review of
     Gerard Manley Hopkins: A Study of Poetic Idiosyncrasy
     in Relation to Poetic Tradition, by W. H. Gardner.
     Britain Today, No. 161 (September, 1949), 42-3.
1922 _____ "A Note on Hopkins's Religious Life," New Verse,
     No. 14 (April, 1935), 3-5.
1923 _____, ed. "Annotation in Abundance." Anonymous
     Review of The Journals and Papers of Gerard Manley
     Hopkins. Economist, (March 21, 1959).
1924 _____, ed. "Aspects of Hopkins's Genius." Anonymous
     Review of The Journals and Papers of Gerard Manley
     Hopkins, edited by Humphry House and The Sermons and
     Devotional Writings of Gerard Manley Hopkins, edited
     by Christopher Devlin, S.J. Scotsman (Edinburgh),
     (March 26, 1959).
1925 _____, ed. "Gerard Manley Hopkins and 'New' English
     Verse." Anonymous Review of The Note-Books and
     Papers of Gerard Manley Hopkins. Republican (Spring-
     field, Massachusetts), (February 28, 1937), 7.
1926 _____, ed. "Gerard Manley Hopkins's Papers: A Journal
     and Early Poems." Anonymous Review of The Note-
     Books and Papers of Gerard Manley Hopkins. Times
     Literary Supplement, (January 23, 1937), 57.
1927 _____, ed. "The Mind of G. M. Hopkins." Anonymous
     Review of The Journals and Papers, edited by Humphry
     House and The Sermons and Devotional Writings,
     edited by Christopher Devlin. Letters and Notices, 64
     (July, 1959), 104-09.
1928 _____, ed. "More Concerning Father Hopkins." Editorial
     Review of The Note-Books and Papers. Commonweal,
     26 (March 12, 1937), 555.

1929 _____, ed. "The Pursuit of Wisdom." Anonymous Review
      of The Note-Books and Papers of Gerard Manley Hopkins.
      Tablet (London), 169 (February 6, 1937), 198-200.
1930 _____, ed. "Rare Ill-Broker'd Talent." Anonymous Review
      of The Journals and Papers, edited by Humphry House
      and The Sermons and Devotional Writings, edited by
      Christopher Devlin, S.J. Times Literary Supplement,
      (September 25, 1959), 544.
1931 Howard, John D. (Letter to the Editor), College English,
      19 (April, 1958), 312.
1932 Howarth, Robert Guy. "Hopkins--A Correction" (Letter to
      the Editor), Notes & Queries, 193 (April 3, 1948), 150.
1933 _____ "Hopkins and Sir Thomas More" (Letter to the
      Editor), Notes & Queries, 192 (September 6, 1947),
      389.
1934 _____ "Hopkins and Sir Thomas More" (Letter to the
      Editor), Notes & Queries, 195 (September 30, 1950),
      438.
1935 _____ "Hopkins's Earlier Poems. The Order of Composi-
      tion," Notes & Queries, 192 (June 14, 1947), 255-56.
1936 _____ "Robert Bridges and Gerard Manley Hopkins." A
      Pot of Gillyflowers: Studies and Notes. Capetown:
      University of Capetown, 1964, 72-9.
1937 _____ "An Unconscious Prophet of Hopkins," Notes &
      Queries, N.S. 6 (December, 1959), 443-44.
1938 _____ "Yeats and Hopkins," Notes & Queries, 188
      (May 19, 1945), 202-04.
1939 Hufstader, Anselm. "The Experience of Nature in Hopkins'
      Journals and Poems," Downside Review, 84 (April,
      1966), 127-49.
1940 Hughes, Emily. "The Innovators," Catholic Digest, 3
      (January, 1939), 77-8. [Condensed from Irish Monthly,
      December, 1938.]
1941 _____ "The Innovators," Irish Monthly, 66 (December,
      1938), 820-24.
1942 _____ "Ripples on a Pool," Irish Monthly, 72 (July,
      1944), 280-85.
1943 Hughes, Nathalie L. "Gerard Manley Hopkins: Toward a
      Synthesis." M.A. thesis, University of Miami, 1967.
1944 Hughes, Riley. "Life of Hopkins." Review of Gerard
      Manley Hopkins, by Eleanor Ruggles. Books on Trial,
      3 (October-November, 1944), 617.
1945 Humiliata, Sister Mary. "Hopkins and the Prometheus
      Myth," PMLA, 70 (March, 1955), 58-68.

1946 Hunter, Jim. <u>Gerard Manley Hopkins</u>. Literature in
        Perspective Series. London: Evans Brothers Limited,
        1966.
1947 Huntley, John F. "Hopkins' 'The Windhover' as a Prayer
        of Request," <u>Renascence</u>, 16 (Spring, 1964), 154-62.
1948 Hutton, Edward. "Catholic English Literature 1850-1950."
        <u>The English Catholics 1850-1950</u>, edited by George
        Andrew Beck. London: Burns Oates, 1950, 534-35.
1949 Huxley, Aldous, ed. <u>Texts and Pretexts: An Anthology
        with Commentaries</u>. New York: W. W. Norton and
        Company, Inc., 1962, 24-6, 28, 34, 44-5, 68, 71,
        291-93.
1950 Hynes, Samuel. <u>The Pattern of Hardy's Poetry</u>. Chapel
        Hill: University of North Carolina Press, 1961.
1951 I.M. "Long Line of Bachelors: Literature and the Single
        State," <u>Melbourne Age</u>, (January 8, 1949).
1952 "The Immediate View," <u>Times Literary Supplement</u>,
        (August 25, 1950).
1953 J. A. Review of <u>Immortal Diamond</u>, edited by Norman
        Weyand, S.J. <u>Times of Malta</u>, (November 25, 1949).
1954 J. D. C. Review of <u>The Psychology of Duns Scotus</u>, by
        Christopher Devlin, S.J.; <u>St. Albert, Patron of
        Scientists</u>, by F. Sherwood Taylor and <u>The Anthropology
        of St. Thomas</u>, by Ian Hislop. <u>Blackfriars</u>, (November,
        1950).
1955 J. F. M. "New Study of Hopkins and his Times." Review
        of <u>Gerard Manley Hopkins</u>, by Eleanor Ruggles. <u>Irish
        Independent</u> (Dublin), (June 26, 1948).
1956 J. H. K. "Listeners' Log," <u>Radio Review</u> (Dublin),
        (August 12, 1949).
1957 J. J. H. "Hopkins and Eliot." Review of <u>Gerard Manley
        Hopkins</u>, by W. A. M. Peters, S.J.; <u>The Prosodic
        Theory of Gerard Manley Hopkins</u>, by Sister Marcella
        Holloway and <u>Poems of Gerard Manley Hopkins</u>, edited
        by W. H. Gardner. 3rd ed. <u>Studies</u>, 37 (December,
        1948), 494-97.
1958 J. J. P. "A Help to the Study of Hopkins." Review of <u>A
        Hopkins Reader</u>, edited by John Pick. <u>Irish Independent</u>
        (Dublin), (June 20, 1953).
1959 J. S. W. "The Cheltenham Festival," <u>Birmingham Post</u>,
        (July 15, 1958).
1960 Jacobson, Bernard. "Songs from Walsall," <u>Music and
        Musicians</u> (London), (January, 1964).
1961 Jagger, J. H. "Pity the Poor Anthologist," <u>Journal of
        Education</u> (London), (January, 1952), 36, 38.

1962 Jakobson, Roman. "Linguistics and Poetics." Essays on the Language of Literature, edited by Seymour Chatman and Samuel R. Levin. Boston: Houghton Mifflin Company, 1967, 296-322. [Reprinted from Style in Language, edited by Thomas A. Sebeok. Cambridge, Massachusetts: Massachusetts Institute of Technology Press, 1960.]

1963 James, Stanley B. "The Blessed Sacrament in English Literature: Father Gerard Manley Hopkins, S.J.," Sentinel of the Blessed Sacrament (New York), 39 (September, 1936), 467-70.

1964 _____ "Priest and Poet." Review of The Letters of Gerard Manley Hopkins to Robert Bridges; The Correspondence of Gerard Manley Hopkins and Richard Watson Dixon, edited by Claude Colleer Abbott. Irish Ecclesiastical Record, 45 (May, 1935), 505-11.

1965 _____ "The Revolution in Literature," Catholic Bookman, 1 (July-August, 1938), 386-88.

1966 _____ "The Sacrifice of Song," Catholic World, 141 (June, 1935), 290-95.

1967 _____ "The Triumph of the Poet," Irish Monthly, 60 (November, 1932), 678-83.

1968 James, Trevor. Review of Sowing the Spring, by James G. Southworth. Life and Letters Today, 29 (May, 1941), 179-80.

1969 Jankowsky, Kurt. "Die Versauffassung bei Gerard Manley Hopkins, den Imagisten und T. S. Eliot. Renaissance Altgermanischen Formgestaltens in der Dichtung des 20. Jahrhunderts." Ph.D., Westfalischen Wilhelms-Universitat, Munster, 1956. [Also manuscript and galley proofs. Munich: Max Hueber, 1967.]

1970 Jannoud, Claude. "Reliquiae de Gerard Manley Hopkins. Un tres Grand Poete Anglais." Review of Reliquiae, translated by Pierre Leyris. Vigie Marocaine (Casablanca), (July 20, 1958).

1971 Jarrett-Kerr, Martin. "Poetry under Religious Discipline: A Sixth-form Broadcast on Gerard Manley Hopkins," British Weekly, (June 29, 1950).

1972 Jaworski, Sister M. Cunegundis. "The Transcendent Victorianism of Gerard Manley Hopkins." M.A. thesis, Creighton University, 1944.

1973 Jennings, Elizabeth. Every Changing Shape. Philadelphia: Dufour Editions, 1962, 95-110.

1974 _____ "The Secular Angels: A Study of Rilke," Blackfriars, 40 (November, 1959), 467-83.

1975 _____ Review of The Shaping Vision of Gerard Manley
Hopkins, by Alan Heuser. London Magazine, 6
(September, 1959), 75-8.

1976 _____ "The Unity of Incarnation: A Study of Gerard
Manley Hopkins," Dublin Review, 234 (Summer, 1960),
170-84. [Reprinted in Every Changing Shape, by
Elizabeth Jennings, 95-110.]

1977 Jeremy, Sister Mary. "Gerard Manley Hopkins: 1844-1944"
(Poem), Poetry, 64 (April, 1944), 11.

1978 _____ "Hopkins and St. Gertrude" (Letter to the Editor),
Times Literary Supplement, (November 14, 1952), 743.

1979 Johnson, Ronald W. "Gerard Manley Hopkins: His
Approach to Literary Criticism." M.A. thesis,
Colorado State University, 1965.

1980 Johnson, Wendell Stacy. "The Imagery of Gerard Manley
Hopkins: Fire, Light and the Incarnation," Victorian
Newsletter, 16 (Fall, 1959), 18-23.

1981 Johnston, J. H. "Reply to Yvor Winters," Renascence, 2
(Spring, 1950), 117-25.

1982 Jones, Glyn. "Hopkins and Welsh Prosody," Life and
Letters Today, 21 (June, 1939), 50-4.

1983 Jones, John. "The Sad and Difficult." Review of The
Journals and Papers of Gerard Manley Hopkins, edited
by Humphry House and The Sermons and Devotional
Writings of Gerard Manley Hopkins, edited by
Christopher Devlin. New Statesman, 57 (March 7,
1959), 338-39.

1984 Joselyn, Sister M., O.S.B. "Herbert and Hopkins: Two
Lyrics," Renascence, 10 (Summer, 1958), 192-95.

1985 Joshi, Baburao N. "Hopkins and T. S. Eliot--A Study in
Linguistic Innovation," Osmania Journal of English
Studies (Hyderabad), (1961), 13-6.

1986 [Junkersfeld], Sister Mary Julienne, S.S.N.D. "The
History and the Critical Reception of the Poems of
Gerard Manley Hopkins, S.J." M.A. thesis, Loyola
University (Chicago), 1935.

1987 K. H. "Hopkins Interpreted." Review of Gerard Manley
Hopkins: A Critical Essay Towards the Understanding
of his Poetry, by W. A. M. Peters, S.J. John
O'Londons Weekly, (May 14, 1948).

1988 Kahler, Erich. "Gerard Manley Hopkins: Gedichte,"
Merkur (Stuttgart), 3 (June, 1949), 565-70.

1989 Kaminsky, Marc. "The Victorian Hopkins." M.A. thesis,
Columbia University, 1967.

1990 Kark, Austen. "Garlic and Sapphires," _Courier_ (London),
(January, 1950), 125-28.

1991 Kearney, Sister Mary Michael. "Gerard Manley Hopkins,
S.J. as Social Worker and Poet." M.A. thesis,
University of Vermont, 1943.

1992 Keating, John E. Review of _Metaphor in Hopkins,_ by
Robert Boyle, S.J. _Journal of English and Germanic
Philology,_ 62 (April, 1963), 413.

1993 _____ "The Wreck of the Deutschland: An Essay and
Commentary," _Kent State University Bulletin, Research
Series VI,_ 51 (January, 1963), 1-110. [Entire issue]

1994 Keating, Joseph Ignatius, S.J. "Disjecta Membra Poetae."
Review of _The Note-Books and Papers of Gerard Manley
Hopkins,_ edited by Humphry House. _Month,_ 169
(February, 1937), 175-76.

1995 _____ "Father Gerard Hopkins and the Spiritual Exercises,"
Month, 166 (September, 1935), 268-70.

1996 _____ "Impressions of Father Gerard Hopkins, S.J." I, II,
III, _Month,_ 114 (July, August, September, 1909), 59-68,
151-60, 246-58.

1997 _____ "Poetry." Review of _The Mind and Poetry of Gerard
Manley Hopkins, S.J.,_ by Bernard Kelly and of _New
Verse,_ April, 1935. _Month,_ 156 (July, 1935), 92-3.

1998 _____ "The Poetry of Father Gerard Hopkins, S.J.,"
Month, N.S. 198 (June, 1913), 643-44.

1999 _____ "Priest and Poet: Gerard Manley Hopkins in his
Letters," _Month,_ 165 (February, 1935), 125-36.

2000 Kelly, Bernard. Review of _Gerard Manley Hopkins,_ by
W. H. Gardner. _Blackfriars,_ 26 (June, 1945), 233-34.

2001 _____ "Gerard Manley Tuncks." Review of _The Note-
Books and Papers of Gerard Manley Hopkins,_ edited by
Humphry House. _Blackfriars,_ 18 (June, 1937), 424-29.

2002 _____ "Hopkins in the Nineteen Thirties," _G.K.'s
Weekly,_ 22 (October 10, 1935), 23-4.

2003 _____ "The Joy of Chastity in the Poetry of Gerard Manley
Hopkins," _Blackfriars,_ 14 (October, 1933), 833-36.

2004 _____ (Letter to the Editor), _G.K.'s Weekly,_ 22 (October
31, 1935), 86.

2005 _____ _The Mind & Poetry of Gerard Manley Hopkins, S.J._
Stones from the Brook No. 2. Ditchling, London:
Pepler & Sewell, 1935. [Number 254 of 300 copies
printed.]

2006 Kelly, Blanche Mary. Review of _The Note-Books and
Papers,_ edited by Humphry House. _Catholic World,_
145 (September, 1937), 750-51.

2007 _____ "Nova et Vetera: Immortal Diamond," Catholic
World, 144 (January, 1937), 481-82. [Reprinted from
The Well of English.]

2008 _____ The Well of English. New York: Harpers, 1936,
276-90, 339, 366.

2009 Kelly, Hugh, S.J. "Father Gerard Hopkins in his Letters."
Review of The Hopkins Letters [sic], edited by Claude
Colleer Abbott. Studies, 25 (June, 1936), 239-52.

2010 _____ Review of Further Letters of Gerard Manley Hopkins,
edited by Claude Colleer Abbott. Studies, 45 (Spring,
1957), 121-23.

2011 _____ Review of Gerard Manley Hopkins, by Eleanor
Ruggles. Studies, 37 (March, 1948), 111-12.

2012 _____ "Gerard Manley Hopkins: Jesuit--Poet." Review of
Gerard Manley Hopkins: Priest and Poet, by John Pick.
Studies, 31 (December, 1942), 438-44.

2013 _____ Review of Mastery and Mercy: A Study of Two
Religious Poems, by Philip M. Martin. Studies, 46
(Winter, 1958), 491-92.

2014 _____ "The Windhover--and Christ," Studies, 45 (Summer,
1956), 188-93.

2015 Kelly, John C., S.J. "Gerard Manley Hopkins: Piety
Versus Poetry." Review of Gerard Manley Hopkins:
Priest and Poet, by John Pick. Studies, 47 (Winter,
1958), 421-30.

2016 _____ Review of The Journals and Papers of Gerard Manley
Hopkins, edited by Humphry House and The Sermons and
Devotional Writings of Gerard Manley Hopkins, edited
by Christopher Devlin, S.J. Studies, 48 (Summer,
1959), 226-30.

2017 _____ "New Hopkinsiana." Review of The Journals and
Papers of Gerard Manley Hopkins, edited by Humphry
House and The Sermons and Devotional Writings of
Gerard Manley Hopkins, edited by Christopher Devlin,
S.J. Irish Times (Dublin), (March 21, 1959).

2018 Kelly, Richard W. "The Intellectual Milieu of Gerard
Manley Hopkins." M.A. thesis, Duke University, 1961.

2019 Kemp, Friedhelm. "Gerard Manley Hopkins." Review of
Gedichte, Ubertragung, Einfuhrung und Erlauterung,
edited by Irene Behn. Hochland (Munich), 41 (April,
1949), 385-89.

2020 Kenmare, Dallas. "The Passionate Christian: A Paper on
Gerard Manley Hopkins." The Face of Truth: Collected
Writings on Poetry and Religion. Oxford: Shakespeare
Head Press, 1939, 92-100.

2021 Kenneally, John Daniel. "The Personal and Literary Relationship of Gerard Manley Hopkins and Richard Watson Dixon." Ph.D., Fordham University, 1966.

2022 Kennedy, Leo. "Fine Life of the Jesuits' Poet." Review of Gerard Manley Hopkins, by Eleanor Ruggles. Chicago Sun Book Week, (August 13, 1944), 9.

2023 _____ "Studies about a Victorian Poet." Review of Gerard Manley Hopkins, by the Kenyon Critics. Chicago Sun Book Week, (February 3, 1946), 2.

2024 Kennedy, R. Dingwall. "Mind Over Matter: An Improper Fraction" (Epigraph only), Theoria (Pietermaritzburg, Natal), 4 (1952), 82.

2025 Kenner, Hugh. The Art of Poetry. New York: Rinehart and Company, Inc., 1959, 31-2, 115.

2026 Kent, Muriel. "Gerard Manley Hopkins: Poet and Prosodist." Review of Gerard Manley Hopkins, by G. F. Lahey, S.J. Bookman (London), 81 (March, 1932), 312-13.

2027 The Kenyon Critics. Gerard Manley Hopkins. London: Dennis Dobson Ltd, 1949.

2028 _____ Anonymous Review of Gerard Manley Hopkins. Listener, 43 (April 13, 1950), 664.

2029 _____ Anonymous Review of Gerard Manley Hopkins. New Yorker, 22 (February 23, 1946), 82-3.

2030 _____ Anonymous Review of Gerard Manley Hopkins. United States Quarterly Book List, 2 (September, 1946), 171-72.

2031 Kermode, Frank. "Characteristicks." Review of The Function of Criticism, by Yvor Winters. New Statesman, 63 (March 16, 1962), 382.

2032 _____ "Hopkins and the Modern Poets." Review of Journals of Gerard Manley Hopkins, edited by Humphry House and The Sermons and Devotional Writings of Gerard Manley Hopkins, edited by Christopher Devlin, S.J. Manchester Guardian Weekly, (February 15 [?], 1959). [Also in Manchester Guardian, February 27, 1959, as "Hopkins and the Moderns."]

2033 Kernan, Sister Mary Noel, S.C. "A Critique of Poetry Compiled from the Prose Writings of Gerard Manley Hopkins." M.A. thesis, Duquesne University, 1962.

2034 Kerr, Sister Marguerite M., R.S.C.J. "Gerard Manley Hopkins: Aspects of his Poetical Theory and Practice." M.A. thesis, University of Detroit, 1942.

2035 Keunen, Jozef. "Guido Gezelle en G. M. Hopkins,"
Dietsche Warande en Belfort (Amsterdam), 112 (1967),
702-11.

2036 Kezys, Algimantas, S.J. "How to Keep Back Beauty/From
Vanishing Away?" Critic, 23 (April-May, 1965), 29-39.
[Photographs, with selections from Gerard Manley
Hopkins.]

2037 Kiely, Robert. "The Spartan as Critic." Review of The
Common Pursuit, by F. R. Leavis. Christian Science
Monitor, (December 3, 1964), 7B.

2038 Kilby, Clyde S., ed. Poetry and Life: An Introduction to
Poetry. New York: Odyssey Press, 1953, 208-09,
273-74.

2039 Kilcoyne, Francis P. "Critical Evaluation of Gerard Manley
Hopkins." Review of Immortal Diamond, edited by
Norman Weyand, S.J. Brooklyn Eagle, (May 11, 1949),
18.

2040 Kilmer, Joyce. Anthology of Catholic Poets. New York:
Halcyon House, 1947, 99-101, 365-67.

2041 _____ Dreams and Images. New York: Boni and Liveright,
1917, 99-101.

2042 _____ "Father Gerard Hopkins, S.J." (Poem). Joyce
Kilmer, edited by Robert Cortes Holliday. Vol. 1. New
York: Doubleday & Company, 1946, 138. [Also in
Studies, 5 (March, 1916), 106.]

2043 _____ "The Poetry of Gerard Hopkins." The Circus and
Other Essays and Fugitive Pieces. New York: Doran,
1921, 180-85. [Also in Poetry, 4 (1914), 241-45.]

2044 Kinerk, Robert. "Should your Child be a Poet?"
(Editorial), Owl (University of Santa Clara), 49
(Winter, 1962), 5-6.

2045 King, Anne R. "Hopkins' 'Windhover' and Blake," English
Studies (Amsterdam), 37 (December, 1956), 245-52.

2046 King, David Ross. "Art and Matter," Commonweal, 45
(April 11, 1947), 632-36.

2047 King, Donald R. "The Vision of 'Being' in Hopkins' Poetry
and Ruskin's 'Modern Painters'," Discourse: A Review
of the Liberal Arts (Moorhead, Minnesota), 9 (Spring,
1966), 316-24.

2048 Kirschbaum, Leo. Review of Gerard Manley Hopkins--A
Life, by Eleanor Ruggles. Modern Language Notes, 60
(March, 1945), 199-201.

2049 Kissane, James. "Classical Echoes in Hopkins' 'Heaven-
Haven'," Modern Language Notes, 73 (November, 1958),
491-92.

2050 Kite, Elizabeth S. "Conflict and Vision in Hopkins,"
     America, 65 (July 19, 1941), 411-12.
2051 Klapp, Brother Frank, S.M. "A Closer Look at this
     Masterful Work of Gerard Manley Hopkins," _Marianist_,
     53 (January, 1962), 22-5.
2052 Kliger, Samuel. "God's 'Plenitude' in the Poetry of Gerard
     Manley Hopkins," _Modern Language Notes_, 59 (June,
     1944), 408-10.
2053 Klotz, Rose Mosen. "Verbal Counterpoint in the Poetry of
     Gerard Manley Hopkins." Ph.D., University of
     Wisconsin, 1966.
2054 Kopper, Edward A., Jr. "Hopkins' 'The Windhover',"
     Explicator, 22 (March, 1964), 54.
2055 Kornacki, Wanda Charlotte. "Thomistic Principles of
     Esthetics in the Poetry of Gerard Manley Hopkins,
     Francis Thompson, and Coventry Patmore." M.A.
     thesis, De Paul University, 1955.
2056 Koszul, A. Review of _Poems of Gerard Manley Hopkins_,
     edited by Robert Bridges. _Revue Anglo-Americaine_
     (Paris), 9 (June, 1932), 451-52.
2057 Kreuzer, James R. _Elements of Poetry_. New York:
     Macmillan Company, 1955, 61.
2058 _____ Review of _Metaphor in Hopkins_, by Robert Boyle,
     S.J. _Criticism_, 5 (Spring, 1963), 191-92.
2059 Krieger, Murray. _A Window to Criticism: Shakespeare's
     "Sonnets" and Modern Poetics_. Princeton, New Jersey:
     Princeton University Press, 1964, 63.
2060 Kunitz, Stanley. "Dilly Tante Observes." Review of
     Gerard Manley Hopkins, by G. F. Lahey, S.J. _Wilson
     Bulletin_, 5 (September, 1930), 61-2.
2061 _____ "Dilly Tante Observes." Review of _Gerard Manley
     Hopkins_, by G. F. Lahey, S.J. and _Poems of Gerard
     Manley Hopkins_, edited by Robert Bridges. _Wilson
     Bulletin_, 5 (December, 1930), 256-58.
2062 _____ "The Letters of Hopkins." Review of _The Letters of
     Gerard Manley Hopkins to Robert Bridges; The
     Correspondence of Gerard Manley Hopkins and Richard
     Watson Dixon_, edited by Claude Colleer Abbott.
     Wilson Bulletin, 9 (May, 1935), 491-92.
2063 _____, ed. "Hopkins, Gerard Manley." _British Authors of
     the Nineteenth Century_. New York: H. W. Wilson Co.,
     1936, 306-08.
2064 Kurz, P. J., S.J. Review of _Schnittpunkte. Gesammelte
     Aufsatze_, by Curt Hohoff. _Stimmen der Zeit_ (Freiburg),
     174 (1964), 77-8.

2065 L. C. "Dylan Thomas." Review of <u>Dylan Thomas</u>, by
      Henry Treece. <u>Yorkshire Post</u> (Leeds), (April 29, 1949).
2066 L. H. Review of <u>A Hopkins Reader</u>, edited by John Pick.
      <u>Dublin Magazine</u>, (January, 1954), 47-8.
2067 _____ "Music Written by Local Composers," <u>Wallington &</u>
      <u>Carshalton Advertiser</u>, (March 21, 1957).
2068 Lackamp, John Jerome, S.J. "The Influence of Music on
      the Life of Gerard Manley Hopkins." M.A. thesis,
      Loyola University (Chicago), 1960.
2069 La Driere, Craig. Review of <u>Poems of Gerard Manley</u>
      <u>Hopkins</u>, edited by W. H. Gardner. 3rd ed.; <u>Gerard</u>
      <u>Manley Hopkins (1844-1889): A Study of Poetic Idiosyn-</u>
      <u>crasy in Relation to Poetic Tradition</u>, by W. H. Gardner.
      Vol. 1; <u>Gerard Manley Hopkins: A Critical Essay</u>
      <u>Towards the Understanding of his Poetry</u>, by W. A. M.
      Peters, S.J. and <u>Immortal Diamond</u>, edited by Norman
      Weyand, S.J. <u>Journal of Aesthetics and Art Criticism</u>,
      9 (December, 1950), 153-54.
2070 _____ "Structure, Sound, and Meaning." <u>Sound and</u>
      <u>Poetry</u>. English Institute Essays 1956. New York:
      Columbia University Press, 1963, 97-8.
2071 Lahey, Gerald F., S.J. <u>Gerard Manley Hopkins</u>. London:
      Humphrey Milford, Oxford University Press, 1930.
2072 _____ Anonymous Review of <u>Gerard Manley Hopkins</u>. <u>New</u>
      <u>York Times Book Review</u>, (July 27, 1930), 12.
2073 _____ Anonymous Review of <u>Gerard Manley Hopkins</u>.
      <u>Times Literary Supplement</u>, (July 17, 1930), 593.
2074 _____ "Gerard Manley Hopkins," <u>America</u>, 39 (October 6,
      1928), 619-20.
2075 _____ "Gerard Manley Hopkins," <u>Commonweal</u>, 18
      (October 20, 1933), 581-84.
2076 _____ Review of <u>Gerard Manley Hopkins, Priest and Poet</u>,
      by John Pick. <u>Thought</u>, 18 (December, 1943), 721-22.
2077 _____ "Hopkins and Newman," <u>Commonweal</u>, 12 (June 25,
      1930), 211-13.
2078 _____ "Preferences." Anonymous Review of <u>Gerard</u>
      <u>Manley Hopkins</u>. <u>Canadian Forum</u> (Toronto), 11
      (October, 1930), 22-3.
2079 _____ "A Victorian who has come into Fashion." Anony-
      mous Review of <u>Gerard Manley Hopkins</u>. <u>New York</u>
      <u>Times Book Review</u>, (July 27, 1930), 12.
2080 Lamont, Corliss. <u>Man Answers Death: An Anthology of</u>
      <u>Poetry</u>. New York: G. P. Putnam's Sons, 1936, 201.

2081 Lanctot, Sister Agnes, C.S.J. "The Liturgical Concept of
Life in Gerard Manley Hopkins and Paul Claudel."
M.A. thesis, University of Notre Dame, 1943.
2082 Landier, Germain. "Lettres de Gerard Manley Hopkins,"
Mesures (Paris), 1 (January, 1935), 103-09.
2083 Langbaum, Robert W. "Browning and the Question of
Myth," PMLA, 81 (October, 1966), 575-84.
2084 _____ The Poetry of Experience: The Dramatic Monologue
in Modern Literary Tradition. London: Chatto and
Windus, 1957, 32, 65-9, 71-2.
2085 Lappin, Henry A. "Gerard Hopkins and his Poetry."
Review of Poems of Gerard Manley Hopkins, edited by
Robert Bridges. Catholic World, 109 (July, 1919),
501-12.
2086 Larsson, Raymond. "Gerard Manley Hopkins." Review of
The Letters of Gerard Manley Hopkins to Robert Bridges
and The Correspondence of Gerard Manley Hopkins and
Richard Watson Dixon, edited by Claude Colleer Abbott.
Commonweal, 22 (June 21, 1935), 219-21.
2087 Laube, Clifford J. Review of Immortal Diamond, edited by
Norman Weyand, S.J. Sign, 28 (May, 1949), 59.
2088 Lawler, Donald L. "Gerard Manley Hopkins: Three
Patterns of his Poetry." M.A. thesis, Columbia
University, 1960.
2089 Leahy, Maurice. "Father Gerard Manley Hopkins, Jesuit
and Poet." Review of Poems of Gerard Manley Hopkins,
edited by Robert Bridges. 2nd ed.; Gerard Manley
Hopkins, by G. F. Lahey, S.J.; The Letters of Gerard
Manley Hopkins to Robert Bridges and The Correspondence of Gerard Manley Hopkins and Richard Watson
Dixon, edited by Claude Colleer Abbott. Irish Monthly,
63 (September, 1935), 567-76.
2090 _____ "Laureate and Levite: Father Gerard Manley
Hopkins, S.J., Convert to the Church," Epistle, 11
(Winter, 1945), 12-4.
2091 _____ "A Priest-Poet: Father Gerard Manley Hopkins,
S.J.," Irish Ecclesiastical Record, 47 (April, 1936),
355-68.
2092 _____ " 'The Terrible Sonnets'," Voice (St. Mary's
Seminary, Baltimore, Maryland), 19 (January, 1942),
19-20, 35. [Summary of address by Maurice Leahy.]
2093 Leary, Jerome V. (Letter to the Editor), New York Times
Book Review, (November 10, 1957), 34.

2094 Leavis, Frank Raymond. "Doughty and Hopkins." Review
of Charles M. Doughty: A Study of his Prose and Verse,
by Anne Treneer. Scrutiny, 4 (December, 1935), 316-17.
2095 _____ "Evaluations (IV): Gerard Manley Hopkins,"
Scrutiny, 12 (Spring, 1944), 82-93. [Reprinted in The
Common Pursuit, 44-58.]
2096 _____ "Gerard Manley Hopkins." New Bearings in
English Poetry: A Study of the Contemporary Situation.
Ann Arbor: University of Michigan Press, 1964, 159-93.
(Also London: Chatto & Windus, 1932.) [Reprinted in
Hopkins: A Collection of Critical Essays, edited by
Geoffrey H. Hartman, 17-36.]
2097 _____ "Hopkins Canonized." Review of The Note-Books
and Papers of Gerard Manley Hopkins, edited by
Humphry House. Cambridge Review, 58 (April 30, 1937),
364.
2098 _____ "The Letters of Gerard Manley Hopkins." Review of
The Letters of Gerard Manley Hopkins to Robert Bridges;
The Correspondence of Gerard Manley Hopkins and
Richard Watson Dixon, edited by Claude Colleer
Abbott. Scrutiny, 4 (September, 1935), 216-31.
[Reprinted in The Common Pursuit, 59-72.]
2099 Lechmere, W. L. "Oxford: 1863-1867," Oxford and
Cambridge Review, 19 (May 12, 1912), 73-113.
2100 Lee, Christopher. Review of Poems of Gerard Manley
Hopkins, edited by W. H. Gardner. Our Time (London),
(October, 1948).
2101 Lee, W. B. (Letter to the Editor), New York Times Book
Review, (November 10, 1957), 34.
2102 Lees, Francis Noel. Gerard Manley Hopkins. Columbia
Essays on Modern Writers No. 21. New York:
Columbia University Press, 1966.
2103 _____ "Gerard Manley Hopkins." The Pelican Guide to
English Literature. Vol. 6: From Dickens to Hardy,
edited by Boris Ford. Baltimore, Maryland: Penguin
Books, 1958, 371-84.
2104 _____ "Hopkinsiana" (Letter to the Editor), Times Literary
Supplement, (September 3, 1954), 557.
2105 _____ "Hopkinsiana" (Letter to the Editor), Times Literary
Supplement, (October 1, 1954), 625.
2106 _____ "Hopkinsiana" (Letter to the Editor), Times Literary
Supplement, (October 22, 1954), 673.
2107 _____ " 'The Windhover'," Scrutiny, 17 (Spring, 1950),
32-7.

2108 _____ Review of The Wreck of the Deutschland: An Essay
     and Commentary, by John E. Keating. Notes & Queries,
     N.S. 12 (February, 1965), 74-5.
2109 Leggett, Barbara Vaughan. (Letter to the Editor), New
     York Times Book Review, (November 10, 1957), 34.
2110 Legouis, Emile and Louis Cazamian. A History of English
     Literature. London: J. M. Dent & Sons, Ltd., 1964,
     1291, 1429-30, 1441-43.
2111 Lehmann, John. New Writing in Europe. London: Allen
     Lane, 1940, 29, 43.
2112 _____ "Poets and Publishers," Observer (London), (March
     19, 1950).
2113 Leishman, James Blair. Review of Further Letters of Gerard
     Manley Hopkins, edited by Claude Colleer Abbott.
     Review of English Studies, 15 (April, 1939), 243-46.
2114 Lenz, Sister Mary Baylon, O.S.F. "The Meditative Style
     in Gerard Manley Hopkins." M.A. thesis, University
     of Notre Dame, 1959.
2115 Lenz, Mildred A. "A Poet's View of Reality: A Study of
     the Works of Gerard Manley Hopkins." M.A. thesis,
     University of Kansas, 1961.
2116 Leslie, Shane. "The Exquisite Doctor." Review of The
     Letters of Gerard Manley Hopkins to Robert Bridges;
     The Correspondence of Gerard Manley Hopkins and
     Richard Watson Dixon, edited by Claude Colleer Abbott.
     Saturday Review, 11 (March 16, 1935), 549-50.
2117 _____ "Introduction." An Anthology of Catholic Poets.
     2nd ed. New York: Macmillan and Company, 1926.
2118 _____ "Letters of Gerard Manley Hopkins." Review of
     The Letters of Gerard Manley Hopkins to Robert Bridges;
     The Correspondence of Gerard Manley Hopkins and
     Richard Watson Dixon, edited by Claude Colleer Abbott.
     Ave Maria, N.S. 41 (April 13, 1935), 456-58.
2119 _____ "New Books: Coventry Patmore." Review of The
     Life and Times of Coventry Patmore, by Derek Patmore.
     Truth (London), (April 29, 1949).
2120 L'Estrange, H. K., S.J. Review of Further Letters of
     Gerard Manley Hopkins, edited by Claude Colleer
     Abbott. Blackfriars, 19 (June, 1938) 465-67.
2121 _____ Review of Further Letters of Gerard Manley Hopkins,
     edited by Claude Colleer Abbott. Month, 171 (June,
     1938), 569-70.

2122 Levi, Peter, S.J. "Hopkins's Progress." Review of Poems
of Gerard Manley Hopkins, edited by W. H. Gardner
and N. H. Mackenzie, 4th ed., and Hopkins Selections,
edited by Graham Storey. Manchester Guardian Weekly,
97 (September 14, 1967), 14.

2123 _____ "Man of Letters." Review of Essays on Literature
and Ideas, by John Wain. Spectator, (November 1,
1963), 506.

2124 Lewis, Dominic Bevan Wyndham. "Blessed David Lewis,"
Month, N.S. 12 (September, 1954), 133-46.

2125 _____ "Catholicism in Modern Poetry" (Preface). An
Anthology of Contemporary Catholic Poetry, compiled by
Maurice Leahy. London: Cecil Palmer, 1931, ix.

2126 Leyris, Pierre, ed. "Hopkins in French." Anonymous
Review of Gerard Manley Hopkins: Reliquiae. Times
Literary Supplement, (April 4, 1958), 184.

2127 _____, trans. "Deux Lettres," Dieu Vivant (Paris), 11
(1948), 29-42.

2128 _____, trans. "Putride Pature," Dieu Vivant (Paris), 3
(1945), 53-9.

2129 Lieder, Paul Robert, ed. Eminent British Poets of the
Nineteenth Century. New York: Harper & Brothers,
1938, 718-23.

2130 Lienhardt, R. G. "Hopkins and Yeats." Review of Gerard
Manley Hopkins, Priest and Poet, by John Pick and The
Development of William Butler Yeats, by V. K. Narayana
Menon. Scrutiny, 11 (Spring, 1943), 220-24.

2131 _____ "Hopkins Commemorated." Review of Gerard Manley
Hopkins, 1844-1889. A Centenary Commemoration, by
W. H. Gardner. Scrutiny, 12 (Autumn, 1944), 296-301.

2132 Liljegren, Sten Bodvar. "Anglistik." Review of Die
Self-Komposita bei Thomas Carlyle, Matthew Arnold und
Gerard Manley Hopkins, by Hans-Werner Ludwig.
Deutsche Literarzeitung (Leipzig), 85 (November-
December, 1964), 1030-34.

2133 Lilly, Gweneth. "The Welsh Influence in the Poetry of
Gerard Manley Hopkins," Modern Language Review, 38
(July, 1943), 192-205.

2134 Linane, Sister Francis Loretto, S.N.D. "Intensification in
G. M. Hopkins' 'The Leaden Echo and the Golden
Echo'." M.A. thesis, Catholic University of America,
1959.

2135 Lincoln, Eleanor. "Giving God Glory," Ariston (College of
St. Catherine, St. Paul, Minnesota), 38 (June, 1944),
4-6.

2136 Lind, L. Roberto. "Gerard Manley Hopkins: Poeta Menor de la Edad Mediavictoriana," Universidad de la Habana Publicacion Bimestral, 36 (May, 1941), 48-55.

2137 Lisca, Peter. "The Return of 'The Windhover'," College English, 19 (December, 1957), 124-26.

2138 Little, Arthur, S.J. "Hopkins and Scotus." Review of Gerard Manley Hopkins: Priest and Poet, by John Pick. Irish Monthly, 71 (February, 1943), 47-59.

2139 _____ "Poetry." Review of The Poems of Gerard Manley Hopkins, edited by Robert Bridges. Studies, 20 (March, 1931), 165-67.

2140 Litzinger, Boyd. Review of The Disappearance of God: Five Nineteenth-Century Writers, by J. Hillis Miller. Journal of English and Germanic Philology, 63 (October, 1964), 818-20.

2141 _____ "The Genesis of Hopkins' 'Heaven-Haven'," Victorian Newsletter, No. 17 (Spring, 1960), 31-3.

2142 _____ "Gerard Manley Hopkins," Critic, 21 (October-November, 1962), 36, 39-40.

2143 _____ "Hopkins' 'Pied Beauty' Once More," Renascence, 13 (Spring, 1961), 136-38.

2144 _____ "Hopkins' 'The Habit of Perfection'," Explicator, 16 (October, 1957), 1.

2145 _____ Review of The Journals and Papers of Gerard Manley Hopkins, edited by Humphry House and The Sermons and Devotional Writings of Gerard Manley Hopkins, edited by Christopher Devlin, S.J. Cithara, 1 (November, 1961), 48-50.

2146 _____ "Once More 'The Windhover'," Victorian Poetry, 5 (Autumn, 1967), 228-30.

2147 _____ "The Pattern of Ascent in Hopkins," Victorian Poetry, 2 (Winter, 1964), 43-7.

2148 _____ " 'The Wreck of the Deutschland'," Stanza 19, Explicator, 20 (October, 1961), 7.

2149 _____ " 'The Wreck of the Deutschland'," Stanza 33, Explicator, 18 (December, 1959), 19.

2150 Lloyd-Jones, Richard. "Common Speech--A Poetic Effect for Hopkins, Browning and Arnold." Ph.D., University of Iowa, 1956.

2151 Lougheed, W. C. "Men of Letters." Review of The Shaping Vision of Gerard Manley Hopkins, by Alan Heuser. Queen's Quarterly (Kingston, Ontario), 66 (Spring, 1959), 173-74.

2152 Louise, Sister Mary, S. L. . . . over the bent World. New York: Sheed & Ward, 1941, xiv.

2153 Louise, Sister Robert, O.P. "Hopkins' 'Spring and Fall:
      To a Young Child'," Explicator, 21 (April, 1963), 65.
2154 Lovas, John Charles. "The Poet and his God: A Study of
      the Religious Verse of Gerard Manley Hopkins." M.A.
      thesis, University of Utah, 1965.
2155 Loveland, Kenneth. "Welsh Composer's View of the
      Seasons," South Wales Argus (Newport), (February 4,
      1960).
2156 Lowell, Robert. "Hopkins and Baudelaire." Review of
      Gerard Manley Hopkins: A Life, by Eleanor Ruggles
      and Baudelaire: A Criticism, by Joseph D. Bennett.
      Sewanee Review, 53 (March, 1945), 136-40.
2157 _____ "The Hopkins Centennial: A Note," Kenyon Review,
      6 (Autumn, 1944), 583-86. [Appears as "Hopkins'
      Sanctity," in Gerard Manley Hopkins, by the Kenyon
      Critics. London: Dennis Dobson Ltd, 1949, 90-4.]
2158 Ludwig, Hans-Werner. Die Self-Komposita bei Thomas
      Carlyle, Matthew Arnold und Gerard Manley Hopkins:
      Untersuchungen zum Geistigen Gehalt einer Sprach-
      lichen Form. Tubingen: Max Niemeyer Verlag, 1963.
      [Studien zur Englischen Philologie, N.F. 2 (Halle).]
2159 Lukanitsch, Ruth Marion. "The Relationship of the Figures
      of Sound to the Rhythm in Certain Poems of Gerard
      Manley Hopkins." Ph.D., Northwestern University,
      1963.
2160 Lynam, Thomas J., S.J. "Self-Portrait of a Major Poet."
      Review of The Letters of Gerard Manley Hopkins to
      Robert Bridges; The Correspondence of Gerard Manley
      Hopkins and Richard Watson Dixon, edited by Claude
      Colleer Abbott. America, 52 (March 23, 1935), 574.
2161 Lynch, John W. "Gerard Manley Hopkins." Hourglass:
      Stories of a Measured Year. New York: Macmillan
      Company, 1952, 151-53.
2162 Lynch, William F., S.J. "Of Rhythm and its End."
      Return to Poetry, edited by John G. Brunini, et al.
      New York: Declan X. McMullen Company, 1947, 85-8.
      [Reprinted from Spirit, November, 1939.]
2163 Lynd, Robert. "Life and Living." Review of Gerard
      Manley Hopkins, by Eleanor Ruggles. Observer
      (London), (November 30, 1947), 3.
2164 _____ Modern Poetry. London: Thomas Nelson and Sons,
      1939, v-ix, 7-9.
2165 M. D. Review of Gerard Manley Hopkins: Priest and
      Poet, by John Pick. Dublin Magazine, N.S. 18
      (January-March, 1943), 63-4.

2166 M. M. C. Review of Selected Poems of Gerard Manley Hopkins, edited by James Reeves. Dominicana, 42 (December, 1957), 369-70.

2167 M. M. W. "Poet in the Tradition of Donne," Rand Daily Mail (South Africa), (April 24, 1948).

2168 M. R. R. Review of The Poetry of Gerard Manley Hopkins: A Survey and Commentary, by E. E. Phare. Oxford Magazine, 52 (May 17, 1934), 714.

2169 M. W. "Eliot's Poetry" (Letter to the Editor), Stafford Newsletter, (April 22, 1950).

2170 M. W. B. "Modern English Poetry: Brilliant Talk to Sino-British Club," South China Sunday Post (Hong Kong), (January 29, 1950).

2171 McBrien, William Augustine. "Likenesses in the Themes and Prosody of Gerard Manley Hopkins and Dylan Thomas." Ph.D., St. John's University, 1959.

2172 _____ "Musical Techniques in the Versification of Gerard Manley Hopkins." M.A. thesis, St. John's University, 1954.

2173 Maccaig, Norman. "Stress Signs." Review of Poems of Gerard Manley Hopkins, edited by W. H. Gardner and N. H. MacKenzie. Listener, 78 (October 26, 1967), 545.

2174 MacCallum, Hugh. "Poetry," University of Toronto Quarterly, 36 (July, 1967), 354-79.

2175 McCarron, Hugh, S.J. "Onomatopoeia, Assonance-- Further Thoughts About Them." Realization. New York: Sheed & Ward, 1937, 38-9.

2176 McCarthy, Adrian James. "The Concept of Inscape in the Poetry of Gerard Manley Hopkins." M.A. thesis, New York University, 1952.

2177 McCarthy, Adrian J., S.M. "Toward a Definition of Hopkins' 'Inscape'," University of Dayton Review, 4 (Autumn, 1967), 55-68.

2178 MacCarthy, Desmond. "Gerard Manley Hopkins." Review of Gerard Manley Hopkins, by W. H. Gardner. Sunday Times (London), (November 12, 1944).

2179 _____ "Gerard Manley Hopkins." Review of Gerard Manley Hopkins, by W. A. M. Peters, S.J. Sunday Times (London), (May 16, 1948), 3.

2180 _____ "Gold and Quartz." Review of Gerard Manley Hopkins, by W. H. Gardner. Sunday Times (London), (November 19, 1944).

2181 _____ "Poetic Idiosyncrasy." Review of Gerard Manley
       Hopkins, 1844-1889: A Study of Poetic Idiosyncrasy
       in Relation to Poetic Tradition, by W. H. Gardner, Vol.
       2. Sunday Times (London), (July 3, 1949).

2182 McChesney, Donald. Review of Hopkins: Selections,
       New Oxford English Series, edited by G. Storey.
       Blackfriars, 49 (October, 1967), 54-5.

2183 MacColl, Dugald Sutherland. "Patmore and Hopkins:
       Sense and Nonsense in English Prosody," London
       Mercury, 38 (July-August, 1938), 217-24, 302.

2184 McCrossan, Sister Joseph Marie, I.H.M. "The Magic
       Baton of Gerard Manley Hopkins." M.A. thesis,
       Villanova College, 1937.

2185 McCrossan, Sister Virginia Elizabeth. "A Study of Two
       Poets of Faith of the Nineteenth Century: Christina
       Rossetti--Gerard M. Hopkins." M.A. thesis,
       University of Hawaii, 1966.

2186 McDonagh, Thomas. Literature in Ireland: Studies Irish
       and Anglo-Irish. London: T. Fisher Unwin, 1916, 229.

2187 McDonald, Gerald D. "Poetry." Review of A Hopkins
       Reader, edited by John Pick. Library Journal, 78
       (August, 1953), 1334.

2188 _____ "Poetry." Review of Poems, edited by W. H.
       Gardner. 3rd ed. Library Journal, 73 (September 15,
       1948), 1277.

2189 McDonald, Sister Mary Roy, O.S.F. "Gerard Manley
       Hopkins as Social Critic." M.A. thesis, Marquette
       University, 1952.

2190 McDonnell, Thomas P. "Hopkins as a Sacramental Poet:
       A Reply to Yvor Winter," Renascence, 14 (Autumn,
       1961), 25-33, 41.

2191 _____ Review of The Shaping Vision of Gerard Manley
       Hopkins, by Alan Heuser. Catholic World, 189 (May,
       1959), 174-75.

2192 McGaughran, Sister Ruth Marie, S.C.N. "The Poetry of
       Gerard Manley Hopkins Embodies Traditional
       Aesthetics." M.A. thesis, Xavier University, 1953.

2193 MacGillivray, Arthur, S.J. Review of Gerard Manley
       Hopkins, Priest and Poet, by John Pick. Poet Lore, 50
       (Autumn, 1944), 276-78.

2194 _____ "Hopkins and Creative Writing." Immortal Diamond:
       Studies in Gerard Manley Hopkins, edited by Norman
       Weyand, S.J. New York: Sheed & Ward, 1949, 51-72.

149

2195 McGowan, Madelon. "The Concept of Nature in the
Poetry of Gerard Manley Hopkins." M.A. thesis,
University of Southern California, 1965.

2196 McGuire, D.P. The Poetry of Gerard Manley Hopkins.
English Association--Adelaide Branch, Pamphlet No. 2.
Adelaide, Australia: Hassell Press, 1934.

2197 McH., R. "A Tribute to Gerard Manley Hopkins." Review
of Immortal Diamond, edited by Norman Weyand, S.J.
Irish Independent (Dublin), (December 5, 1949).

2198 Mack, Maynard. "Hopkins: His Poetry and Prose."
Review of Gerard Manley Hopkins, by the Kenyon
Critics. Yale Review, 35 (March, 1946), 539-42.

2199 _____, Leonard Dean and William Frost, eds. "Introduction." English Masterpieces. Vol. 7: Modern Poetry,
2nd ed. Englewood Cliffs, New Jersey: Prentice-Hall,
Inc., 1961, 1-27.

2200 McKenzie, Gordon. "Great and Odd Poet and Some of his
Great and Odd Poetry." Review of Poems of Gerard
Manley Hopkins, edited by W. H. Gardner and Gerard
Manley Hopkins, by W. H. Gardner. San Francisco
Chronicle, "This World" Supplement, (September 26,
1948), 19.

2201 MacKenzie, Norman H. "Bridges's Debt to Hopkins"
(Letter to the Editor), Times Literary Supplement,
(September 1, 1961), 588.

2202 _____ "The Classicism of Hopkins." Review of Gerard
Manley Hopkins, the Classical Background and Critical
Reception of his Work, by Todd K. Bender. Queen's
Quarterly (Kingston, Ontario), 74 (Autumn, 1967),
547-48.

2203 _____ "Gerard and Grace Hopkins: Some New Links,"
Month, N.S. 33 (June, 1965), 347-50.

2204 _____ "Hopkins Among the Victorians: Form in Art and
Nature." English Studies Today, 3rd series, edited by
G. I. Duthie. Edinburgh: University Press, 1964,
155-68. [Lectures and Papers read at the fifth confer-
ence of the International Association of Professors of
English held at Edinburgh and Glasgow, August 1962.]

2205 _____ "A Hopkins Fragment" (Letter to the Editor),
Times Literary Supplement, (February 10, 1966), 110.

2206 _____ "Hopkins MSS.: Old Losses and New Finds,"
Times Literary Supplement, (March 18, 1965), 220.

2207 McKinney, John F. The Poetry of Gerard Manley Hopkins.
Monarch Notes and Study Guides. New York: Monarch
Press, 1965.

2208 Mackworth, Cecily. "Mallarme en Angleterre," Lettres (Paris), Special Number, n.d., 217-24.

2209 McLaughlin, John, S.J. "The Influence of St. Paul on Gerard Manley Hopkins." M.A. thesis, Boston College, 1961.

2210 _____ "The Pulpit Rhetoric of Gerard Manley Hopkins." Ph.D., Columbia University, 1967.

2211 McLuhan, Herbert Marshall. "The Analogical Mirrors," Kenyon Review, 6 (Summer, 1944), 322-32. [Reprinted in Gerard Manley Hopkins, by the Kenyon Critics, 21-32, and in Hopkins: A Collection of Critical Essays, edited by Geoffrey H. Hartman, 80-8.]

2212 _____ "Gerard Hopkins and his World." Review of Gerard Manley Hopkins--A Life, by Eleanor Ruggles. New York Times Book Review, (September 3, 1944), 7, 14.

2213 _____ "Literary Criticism." Review of The Forlorn Demon, by Allen Tate; A Hopkins Reader, edited by John Pick and The Alien Vision of Victorian Poetry, by E. D. H. Johnson. Queen's Quarterly (Toronto, Ontario), 61 (Summer, 1954), 268-70.

2214 _____ "A Victorian Proto-Martyr of the Arts." Review of A Hopkins Reader, edited by John Pick. Commonweal, 58 (July 3, 1953), 326-27.

2215 MacManus, Francis. Review of Further Letters of Gerard Manley Hopkins, edited by Claude Colleer Abbott. Irish Monthly, 66 (August, 1937), 508-10.

2216 _____ "Gerard Manley Hopkins, S.J. Part I.--Return of a Victorian. Part II.--The Poet who Knew too Much," Irish Monthly, 65 (May, June, 1937), 327-35, 389-99.

2217 _____ "Jesuit who Led Literary World a Fine Dance." Review of Immortal Diamond, edited by Norman Weyand, S.J. Irish Press (Dublin), (November 17, 1949).

2218 _____ "This English Jesuit had the Makings of a Rebel." Review of Poems and Prose of Gerard Manley Hopkins, edited by W. H. Gardner. (Penguin Books). Irish Press (Dublin), (October 4, 1953).

2219 McNamara, Peter L. "Gerard Manley Hopkins: A Study," Motley (Spring Hill College, Mobile, Alabama), 9 (Spring, 1958), 24-6.

2220 _____ "Motivation and Meaning in the 'Terrible Sonnets'," Renascence, 16 (Winter, 1964), 78-80, 94.

2221 McNamee, Maurice B., S.J. "Hopkins, Poet of Nature and of the Supernatural." Immortal Diamond, edited by Norman Weyand, S.J. New York: Sheed & Ward, 1949, 222-51.

2222 _____ "Mastery and Mercy in 'The Wreck of the Deutschland'," College English, 23 (January, 1962), 267-76.

2223 MacNeice, Louis. "A Comment," New Verse, 14 (April, 1935), 26-7.

2224 _____ "English Poetry Today," Listener, 40 (September 2, 1948), 346-47.

2225 _____ Review of The Note-Books and Papers of Gerard Manley Hopkins, edited by Humphry House. Criterion, 16 (July, 1937), 698-700.

2226 _____ "Poets Conditioned by their Times," London Calling, (February 10, 1949), 12.

2227 _____ "Rhythm and Rhyme." Modern Poetry: A Personal Essay. London: Oxford University Press, 1938, 114-25.

2228 MacNeil, Stella Therese. "The Poetry of Thomas Merton Considered in Relation to that of Gerard Manley Hopkins and T. S. Eliot." M.A. thesis, New York University, 1953.

2229 McQueen, William A. " 'The Windhover' and 'St. Alphonsus Rodriguez'," Victorian Newsletter, 23 (Spring, 1963), 23, 25-6.

2230 Macri, Clare Grace. "Gerard Manley Hopkins and Robert Bridges." M.A. thesis, Columbia University, 1945.

2231 MacS., J. Review of Essay on Poetry, by George O'Neill, S.J. Irish Ecclesiastical Record, (January, 1920), 83-6.

2232 Madeleva, Sister Mary, C.S.C. Chaucer's Nuns and Other Essays. New York: D. Appleton and Company, 1925, ix, 93, 96-8, 117, 125-29.

2233 _____ "The Religious Poetry of the Nineteenth Century," Catholic World, 120 (November, 1924), 212-24.

2234 _____ "What Shall I Sing?" Spirit, 14 (July, 1947), 80-6.

2235 Madge, Charles. "What is all this Juice?" New Verse, 14 (April, 1935), 17-21.

2236 Magny, Olivier de. "Gerard Manley Hopkins et le Coeur des Choses," Lettres Nouvelles (Paris), 6 (February, 1958), 248-56.

2237 Maguire, Alice Marie. "A Study of the Poetry of Gerard Manley Hopkins." M.A. thesis, Brown University, 1946.

2238 Mais, Stuart Petre Brodie. A Chronicle of English Literature. London: William Heinemann Ltd., 1936, 360-61.

2239 "The Making of a Poet." Anonymous Review of Dylan
Thomas, by Henry Treece. Times Literary Supplement,
(July 22, 1949).

2240 Malloy, Margaret Gladys. "Desolation and Delight: A
Study of Recurring Themes in the Poetry of Gerard
Manley Hopkins." M.A. thesis, University of
Manitoba, 1963.

2241 Mambrino, Jean. Review of Reliquiae, edited by Pierre
Leyris. Etudes (Paris), 296 (April, 1958), 136-37.

2242 Mandelbaum, Allen. "Of Mind and Metaphor: A Study in
Richard Crashaw and Gerard Manley Hopkins." M.A.
thesis, Columbia University, 1946.

2243 Mann, John S. "A Study in the Relation of Structure to
Thought in the Poetry of Gerard Manley Hopkins."
M.A. thesis, Columbia University, 1959.

2244 Mansfield, Margery. "Gerard Manley Hopkins." Workers
in Fire. New York: Longmans, Green, and Co., 1937,
71, 130, 147-49, 161-65.

2245 "Manuscripts of Gerard Manley Hopkins Seen, Notre Dame
College," Catholic Review (Washington, D. C.,
Baltimore), 7 (March 4, 1949), 12.

2246 Marchant, James. The Madonna: An Anthology. London:
Longmans, Green and Co., 1928, 78-82.

2247 Marcotte, Paul John. "Gerard Manley Hopkins: Mortal
Without Glitter," Inscape (University of Ottawa),
No. 1 (Spring, 1959), 4-17.

2248 _____ "A Philosophical Presentation of the Aesthetic-
Poetics of Gerard Manley Hopkins as Inferred from
Scape and Inscape, with its Significance as a new
Critique." M.A. thesis, St. John's University
(Brooklyn), 1953.

2249 Margoliouth, Herschel Maurice. Review of The Unmediated
Vision: An Interpretation of Wordsworth, Hopkins, Rilke
and Valery, by Geoffrey H. Hartman. Review of English
Studies, N.S. 7 (October, 1956), 436-37.

2250 Mariani, Paul Louis. "Hopkins' 'Felix Randall' [sic] as
Sacramental Vision," Renascence, 19 (Summer, 1967),
217-20.

2251 Maritain, Jacques. Art and Scholasticism. New York:
Scribner's Sons, 1935, 28-9.

2252 _____ "Poetic Experience," Review of Politics, 6
(October, 1944), 387-402.

2253 _____ "The Poetic Sense," Poetry, 81 (March, 1953),
369-82. [Reprinted in Creative Intuition in Art and
Poetry. The A. W. Mellon Lectures in the Fine Arts.
Bollingen Series 35. New York: Meridian Books, 1955,
191-201.]

2254 Markert, Marilyn Rose. "Gerard Manley Hopkins' Use of
the Sonnet Form." M.A. thesis, John Carroll University,
1961.

2255 Marryat, Phillip. "Gerard Manley Hopkins: Priest, Poet
and Music-Lover," Canon (Hunter's Hill, Australia),
11 (August, 1957), 6-10.

2256 Marsden, M. Review of The Letters of Gerard Manley
Hopkins to Robert Bridges and The Correspondence of
Gerard Manley Hopkins and Richard Watson Dixon,
edited by Claude Colleer Abbott. Music and Letters,
16 (April, 1935), 158-59.

2257 Marsh, Derick. "Part, Pen, Pack: A Critical Reading of
Two Poems by G. M. Hopkins," Balcony: The Sydney
Review, No. 2 (1965), 19-27.

2258 Martin, Philip Montague. "Interpretations." Anonymous
Review of Mastery and Mercy. Times Literary Supplement, (June 28, 1957), 398.

2259 _____ Mastery and Mercy: A Study of Two Religious
Poems: 'The Wreck of the Deutschland' by G. M.
Hopkins and 'Ash Wednesday' by T. S. Eliot. London:
Oxford University Press, 1957.

2260 Martz, Louis Lohr. The Poetry of Meditation. Vol. 125:
Yale Studies in English. New Haven: Yale University
Press, 1954.

2261 Marx, Carola Maxine. "Gerard Manley Hopkins, 'Spring
and Fall: To a Young Child': A Study of Poetic
Compression." M.A. thesis, Cornell University, 1964.

2262 Mason, Colin. "New Music in London," Guardian
(Manchester & London), (March 10, 1964).

2263 Masson, David I. "Sound and Sense in a Line of Poetry."
British Journal of Aesthetics, 3 (January, 1963), 70-2.

2264 _____ "Thematic Analysis of Sounds in Poetry." Essays
on the Language of Literature, edited by Seymour
Chatman and Samuel R. Levin. Boston: Houghton
Mifflin Company, 1967, 54-70. [Reprinted from
Proceedings (Literary and Historical) of the Leeds
Philosophical and Literary Society.]

2265 _____ "Vowel and Consonant Patterns in Poetry." Essays on the Language of Literature, edited by Seymour Chatman and Samuel R. Levin. Boston: Houghton Mifflin Company, 1967, 3-18. [Reprinted from Journal of Aesthetics and Art Criticism, 12 (December, 1953).]

2266 _____ "Wilfred Owen's Free Phonetic Patterns: Their Style and Function," Journal of Aesthetics and Art Criticism, 13 (March, 1955), 360-69.

2267 Matchett, William H. "Notes, Documents, and Critical Comment: An Analysis of 'The Windhover'," PMLA, 72 (March, 1957), 310-11.

2268 Mathew, David. Catholicism in England 1535-1935; Portrait of a Minority: Its Culture and Tradition. London: Longmans, Green and Co., 1937, 228-29.

2269 _____ "Old Catholics and Converts." The English Catholics 1850-1950, edited by George Andrew Beck. London: Burns Oates, 1950, 236.

2270 Mathison, John K. "The Poetic Theory of Gerard Manley Hopkins," Philological Quarterly, 26 (January, 1947), 21-35.

2271 _____ "The Poetical Relationship of Gerard Manley Hopkins, Coventry Patmore, and Francis Thompson." Ph.D., Princeton University, 1943.

2272 Matthai, A. P. "Hopkins the Jesuit," New Review (Calcutta), 13 (April, 1941), 306-17.

2273 Matthiessen, Francis Otto. American Renaissance: Art and Expression in the Age of Emerson and Whitman. New York: Oxford University Press, 1946, 440, 584-92, 600. [Pages 584-91 reprinted as "Hopkins and Whitman" in Hopkins: A Collection of Critical Essays, edited by Geoffrey H. Hartman, 144-50.]

2274 Maude, Mother Mary, CSM. "A New Collection of Gerard Manley Hopkins' Letters." Review of Further Letters of Gerard Manley Hopkins, edited by Claude Colleer Abbott. Living Church, 99 (September 7, 1938), 214.

2275 _____ "Notebooks with Sketches of Gerard Manley Hopkins." Review of The Notebooks and Papers of Gerard Manley Hopkins, edited by Humphry House. Living Church, 96 (April 17, 1937), 495-96.

2276 Mauriac, Claude. "Pierre Leyris Traduit Hopkins." Review of Reliquae, translated by Pierre Leyris. Figaro (Paris), (March 4, 1964).

2277 Mauriac, Francois. "Faith and the Writer." Catholicism in the Cross Currents of the Present, edited by Joseph Roggendorf. Tokyo: Sobunsha, 1959, 379-90. [In Japanese]

2278 _____ Memoires Interieurs, translated by Gerard Hopkins. New York: Farrar, Straus & Cudahy, Inc., 1960, 137-40.

2279 Maxwell, J. C. Review of Gerard Manley Hopkins, by Frances Noel Lees. Notes & Queries, 14 (October, 1967), 398-99.

2280 Mayhead, Robin. "Poets in Perspective." Understanding Literature. New York: Cambridge University Press, 1965, 178, 192.

2281 Maynard, Theodore. "The Artist as Hero." Review of Poems of Gerard Manley Hopkins, edited by Robert Bridges. New Witness, 13 (January 24, 1919), 259-60.

2282 _____ The Book of Modern Catholic Verse. New York: Henry Holt and Company, 1926, 161-66.

2283 _____ "The Poems of Father Hopkins," Freeman, 8 (October 24, 1923), 156-57.

2284 _____ "The Poet's Need for a Center." Return to Poetry, edited by John G. Brunini, et al. New York: Declan X. McMullen Company, 1947, 119-22. [Reprinted from address given at First Congress, Catholic Poetry Society of America, Fordham University, 1941.]

2285 _____ Preface to Poetry. New York: Century Company, 1933, 14, 116, 162, 271.

2286 _____ "The Solitary of Song," America, 20 (March 1, 1919), 533-34.

2287 _____ "When the Pie was Opened," Commonweal, 22 (August 2, 1935), 339-41.

2288 Mazza, Maria Serafina, S.C. Not for Art's Sake: The Story of 'Il Frontespizio.' New York: King's Crown Press, Columbia University, 1948, 137-41, 172-73, 211.

2289 Meagher, Edward F. Review of Poems of Gerard Manley Hopkins, edited by W. H. Gardner, 3rd ed., and Gerard Manley Hopkins, by W. H. Gardner. Commonweal, 48 (September 3, 1948), 505.

2290 M[eagher], M[argaret] C. Review of Further Letters of Gerard Manley Hopkins, edited by Claude Colleer Abbott. Catholic World, 147 (September, 1938), 758-59.

2291 _____ Review of Gerard Manley Hopkins, by the Kenyon Critics. Catholic World, 163 (May, 1946), 181-82.

2292 _____ Review of Gerard Manley Hopkins, by G. F. Lahey, S.J. and Poems of Gerard Manley Hopkins, edited by Robert Bridges. Catholic World, 132 (March, 1931), 754-56.

2293 _____ Review of Gerard Manley Hopkins, Priest and Poet, by John Pick. Catholic World, 157 (July, 1943), 439-41.

2294 _____ Review of The Letters of Gerard Manley Hopkins to Robert Bridges; The Correspondence of Gerard Manley Hopkins and Richard Watson Dixon, edited by Claude Colleer Abbott. Catholic World, 142 (October, 1935), 119-20.

2295 _____ Review of The Poetry of Gerard Manley Hopkins; a Survey and Commentary, by Elsie Elizabeth Phare. Catholic World, 139 (July, 1934), 499.

2296 Measure: The Journal of the Gerard Manley Hopkins Poetry Society (Georgetown University, Washington, D. C.). Vol. 1--2, No. 1. (Christmas, 1932--Christmas, 1933). [All published]

2297 Meath, Gerard, O.P. "Bridges and Hopkins." Review of Robert Bridges and Gerard Hopkins, 1863-1889. A Literary Friendship, by Jean-Georges Ritz. Tablet (London), 204 (July 30, 1960), 721-22.

2298 _____ "Elders and Betters?" Review of The Oxford Book of Nineteenth-Century English Verse. Tablet (London), (July 4, 1964).

2299 _____ "Gerard Manley Hopkins." Review of The Journals and Papers of Gerard Manley Hopkins, edited by Humphry House and The Sermons and Devotional Writings of Gerard Manley Hopkins, edited by Christopher Devlin, S.J. Tablet (London), 213 (February 14, 1959), 154-55.

2300 _____ "Poetry and Religion." Review of Studies in Structure, by Robert J. Andreach. Tablet (London), (September 25, 1965).

2301 _____ Review of Selected Poems of Gerard Manley Hopkins, edited by James Reeves and A Hopkins Reader, edited by John Pick. Blackfriars, 34 (September, 1953), 413-16.

2302 "A Medley of Verse," Spectator, 122 (May 10, 1919), 598-99.

2303 Meehan, Francis Joseph Gallagher. English Literature: A Survey and a Commentary, by "Brother Leo." Boston: Ginn and Company, 1928, 483.

2304 Megroz, Rodolphe Louis. Modern English Poetry 1882-1932. London: Ivor Nicholson & Watson, Ltd., 1933.

2305 Melchiori, Giorgio. "Due Manieristi: Henry James e G.
M. Hopkins," Spettatore Italiano (Rome), 6 (January,
1953), 20-7.

2306 _____ "Poesia Inglese Contemporanea," Spettatore
Italiano (Rome), (March, 1955), 101-07.

2307 _____ Poeti Cattolici in Inghilterra," Fiera Letteraria
(Rome), 3 (March 28, 1948), 4.

2308 _____ Review of The Poetry of Gerard Manley Hopkins and
T. S. Eliot in the Light of the Donne Tradition, by D.
Morris. English Studies (Amsterdam), 41 (1960),
211-13.

2309 _____ "Stylistic View of Modern Writing." Anonymous
Review of The Tightrope Walkers. Times Literary
Supplement, (May 4, 1956), 270.

2310 _____ The Tightrope Walkers. London: Routledge &
Kegan Paul, 1956, 4, 12-33, 192, 222-29, 235, 237,
241.

2311 _____ Anonymous Review of The Tightrope Walkers.
Month, N.S. 15 (May, 1956), 316-17.

2312 _____ "Two Mannerists: James and Hopkins." The
Tightrope Walkers. London: Routledge & Kegan Paul,
1956. [Translation of "Due Manieristi: Henry James e
G. M. Hopkins," Spettatore Italiano, January, 1953,
20-7. Reprinted in Hopkins: A Collection of Critical
Essays, edited by Geoffrey H. Hartman, 131-43.]

2313 Melchner, Sister Mary Roberta, S.S.N.D. "Hopkins and
the Common Man." M.A. thesis, Boston College, 1942.

2314 Mellers, Wilfrid. "Egon Wellesz: An 80th Birthday
Tribute," Musical Times (London), (October, 1965),
766-68.

2315 Mellown, Elgin W. "Gerard Manley Hopkins and his
Public, 1889-1918," Modern Philology, 57 (November,
1959), 94-9.

2316 _____ "Hopkins, Hall Caine, and D. G. Rossetti," Notes
& Queries, N.S. 6 (March, 1959), 109-10.

2317 _____ "The Reception of Gerard Manley Hopkins' 'Poems,'
1918-30," Modern Philology, 63 (August, 1965), 38-51.

2318 Melody, Sister M. Winifred, O.S.U. "Gerard Manley
Hopkins, Critic of English Poetry." M.A. thesis,
University of Notre Dame, 1941.

2319 Mendel, Sydney. Review of The Disappearance of God:
Five Nineteenth-Century Writers, by J. Hillis Miller.
Dalhousie Review, 44 (1964-1965), 107-09.

2320 Mercer, W. C. "G. M. Hopkins and Richard Jefferies,"
Notes & Queries, 197 (May 10, 1952), 217.

2321 Merchant, W. Moelwyn. "The Vision of G. M. Hopkins."
Review of The Shaping Vision of Gerard Manley Hopkins,
by Alan Heuser. Church Quarterly Review, 161 (1960),
124-25.

2322 Merton, Thomas. The Seven Storey Mountain. New York:
Harcourt, Brace and Company, 1948, 100, 175, 211,
215-16, 235.

2323 _____ "Todo y Nada: Writing and Contemplation."
Unpublished material on 'Writing and Contemplation'
from the original manuscript of Thomas Merton's Seven
Storey Mountain. Introduction by Sister M. Therese,
S.D.S. Renascence, 2 (Spring, 1950), 87-101.

2324 Mesterton, Erik and J. C. A. Rathmell. (Correspondence),
London Magazine, 6 (December, 1959), 60.

2325 Methuen, Algernon, comp. An Anthology of Modern Verse.
3rd ed. London: Methuen & Co. Ltd., 1921.

2326 Meuth, Georgeanna S. "Gerard Manley Hopkins: Creator
and Created." M.A. thesis, Columbia University,
1952.

2327 Meyer, Gerard Previn. "For Gerard Manley Hopkins, S.J."
(Poem), Commonweal, 27 (January 14, 1938), 318.

2328 Meyerstein, Edward Harry William. "Note on 'The Loss of
the Eurydice' " (Letter to the Editor), Times Literary
Supplement, (November 11, 1949), 733.

2329 Micklewright, F. H. Amphlett. "G. M. Hopkins and
Provost Fortescue," Notes & Queries, 197 (April 12,
1952), 169-72.

2330 _____ "G. M. Hopkins and Provost Fortescue," Notes &
Queries, 197 (August 16, 1952), 365-66.

2331 _____ "Hopkins and Fortescue: A Correction," Notes &
Queries, 197 (April 12, 1952), 174.

2332 Miles, Alfred H., ed. The Poets and the Poetry of the
Century. 10 vols. London: Hutchinson & Co., 1898.

2333 Miles, Josephine. "Eras in English Poetry." Essays on
the Language of Literature, edited by Seymour Chatman
and Samuel R. Levin. Boston: Houghton Mifflin
Company, 1967, 175-96. [Reprinted from PMLA, 70
(September, 1955, Part I), 853-75.]

2334 _____ "Hopkins as Poet." Review of Gerard Manley
Hopkins, 1844-1889, by W. H. Gardner. Yale Review,
39 (December, 1950), 368-70.

2335 _____ "Hopkins: The Sweet and Lovely Language."
Eras and Modes in English Poetry. Berkeley: University
of California Press, 1964, 164-77. [Reprinted from
Kenyon Review, Summer, 1944, 355-68. Also in Gerard
Manley Hopkins, by the Kenyon Critics, 58-73.]
2336 Millay, Edna St. Vincent. Letters of Edna St. Vincent
Millay, edited by Allan Ross MacDougall. New York:
Harper and Brothers, 1952, 314, 332, 334-35, 350.
2337 Miller, A. J., S.J. Review of Selections from the Note-
Books of Gerard Manley Hopkins, edited by T. Weiss.
Catholic Library World, 17 (January, 1946), 128.
2338 Miller, Betty. Review of Further Letters of Gerard Manley
Hopkins, edited by Claude Colleer Abbott. 2nd ed.
Twentieth Century, 161 (March, 1957), 306-08.
2339 Miller, Bruce E. "On 'The Windhover'," Victorian Poetry,
2 (Spring, 1964), 115-19.
2340 Miller, Joseph Hillis. "The Creation of the Self in Gerard
Manley Hopkins," ELH, 22 (December, 1955), 293-319.
2341 _____ The Disappearance of God: Five Nineteenth-Century
Writers. Cambridge, Massachusetts: Belknap Press of
Harvard University Press, 1963, 270-359.
2342 _____ Anonymous Review of The Disappearance of God.
Virginia Quarterly Review, 40 (Winter, 1964), xvii.
2343 _____ " 'Orion' in 'The Wreck of the Deutschland',"
Modern Language Notes, 76 (June, 1961), 509-14.
2344 _____ Poets of Reality: Six Twentieth-Century Writers.
Cambridge, Massachusetts: Belknap Press of Harvard
University Press, 1965, 2, 138, 267, 283, 297.
2345 _____ "Surveying the Inscape." Anonymous Review of
The Disappearance of God: Five Nineteenth-Century
Writers. Times Literary Supplement, (February 27,
1964), 168.
2346 _____ "The Theme of the Disappearance of God in
Victorian Poetry," Victorian Studies, 6 (March, 1962),
207-27.
2347 _____ "The Univocal Chiming." Hopkins: A Collection of
Critical Essays, edited by Geoffrey H. Hartman.
Englewood Cliffs, New Jersey: Prentice-Hall, Inc.,
1966, 89-116. [Reprinted from The Disappearance of
God, 276-317.]
2348 Miller, Nancy Lou. "Hopkins and Science," Spheres
(Mount St. Agnes College, Baltimore, Maryland),
(Spring, 1948), 17-8.
2349 Millspaugh, Clarence Arthur. "To Gerard Manley Hopkins"
(Poem), Commonweal, 26 (November 13, 1936), 68.

2350 Milward, Peter, S.J. "The Formation of Hopkins as a
     Modern Poet," Sophia (Sophia University, Tokyo),
     4 (Autumn, 1955), 307-26, 388. [In Japanese]
2351 _____ "Shakespeare in Japanese Translation." Studies in
     Japanese Culture, edited by Joseph Roggendorf. Tokyo:
     Sophia University, 1963, 187-207.
2352 _____ "The Underthought of Shakespeare in Hopkins,"
     Studies in English Literature (Tokyo), 39 (1963), 1-9.
2353 Mims, Edwin. "Gerard Manley Hopkins: Jesuit Scholar."
     The Christ of the Poets. New York: Abingdon-Cokesbury
     Press, 1948, 204-11, 213, 232.
2354 Minerof, Arthur F. "Recent Publications: A Selected List.
     March 1966--August 1966," Victorian Newsletter, 30
     (Fall, 1966), 28-32.
2355 _____ "Recent Publications: A Selected List. September
     1966--February 1967," Victorian Newsletter, 31
     (Spring, 1967), 59-64.
2356 _____ "Recent Publications: A Selected List. March
     1967--August 1967," Victorian Newsletter, 32 (Fall,
     1967), 28-32.
2357 Minten, Sister Grace Ellen, O.P. "The Literary Reputation
     of Gerard Manley Hopkins." M.A. thesis, De Paul
     University, 1946.
2358 Mitchell, Donald. "Modernist Music in Historic Hall,"
     Daily Telegraph (London), (February 1, 1960).
2359 Mizener, Arthur. "Victorian Hopkins," Kenyon Review, 6
     (Autumn, 1944), 590-606. [Reprinted in Gerard Manley
     Hopkins, by the Kenyon Critics, 95-112.]
2360 Mlodzik, Sister Mary Nazaria, O.P. "A Study of the
     Parallelism and Evolution in the Imagery of Gerard
     Manley Hopkins." M.A. thesis, University of Detroit,
     1951.
2361 Moakler, Kenneth. "The Dark Night of the Self: The
     Unifying Vision in Gerard Manley Hopkins." M.A.
     thesis, Western Illinois University, 1966.
2362 Molloy, Eugene Joseph. "The True Humanism of Gerard
     Manley Hopkins." M.A. thesis, St. John's University,
     1946.
2363 Moloney, Michael F. Review of A Hopkins Reader, edited
     by John Pick. America, 89 (September 5, 1953), 555-56.
2364 Monroe, Harriet and Alice Corbin Henderson. "Introduction
     to the Present Edition." The New Poetry: An Anthology
     of Twentieth Century Verse in English. new and enl. ed.
     New York: Macmillan Co., 1932, xlv-xlviii.

2365 Montag, George E. "Hopkins' 'God's Grandeur' and 'The Ooze of Oil Crushed'," <u>Victorian Poetry</u>, 1 (November, 1963), 302-03.

2366 _____ " 'The Windhover': Crucifixion and Redemption," <u>Victorian Poetry</u>, 3 (Spring, 1965), 109-18.

2367 Moody, William Vaughn and Robert Lovett. <u>A History of English Literature</u>. rev. ed. New York: Charles Scribner's Sons, 1935, 464-66.

2368 Moon, Nelson Ferdinand. "Gerard Manley Hopkins' Use of Imagery." M.A. thesis, University of Oklahoma, 1948.

2369 Mooney, Margaret Elizabeth. "Gerard Manley Hopkins and Vincent Van Gogh." M.A. thesis, Columbia University, 1947.

2370 Mooney, Stephen. "Hopkins and Counterpoint," <u>Victorian Newsletter</u>, 18 (Fall, 1960), 21-2.

2371 Moore, Carlisle. Review of <u>The Shaping Vision of Gerard Manley Hopkins</u>, by Alan Heuser. <u>Comparative Literature</u>, 12 (Spring, 1960), 172-75.

2372 Moore, Dom Sebastian. "Gerard Manley Hopkins," <u>Downside Review</u>, 62 (October, 1944), 184-95.

2373 Moore, Rosalie (Brown). "Stand Before Him as Would (For G. M. Hopkins)" (Poem). <u>The Grasshopper's Man and Other Poems</u>. Yale Series of Younger Poets, No. 47. New Haven: Yale University Press; London: Geoffrey Cumberlege, Oxford University Press, 1949, 63-4.

2374 _____ "Two American Poets." Anonymous Review of <u>The Grasshopper's Man</u>, by Rosalie Moore and <u>The Lost Son</u>, by Theodore Roethke. <u>Times Literary Supplement</u>, (February 17, 1950), 107.

2375 _____ "The Weather." Review of <u>Further Letters of Gerard Manley Hopkins</u>, edited by Claude Colleer Abbott. 2nd ed. <u>Poetry</u>, 92 (May, 1958), 113-15.

2376 Moore, Thomas Sturge. "Style or Beauty in Literature," <u>Criterion</u>, 9 (July, 1930), 591-603.

2377 Moran, Eugene A. "Gerard Manley Hopkins" (Letter to the Editor), <u>Commonweal</u>, 12 (October 8, 1930), 582.

2378 Morati, Luciano, S.J. "Spiritualita e Ispirazione nella Poesia di Gerard Manley Hopkins," <u>Letture</u> (Milan), 15 (1960), 563-70. [Also in <u>Profili di Scrittori</u> (<u>Inchieste Teologiche</u>) (Milan), 1961, 127-36.]

2379 Morgan, Diane. "Margaret" (for high voice and piano),
words by Gerard Manley Hopkins. Toronto: BMI
Canada Limited; New York: Associated Music
Publishers, Inc., [1957]. [Musical Setting]
2380 Morgan, Edwin. "A Hopkins Phrase," Times Literary
Supplement, (May 27, 1949), 347.
2381 Morgan, William. "A Religious Poet." Review of Gerard
Manley Hopkins, by W. A. M. Peters. New English
Review (London), 16 (June, 1948), 570-72.
2382 Morison, W. "The Affinity Between Poetry and Religion,"
Poetry Review, 10 (1919), 57-68.
2383 Morley, Christopher. " 'The Wreck of the Deutschland', "
Saturday Review, 14 (August 15, 1936), 12.
2384 Morris, David John. The Poetry of Gerard Manley Hopkins
and T. S. Eliot in the Light of the Donne Tradition: A
Comparative Study. Swiss Studies in English, No. 33.
Bern: A. Francke, 1953. [Inaugural Dissertation,
Bern University, 1951.]
2385 Morrison, James Dalton, ed. Masterpieces of Religious
Verse. New York: Harper & Brothers, 1948, 121.
2386 Morrison, Theodore. "The Man of the Month: Gerard
Manley Hopkins." Review of The Letters of Gerard
Manley Hopkins to Robert Bridges; The Correspondence
of Gerard Manley Hopkins and Richard Watson Dixon,
edited by Claude Colleer Abbott. Atlantic, 156
(September, 1935), 6, 8.
2387 Morse, Samuel French. "The Image of a Poet in his Own
Words." Review of The Journals and Papers of Gerard
Manley Hopkins, edited by Humphry House and The
Sermons and Devotional Writings of Gerard Hopkins,
edited by Christopher Devlin, S.J. New York Times
Book Review, (April 5, 1959), 4-5.
2388 Mortimer, Raymond. "The Emergence of a Great Poet."
Review of Robert Bridges and Gerard Hopkins, 1863-
1889: A Literary Friendship. Sunday Times (London),
(May 15, 1960).
2389 Moss, Ernest. Review of The Note-Books and Papers of
Gerard Manley Hopkins, edited by Humphry House.
Dublin Review, 201 (July, 1937), 165-67.
2390 Mowrer, Deane. Review of Gerard Manley Hopkins, by
the Kenyon Critics and Selections from the Note-Books
of Gerard Manley Hopkins, edited by T. Weiss. New
Mexico Quarterly Review, 17 (Autumn, 1947), 383-85.
2391 Muhlberger, Josef. "Der Englische Lyriker Hopkins,"
Berliner Anzeigenblatt, (August 18, 1949).

2392 Muir, Edwin. "Hopkins's Note-Books." Review of The Note-Books and Papers of Gerard Manley Hopkins, edited by Humphry House. London Mercury, 35 (March, 1937), 511-12.

2393 _____ "Modern Criticism." Review of Gerard Manley Hopkins: A Study of Poetic Idiosyncrasy in Relation to Poetic Tradition, by W. H. Gardner. Vol. 2. Observer (London), (July 10, 1949).

2394 _____ The Present Age from 1914. Vol. 5: Introductions to English Literature, edited by Bonamy Dobree. New York: Robert McBride and Company, 1940, 44, 86-93, 119, 191.

2395 Mulgan, John and D. M. Davis. An Introduction to English Literature. Oxford: Clarendon Press, 1947, 139.

2396 Mullaney, Stephen William. "Religious Elements in Hopkins' Poetry." M.A. thesis, University of Iowa, 1950.

2397 Muller-Schwefe, Gerhard. "G. M. Hopkins--der Victorianer." Festschrift zum 75. Geburtstag von Theodor Spira, edited by Helmut Viebrock and Willi Erzgraber. Heidelberg: Carl Winter, 1961, 233-39.

2398 _____ "Gerard Manley Hopkins' 'Spelt from Sibyl's Leaves'." Die Moderne Englische Lyrik: Interpreta-tionen, edited by Horst Oppel. Berlin: Erich Schmidt, 1967, 39-48.

2399 Munoz Rojas, Jose A. "En el Centenario de Gerard Manley Hopkins, S.J. (1844-1889)," Razon y Fe (Madrid), 132 (November, 1945), 569-74.

2400 _____ "Gerard Manley Hopkins," Cruz y Raja (Madrid), No. 34 (January, 1936), 107-18.

2401 Murphy, Gwendolen, ed. The Modern Poet: An Anthology. London: Sidgwick & Jackson, Ltd., 1938.

2402 _____, ed. The Modern Poet: An Anthology. London: Sidgwick & Jackson, Ltd., 1947.

2403 [Murphy], L. D. "G. M. Hopkins." Review of Gerard Manley Hopkins: The Man and the Poet, by K. R. Srinivasa Iyengar. Sunday Hindu (Madras), (August 1, 1948), 10.

2404 _____ "Inscape." Review of Gerard Manley Hopkins: A Critical Essay Towards the Understanding of his Poetry, by W. A. M. Peters, S.J. Sunday Hindu (Madras), (June 27, 1948).

2405 Murphy, Sister Miriam Joseph. "Gerard Manley Hopkins, Critic of his Contemporaries in the Nineteenth Century." M.A. thesis, Duquesne University, 1943.

2406 Murray, John, S.J. "Gerard Manley Hopkins" (Editorial Comment), Month, 172 (April, 1939), 293-94.

2407 Murray, W. H. "Words from on High." Review of The Climber's Fireside Book, compiled by Wilfred Noyce and Four Against Everest, by Woodrow Wilson Sayre. Glasgow Herald, (November 7, 1964).

2408 Murray, Rosalind. The Forsaken Fountain. New York: Longmans, Green and Co., 1948, 75.

2409 Murry, John Middleton. "Gerard Manley Hopkins." Aspects of Literature. 2nd ed. London: W. Collins Sons & Co. Ltd., 1921, 52-61.

2410 _____ "Gerard Manley Hopkins." Review of Poems of Gerard Manley Hopkins, edited by Robert Bridges. Athenaeum, No. 4649 (June 6, 1919), 425-26.

2411 _____ The Problem of Style. London: Oxford University Press, 1967.

2412 " 'Music in Our Time' Festival Pursues Sober Course," Times (London), (October 17, 1963).

2413 Musser, Benjamin Francis. "The Newness of New Poetry," America, 44 (March 21, 1931), 579-80.

2414 Myers, John A., Jr. "Intimations of Mortality: An Analysis of Hopkins' 'Spring and Fall'," English Journal, 51 (November, 1962), 585-87.

2415 N. C. S. Review of The Note-Books and Papers of Gerard Manley Hopkins, edited by Humphry House. Oxford Magazine, 56 (March 10, 1938), 522-23.

2416 N. K. D. Review of Further Letters of Gerard Manley Hopkins, edited by Claude Colleer Abbott. San Francisco Chronicle "This World" Supplement, (February 24, 1957), 22.

2417 Napier, Murray. "A Study of the Sermons of Gerard Manley Hopkins." M.A. thesis, McGill University, 1961.

2418 Nassar, Eugene. "Hopkins, 'Figura,' and Grace: God's Better Beauty," Renascence, 17 (Spring, 1965), 128-30, 136.

2419 Needham, Joseph. "Chinese Writing." Review of The Six Scripts, or: The Principles of Chinese Writing, by Tai T'ung, translated by Lionel Charles Hopkins. Cambridge Review, (November 27, 1954).

2420 Neenan, Sister Mary Pius. "Some Evidences of Mysticism in English Poetry of the Nineteenth Century." Ph.D., Catholic University of America, 1916.

2421 Nelson, Elizabeth. Review of <u>Poetry and Prayer</u>, by
William T. Noon, S.J. <u>Library Journal</u>, 92 (June 1,
1967), 2160.
2422 Nelson, Norman Kent. "Gerard Manley Hopkins: Analysis
and Interpretation of Three Representative Sonnets."
M.A. thesis, Duke University, 1949. ["The Starlight
Night," "Spelt from Sibyl's Leaves," and "The
Windhover."]
2423 <u>New Verse</u>, No. 14 (April, 1935), Gerard Manley Hopkins
issue, 1-30.
2424 Nicholl, Donald. "A Ruthless Scrutiny of the Spirit."
Review of <u>The Journals and Papers of Gerard Manley
Hopkins</u>, edited by Humphry House and <u>The Sermons
and Devotional Writings of Gerard Manley Hopkins</u>,
edited by Christopher Devlin, S.J. <u>Cambridge Review</u>,
80 (March 7, 1959), 405, 407, 409.
2425 Nicholson, Daniel Howard Sinclair and A. H. E. Lee, eds.
<u>The Oxford Book of English Mystical Verse</u>. Oxford:
Clarendon Press, 1945, 353-59.
2426 Nicholson, Norman. Review of <u>Gerard Manley Hopkins:
A Study of Poetic Idiosyncrasy in Relation to Poetic
Tradition</u>, by W. H. Gardner. Vol. 2. <u>Fortnightly
Review</u>, N.S. 166 (July, 1949), 65-6.
2427 Nicol, B. De Bear. "A Hopkins Phrase" (Letter to the
Editor), <u>Times Literary Supplement</u>, (May 13, 1949),
313.
2428 Nielsen, Anne E. (Sister Ancilla of the Immaculate, D.W.)
"The Scotist Element in Hopkins." M.A. thesis,
Saint John's University, 1964.
2429 Nims, John Frederick. "Eleven Essays on Poetry of
Gerard Manley Hopkins." Review of <u>Immortal Diamond</u>,
edited by Norman Weyand, S.J. <u>Chicago Sunday
Tribune</u>, (May 29, 1949), part 4, page 6.
2430 Nist, John. "Gerard Manley Hopkins and Textural
Intensity: A Linguistic Analysis," <u>College English</u>, 22
(April, 1961), 497-500. [Adapted from a lecture
delivered to the Associacao de Cultura Brasil-Estados
Unidos in Ribeirao Preto on March 9, 1959.]
2431 _____ Review of <u>Hopkins: A Collection of Critical Essays</u>,
edited by Geoffrey H. Hartman. <u>Western Humanities
Review</u>, 21 (Winter, 1967), 72-3.
2432 _____ "Sound and Sense: Some Structures of Poetry,"
<u>College English</u>, 23 (January, 1962), 291-95.

2433 Noel, Sister Mary, S.C. "Gathering to a Greatness: A Study of 'God's Grandeur'," English Journal, 53 (April, 1964), 285-87.

2434 Nolan, Gerald L. "The 'Windhover' " (Letter to the Editor), Times Literary Supplement, (June 24, 1955), 349.

2435 _____ "The 'Windhover' " (Letter to the Editor), Times Literary Supplement, (August 5, 1955), 445.

2436 Noon, William T., S.J. "The Art Principles of Gerard Manley Hopkins." M.A. thesis, Loyola University (Chicago), 1943.

2437 _____ "Hopkins: Christian Humanist," America, 74 (October 20, 1945), 73-5.

2438 _____ Poetry and Prayer. New Brunswick, New Jersey: Rutgers University Press, 1967.

2439 _____ "The Three Languages of Poetry." Immortal Diamond, edited by Norman Weyand, S.J. New York: Sheed & Ward, 1949, 252-74.

2440 Noonan, James Joseph. "Evidences of the Supernatural in the Poetry of Gerard Manley Hopkins, S.J." M.A. thesis, Boston College, 1937.

2441 Norris, Carolyn Brimley. " 'Fused Images' in the Sermons of Gerard Manley Hopkins," Tennessee Studies in Literature, 7 (1962), 127-33.

2442 _____ "Gerard Manley Hopkins in his Sermons and Poetry," Notes & Queries, N.S. 10 (January, 1963), 27.

2443 _____ "Rhetoric and Poetic Language in the Sermons of Gerard Manley Hopkins." M.A. thesis, University of Tennessee, 1961.

2444 N[orth], J[essica] N. "Quality in Madness," Poetry, 34 (August, 1929), 270-73.

2445 Northup, Eileen. "Hopkins as a Student of Pater." M.A. thesis, University of Rhode Island, 1958.

2446 Novelli, Gino. "Discorso su Hopkins," Giornale di Sicilia (Palermo), (December 10, 1958).

2447 Nowell-Smith, Simon. "Bridges, Hopkins and Dr. Daniel," Times Literary Supplement, (December 13, 1957), 764

2448 _____ "Bridges's Debt to Hopkins" (Letter to the Editor), Times Literary Supplement, (May 12, 1961), 293.

2449 _____ "Housman Inscriptions" (Letter to the Editor), Times Literary Supplement, (November 6, 1959), 643.

2450 Nowottny, Winifred. The Language Poets Use. Oxford: Athlone Press, 1962, 50, 115-16, 210.

2451 Noyes, Alfred. The Golden Book of Catholic Poetry. New York: J. B. Lippincott Company, 1946, 226-29.

2452 Nye, Robert. "Essayists Anonymous." Review of The Concise Encyclopaedia of Modern World Literature, edited by Geoffrey Grigson. Tribune (London), (June 14, 1963).

2453 _____ "God Among the Poets: The Old Misalliance," Scotsman (Edinburgh), (May 27, 1967).

2454 _____ "Parnassian Quartets," Western Mail (Cardiff), (January 16, 1965).

2455 _____ "Poet who brought Voice back to Poetry," Scotsman (Edinburgh), (April 29, 1963).

2456 _____ "Two Strides Back from Lit to Life." Review of Studies in Structure: The Stages of the Spiritual Life in Four Modern Authors, by Robert J. Andreach. Scotsman (Edinburgh), (June 19, 1965).

2457 "Obituary: Gerard Manley Hopkins," Cholmeleian: or, Highgate School Magazine, 16 (October, 1889), 179.

2458 O'Brien, A. P. "Structure Complex of Hopkins's Words," Indian Journal of English Studies (Calcutta), 1 (1960), 48-56.

2459 O'Brien, Justin. Review of Gerard Manley Hopkins, by G. F. Lahey, S.J. Bookman, 71 (July, 1930), 447.

2460 _____ Review of The Poems of Gerard Manley Hopkins, edited by Robert Bridges. Bookman, 73 (April, 1931), 206-08.

2461 O'Brien, Kate and W. J. Turner. The Romance of English Literature (Britain in Pictures). New York: Hastings House, 1944, 94-5.

2462 O'Brien, Robert David, S.J. "The Critical Mind of Gerard Manley Hopkins." M.A. thesis, Boston College, 1942.

2463 _____ Review of Gerard Manley Hopkins, by Eleanor Ruggles. Boston Globe, (August 16, 1944), 15.

2464 Ochshorn, Myron Gustav. "Hopkins the Critic: The Literary Judgment and Taste of Gerard Manley Hopkins, with an Appendix on his Verse Theory." Ph.D., University of New Mexico, 1963.

2465 _____ "Hopkins the Critic," Yale Review, 54 (Spring, 1965), 346-67.

2466 O'Connor, Sister M. Elizabeth Therese, R.S.M. "Gerard Manley Hopkins' 'The Wreck of the Deutschland': A Plea for Structural Analysis." M.A. thesis, University of Scranton, 1965.

2467 O'Connor, William Van. Sense and Sensibility in Modern Poetry. Chicago: University of Chicago Press, 1948.

2468 O'Dea, Richard J. " 'The Loss of the Eurydice': A Possible Key to the Reading of Hopkins," Victorian Poetry, 4 (Autumn, 1966), 291-93.

2469 O'Donnell, Margaret J. Feet on the Ground Being an Approach to Modern Verse. London: Blackie & Son Limited, 1952.

2470 Ogden, Charles Kay. (Editorial), Psyche (Cambridge), 15 (1935), 5-18.

2471 O'Gorman, Ned. "The Poet Revealed to his Friends." Review of The Correspondence of Gerard Manley Hopkins and R. W. Dixon; The Letters of Gerard Manley Hopkins to Robert Bridges, edited by Claude Colleer Abbott. Commonweal, 62 (July 22, 1955), 403-04.

2472 "Old Alumni," Stonyhurst Magazine, 23 (March, 1936), 394.

2473 Oldfield, Sybil. Review of The Disappearance of God: Five Nineteenth-Century Writers, by J. Hillis Miller. Victorian Studies, 8 (December, 1964), 195-96.

2474 Olivero, Federico. "Gerard Hopkins." Correnti Mistiche nella Letteratura Inglese Moderna. Torino: Fratelli Bocca, 1932, 10, 16, 73-100.

2475 Olney, James Leslie. "George Herbert and Gerard Manley Hopkins: A Comparative Study in Two Religious Poets." Ph.D., Columbia University, 1963.

2476 O'London, John. "John O'London's," Time and Tide (London), 45 (April 2-8, 1964), 16.

2477 Olson, Signe. "Meaning and Obscurity--Gerard Manley Hopkins," Discourse: A Review of the Liberal Arts, 7 (Spring, 1964), 188-200.

2478 Omond, Thomas Stewart. "Postscript." English Metrists. Oxford: Clarendon Press, 1921, 263.

2479 O'Neill, George, S.J. Essays on Poetry. Dublin: Talbot Press Ltd.; London: T. Fisher Unwin Ltd., 1919, 117-38.

2480 _____ "Poetry." Review of Poems of Gerard Manley Hopkins, edited by Robert Bridges. Studies, 8 (June, 1919), 331-35.

2481 Onesta, P. A. "The Self in Hopkins," English Studies in Africa, 4 (September, 1961), 174-81.

2482 Ong, Walter J., S.J. "Evolution, Myth, and Poetic Vision," Comparative Literature Studies, 3 (1966), 1-20. [Reprinted in In the Human Grain: Further Explorations of Contemporary Culture. New York: Macmillan Co., 1967, 99-126.]

2483 _____ "Historical Backgrounds of Sprung Rhythm in Modern English Verse: A Preliminary Survey." M.A. thesis, St. Louis University, 1941.

2484 _____ "Hopkins: Not for Burning" (Letter to the Editor), College English, 23 (October, 1961), 60.

2485 _____ "Hopkins' Sprung Rhythm and the Life of English Poetry." Immortal Diamond, edited by Norman Weyand, S.J. New York: Sheed & Ward, 1949, 93-174.

2486 _____ Review of The Journals and Papers of Gerard Manley Hopkins, edited by Humphry House; The Sermons and Devotional Writings of Gerard Manley Hopkins, edited by Christopher Devlin, S.J. and The Shaping Vision of Gerard Manley Hopkins, by Alan Heuser. Victorian Studies, 3 (March, 1959), 305-08.

2487 _____ The Presence of the Word. New Haven: Yale University Press, 1967, 170-71.

2488 _____ "Sprung Rhythm and English Tradition." Hopkins: A Collection of Critical Essays, edited by Geoffrey Hartman. Englewood Cliffs, New Jersey: Prentice-Hall, Inc., 1966, 151-59. [Reprinted from "Hopkins' Sprung Rhythm and the Life of English Poetry." Immortal Diamond, edited by Norman Weyand, S.J., 159-68, 170-72.]

2489 Oras, Ants. "Spenser and Milton: Some Parallels and Contrasts in the Handling of Sound." Essays on the Language of Literature, edited by Seymour Chatman and Samuel R. Levin. Boston: Houghton Mifflin Company, 1967, 19-32. [Reprinted from Sound and Poetry, English Institute Essays 1956. New York: Columbia University Press, 1957, 109-33.]

2490 Orr, Paul Anthony. "The Artistic Principles of Gerard Manley Hopkins." M.A. thesis, McGill University, 1949.

2491 _____ "The Artistic Principles of Gerard Manley Hopkins." Ph.D., University of Notre Dame, 1964.

2492 Orwell, George. "Poet and Priest." Review of Gerard Manley Hopkins, by W. H. Gardner. Observer (London), (November 12, 1944), 3.

2493 O'Shannon, Cathal. "Three Paradoxes of the Irish Revival," Dublin Evening Press, (July 6, 1956).

2494 Owen, B. Evan. "Dylan's Favourites." Review of The Colour of Saying, edited by Ralph Maud and Aneirin Talfan Davies. Teacher (London), (February 7, 1964).

2495 _____ "A Gallery of Mixed Greats." Review of English Literature: A Portrait Gallery, by Oliver Warner. Teacher (London), (March 19, 1965).

2496 _____ "Gerard Manley Hopkins," Fortnightly, 174 (July, 1950), 38-42.

2497 _____ "In Defence of Hopkins," British Weekly (London), (February 3, 1949), 4.

2498 Oxford University. Alumni Oxonienses: The Members of the University of Oxford, 1715-1886: Their Parentage, Birthplace, and Year of Birth, with a Record of their Degrees. Being the Matriculation Register of the University, edited by Joseph Foster. 4 vols. Oxford: Parker and Co., 1888. [Hopkins listed in Vol. 2, 688.]

2499 _____ The Historical Register of the University of Oxford being a Supplement to the Oxford University Calendar with an Alphabetical Record of the University Honours and Distinctions Completed to the end of Trinity Term 1900. Oxford: Clarendon Press, 1900.

2500 Pace, George B. "On the Octave Rhymes of 'The Windhover'," English Language Notes, 2 (June, 1965), 285-86.

2501 "The Pack of Autolycus," Ethos (Emmanuel College, Boston), 12 (November, 1939), 217-21.

2502 Page, Frederick G. "Father Gerard Hopkins. I.--His Poetry." Review of Poems of Gerard Manley Hopkins, edited by Robert Bridges. Dublin Review, 167 (July, 1920), 40-5.

2503 Palgrave, Francis Turner, comp. The Golden Treasury of the Best Songs and Lyrical Poems in the English Language. London: Collins, 1954.

2504 _____, comp. The Golden Treasury of the Best Songs and Lyrical Poems in the English Language. rev. and enl. New York: New American Library, 1964.

2505 Palmer, Herbert. "William Wordsworth and other Lake Poets," Methodist Recorder, (April 20, 1950), 9.

2506 Panhuysen, Jos. "De Poezie van Gerard Manley Hopkins," Boekenschouw (Amsterdam), 32 (November, 1938), 313-18.

2507 Park, B. A. Review of The Journals and Papers of Gerard Manley Hopkins, edited by Humphry House. Books Abroad, 33 (Autumn, 1959), 461.

2508 _____ Review of The Shaping Vision of Gerard Manley Hopkins, by Alan Heuser. Books Abroad, 33 (Summer, 1959), 351.

2509 Parker, Dorothy Elizabeth Hagman. "Gerard Manley
Hopkins and the Critics." Ph.D., University of Texas,
1961.

2510 Parker, Mary. "Gerard Manley Hopkins," Mount Mary
Quarterly (Mount Mary College, Milwaukee, Wisconsin),
19 (January, 1943), 21-34.

2511 Parrott, Thomas M. and Willard Thorp. "Gerard Manley
Hopkins." Poetry of the Transition 1850-1914. New
York: Oxford University Press, 1936, 300-09.

2512 Parsons, Ian Macnaghten, ed. The Progress of Poetry: An
Anthology of Verse from Hardy to the Present Day.
London: Chatto and Windus, 1937, xiv-xvi, xxxiii,
16-24.

2513 "Passionate Science" (Editorial), Times Literary Supplement, (March 18, 1955), 165.

2514 Patmore, Derek. "Three Poets Discuss New Verse Forms:
The Correspondence of Gerard Manley Hopkins, Robert
Bridges, and Coventry Patmore," Month, N.S. 6
(August, 1951), 69-78.

2515 Patricia, Sister Mary, C.S.J. "Forty Years of Criticism:
A Chronological Check List of Criticism of the Works of
Gerard Manley Hopkins from 1909 to 1949." Parts I
and II. Bulletin of Bibliography and Dramatic Index,
20 (May-August, September-December, 1950), 38-44,
63-7.

2516 Patterson, Jean Kenny. "The Influence of Welsh Alliteration upon the Poetry of Gerard Manley Hopkins."
M.A. thesis, Fordham University, 1954.

2517 Paye, Sister Mary Paul, R.S.M. "The Logical Structure
of the Sonnets of Gerard Manley Hopkins." M.A.
thesis, Catholic University of America, 1956.

2518 Payne, Mervyn. "Greatness of a Jesuit Poet." Review of
Poems of Gerard Manley Hopkins, edited by W. H.
Gardner and N. H. MacKenzie. Eastern Daily Press
(Norwich), (October 9, 1967).

2519 Payne, Michael. "Syntactical Analysis and 'The Windhover'," Renascence, 19 (Winter, 1967), 88-92.

2520 Peach, William W. "Gerard Manley Hopkins: His Outlook
on External Reality as it is Revealed in his Works."
B.A. thesis, University of Santa Clara, 1949.

2521 Pearson, Norman Holmes. "Priest and Professional Poet."
Review of Gerard Manley Hopkins, by W. H. Gardner.
Saturday Review, 32 (September 17, 1949), 16-7.

2522   "Two Victories in the Present Tense." Review of Gerard Manley Hopkins, by W. H. Gardner and Tennyson: Sixty Years After, by Paull F. Baum. Saturday Review, 31 (October 30, 1948), 26-7.

2523 Pearson, W. H. "G. M. Hopkins and 'Gifted Hopkins'," Notes & Queries, 6 (December, 1959), 452-53.

2524   "G. M. Hopkins and Provost Fortescue," Notes & Queries, 196 (September 29, 1951), 431-33.

2525 Peel, John Hugh Brignall. "The Echoes in a Booming Voice," New York Times Book Review, (October 20, 1957), 40-1.

2526 Pendergrass, Paula Belcher. "The Dark Sonnets of Gerard Manley Hopkins: A Critical Study." M.A. thesis, University of Florida, 1967.

2527 Pendexter, Hugh. "Hopkins' 'God's Grandeur'," Explicator, 23 (September, 1964), 2.

2528 Pepler, Conrad. "Hopkins, the Priest and Poet." Review of Immortal Diamond, edited by Norman Weyand, S.J. Universe (London), (February 10, 1950).

2529 Pepper, Stephen Coburn. The Basis of Criticism in the Arts. Cambridge, Massachusetts: Harvard University Press, 1945.

2530 Perkins, Robert L. Review of The Disappearance of God: Five Nineteenth-Century Writers, by J. Hillis Miller. Library Journal, 88 (November 1, 1963), 4222.

2531 Perrine, Laurence. Sound and Sense: An Introduction to Poetry. New York: Harcourt, Brace and Company, 1956, 142-43, 205.

2532 Perry, John Oliver. "The Relationship Between Rhythm and Meaning," Criticism, 7 (1965), 373-78.

2533 Peschmann, Hermann. Review of Gerard Manley Hopkins (1844-1889). A Study of Poetic Idiosyncrasy in Relation to Poetic Tradition, by W. H. Gardner. Vol. 2. English, 7 (Spring, 1949), 295-96.

2534   "Poetic Pattern." Review of Form in Modern Poetry, by Herbert Read. New English Weekly (London), (December 2, 1948).

2535   Review of Selected Poems of Gerard Manley Hopkins, edited by James Reeves and A Hopkins Reader, edited by John Pick. English, 9 (Autumn, 1953), 224-25.

2536 Peters, Wilhelmus Antonius Maria, S.J. "De Engelsche Dichter Gerard Manley Hopkins, S.J.: De Controverse Rond Zijn Persoon," Studien: Katholiek Cultureel Tijdschrift (Gravenhage), 71 (November, 1939), 448-59.

2537 _____ "Duns Scotus and Hopkins." Anonymous Review of
Gerard Manley Hopkins. Times Literary Supplement,
(July 10, 1948), 386.

2538 _____ "Gerard Manley Hopkins," Katholiek Cultureel
Tijdschrift Streven (Brussels), No. 2 (November, 1949),
200-01.

2539 _____ "Gerard Manley Hopkins." Review of Gerard
Manley Hopkins: A Study of Poetic Idiosyncracy in
Relation to Poetic Tradition, by W. H. Gardner. Vol.
2. Month, N.S. 2 (October, 1949), 269-73.

2540 _____ Gerard Manley Hopkins: A Critical Essay Towards
the Understanding of his Poetry. London: Geoffrey
Cumberlege, Oxford University Press, 1947. [Cover,
1948]

2541 _____ Gerard Manley Hopkins: A Critical Essay Towards
the Understanding of his Poetry. London: Geoffrey
Cumberlege, Oxford University Press, 1948.

2542 _____ Anonymous Review of Gerard Manley Hopkins: A
Critical Essay Towards the Understanding of his Poetry.
Durham University Journal, N.S. 9 (June, 1948), 98-9.

2543 _____ Anonymous Review of Gerard Manley Hopkins: A
Critical Essay Towards the Understanding of his Poetry.
Listener, 40 (September 30, 1948), 495-96.

2544 _____ "Hopkinsiana" (Letter to the Editor), Times Literary
Supplement, (October 29, 1954), 689.

2545 _____ "The Poet and 'The Dunce'." Anonymous Review of
Gerard Manley Hopkins, a Critical Essay Towards the
Understanding of his Poetry. Melbourne Age,
(October 2, 1948).

2546 _____ "25 Jaren Hopkins-critiek," Streven (Brussels), 9
(1955), 208-16.

2547 Peyre, Henri. Writers and their Critics. Ithaca, New
York: Cornell University Press, 1944.

2548 Phare, Elsie Elizabeth (Mrs. Austin Duncan-Jones).
"Gerard Hopkins and Richard Jefferies," Notes &
Queries, N.S. 2 (July, 1955), 318.

2549 _____ Review of The Journals and Papers of Gerard Manley
Hopkins, edited by Humphry House; The Sermons and
Devotional Writings of Gerard Manley Hopkins, edited
by Christopher Devlin, S.J. and Gerard Manley
Hopkins: An Idiom of Desperation, by John Wain.
Modern Language Review, 57 (July, 1962), 431-33.

2550 _____ "Poet and Priest." Review of Gerard Manley
Hopkins, by W. A. M. Peters, S.J. Birmingham Post,
(April 13, 1948).

2551 _____ The Poetry of Gerard Manley Hopkins: A Survey and Commentary. Cambridge: University Press, 1933.
2552 _____ Anonymous Review of The Poetry of Gerard Manley Hopkins: A Survey and Commentary. Month, 163 (January, 1934), 93.
2553 _____ Anonymous Review of The Poetry of Gerard Manley Hopkins: A Survey and Commentary. Nation, 138 (January 24, 1934), 109.
2554 _____ Anonymous Review of The Poetry of Gerard Manley Hopkins: A Survey and Commentary. Notes & Queries, 165 (November 25, 1933), 378.
2555 _____ Anonymous Review of The Poetry of Gerard Manley Hopkins: A Survey and Commentary. Times Literary Supplement, (January 25, 1934), 57.
2556 _____ "R. W. Dixon's 'Terrible Crystal' " (Letter to the Editor), Notes & Queries, N.S. 3 (June, 1956), 267.
2557 Phillips, Marjorie. "Muse's Library." Review of Thomas Lovell Beddoes, edited by H. W. Donner and Selected Poems of William Barnes, edited by Geoffrey Grigson. Books of the Month (London), (October, 1950), 9-10.
2558 Phillipson, Dom Wulstan, O.S.B. "Gerard Hopkins and Coventry Patmore." Review of Further Letters of Gerard Manley Hopkins, edited by Claude Colleer Abbott. Downside Review, 57 (July, 1939), 389-98.
2559 _____ "Gerard Hopkins, Priest," Downside Review, 56 (July, 1938), 311-23.
2560 _____ "Gerard Manley Hopkins," Downside Review, 51 (April, 1933), 326-48.
2561 _____ Review of Gerard Manley Hopkins, by John Pick. Downside Review, 61 (January, 1943), 44.
2562 _____ Review of Gerard Manley Hopkins, 1844-1889, by W. H. Gardner. Vol. 1. Downside Review, 63 (1945), 135-36.
2563 _____ "Hopkins Again." Review of The Journals and Papers of Gerard Manley Hopkins, edited by Humphry House and The Sermons and Devotional Writings of Gerard Manley Hopkins, edited by Christopher Devlin, S.J. Downside Review, 78 (Summer, 1960), 213-17.
2564 _____ "The Journals of G. M. Hopkins." Review of Note-Books and Papers of Gerard Manley Hopkins, edited by Humphry House. Downside Review, 55 (October, 1937), 526-36.

2565 _____ "The Letters of Gerard Manley Hopkins." Review of The Letters of Gerard Manley Hopkins to Robert Bridges and The Correspondence of Gerard Manley Hopkins and Richard Watson Dixon, edited by Claude Colleer Abbott. Downside Review, 53 (April, 1935), 210-28.

2566 _____ Review of The Mind and Poetry of Gerard Manley Hopkins, S.J. by Bernard Kelly. Downside Review, 53 (July, 1935), 407.

2567 _____ "More Light on Hopkins." Review of Further Letters of Gerard Manley Hopkins, edited by Claude Colleer Abbott. Downside Review, 76 (Fall, 1958), 402-10.

2568 "Philomathic Society: Paradox of Modern Poetry," Warrington Examiner (Warrington, England), (February 7, 1951).

2569 Piatier, Jacqueline. "Une These de Sorbonne sur le Poete Anglais: Gerard Manley Hopkins," Monde (Paris), (May 14, 1958).

2570 Pick, John. "The Centenary of Gerard Manley Hopkins," Thought, 19 (December, 1944), 590-93.

2571 _____ "Christian Poet." Review of A Hopkins Reader, edited by John Pick. Time, 61 (May 25, 1953), 106. [Includes "A Gerard Manley Hopkins Sampler" comprising "Pied Beauty," "Duns Scotus's Oxford," and "God's Grandeur."]

2572 _____ Review of Further Letters of Gerard Manley Hopkins, edited by Claude Colleer Abbott. Commonweal, 28 (July 8, 1938), 302-03.

2573 _____ Review of Further Letters of Gerard Manley Hopkins, edited by Claude Colleer Abbott. Victorian Studies, 1 (September, 1959), 91-3.

2574 _____ "Gerard Manley Hopkins: A Poet's Conflict, the Divine and the Earthly." Anonymous Review of Gerard Manley Hopkins, Priest and Poet. Times Literary Supplement, (September 26, 1942), 474.

2575 _____ "Gerard Manley Hopkins." The Victorian Poets: A Guide to Research, edited by Frederic E. Faverty. Cambridge, Massachusetts: Harvard University Press, 1956, 196-227.

2576 _____ Review of Gerard Manley Hopkins, by the Kenyon Critics. Thought, 21 (June, 1946), 323-24.

2577 _____ Review of Gerard Manley Hopkins, by W. A. M. Peters, S.J. Thought, 24 (September, 1949), 534-36.

2578 _____ "Gerard Manley Hopkins." Review of Gerard
Manley Hopkins: A Life, by Eleanor Ruggles.
Commonweal, 40 (August 25, 1944), 447-48.

2579 _____ Review of Gerard Manley Hopkins: The Man and
the Poet, by K. R. Srinivasa Iyengar. Renascence, 1
(Spring, 1949), 57-8.

2580 _____ Review of Gerard Manley Hopkins: A Study of
Poetic Idiosyncrasy in Relation to Poetic Tradition, by
W. H. Gardner. Catholic World, 168 (October, 1948),
90-1.

2581 _____ Review of Gerard Manley Hopkins: A Study of
Poetic Idiosyncrasy in Relation to Poetic Tradition, by
W. H. Gardner. Thought, 20 (June, 1945), 347-49.

2582 _____ Review of Gerard Manley Hopkins: A Study of
Poetic Idiosyncrasy in Relation to Poetic Tradition, by
W. H. Gardner. Vol. 2. Catholic World, 170
(December, 1949), 238-39.

2583 _____ Gerard Manley Hopkins: Priest and Poet. London:
Oxford University Press, 1942. [Inscribed "John Pick,
September 4, 1948, New Haven".]

2584 _____ Gerard Manley Hopkins: Priest and Poet. London:
Geoffrey Cumberlege, Oxford University Press, 1946.
[Inscribed "John Pick, Sept. 4, 1948, New Haven".]

2585 _____ Gerard Manley Hopkins: Priest and Poet. 2nd ed.
London: Oxford University Press, 1966.

2586 _____ Gerard Manley Hopkins: Priest and Poet. 2nd ed.
Galaxy Book. New York: Oxford University Press,
1966.

2587 _____ Anonymous Review of Gerard Manley Hopkins:
Priest and Poet. Durham University Journal, N.S. 3
(December, 1942), 34-5.

2588 _____ Anonymous Review of Gerard Manley Hopkins:
Priest and Poet. Notes & Queries, 185 (October 9,
1943), 240.

2589 _____ Anonymous Review of Gerard Manley Hopkins:
Priest and Poet. Virginia Quarterly Review, 19
(Autumn, 1943), lxxxvi-lxxxvii.

2590 _____ "Gerard Manley Hopkins: The Problem of Religious
Poetry," Stylus (Boston College), 55 (February, 1942),
14-21.

2591 _____ "Great Catholic Authors." Review of The Shaping
Vision of Gerard Manley Hopkins, by Alan Heuser.
America, 100 (January 10, 1959), 431-32.

2592 _____ "The Growth of a Poet: Gerard Manley Hopkins, S.J." Parts I and II, Month, 175 (January, February, 1940), 39-46, 106-13.

2593 _____ "Hopkins' Imagery: The Relation of his Journal to his Poetry," Renascence, 7 (Autumn, 1954), 30-8.

2594 _____ Review of Immortal Diamond: Studies in Gerard Manley Hopkins, edited by Norman Weyand, S.J.; Gerard Manley Hopkins: A Study of Poetic Idiosyncrasy in Relation to Poetic Tradition, by W. H. Gardner and Gerard Manley Hopkins: A Critical Essay towards the Understanding of his Poetry, by W. A. M. Peters, S.J. Thomist, 13 (April, 1950), 289-96.

2595 _____ "The Inspiration of Hopkins' Poetry," America, 68 (January 23, 1943), 437-38.

2596 _____ (Letter to the Editor), Catholic Book Club Newsletter, 3 (June, 1943), 1-2.

2597 _____ "The Listener's Book Chronicle." Anonymous Review of Priest and Poet. Listener, 28 (November 12, 1942), 632, 635.

2598 _____ "Manresa." Review of Gerard Manley Hopkins: A Study of his Ignatian Spirit, by David A. Downes. Renascence, 16 (Spring, 1964), 163-65.

2599 _____ "More About Hopkins." Review of Poems of Gerard Manley Hopkins, edited by W. H. Gardner. 3rd ed.; Gerard Manley Hopkins: A Study of Poetic Idiosyncrasy in Relation to Poetic Tradition, by W. H. Gardner, Vol. 1; Gerard Manley Hopkins: A Critical Essay towards the Understanding of his Poetry, by W. A. M. Peters, S.J., and Immortal Diamond, edited by Norman Weyand, S.J. Kenyon Review, 11 (Winter, 1949), 155-59.

2600 _____ "Newman the Poet," Renascence, 8 (Spring, 1956), 127-35.

2601 _____ "An Original Bouquet." Review of An Anthology of Catholic Poets, edited by Shane Leslie. Renascence, 7 (Autumn, 1954), 42-3.

2602 _____ "Religious Thought and Experience in the Poetry of Gerard Manley Hopkins." Ph.D., University of Wisconsin, 1938.

2603 _____ "Revolutionary Traditionalist." Review of Gerard Manley Hopkins: A Study of Poetic Idiosyncrasy in Relation to Poetic Tradition, by W. H. Gardner and Poems of Gerard Manley Hopkins, edited by W. H. Gardner, 3rd ed. America, 80 (October 9, 1948), 19.

2604 _____ "Right Directions in Criticism." Review of Gerard Manley Hopkins, by the Kenyon Critics. America, 74 (February 16, 1946), 539.

2605 _____ Review of Selections from the Note-Books of Gerard Manley Hopkins, edited by T. Weiss. Thought, 21 (March, 1946), 159-60.

2606 _____ Review of The Sermons and Devotional Writings of Gerard Manley Hopkins, edited by Christopher Devlin, S.J. Modern Philology, 57 (November, 1959), 137-38.

2607 _____ Review of The Shaping Vision of Gerard Manley Hopkins, by Alan Heuser. Modern Philology, 56 (May, 1959), 282-83.

2608 _____ "A Steady Growth." Review of The Letters of Gerard Manley Hopkins to Robert Bridges and The Correspondence of Gerard Manley Hopkins and Richard Watson Dixon, edited by Claude Colleer Abbott. Renascence, 8 (Summer, 1956), 216-17.

2609 _____ Review of Victorian Portraits: Hopkins and Pater, by David Anthony Downes. Renascence, 18 (Autumn, 1965), 53.

2610 _____, ed. "Greatness and Oddness." Anonymous Review of A Hopkins Reader. Nation, 176 (June 6, 1963), 486.

2611 _____, ed. "Hopkins as Poet and Critic." Anonymous Review of Selected Poems of Gerard Manley Hopkins, edited by James Reeves and A Hopkins Reader, edited by John Pick. Times Literary Supplement, (June 5, 1953), 366.

2612 _____, ed. Anonymous Review of A Hopkins Reader. New Yorker, 29 (September 12, 1953), 147-48.

2613 _____, ed. Anonymous Review of A Hopkins Reader. Notes & Queries, N.S. 1 (September, 1954), 411-12.

2614 Pickman, Hester. "Gerard Manley Hopkins, S.J." Review of Gerard Manley Hopkins, S.J., by G. F. Lahey, S. J. and The Poems of Gerard Manley Hopkins, S.J., edited by Robert Bridges. Hound and Horn, 4 (October-December, 1930), 118-27.

2615 Pietrikiewicz, Jerzy. "Introducing Norwid," Slavonic and East European Review, 27 (December 28, 1948), 228-47.

2616 Pinto, Vivian de Sola. Crisis in English Poetry 1880-1940. London: Hutchinson's University Library, 1951.

2617 _____ Crisis in English Poetry 1880-1940. 4th ed. London: Hutchinson University Library, 1965.

2618 _____ Crisis in English Poetry 1880-1940. 5th ed. London: Hutchinson University Library, 1967.

2619 _____ "A Dynamic Friendship." Review of Robert Bridges and Gerard Hopkins, 1863-1889. A Literary Friendship, by Jean-Georges Ritz. Critical Quarterly, 2 (Autumn, 1960), 281-82.

2620 _____ "Hopkins and 'The Trewnesse of the Christian Religion' " (Letter to the Editor), Times Literary Supplement, (June 10, 1955), 317.

2621 Piontek, Heinz. "Dienst als Dank. Gerard Manley Hopkins in Neuen Ubertragungen," Zeitwende (Hamburg), 35 (1964), 317-26.

2622 Pirie, Peter J. "Michael Tippet: A Child of Our Time," Musical Opinion (London), (January, 1959), 235-38.

2623 Pisanti, Tommaso. Review of I Funamboli: Il Manierismo nella Letteratura Inglese Contemporanea, by Giorgio Melchiori. l'Italia Che Scrive (Rome), (February, 1964).

2624 Pitchford, Lois W. "The Curtal Sonnets of Gerard Manley Hopkins," Modern Language Notes, 67 (March, 1952), 165-69.

2625 Pitts, Arthur W., Jr. "Hopkins' 'The Wreck of the Deutschland,' Stanza 29," Explicator, 24 (September, 1965), 7.

2626 "The Place of Robert Bridges" (Editor's Commentary), Criterion, 9 (July, 1930), 587-88.

2627 Plomer, William. "Gerard Manley Hopkins." Review of The Poetry of Gerard Manley Hopkins: A Survey and Commentary, by Elsie Elizabeth Phare. Spectator, 151 (November 17, 1933), 712.

2628 Plomteux, R. "Une Nouvelle Etude sur Gerard Manley Hopkins." Review of Le Poete Gerard Manley Hopkins, S.J., by Jean-Georges Ritz. Revue des Langues Vivantes (Brussels), 32 (1966), 434-36.

2629 Plowman, Max. "Gerard Hopkins's Birthday" (Letter to the Editor), Times Literary Supplement, (February 28, 1935), 124.

2630 _____ "Gerard Manley Hopkins." Review of The Letters of Gerard Manley Hopkins to Robert Bridges and The Correspondence of Gerard Manley Hopkins and Richard Watson Dixon, edited by Claude Colleer Abbott. Adelphi, 9 (1935), 356-61.

2631 Pocs, John A. "Nationalism in the Poetry of Gerard Manley Hopkins." M.A. thesis, Bowling Green State University, 1961.

2632 "Poet and Priest. Gerard Hopkins: 1844-1889. The 'Dare-Gale Skylark'," Times Literary Supplement, (June 10, 1944), 282, 284.

2633 "Poet's Travail," British Weekly (London), (June 29, 1950).

2634 Pol, Osvaldo, S.J. "Hopkins: Una Extrana Experiencia,"
Estudios (Buenos Aires), (January–February, 1964),
52–60.

2635 Pompen, Aurelius, O.F.M. "Gerard Manley Hopkins,
S.J.," Onze Taaltuin (Rotterdam), 6 (May, 1937),
95–102.

2636 Porter, Alan. "Difficult Beauty," Spectator, 130 (January
13, 1923), 66.

2637 Pouncey, Lorene. "An Analysis of Hopkins' 'Terrible'
Sonnet No. 65: 'No Worst'," Critical Survey, (Summer,
1966), 242–45.

2638 _____ "Gerard Manley Hopkins' Sextet of 'Terrible'
Sonnets: An Analytical Study." M.A. thesis, University of Houston, 1963.

2639 Power, Ellen M. (Letter to the Editor), G. K.'s Weekly,
22 (November 21, 1935), 134.

2640 Prasad, Shreekrishna. "G. M. Hopkins: The Pioneer-
Artist of the Psychic Life in Modern English Poetry,"
Sri Aurobindo Circle (Bombay), No. 13 (1957), 104–15.

2641 Praz, Mario. "Due Poeti Cattolici: Nell'Inghilterra
dell'Ottocento," Nazione Italiana (Florence), (October
10, 1957), 3.

2642 Prenderville, Brendan. "Visible Thought," British Journal
of Aesthetics, 7 (October, 1967), 339–49.

2643 Press, John. The Chequer'd Shade: Reflections on
Obscurity in Poetry. London: Oxford University Press,
1958.

2644 _____ The Fire and the Fountain: An Essay on Poetry.
London: Geoffrey Cumberlege, Oxford University
Press, 1955.

2645 _____, comp. Poetic Heritage: A Sunday Times Anthology
of English Verse from the 16th to the 20th Century.
London: Andre Deutsch, 1957, 14, 96.

2646 Price, Fanny. "G. M. Hopkins on Robert Bridges,"
Notes & Queries, 186 (January 15, 1944), 49.

2647 Price, R. G. G. "Gerard Manley Hopkins." Review of
Gerard Manley Hopkins, by W. H. Gardner. Vol. 2.
English Review Magazine (London), 3 (September,
1949), 212.

2648 Pridie, F. M. "Gerard Manley Hopkins: Priest and Poet."
Review of A Hopkins Reader, edited by John Pick.
Westminster Cathedral Chronicle (London), 47
(September, 1953), 147–48.

2649 "Prince of Celtic Bards: Singer of Love and Woodlands." Review of Dafydd Ap Gwilym: Fifty Poems, edited by H. Idris Bell and David Bell. Times Literary Supplement, (May 30, 1942), 273.

2650 Prosen, Anthony J., S.J. "Suffering in Aeschylus and Hopkins," Classical Bulletin, 41 (November, 1964), 11-3.

2651 Pryce-Jones, Alan. "Gerard Manley Hopkins." Review of The Collected Poems of Gerard Manley Hopkins. London Mercury, 24 (May, 1931), 45-52.

2652 _____ "The Rococo Spirit," Listener, 61 (March 19, 1959), 506-08.

2653 Przywara, Sister Benice. " ' The Wreck of the Deutschland': Story and Analysis." M.A. thesis, Niagara University, 1951.

2654 Purcell, J. M. "The Poetry of Gerard Manley Hopkins," Cronos (Ohio State University, Columbus), 1 (Summer, 1947), 21-5.

2655 "Purchase of Manuscripts of Gerard Manley Hopkins," Bodleian Library Record, 4 (1953), 290.

2656 Putnam, Sam. "Gerard Manley Hopkins." Review of Poems of Gerard Manley Hopkins, edited by Robert Bridges. Chicago Evening Post, (May 30, 1924), 7.

2657 Quennell, Peter. "Books in General." Review of The Life and Times of Coventry Patmore, by Derek Patmore. New Statesman and Nation, (April 30, 1949), 445-46.

2658 Quiller-Couch, Arthur, ed. The Oxford Book of English Verse. 1250-1918. Oxford: Clarendon Press, 1939, 1010-13.

2659 _____ The Oxford Book of Victorian Verse. Oxford: Clarendon Press, 1912, 691.

2660 Quinn, Kerker. "Portrait in Letters." Review of Further Letters of Gerard Manley Hopkins, edited by Claude Colleer Abbott. Poetry, 53 (December, 1938), 150-55.

2661 Quintana, Ricardo, ed. Two Hundred Poems. London: Longmans, Green and Company, 1947, 307-09.

2662 Quirk, Charles J., S.J. "Gerard Manley Hopkins, S.J. 1844-1944" (Poem), Catholic World, 160 (December, 1944), 240.

2663 R.B.H. Review of Gerard Manley Hopkins, by Eleanor Ruggles. Orate Fratres, 19 (December 3, 1944), 47-8.

2664 R.B.O'B. "Literary Society," Stonyhurst Magazine, 29 (July, 1948), 169-70.

2665 R.G. Review of Gerard Manley Hopkins, by G. F. Lahey, S.J. America, 43 (September 10, 1930), 600.

2666 R.J.L. "Poet and Priest." Review of Poems of Gerard
     Manley Hopkins, edited by W. H. Gardner. 3rd ed.
     New Haven Register, (August 28, 1948), 6.
2667 Rader, Louis. "The Dark Sonnets of Gerard Manley
     Hopkins." M.A. thesis, Cornell University, 1961.
     [Microfilm]
2668 _____ "Hopkins' Dark Sonnets: Another New Expression,"
     Victorian Poetry, 5 (Spring, 1967), 13-20.
2669 _____ "Major Problems in Hopkins Criticism." Ph.D.,
     Cornell University, 1964.
2670 Raine, Kathleen. Blake and Tradition. Vol. 2. The A. W.
     Mellon Lectures in the Fine Arts 1962. Bollingen Series
     35. Princeton, New Jersey: Princeton University Press,
     1968, 26.
2671 _____ "Gerard Manley Hopkins." Review of Gerard
     Manley Hopkins: A Critical Essay Towards the Under-
     standing of his Poetry, by W. A. M. Peters, S.J. Time
     and Tide, 29 (April 24, 1948).
2672 Ransom, John Crowe. The New Criticism. Norfolk,
     Connecticut: New Directions, 1941, 212, 231.
2673 Rathmell, J. C. A. "Explorations and Recoveries--I.
     Hopkins, Ruskin and the Sidney Psalter," London
     Magazine, 6 (September, 1959), 51-66.
2674 Ratliff, John D. "Hopkins' 'The May Magnificat,' 19-22,"
     Explicator, 16 (December, 1957), 17.
2675 Ray, Randolph. 100 Great Religious Poems. New York:
     World Publishing Company, 1951, 23.
2676 Raymond, William O. " 'The Mind's Internal Heaven' in
     Poetry," University of Toronto Quarterly, 20 (April,
     1951), 215-32.
2677 Read, Herbert. "Americans on Hopkins." Review of
     Gerard Manley Hopkins, by the Kenyon Critics.
     Tribune (London), (April 21, 1950).
2678 _____ Form in Modern Poetry. Essays in Order, No. 11
     New York: Sheed & Ward, 1933, 35, 41, 44-55.
2679 _____ "Gerard Hopkins's Metres" (Letter to the Editor),
     Times Literary Supplement, (February 23, 1933), 127.
2680 _____ "Gerard Manley Hopkins." Collected Essays in
     Literary Criticism. London: Faber and Faber Ltd,
     1938, 331-53.
2681 _____ Review of Gerard Manley Hopkins, by G. F. Lahey,
     S.J. and Poems of Gerard Manley Hopkins, edited by
     Robert Bridges. Criterion, 10 (April, 1931), 552-59.
2682 _____ "Gerard Manley Hopkins." In Defence of Shelley
     and Other Essays. London: Heinemann, 1936, 111-14.

2683 _____ "In Defence of Shelley: New Essays by Mr. Herbert Read." Anonymous Review of In Defence of Shelley and Other Essays. Times Literary Supplement, (February 22, 1936), 157.

2684 _____ "Inscape and Gestalt: Hopkins." The True Voice of Feeling. London: Faber and Faber, 1953.

2685 _____ Review of The Letters of Gerard Manley Hopkins to Robert Bridges; The Correspondence of Gerard Manley Hopkins and Richard Watson Dixon, edited by Claude Colleer Abbott. Criterion, 14 (April, 1935), 478-82.

2686 _____ Review of The Mind and Poetry of Gerard Manley Hopkins, S.J., by Bernard Kelly. Criterion, 58 (October, 1935), 174.

2687 _____ The Nature of Literature. New York: Horizon Press, 1956, 41, 45, 48, 323, 327-28, 331-53.

2688 _____ Phases of English Poetry. Norfolk, Connecticut: New Directions, 1951, 123-24.

2689 _____ "Poetry and Belief in Gerard Manley Hopkins," New Verse, 1 (January, 1933), 11-15.

2690 _____ "Poetry in the Present." Anonymous Review of Form in Modern Poetry. Times Literary Supplement, (February 9, 1933), 81-2.

2691 _____ "The Poetry of Gerard Manly [sic] Hopkins," Direction, 1 (1934), 32-43. [Reprinted from English Critical Essays: Twentieth Century, edited by Phyllis M. Jones, 1933, 351-74. Also reprinted as "Gerard Manley Hopkins" in Collected Essays in Literary Criticism, by Herbert Read, 1938, 331-53 and in In Defence of Shelley and Other Essays, by Herbert Read, 1936, 111-44.]

2692 _____, ed. The Knapsack: A Pocket-Book of Prose and Verse. 7th ed. London: George Routledge & Sons, 1947, 204, 345-47.

2693 Reeves, James. The Critical Sense. Melbourne: William Heinemann Ltd., 1956, 101-04.

2694 _____ "Fire and Clay." Review of Robert Bridges and Gerard Hopkins: A Literary Friendship, by Jean-Georges Ritz. New Statesman, 59 (May 14, 1960), 724.

2695 _____ "A Poet's Prose." Review of A Hopkins Reader, edited by John Pick. Listener, 49 (June 25, 1953), 1060, 1063.

2696 _____ "The Study of Poetry with Notes on Gerard Manley Hopkins," Use of English, 2 (1951), 130-36.

2697 _____, ed. "Hopkins as Poet and Critic." Anonymous
Review of Selected Poems of Gerard Manley Hopkins,
edited by James Reeves and A Hopkins Reader, edited
by John Pick. Times Literary Supplement, (June 5,
1953), 366.
2698 _____, ed. The Modern Poet's World. London: William
Heinemann Ltd., 1957, 114-16.
2699 _____, ed. "Reviews in Brief." Anonymous Review of
Selected Poems of Gerard Manley Hopkins. Times
Educational Supplement (London), (June 19, 1953).
2700 Reid, John Cowie. Gerard Manley Hopkins, Priest and
Poet: A Centennial Tribute. Wellington, New Zealand:
Published for the Catholic Writers' Movement by
Catholic Supplies Ltd., [1944].
2701 _____ Review of Robert Bridges and Gerard Hopkins, 1863-
1889: A Literary Friendship, by Jean-Georges Ritz.
Victorian Studies, 4 (December, 1960), 182-83.
2702 Reiman, Donald H. "Hopkins' 'Oooze of Oil' Rises
Again," Victorian Poetry, 4 (Winter, 1966), 39-42.
2703 Reizenstein, Franz. "Genesis" (Oratorio for soprano and
baritone soli, chorus and orchestra), text arranged by
Christopher Hassall. London: Alfred Lengnick & Co.,
Ltd., 1958. [Musical Setting. Lines from "The
Starlight Night," 15-9.]
2704 Remes, Sister Honora, D. C. "Positively Speaking:
Gerard Manley Hopkins," Delta Epsilon Sigma Bulletin,
10 (October, 1965), 69-77.
2705 Retinger, Sister Antony Mary, S.S.N.D. "Gerard Manley
Hopkins as a Critic of English Literature." M.A.
thesis, De Paul University, 1951.
2706 Revol, Enrique Luis. "La Poesia de Gerard Manley
Hopkins." Al Pie de las Letras: Pequenos Ensayos
Literarios. Buenos Aires: Reunion, 1949, 55-71.
2707 Rice, W. I. "A Hundred Years of Catholic Writing,"
Catholic Times (London), (September 29, 1950).
2708 Richards, Ivor Armstrong. Coleridge on Imagination. New
York: W. W. Norton and Company, 1950, 192, 208,
215.
2709 _____ "Gerard Hopkins," Dial, 81 (September, 1926),
195-203.
2710 _____ "Gerard Hopkins," Cambridge Review, 49 (October
28, 1927), 49-51. [Condensed from "Gerard Hopkins"
in Dial, September, 1926.]

2711 Richardson, Joanna. "Poetry of Stress." Review of A
Hopkins Reader, edited by John Pick and Selected
Poems of Gerard Manley Hopkins, edited by James
Reeves. Spectator, 190 (August 28, 1953), 226.
2712 Richmond, William Kenneth. Poetry and the People.
London: George Routledge & Sons, Ltd., 1947, 223-24.
2713 Ricker, Elizabeth Ann. "The Relation of Hopkins' Theories
of Poetry to his Applied Criticisms." M.A. thesis,
Boston College, 1949.
2714 Riding, Laura and Robert Graves. A Survey of Modernist
Poetry. London: William Heinemann Ltd., 1929.
2715 Ridler, Anne. "Gerard Hopkins (1844-1889)," Periodical
(Oxford), 26 (July, 1944), 109-13.
2716 Riffaterre, Michael. "Stylistic Context." Essays on the
Language of Literature, edited by Seymour Chatman and
Samuel R. Levin. Boston: Houghton Mifflin Company,
1967, 431-41. [Reprinted from Word, 16 (August,
1960).]
2717 Riley, Sister Maria Amabilis, O.P. "A Comparative Study
Showing the Influence of John Keats on Gerard Manley
Hopkins." M.A. thesis, Florida State University,
1963.
2718 Rillie, John A. M. Review of Further Letters of Gerard
Manley Hopkins Including his Correspondence with
Coventry Patmore, edited by Claude Colleer Abbott.
Review of English Studies, 9 (August, 1958), 334-36.
2719 Riordan, Mary Marguerite. "A Study of the Similarities in
the Works of Gerard Manley Hopkins and Walt
Whitman." M.A. thesis, San Francisco State College,
1961.
2720 Rippy, Frances Mayhew. "Brevity, Music, Particularity,
Change: Four Premises of Modern Literature." Muncie,
Indiana: Ball State University Faculty Lecture Series,
1965-1966, 36-56.
2721 Ritz, Jean-Georges. "Bridges's Debt to Hopkins" (Letter
to the Editor), Times Literary Supplement, (June 30,
1961), 408.
2722 _____ "Dans quel Ordre Convient-il de Lire les 'Terribles
Sonnets' de G. M. Hopkins," Etudes Anglaises (Paris),
23 (1964), 161-73.
2723 _____ "La Glorification de Dieu dans les Poemes de G.
M. Hopkins," Travaux et Jours (Beyrouth), Nos. 14-5
(1964), 3-23.

2724 _____ Review of A Hopkins Reader, edited by John Pick; Selected Poems of Gerard Manley Hopkins, edited by James Reeves and Poems and Prose of Gerard Manley Hopkins, edited by W. H. Gardner. Etudes Anglaises, 7 (July, 1954), 342-43.

2725 _____ "Un Poete Anglais: le R. P. Gerard Manley Hopkins, S.J.," Bulletin des Lettres (Lyons), 20 (May 15, 1958), 189-96.

2726 _____ Le Poete Gerard Manley Hopkins, S.J. 1844-1889: L'Homme et l'Oeuvre. Etudes Anglaises 16. Paris: Didier, 1963.

2727 _____ Robert Bridges and Gerard Hopkins 1863-1889: A Literary Friendship. London: Oxford University Press, 1960.

2728 _____ "A Strong Fire of Love." Anonymous Review of Robert Bridges and Gerard Hopkins 1863-1889: A Literary Friendship. Times Literary Supplement, (May 6, 1960), 288.

2729 _____ Review of The Unmediated Vision, by Geoffrey H. Hartman. Etudes Anglaises, 12 (1959), 69.

2730 _____ " 'The Windhover' " (Letter to the Editor), Times Literary Supplement, (May 6, 1955), 237.

2731 _____ " 'The Windhover' de G. M. Hopkins," Etudes Anglaises, 9 (January-March, 1956), 14-22.

2732 Robbins, R. H. "Choral Speaking at the Oxford Festivals," Quarterly Journal of Speech, 25 (April, 1939), 227-35.

2733 Roberts, Denys Kilham. The Centuries' Poetry: An Anthology. 4: Hood to Hardy. Pelican Book. Harmondsworth: Penguin Books, 1945.

2734 Roberts, Donald A. "The Technical Influence of Gerard Manley Hopkins in Modern British Poetry." M.A. thesis, Columbia University, 1948.

2735 Roberts, Michael. "A Hopkins Number." Review of New Verse, April, 1935. Spectator, 154 (May 17, 1935), 844.

2736 _____ "Notes on English Poets," Poetry, 39 (May, 1932), 271-79.

2737 _____ Review of The Poetry of Gerard Manley Hopkins. A Survey and Commentary, by E. E. Phare. Adelphi, 8 (April, 1934), 76-7.

2738 _____ "Reflections of Gerard Manley Hopkins." Review of The Letters of Gerard Manley Hopkins to Robert Bridges and to Richard Watson Dixon, edited by Claude Colleer Abbott. London Mercury, 31 (March, 1935), 480-81.

2739 _____, ed. The Faber Book of Modern Verse. London: Faber and Faber, 1938, 39-60.

2740 Robie, Burton A. Review of The Journals and Papers of Gerard Manley Hopkins, edited by Humphry House. Library Journal, 84 (April 1, 1959), 1133-34.

2741 _____ Review of Metaphor in Hopkins, by Robert Boyle, S.J. Library Journal, 86 (September 15, 1961), 2945.

2742 Robinson, Brian L. "Nature in the Poetry of Gerard Manley Hopkins." M.A. thesis, Columbia University, 1951.

2743 Robinson, Henry Morton. "Gerard Manley Hopkins: A Preface," Commonweal, 7 (December 28, 1927), 869-71.

2744 Robson, William Wallace. "Choice of Life." Review of The Journals and Papers of Gerard Manley Hopkins, edited by Humphry House and The Sermons and Devotional Writings of Gerard Manley Hopkins, edited by Christopher Devlin, S.J. Spectator, 201 (February 27, 1959), 300.

2745 _____ "Hopkins and Congreve" (Letter to the Editor), Times Literary Supplement, (February 24, 1950), 121.

2746 Roditi, Edouard. "Gerard Manley Hopkins," Cahiers du Sud (Marseilles), 19 (April, 1940), 229-32.

2747 _____ "Poemes de Gerard Manley Hopkins," Mesures (Paris), 1 (January 15, 1935), 91-102.

2748 Rodman, Selden, ed. A New Anthology of Modern Poetry. New York: Random House, 1946, 9-12.

2749 _____, ed. 100 Modern Poems. Mentor Book. New York: New American Library, 1952.

2750 Roeder, Raymond Louis, Jr. "The Sonnet Tradition and Gerard Manley Hopkins." B.A. thesis, University of Santa Clara, 1961.

2751 Roethke, Theodore. "Two American Poets." Anonymous Review of The Grasshopper's Man, by Rosalie Moore and The Lost Son, by Theodore Roethke. Times Literary Supplement, (February 17, 1950), 107.

2752 Roggen, F. N. "Gerard Manley Hopkins," Studies in English Literature (Tokyo), 15 (1935), 517-34.

2753 Roig, Jose Antonio, S.J. and Jose Vicente, S.J. "Dos Poemas Marianos de Hopkins." Razon y Fe (Madrid), 150 (July-August, 1954), 110-16.

2754 Rolfs, Alvin R. "First of Modern Poets." Review of Immortal Diamond, edited by Norman Weyand, S.J. St. Louis Post-Dispatch, (April 15, 1949), Section C, 2.

2755 Rooney, William Joseph. "The Problem of Poetry and
Belief in Contemporary Criticism." Ph.D., Catholic
University of America, 1949, 35, 103-04, 155.
[Published by Catholic University of America Press,
Washington, D. C.]

2756 _____ " 'Spelt from Sibyl's Leaves'--A Study in Contrast-
ing Methods of Evaluation," Journal of Aesthetics and
Art Criticism, 13 (June, 1955), 507-19.

2757 Rose, E. J. Review of Metaphor in Hopkins, by Robert
Boyle, S.J. Dalhousie Review, 43 (Spring, 1963),
110-11.

2758 Rose, Leslie. " 'Plumage of Far Wonder'," Sentinel of the
Blessed Sacrament, 46 (February, 1943), 65-7.

2759 Roseliep, Raymond. "Two Poems for Gerard Hopkins"
(Poems), Catholic World, 185 (April, 1957),33.

2760 _____ "With a Book of Verse Beneath the Bough" (Poem),
Tablet (London), (July 28, 1962.)

2761 Rosenthal, Macha Louis. The Modern Poets: A Critical
Introduction. New York: Oxford University Press,
1960.

2762 _____ The New Poets: American and British Poetry Since
World War II. New York: Oxford University Press,
1967.

2763 _____ and Arthur James Marshall Smith. Exploring Poetry.
New York: Macmillan Company, 1955, xix-xx, 62-6,
94-8, 257-62, 584, 599-600.

2764 Rothenstein, Elizabeth (Smith). "The Pre-Raphaelites and
Ourselves," Month, N.S. 1 (March, 1949), 180-98.

2765 _____, ed. The Virgin and the Child: An Anthology of
Paintings and Poems. London: William Collins Sons
and Co. Ltd.; New York: Charles Scribner's Sons,
1951.

2766 Rottiers, A. K. "Engelse Letteren: De Kunst der Dichters."
Review of Gerard Manley Hopkins, by W. H. Gardner.
Vol. 1 and 2. Band Kalina, No. 4 (1950), 156-58.

2767 Routh, Harold Victor. English Literature and Ideas in the
Twentieth Century. New York: Longmans, Green & Co.,
1948.

2768 _____ Review of Immortal Diamond, edited by Norman
Weyand, S.J. Adelphi, N.S. 26 (January-March,
1950), 210-11.

2769 _____ Review of Letters of Gerard Manley Hopkins to
Robert Bridges; Correspondence of Gerard Manley
Hopkins and Richard Watson Dixon, edited by C. C.
Abbott. Year's Work in English Studies, 16 (1935),331.

2770 _____ Review of Poems of Gerard Manley Hopkins, edited
by Robert Bridges. 2nd ed. Year's Work in English
Studies, 12 (1931), 286-87.

2771 Routley, Erik. Hymns and Human Life. Grand Rapids,
Michigan: Wm. B. Eerdmans Publishing Co., 1952,
162, 178-79.

2772 Rubbra, Edmund. "Inscape" (Suite for mixed voices,
strings and harp, Op. 122), words by Gerard Manley
Hopkins. South Croydon, Surrey: Alfred Lengnick &
Co., Ltd., 1965. [Musical Setting. I. "Pied Beauty."
II. "The Lantern Out of Doors." III. "Spring."
IV. "God's Grandeur." V. "Summa" (lines from a
fragment).]

2773 Rubenstein, Gladys. "A Study of Gerard Manley Hopkins'
Reputation as a Poet." M.A. thesis, Claremont
College, 1955.

2774 Ruggles, Eleanor. Gerard Manley Hopkins: A Life.
London: John Lane the Bodley Head, 1947.

2775 _____ Anonymous Review of Gerard Manley Hopkins: A
Life. New Yorker, 20 (August 12, 1944), 56.

2776 _____ "A Great Precursor." Anonymous Review of Gerard
Manley Hopkins: A Life. Times Literary Supplement,
(January 3, 1948), 11.

2777 _____ "Poet's Poet." Anonymous Review of Gerard Manley
Hopkins: A Life. Time, 44 (August 14, 1944), 99,
102, 104.

2778 Russell, Matthew, S.J. "Father Gerard Hopkins, S.J.,
and his Poetry," Irish Monthly, 47 (August, 1919),
441-48.

2779 _____ "Poets I have Known. V. Katharine Tynan,"
Donahoe's Magazine, 47 (April, 1902), 389-406.
[Also appears, without illustrations, in Irish Monthly,
31 (May, 1903), 250-67.]

2780 Russell, Peter. "Poetry is Dead but it Won't Lie Down,"
Cavalcade (London), (July 8, 1950), 18.

2781 _____ "Why Hopkins Wrote as he Did." Review of The
Journals and Papers of Gerard Manley Hopkins, edited
by Humphry House and The Sermons and Devotional
Writings of Gerard Manley Hopkins, edited by
Christopher Devlin, S.J. Liverpool Daily Post,
(March 11, 1959).

2782 Ryan, Francis. " 'The Wreck of the Deutschland': An
Introduction and a Paraphrase," Dublin Review, 221
(Second Quarter, 1948), 124-41.

2783 Ryan, Sister Mary Philip, O.P. "Gerard Manley Hopkins: The Physical Basis of his Poetical Forms." M.A. thesis, University of Detroit, 1935.

2784 Rylands, George. Review of Gerard Manley Hopkins, by W. H. Gardner. Vol. 2. Cambridge Review, (February 25, 1950).

2785 S. D. "Writers and their Work." Review of Gerard Manley Hopkins, by Geoffrey Grigson; Lytton Strachey, by R. A. Scott and Charles Williams, by John Heath-Stubbs. Thought (Delhi, India), (April 28, 1956).

2786 Sackett, S.J., comp. "Master's Theses in Literature Presented at American Colleges and Universities July 1, 1964 - June 30, 1965," LIT, No. 7 (Spring, 1966), 89-165.

2787 _____, comp. "Master's Theses in Literature Presented at American Colleges and Universities July 1, 1965 - August 31, 1966," LIT, 8 (November, 1967), 45-174. [Entire issue]

2788 Sackville, Lady Margaret. "Victorian Age of Giants." Review of The Life and Times of Coventry Patmore, by Derek Patmore. Gloucester Echo, (July 2, 1949).

2789 St. Virginia, Sister Mary, B.V.M. "Poetry: the Word." Return to Poetry, edited by John G. Brunini, et al. New York: Declan X. McMullen Company, 1947, 178-90. [Reprinted from Panel Discussion Paper, First Congress, Catholic Poetry Society of America, Fordham University, 1941.]

2790 Saintsbury, George. Cambridge History of English Literature, edited by Adolphus William Ward and A. R. Walker. Vol. 13. New York: G. P. Putnam's Sons; Cambridge, England: University Press, 1917, 230-31, 234.

2791 _____ A History of English Prosody. Vol. 3. London: Macmillan & Co., Ltd., 1910, 391.

2792 Sale, William M., Jr. "Gerard Manley Hopkins: Poet and Convert," Poetry, 65 (December, 1944), 142-49.

2793 Sambrook, James. A Poet Hidden: The Life of Richard Watson Dixon 1833-1900. London: Athlone Press, University of London, 1962.

2794 Sampson, George. The Concise Cambridge History of English Literature. New York: Macmillan Company, 1941, 54, 739, 1005.

2795 Sanders, Gerald DeWitt and J. H. Nelson. "Gerard Manley Hopkins." Chief Modern Poets of England and America. New York: Macmillan, 1950, 39-50, 932.

2796 Sansom, Clive. "A Hopkins Phrase" (Letter to the Editor), Times Literary Supplement, (May 20, 1949), 329.

2797 Sapir, Edward. Review of Poems of Gerard Manley Hopkins, edited by Robert Bridges. Poetry, 18 (September, 1921), 330-36.

2798 Sargent, Daniel. "The Charm and the Strangeness: Gerard Manley Hopkins," Atlantic, 184 (August, 1949), 73-7.

2799 _____ "Four Literary Converts." Anonymous Review of Four Independents. Times Literary Supplement, (November 30, 1935), 799.

2800 _____ "Gerard Manley Hopkins." Four Independents. London: Sheed & Ward, 1935, 117-83.

2801 _____ "Gerard Manley Hopkins," From the Housetops, 1 (September, 1946), 12-21.

2802 Sarma, G. V. L. N. "The Growth of Poetic Sensibility in G. M. Hopkins," Journal of the University of Gauhati, (1958), 73-94.

2803 Savant, John J. "The Rhetorical Effect of Sentence Patterns in Gerard Manley Hopkins' Poem 'The Blessed Virgin Compared to the Air we Breathe'." M.A. thesis, Dominican College of San Rafael, 1966.

2804 Scarfe, Francis. Review of Robert Bridges and Gerard Hopkins, 1863-1889, A Literary Friendship, by Jean-Georges Ritz. Etudes Anglaises, 15 (1962), 85-6.

2805 Schappes, Morris U. Review of Gerard Manley Hopkins, by G. F. Lahey, S. J. and Poems of Gerard Manley Hopkins, edited by Robert Bridges. 2nd ed. Symposium, 2 (January, 1931), 129-36.

2806 Schaumberg, Hans-Hubert. "Gerard Manley Hopkins' Naturauffassung (Eine Untersuchung der Tagebucher)." Ph.D., Georg August-Universitat of Gottingen, 1957.

2807 Scheetz, Sister M. Johannina. "Gerard Manley Hopkins: A Modern Victorian." M.A. thesis, Creighton University, 1937.

2808 Scheve, Brother Adelbert, F.S.C. "Hopkins' 'The Wreck of the Deutschland,' Stanza 33," Explicator, 17 (June, 1959), 60.

2809 Schlauch, Margaret. The Gift of Tongues. New York: Viking Press, 1942, 239-40, 251-52.

2810 Schlegel, Desmond, O.S.B. "Culture and the Contemplative Life," Blackfriars, 40 (July, 1959), 335-41.

2811 Schmidt, Kenneth J. (Letter to the Editor), New York Times Book Review, (November 10, 1957), 34.

2812 Schneider, Elisabeth Wintersteen. "Hopkins' 'My Own Heart Let me More have Pity On'," Explicator, 5 (May 1947), 51.

2813 _____ "Hopkins' 'My Own Heart Let me More have Pity On'," Explicator, 7 (May, 1949), 49.

2814 _____ "Hopkins' 'The Windhover'," Explicator, 18 (January, 1960), 22.

2815 _____ "Hopkins' 'The Wreck of the Deutschland,' Stanza 33," Explicator, 16 (May, 1958), 46.

2816 _____ Poems and Poetry. New York: American Book Company, 1964, 470-71.

2817 _____ "Sprung Rhythm: A Chapter in the Evolution of Nineteenth-Century Verse." PMLA, 80 (June, 1965), 237-53.

2818 _____ "Two Metaphysical Images in Hopkins's 'The Wreck of the Deutschland'," Modern Language Notes, 65 (May, 1950), 306-11.

2819 _____ " 'The Wreck of the Deutschland': A New Reading," PMLA, 81 (March, 1966), 110-22.

2820 Schneider, Isidor. "A Great Poet." Review of A Vision of the Mermaids, by Gerard Manley Hopkins and The Life of Father Gerard Manley Hopkins, S.J., by G. F. Lahey, S.J. Nation, 130 (April 16, 1930), 456, 458.

2821 Schoder, Raymond V., S.J. Review of A Hopkins Reader, by John Pick. Thought, 28 (Winter, 1953-1954), 619-21.

2822 _____ "An Interpretive Glossary of Difficult Words in the Poems." Immortal Diamond, edited by Norman Weyand, S.J. New York: Sheed & Ward, 1949, 192-221.

2823 _____ "Spelt from Sibyl's Leaves," Thought, 19 (December, 1944), 633-48.

2824 _____ "What Does 'The Windhover' Mean?" Immortal Diamond, edited by Norman Weyand, S.J. New York: Sheed & Ward, 1949, 275-306.

2825 Schoeck, R. J. "Influence and Originality in the Poetry of Hopkins," Renascence, 9 (Winter, 1956), 77-84.

2826 _____ "Peine Forte et Dure and Hopkins' 'Margaret Clitheroe'," Modern Language Notes, 74 (March, 1959), 220-24.

2827 Schoffler, Heinz. "Hinautgerissen in den Bannkreis der Schopfung: Ein Unbekannter Englischer Lyriker: Gerard Manley Hopkins," Rheinpfalz (Ludwigshafen), (February 24, 1955).

2828 Schonauer, Franz. "Entdeckung eines grossen Dichters," Deutsche Rundschau (Baden-Baden), (October, 1955), 1101-02.

2829 Schorer, Mark. William Blake: The Politics of Vision.
New York: Henry Holt and Company, 1946, 64-5, 97,
134, 151, 416, 433.

2830 Schreiber, Annette Claire. "Hopkins' 'The Wreck of the
Deutschland': A Study." Ph.D., Cornell University,
1960. [Microfilm]

2831 Schrickx, Wim. "De Dichter Dylan Thomas," Vlaamse
Gids (Brussels), (September, 1955), 529-42.

2832 Schulze, F. W. Review of Gerard Manley Hopkins
(Writers and Their Work, No. 59), by Geoffrey Grigson.
Zeitschrift fur Anglistik und Amerikakunde, 4 (1955?),
363-65.

2833 Schwartz, Delmore. "The Poetry of Hopkins." Review of
Gerard Manley Hopkins, by the Kenyon Critics. Nation,
162 (March 23, 1946), 347-48.

2834 Schwartz, Joseph Michael. "Gerard Manley Hopkins as
Literary Critic: With Specific Reference to the Criticism of his Significant Contemporaries as seen in his
Correspondence." M.A. thesis, Marquette University,
1947.

2835 Scott, Arthur Finlay. The Poet's Craft: A Course in the
Critical Appreciation of Poetry. Cambridge, England:
University Press, 1957.

2836 Scott, Michael M., S.J. "Gerard Manley Hopkins, S.J.,"
Irish Monthly, 61 (November-December, 1933), 715-20,
786-92.

2837 Scott, Nathan A., Jr. Review of Poetry and Prayer, by
William T. Noon. Thought, 42 (Winter, 1967), 622-24.

2838 Scott, Rebecca Kathryn. "The Individualism of Gerard
Manley Hopkins." M.A. thesis, University of Missouri,
1943.

2839 Scott, W. T. Review of Immortal Diamond, edited by
Norman Weyand, S.J. Providence Sunday Journal, (May
8, 1949), Section vi, 10.

2840 Scott-James, Rolfe Arnold. Fifty Years of English Literature.
London: Longmans, Green and Co., 1951, 109.

2841 Scott-Moncrieff, George. "Studies in Hopkins." Review
of Gerard Manley Hopkins, by Geoffrey Grigson and
Selected Poems of Gerard Manley Hopkins, published by
Nonesuch Press. Tablet (London), (June 25, 1955).

2842 Scully, James, ed. "Gerard Manley Hopkins." Modern
Poetics. New York: McGraw-Hill Company, 1965, 73-9.
[Includes reprint of "Author's Preface" from Poems of
Gerard Manley Hopkins, a manuscript collection in the
possession of Robert Bridges.]

2843 Seddon, Richard. "Poetic Licence," Sheffield Telegraph, (September 28, 1963).

2844 Seelhammer, Ruth. "One Morning when it Rained," America, 99 (May 24, 1958), 261-62.

2845 Sehrt, Ernst Th. "Gerard Manly [sic] Hopkins: Eine Deutsche Ausgabe," Sammlung (Gottingen), 10 (April, 1953), 215-19.

2846 Seraphim, Sister Mary, O.S.F. "With the Poets at Prayer," Burnished Gold (College of St. Francis, Joliet, Illinois), 1 (1936), 10-7.

2847 Sergeant, Howard. "The Innovations of Gerard Manley Hopkins," Aryan Path (Bombay), 35 (December, 1964), 540-45.

2848 _____ "Music in Modern Poetry," British Weekly, (August 25, 1949).

2849 _____ "Poetry and the Sense of Tradition," Aryan Path (Bombay), 36 (February, 1965), 78-82.

2850 Sewell, Brocard, O. Carm. "Hopkins' Best Friend." Review of Robert Bridges and Gerard Hopkins: A Literary Friendship, by Jean-Georges Ritz. Catholic Herald (London), (June 3, 1960).

2851 Sewell, Elizabeth. The Human Metaphor. Notre Dame: University of Notre Dame Press, 1964, 48, 88, 193.

2852 _____ "Humour and Hopkins," Duckett's Register, 5 (March, 1950), 41-2.

2853 Seymour-Smith, Martin. "An Unrecommended View of Poetry." Review of English Poetry: A Short History, by Kenneth Hopkins. Scotsman (Edinburgh), (March 16, 1963).

2854 Shanks, Edward. "The Technique of the Poet," Truth (London), (April 27, 1951), 429-30.

2855 Shapiro, Karl. Essay on Rime. New York: Reynal & Hitchcock, 1945, 8, 15, 33, 55.

2856 _____ Review of The Prosodic Theory of Gerard Manley Hopkins, by Sister Marcella Marie Holloway. Modern Language Notes, 64 (March, 1949), 200-01.

2857 Sharpe, Garold. "Gerard Manley Hopkins: The Dublin Years." M.A. thesis, Columbia University, 1948.

2858 Sharples, Sister Marian, IHM. "Conjecturing a Date for Hopkins' 'St. Thecla'," Victorian Poetry, 4 (Summer, 1966), 204-09.

2859 _____ "Hopkins and Joyce: A Point of Similarity," Renascence, 19 (Spring, 1967), 156-60.

2860 Sharrock, Roger. Review of The Poetry of Gerard Manley Hopkins and T. S. Eliot in the Light of the Donne Tradition, by David Morris. Modern Language Review, 50 (April, 1955), 242-43.

2861 Shaw, James Gerard. "Among Ourselves," Canadian Register (October 28, 1944), 8.

2862 _____ "Mr. Fletcher on Hopkins," Commonweal, 25 (November 13, 1936), 69-71,

2863 _____ "New Hopkins Studies Written by Jesuits." Review of Immortal Diamond, edited by Norman Weyand, S.J. Ensign (Kingston, Ontario), 2 (May 14, 1949), 10.

2864 Shaw, Martin. "God's Grandeur," for mixed voices and organ. London: Oxford University Press, 1948. [Musical Setting. For the Aldeburgh Festival, June, 1948.]

2865 Shaw, Priscilla W. Review of The Disappearance of God, by J. Hillis Miller and Studies in Structure, by Robert J. Andreach. Yale Review, 55 (Winter, 1966), 310-12.

2866 Shea, Dennis Donald David. "An Organization of Gerard Manley Hopkins' Critical Opinions." M.A. thesis, Columbia University, 1948.

2867 Shea, F. X., S.J. "Another Look at 'The Windhover'," Victorian Poetry, 2 (Autumn, 1964), 219-39.

2868 Sheean, Vincent. The Indigo Bunting: A Memoir of Edna St. Vincent Millay. New York: Harper & Brothers, 1949, 10, 14, 43-4.

2869 Sheed, Francis Joseph, comp. Poetry and Life: An Anthology of English Catholic Poetry. New York: Sheed & Ward, 1942.

2870 Sherwood, H. C. "Hopkins' 'Spelt from Sibyl's Leaves'," Explicator, 15 (October, 1956), 5.

2871 Shewring, Walter. "Gerard Manley Hopkins 1844-1944," Weekly Review (London), 40 (November 30, 1944), 115-16.

2872 _____ "The Letters of Father Hopkins." Review of The Letters of Gerard Manley Hopkins to Robert Bridges; The Correspondence of Gerard Manley Hopkins and Richard Watson Dixon, edited by Claude Colleer Abbott. Blackfriars, 16 (April, 1935), 265-71.

2873 Shields, John. "The Poetry of Gerard Manley Hopkins," Georgetown University French Review, 5 (1937), 29-44.

2874 Shipley, Orby, ed. Carmina Mariana: An Anthology in Verse in Honor of and in Relation to the Blessed Virgin Mary. Second Series. Roehampton: John Griffin, Manresa Press, 1902.

2875 Shkolnick, Sylvia. "Gerard Manley Hopkins: A Study in the Poetry of Meditation." M.A. thesis, Columbia University, 1959.

2876 Shuster, George Newman. The English Ode from Milton to Keats. Gloucester, Massachusetts: Peter Smith, 1964, 41, 92, 184.

2877 _____ "Poetry and Three Poets." The Catholic Spirit in Modern English Literature. New York, Macmillan and Company, 1922, 115-21.

2878 _____ "A Poet's By-paths." Review of The Note-Books and Papers of Gerard Manley Hopkins, edited by Humphry House. Commonweal, 26 (June 4, 1937), 164.

2879 _____ "Summons from the Dark." Review of Immortal Diamond, edited by Norman Weyand, S.J. New York Herald Tribune Weekly Book Review, (April 17, 1949), 7.

2880 _____ "The Varied Flavor of Hopkins." Review of Gerard Manley Hopkins, Priest and Poet, by John Pick. Saturday Review, 26 (June 5, 1943), 31.

2881 _____ The World's Great Catholic Literature. New York: Macmillan Company, 1942, 383-85.

2882 Sieveking, Lancelot de Giberne. "Gerard Manley Hopkins." The Eye of the Beholder. London: Hutton Press, 1957, 20, 93, 275-85.

2883 _____ "Gerard Manley Hopkins," Poetry Review, 33 (September-October, 1942), 323-25.

2884 _____ "Remembering Gerard Manley Hopkins," Listener, 57 (January 24, 1957), 151-52.

2885 Silkin, Jon. "An Interview with Jon Silkin, Editor of the Magazine Stand," Adelphi, 4 (April-May, 1965), 41-8.

2886 Silverstein, Henry. "On 'Tom's Garland'," Accent, 7 (Winter, 1947), 67-81.

2887 _____ "On 'Tom's Garland'." M.A. thesis, New York University, 1959.

2888 Simoes, Joao Gaspar. "Critica Literaria." Review of Tempo do Silencio, by Jose Ferreira Monte; O Pinhal das Dunas, by Sant'Iago Prezado and Esta Riqueza que o Senhor me Deu: Poemas, by Joao Braz. Dia'Rio Popular (Lisbon), 12 (October 28, 1953), 5, 15.

2889 Simons, John W. "The Credentials of the Catholic Poet," Spirit, 13 (November, 1946), 144-50.

2890 _____ "Hopkins in his Sermons," Commonweal, 26 (September 24, 1937), 491-93.

2891 Sinclair, John. "Poetry from Behind the Canvas." Review of Prose Keys to Modern Poetry, by J. J. Shapiro. Scotsman (Edinburgh), (February 23, 1963).

2892 Sitwell, Edith. The Atlantic Book of British and American
      Poetry. Boston: Little, Brown and Co., 1958, xiii-xiv,
      757-72.

2893 _____ "Gerard Manley Hopkins." Aspects of Modern
      Poetry. London: Duckworth, 1934, 51-72.

2894 _____ A Poet's Notebook. London: Macmillan and Co.,
      Ltd., 1944, 94-6.

2895 _____, ed. A Book of Winter. London: Macmillan Co.,
      Ltd., 1950, 75-6.

2896 Slater, John. "Gerard Manley Hopkins." Recent Literature
      and Religion. New York: Harper, 1938, 186-89.

2897 Slattery, James J. "Some Bibliographical References on
      Gerard Manley Hopkins, S.J." Catholic Library World,
      5 (January, 1934), 36.

2898 Slevin, Gerard. "Gerard Manley Hopkins." Review of
      Selected Poems of Gerard Manley Hopkins, edited by
      James Reeves and A Hopkins Reader, edited by John
      Pick. Tablet (London), 202 (August 8, 1953), 133-34.

2899 Slocombe, George. Review of Trois Poetes, by Georges
      Cattaui. New York Herald Tribune (Paris Edition),
      (December 1, 1948).

2900 Small, Christopher. "Hopkins: Pattern in the Poet's Eye."
      Review of The Journals and Papers of Gerard Manley
      Hopkins, edited by Humphry House and The Sermons
      and Devotional Writings of Gerard Manley Hopkins,
      edited by Christopher Devlin, S.J. Glasgow Herald,
      (February 19, 1959).

2901 Smalley, T., S.J. "Gerard Manley Hopkins: His Place in
      the European Poetic Tradition." Review of Gerard
      Manley Hopkins, by W. H. Gardner. Vol. 1. Catholic
      Herald (London), (November 24, 1944), 3.

2902 Smith, Grover. "A Source for Hopkins' 'Spring and Fall' in
      'The Mill on the Floss'?" English Language Notes, 1
      (September, 1963), 43-6.

2903 Smith, Helen. "A Study of the Treatment of Nature in the
      Poetry of Gerard Manley Hopkins." M.A. thesis,
      Ohio University, 1948.

2904 Smith, Charles Nowell. Notes on 'The Testament of
      Beauty.' London: Humphrey Milford, Oxford University
      Press, 1931, xxv, 64.

2905 Smith, R. L. "The Literary Club," Stonyhurst Magazine,
      14 (February, 1919), 632.

2906 Smullen, George J. "The Sonnet Forms of Gerard Manley
      Hopkins and Robert Bridges." M.A. thesis, Kent
      State University, 1967.

2907 Snavely, Robert Carl. "Gerard Manley Hopkins: Mystic or Metaphysical." M.A. thesis, University of Omaha, 1966.

2908 Snyder, Franklin Bliss and Robert Grant Martin. A Book of English Literature. Vol. 2. New York: Macmillan Co., Ltd., 1947, 946-48, 955-60.

2909 Soderberg, Lasse. "Prast och Poet: G. M. Hopkins," Arbetaren (Stockholm), (January 16, 1954).

2910 Sonstroem, David. "Making Earnest of Game: G. M. Hopkins and Nonsense Poetry," Modern Language Quarterly, 28 (June, 1967), 192-206.

2911 Southworth, James Granville. "Gerard Manley Hopkins." Sowing the Spring: Studies in British Poets from Hopkins to MacNeice. Oxford: Basil Blackwell, 1940, 15-32.

2912 Spanos, William V. The Christian Tradition in Modern British Verse Drama: The Poetics of Sacramental Time. New Jersey: Rutgers University Press, 1967, 122, 322-23.

2913 Spark, Muriel. The Girls of Slender Means. New York: Alfred A. Knopf, 1963, 9, 22, 48, 60, 122, 131, 162-65.

2914 Sparrow, John. "Disciple of Beauty," Time and Tide, (July 4, 1953).

2915 Sparshott, F. E. The Structure of Aesthetics. Toronto: University of Toronto Press, 1963, 396-97, 411.

2916 Speaight, Robert. "Gerard Manley Hopkins, S.J.," Commonweal, 33 (March 28, 1941), 562-65.

2917 _____ "The Price of Poetry." Review of Rimbaud's Illuminations: A Study in Angelism, by Wallace Fowlie; A Hopkins Reader, edited by John Pick and Selected Poems of Gerard Manley Hopkins, edited by James Reeves. Dublin Review, 227 (Winter, 1953), 371-80.

2918 Spehar, Elizabeth Marie. "Gerard Manley Hopkins as a Literary Critic." M.A. thesis, University of Colorado, 1946.

2919 Spellanzon, Giannina. "Il Dramma di Hopkins: La Vita Estranea," l'Avvenire d'Italia (Bologna), (November 27, 1958).

2920 _____ "Gerard Manley Hopkins," l'Indice d'Oro (Rome), (October, 1958), 369-70.

2921 Spencer, Theodore. "Poet in Search of 'Inescape'." [sic] Review of Gerard Manley Hopkins. A Life, by Eleanor Ruggles. Saturday Review, 27 (September 2, 1944), 20.

2922 Spender, Stephen. The Creative Element: A Study of
       Vision, Despair and Orthodoxy among some Modern
       Writers. London: Hamish Hamilton, 1953, 29.

2923 _____ The Destructive Element: A Study of Modern
       Writers and Beliefs. Philadelphia: Albert Saifer, 1953,
       173, 220.

2924 _____ Review of Further Letters of Gerard Manley Hopkins
       Including his Correspondence with Coventry Patmore,
       edited by Claude Colleer Abbott and The Mind and Art
       of Coventry Patmore, by J. C. Reid. London Magazine,
       4 (April, 1959), 58-61.

2925 _____ Review of Immortal Diamond, edited by Norman
       Weyand, S.J. Universities Quarterly (London), 4 (May
       1950), 293-95.

2926 _____ "The Modern Necessity." The Struggle of the
       Moderns. Berkeley: University of California Press,
       1963, 98-109.

2927 _____ "Shook Foil" (Letter to the Editor), New Statesman
       (London), (May 17, 1963). [Reply by Donald Davie.]

2928 Speyrer, Anna Elizabeth. "Bibliography of the Gerard
       Manley Hopkins Collection in the Crosby Library,
       Gonzaga University." M.A. thesis, Gonzaga Univer-
       sity, 1962.

2929 Spheres (Mount St. Agnes College, Baltimore, Maryland).
       "Gerard Manley Hopkins Issue," (Spring, 1948), 1-35.

2930 Spira, Theodor. "Gerard Manley Hopkins: Zu Einer
       Deutschen Neuerscheinung," Anglia (Tubingen), 74
       (1956), 333-44.

2931 Squire, John Collings. The Cambridge Book of Lesser
       Poets. Cambridge, England: University Press, 1927,
       443.

2932 Srinivasa Iyengar, Kodaganallur Ranaswami. "Gerard
       Manley Hopkins" (in three parts), New Review
       (Calcutta), 7 (January, February, March, 1938), 1-11,
       115-25, 264-73.

2933 _____ Gerard Manley Hopkins: The Man and the Poet.
       Oxford: Geoffrey Cumberlege, Oxford University
       Press, Indian Branch, 1948.

2934 Stadlen, Peter. "Manley Hopkins Poems set by Rubbra,"
       Daily Telegraph (London), (April 1, 1967).

2935 Stageberg, Norman C. and Wallace L. Anderson. Poetry
       as Experience. New York: American Book Company,
       1952.

2936 Stallknecht, Newton P. "On Metaphor." Review of
Models and Metaphors: Studies in Language and
Philosophy, by Max Black; Metaphor in Hopkins, by
Robert Boyle, S.J. and Metaphor and Reality, by
Philip Wheelwright. Yale Review, 51 (Summer, 1962),
637-42.
2937 Stallman, Robert. "A Selective Bibliography on the
Criticism of Poetry 1920-1942," University Review, 10
(Autumn, 1943), 65-71.
2938 Stanek, Rose Marie. "Hopkins and Philosophy," Spheres
(Mount St. Agnes College, Baltimore, Maryland),
(Spring, 1948), 19-21.
2939 Stanford, Derek. "Christian Humanist: Recent Works on
Hopkins," Month, N.S. 24 (September, 1960), 158-64.
2940 _____ Review of The Journals and Papers of Gerard Manley
Hopkins, edited by Humphry House and The Sermons and
Devotional Writings of Gerard Manley Hopkins, edited
by Christopher Devlin, S.J. English, 12 (Summer,
1959), 191-92.
2941 _____ "The Lineage of English Poetry," Poetry Review, 49
(May, 1948), 188-92.
2942 _____ Review of The Power of Blackness: Hawthorne,
Poe, and Melville, by Harry Levin; Poets' Grammar, by
Francis Berry and The Shaping Vision of Gerard Manley
Hopkins, by Alan Heuser. English, 12 (Spring, 1959),
146-48.
2943 _____ "Their Bond was Poetry." Review of Chaucer, by
D. S. Brewer; Sir Walter Ralegh, by Philip Edwards
and Gerard Manley Hopkins--A Selection of his Poems
and Prose, edited by W. H. Gardner. Yorkshire
Observer (Bradford, Yorks), (November 19, 1953).
2944 Stanford, William Bedell. "Gerard Manley Hopkins,"
Sheed & Ward's Own Trumpet, 23 (May, 1950), 8.
[Book talk given from Radio Eireann.]
2945 _____ "Gerard Manley Hopkins and Aeschylus," Studies,
30 (September, 1941), 359-68.
2946 Stanier, R. S. "Gerard Hopkins's Metres" (Letter to the
Editor), Times Literary Supplement, (February 23, 1933),
127.
2947 Stanzel, Franz. "G. M. Hopkins, W. B. Yeats, D. H.
Lawrence und die Spontaneitat der Dichtung."
Anglistische Studien: Friedrich Wild zum 70 Geburtstag
Festschrift, edited by Karl Brunner, Herbert Koziol,
and Siegfried Korninger. Wien: Wilhem Braumuller,
1958, 179-93.

2948 "Star of Balliol" (Editorial), Catholic Times (London),
     (June 19, 1953).
2949 Stauffer, Donald A. The Nature of Poetry. New York:
     W. W. Norton & Company, Inc., 1946, 40-2, 74-6,
     155, 214, 247-48.
2950 Stauffer, Robert E. "To the Greater Glory of God." Review
     of A Hopkins Reader, edited by John Pick. Voices: A
     Journal of Poetry, No. 152 (September-December, 1953),
     55-7.
2951 Stein, Karen F. "Hopkins' 'The Wreck of the Deutschland':
     An Aesthetic Analysis." M.A. thesis, Pennsylvania
     State University, 1966.
2952 Steiner, George, ed. The Penguin Book of Modern Verse
     Translation. Harmondsworth, Middlesex: Penguin
     Books, 1966.
2953 Stempel, Daniel. "A Reading of 'The Windhover', "
     College English, 23 (January, 1962), 305-07.
2954 Stenten, Cathryn Davis. "A Study of the Poetic Theories
     of Coventry Patmore, Robert Bridges and Gerard Hopkins
     as the Basis for a System of Modern Prosody." M.A.
     thesis, University of Nebraska, 1963.
2955 Stenzel, H., S.J. "Geistliches Wort." Review of
     Hopkins, G.M.: Gedichte--Schriften--Briefe, edited
     by Wolfgang Clemen. Stimmen der Zeit, 157
     (December, 1955), 233.
2956 Stephens, James, Edwin Beck and Royall Snow. English
     Poets, Romantic, Victorian and Later. New York:
     American Book Company, 1933, xxxi, xl.
2957 _____, Edwin Beck and Royall Snow. Victorian and Later
     English Poets. New York: American Book Company,
     1937, xxxi, xl, 928-33, 1307-10.
2958 Stephenson, A. A., S.J. "G. M. Hopkins and John
     Donne, " Downside Review, 77 (Fall, 1959), 300-20.
2959 _____ "Gerard Manley Hopkins: A Poet Utterly Given to
     Christ." Review of The Journals and Papers of Gerard
     Manley Hopkins, edited by Humphry House and The
     Sermons and Devotional Writings of Gerard Manley
     Hopkins, edited by Christopher Devlin, S.J. Catholic
     Herald (London), (March 26, 1959), 3.
2960 _____ Review of Gerard Manley Hopkins: Priest and Poet,
     by John Pick. Dublin Review, 212 (April, 1943), 170-74.
2961 Sternfeld, Frederick W. "Poetry and Music--Joyce's
     Ulysses." Sound and Poetry. English Institute Essays
     1956. New York: Columbia University Press, 1963,
     35, 38-9, 41.

2962 Steuert, Dom Hilary. Review of A Hopkins Reader, edited by John Pick. Downside Review, 71 (Autumn, 1953), 459-61.

2963 Stevens, Sister Mary Dominic, O.P. "Hopkins' 'That Nature is a Heraclitean Fire'," Explicator, 22 (November, 1963), 18.

2964 Stillinger, Jack. "Hopkins' 'Skate's Heel' in 'The Windhover'," Notes & Queries, N.S. 6 (June, 1959), 215-16.

2965 Stobie, Margaret R. "Patmore's Theory and Hopkins' Practice," University of Toronto Quarterly, 19 (October, 1949), 64-80.

2966 Stonier, George Walter. "Books in General." Review of Gerard Manley Hopkins, Priest and Poet, by John Pick. New Statesman and Nation, 24 (September 26, 1942), 207.

2967 _____ "Books in General." Review of Letters of Gerard Manley Hopkins and Robert Bridges, edited by Claude Colleer Abbott. New Statesman and Nation, N.S. 9 (January 26, 1935), 108.

2968 _____ "Gerard Manley Hopkins." Gog Magog and Other Critical Essays. Essay Index Reprint Series. Freeport, New York: Books for Libraries Press, Inc., 1966, 43-63.

2969 _____ "Gerard Manley Hopkins." Review of Poems of G. M. Hopkins, edited by Charles Williams. New Statesman and Nation, N.S. 3 (June 25, 1932), 836-38.

2970 _____ "Hopkins." Review of Gerard Manley Hopkins (1844-1889). A Study of Poetic Idiosyncrasy in Relation to Poetic Tradition, by W. H. Gardner. New Statesman and Nation, N.S. 28 (November 4, 1944), 307-08.

2971 _____ "More Hopkins Letters." Review of Further Letters of Gerard Manley Hopkins, edited by Claude Colleer Abbott. New Statesman and Nation, 15 (May 14, 1938), 840-42.

2972 _____ Review of The Poetry of Gerard Manley Hopkins, by E. E. Phare. Fortnightly Review, 135 (March, 1934), 374.

2973 _____ "The Young Hopkins." Review of The Note-Books and Papers of Gerard Manley Hopkins, edited by Humphry House. New Statesman and Nation, N.S. 13 (January 23, 1937), 124-26.

2974 Storey, Graham. "Hopkins" (Letter to the Editor), Encounter, 13 (July, 1959), 86-7.

2975 _____ "The Notebooks and Papers of Gerard Manley
     Hopkins: A New Edition," Month, N.S. 20 (November
     1958), 273-81. [A talk given in the B.B.C. Third
     Programme, 23 February 1958.]
2976 _____ "Six New Letters of Gerard Manley Hopkins,"
     Month, N.S. 19 (May, 1958), 263-70.
2977 Storm, Melvin G. "Gerard Manley Hopkins: The Poet as
     Critic." M.A. thesis, University of Wyoming, 1966.
2978 Strecto, James. (Letter to the Editor). New York Times
     Book Review, (November 10, 1957), 34.
2979 "Stroud Festival of Religious Drama and the Arts," Musical
     Events (London), (October, 1965), 30-2.
2980 Stutterheim, Cornelius Ferdinand Petrus. Review of Gerard
     Manley Hopkins: A Critical Essay Towards the Under-
     standing of his Poetry, by W. A. M. Peters. Lingua
     (Haarlem, Netherlands), 3 (1952), 109-13.
2981 Surtz, Edward L. "The Religious Aspect of the Poetry of
     Gerard Manley Hopkins." M.A. thesis, Xavier Univer-
     sity, 1934.
2982 Sutcliffe, Edmund Felix. Bibliography of the English
     Province of the Society of Jesus 1773-1953. Roehampton,
     London: Manresa Press, 1957, 206-08.
2983 Sutherland, Donald. "Hopkins Again," Prairie Schooner,
     35 (Fall, 1961), 197-242.
2984 Swallow, Alan, ed. Rinehart Book of Verse. New York:
     Rinehart and Company, 1952, 312-13, 361.
2985 Sweeney, Maxwell. "Going Your Way: When the First
     Christmas Card was Sent, and Now," Evening Herald
     (Dublin), (December 28, 1955).
2986 Sylvester, Howard E. "A Study of Gerard Manley Hopkins."
     M.A. thesis, University of New Mexico, 1941.
2987 Symes, Gordon. "Hopkins, Herbert and Contemporary
     Modes," Hibbert Journal, 47 (July, 1949), 389-94.
2988 Symons, Julian. "The Virtuous Victorian," Tribune
     (London), (December 28, 1956).
2989 Szlosek, J. F. "Gerard Manley Hopkins, S.J.," Stylus
     (Boston College), 58 (Spring, 1945), 54-6, 60.
2990 Talbot, Norman. "A Note on 'God's Granduer" [sic],
     Balcony: The Sydney Review, No. 3 (1965), 46.
2991 "Talk on Difficult Verse," Chichester Observer, (November
     24, 1951). [Report of talk by Anthony Bertram.]
2992 Tamplin, John C. "The Forsaken Forged Feature: A Study
     of Gerard Manley Hopkins' Sonnet, 'Henry Purcell'."
     M.A. thesis, Kent State University, 1966.

2993 Tate, Allen. "Foreword." Selected Writings: Poetry and Criticism, by Herbert Read. London: Faber & Faber, Ltd., 1963; New York: Horizon Press, 1964.

2994 _____ "Miss Emily and the Bibliographer." On the Limits of Poetry. New York: William Morrow & Company, 1948, 60. [Also in Reason in Madness: Critical Essays. New York: G. P. Putnam's Sons, 1941.]

2995 Taylor, E. K. "Gerard Manley Hopkins: A Poet for Priests," Clergy Review, 37 (July, 1952), 394-404.

2996 Taylor, Frajam. "The Rebellious Will of Gerard Manley Hopkins," Poetry, 59 (February, 1942), 270-78.

2997 Taylor, Griffin. "The Province of the Poem is not Dark: Some Views of the Recovery of Immanence." Review of The Disappearance of God, by J. Hillis Miller. Sewanee Review, 72 (October-December, 1964), 698-709.

2998 Taylor, Michael. "Hopkins' 'God's Grandeur,' 3-4," Explicator, 25 (April, 1967), 68.

2999 Taylor, Robert A., S.J. "Poetic Meaning." M.A. thesis, Gonzaga University, 1954, 61.

3000 Teeling, John. "Admirable Criticism." Review of Metaphor in Hopkins, by Robert Boyle, S.J. America, 106 (October 14, 1961), 50-1.

3001 Templeman, William Darby. "Hopkins and Whitman: Evidence of Influence and Echoes," Philological Quarterly, 33 (January, 1954), 48-65.

3002 _____ "Ruskin's Ploughshare and Hopkins' 'The Wind-hover'," English Studies (Amsterdam), 43 (April, 1962), 103-06.

3003 Therese, Sister M. I Sing of a Maiden: The Mary Book of Verse. New York: Macmillan Company, 1947, 189-94, 402.

3004 Therese, Sister, S.N.D. "Hopkins' 'Spelt from Sibyl's Leaves'," Explicator, 17 (April, 1959), 45.

3005 They Look at Wales: An Anthology of Prose and Verse. Cardiff: University of Wales Press Board, 1941, 16.

3006 Thomas, Alfred, S.J. "G. M. Hopkins: An Unpublished Triolet," Modern Language Review, 61 (April, 1966),

3007 _____ "G. M. Hopkins and the Silver Jubilee Album," Library, 5th Series, 20 (June, 1965), 148-52.

3008 _____ "G. M. Hopkins and 'Tones'," Notes & Queries, N.S. 12 (November, 1965), 429-30.

3009 _____ "Gerard Manley Hopkins: 'Doomed to Succeed by Failure'," Dublin Review, 240 (Summer, 1966), 161-75.

3010 _____ "Hopkins, Welsh and Wales," Cymmrodorion
Society Transactions (London), (1965), 272-85.
3011 _____ "A Hopkins Fragment Replaced" (Letter to the Editor),
Times Literary Supplement, (January 20, 1966), 48.
3012 _____ "A Note on Gerard Manley Hopkins and his
Superiors, 1868-77," Irish Ecclesiastical Record,
5th Series, 104 (October-November, 1965), 286-91.
3013 _____ "Odd Priest Out" (Letter to the Editor), Times
Literary Supplement, (October 27, 1966), 981.
3014 Thomas, Anthony Leighton. "Evaluating a Composer of
Note," Western Mail (Cardiff), (July 22, 1961).
3015 Thomas, Gilbert. "Difficult Nonage." Review of The
Golden Echo, by David Garnett. Birmingham Post,
(January 12, 1954).
3016 _____ "Round the Shelves." Review of Further Letters of
Gerard Manley Hopkins, edited by Claude Colleer
Abbott. Birmingham Post, (December 18, 1956).
3017 _____ "Round the Shelves." Review of The Journals and
Papers of Gerard Manley Hopkins, edited by Humphry
House and The Sermons and Devotional Writings of
Gerard Manley Hopkins, edited by Christopher Devlin,
S.J. Birmingham Post (February 17, 1959).
3018 Thomas, Henri. "Gerard Manley Hopkins." Review of
Gerard Manley Hopkins, Reliquiae, edited by Pierre
Leyris. Nouvelle Revue Francaise (Paris), 6 (January 1,
1958), 122-25.
3019 Thomas, J. D. "Hopkins' 'The Windhover'," Explicator,
20 (December, 1961), 31.
3020 Thomas, M. G. Lloyd. Review of Gerard Manley Hopkins:
A Critical Essay Towards the Understanding of his
Poetry, by W. A. M. Peters, S.J. Cambridge Journal,
2 (April, 1949), 438-40.
3021 _____ "Hopkins as Critic," Essays and Studies, 32
(1946), 61-73.
3022 _____ Review of Immortal Diamond, edited by Norman
Weyand, S.J. Review of English Studies, N.S. 2
(October, 1951), 397-99.
3023 Thomas, Marie A. "Gerard Manley Hopkins 1844-1944,"
Ethos (Emmanuel College, Boston, Massachusetts),
17 (June, 1944), 142-53.
3024 Thomas, Neville Penry. "Dylan Thomas--Roaring Angel of
English Poetry." Review of Dylan Thomas: A Literary
Study, by Derek Stanford and Quite Early One Morning:
Broadcasts by Dylan Thomas. Church of England Newspaper (London), (December 3, 1954).

3025 Thomas, R. George. "Private Poetry." Review of Language as Gesture, by R. P. Blackmur. Western Mail (Cardiff), (January 19, 1955).

3026 Thomas, Ronald Stuart. "A Frame for Poetry," Times Literary Supplement, (March 3, 1966).

3027 _____, ed. The Penguin Book of Religious Verse. Baltimore, Maryland: Penguin Books, 1963, 11, 21-3, 90, 105, 181.

3028 Thomas, Wright and Stuart Gerry Brown. Reading Poems: An Introduction to Critical Study. New York: Oxford University Press, 1941, 494-97, 505, 587-88.

3029 Thomson, J. A. K. The Classical Background of English Literature. London: Allen and Unwin, 1948, 259.

3030 "Thorndike in 'Some Men and Women'," Stage (London), (March 28, 1963).

3031 Thornton, Francis Beauchesne. "Essay on 'The Wreck of the Deutschland'," Catholic World, 160 (October, 1944), 41-6.

3032 _____ "Gerard Manley Hopkins: Major Poet or Major Craftsman?" America, 56 (January 23, 1937), 379-80.

3033 _____ Review of A Gerard Manley Hopkins Reader, edited by John Pick. Catholic Digest, 18 (November, 1953), 105-06.

3034 _____ "Hopkins Again" (Letter to the Editor), America, 56 (February 20, 1937), 475.

3035 _____, ed. "Gerard Manley Hopkins, S.J." Return to Tradition: A Directive Anthology. Milwaukee: Bruce Publishing Company, 1948, 62-72.

3036 Thwaite, Anthony. "Gerard Manley Hopkins." Contemporary English Poetry: An Introduction. Melbourne: Heinemann, 1959, viii, 2, 15-27, 60, 96-7, 105, 110, 134.

3037 _____ "Gerard Manley Hopkins." Contemporary English Poetry: An Introduction, 3rd ed. London: Heinemann, 1964, viii, 2, 15-27, 62, 98-9, 107, 112, 137.

3038 Thwaites, Michael. "The Devoted Doorkeeper: A Searching Sonnet," Melbourne Age (Australia), (January 19, 1952). ["St. Alphonsus Rodriguez"]

3039 _____ "G. M. Hopkins--Forerunner of the Moderns," Melbourne Age (Australia), (June 24, 1950).

3040 _____ "The Pros and Cons of Originality," Melbourne Age (Australia), (February 14, 1953).

3041 _____ "The Victorian Age," Melbourne Age (Australia), (June 10, 1950).

3042 Tierney, Michael. "Gerard Hopkins's Metres" (Letter to the Editor), Times Literary Supplement, (February 16, 1933), 108.

3043 _____ "Gerard Hopkins's Metres" (Letter to the Editor), Times Literary Supplement, (March 9, 1933), 167.

3044 _____ "Studies in Literature." Review of The Poetry of Gerard Manley Hopkins, by E. E. Phare and Patmore: A Study in Poetry, by Frederick Page. Studies, 23 (March, 1934), 180-81.

3045 Tillemans, Th. "Is Hopkins a Modern Poet?" English Studies (Amsterdam), 24 (June, 1942), 90-5.

3046 Tiller, Terence. "Major or Minor?" Review of Gerard Manley Hopkins: A Study of Poetic Idiosyncrasy in Relation to Poetic Tradition, by W. H. Gardner. Vol. 2. Tribune (London), (July 15, 1949).

3047 Tillotson, Geoffrey. "Bridges's Debt to Hopkins" (Letter to the Editor), Times Literary Supplement, (June 30, 1961), 408.

3048 _____ "Hopkins and Ruskin" (Letter to the Editor), Times Literary Supplement, (January 6, 1956), 7.

3049 _____ "Matthew Arnold in 1954." Review of Matthew Arnold: Poetry and Prose, edited by John Bryson. Spectator (London), (April 2, 1954).

3050 Tillyard, Eustace Mandeville Wetenhall. Poetry and its Background: Illustrated by Five Poems 1470-1870. London: Chatto & Windus, 1961, 76. [Covered by label reading "New York, Barnes & Noble." First published in 1948 under title Five Poems 1470-1870: An Elementary Essay on the Background of English Literature. London: Chatto & Windus.]

3051 The Times, London. Literary Supplement. American Writing Today: Its Independence and Vigor, edited by Allan Angoff. New York: New York University Press, 1957, 15, 23, 70, 388.

3052 Tindall, William York. Forces in Modern British Literature 1885-1946. New York: Alfred A. Knopf, 1947.

3053 _____ The Literary Symbol. Bloomington: Indiana University Press, 1955.

3054 Tobias, R. C. "The Year's Work in Victorian Poetry: 1962," Victorian Poetry, 1 (August, 1963), 223-30.

3055 _____ "The Year's Work in Victorian Poetry: 1963," Victorian Poetry, 2 (Summer, 1964), 187-202.

3056 _____ "The Year's Work in Victorian Poetry: 1964," Victorian Poetry, 3 (Spring, 1965), 119-35.

3057 _____ "The Year's Work in Victorian Poetry: 1965,"
Victorian Poetry, 4 (Summer, 1966), 175-98.

3058 _____ "The Year's Work in Victorian Poetry: 1966,"
Victorian Poetry, 5 (Autumn, 1967), 183-215.

3059 Tonnac-Villeneuve, G. de. "Le Choix Difficile," Suisse
(Geneva), (April 13, 1950).

3060 Topliss, John. (Letter to the Editor), G.K.'s Weekly, 22
(October 31, 1935), 86.

3061 Torchiana, Donald Thornhill. "Pater, Newman and the
Poetic Development of G. M. Hopkins." M.A. thesis,
University of Iowa, 1949.

3062 Towner, Annemarie Ewing. "Welsh Bardic Meters and
English Poetry," Massachusetts Review, 6 (Spring-
Summer, 1965), 614-24.

3063 Townsend, Francis G. Review of The Unmediated Vision:
An Interpretation of Wordsworth, Hopkins, Rilke, and
Valery, by Geoffrey F. Hartman. Journal of English and
Germanic Philology, 55 (January, 1956), 166-68.

3064 Townsend, Gerard James. "A Comparative Study of 'The
Wreck of the Deutschland' by Gerard Manley Hopkins
and 'The Dark Night of the Soul' by St. John of the
Cross." M.A. thesis, Tulane University, 1963.

3065 Toynbee, Philip. "The Man in the Centre." Review of
Essays on Literature and Ideas, by John Wain.
Observer (London), (October 6, 1963).

3066 _____ "The Modern Philosophy Game." Review of
Freedom and the Will, edited by David Pears.
Observer (London), (March 10, 1963).

3067 _____ "Today, There is no such Thing as a Fashion in
Literature," Times of Ceylon (Colombo), (April 18,
1954). [Reprinted under title "Literary Fashions" in
East African Standard (Nairobi), (April 23, 1954).]

3068 Trapanese, Vincenzo. "Coventry Patmore: Mistico Poeta
dell'Amore," Campana (Naples), (December 4, 1955).

3069 Trappes-Lomax, M. "The Literary Club," Stonyhurst
Magazine, 14 (February, 1919), 632-33.

3070 Traversi, Derek. "La Poesia de Gerard Manley Hopkins,"
Nuestro Tiempo (Madrid), 15 (1961), 1330-47.

3071 Treece, Henry. "The Debt to Hopkins." Dylan Thomas.
London: Lindsay Drummond, 1949, 58-71.

3072 _____ "Gerard Manley Hopkins and Dylan Thomas." How
I See Apocalypse. London: Lindsay Drummond, 1946,
129-39.

3073 _____ "Treece on Thomas." Anonymous Review of Dylan
       Thomas, by Henry Treece. Liverpool Daily Post,
       (September 7, 1949).

3074 Treneer, Anne. "Beauty Past Change." Review of Gerard
       Manley Hopkins, by W. H. Gardner. Time and Tide,
       30 (July 16, 1949), 726-27.

3075 _____ "The Criticism of Gerard Manley Hopkins."
       Penguin New Writing, No. 40, edited by John Lehmann.
       Harmondsworth, Middlesex: Penguin Books Ltd.,
       1950, 98-115.

3076 Trethowan, Dom Illtyd. Review of Gerard Manley Hopkins,
       by W. A. M. Peters, S.J. Downside Review, 66
       (October, 1948), 479.

3077 Trewin, J. C. "Fire in the Ears," John O'London's Weekly,
       (February 29, 1952), 198.

3078 Tripp, Kathryn Stewart. "Gerard Manley Hopkins and the
       Self." M.A. thesis, Columbia University, 1965.

3079 Trower, Philip. "The Priest as Artist." Review of Gerard
       Manley Hopkins, a Life, by Eleanor Ruggles.
       Spectator, 178 (December 19, 1947), 776, 778.

3080 Troy, William. " 'Gloried from Within'." Review of The
       Notebooks and Papers of Gerard Manley Hopkins, edited
       by Humphry House. Nation, 144 (May 1, 1937),
       511-12.

3081 _____ "The New Parnassianism and Recent Poetry,"
       Chimera, (Winter-Spring, 1944), 3-16.

3082 Trudeau, Sister Paul Augusta, O.P. "A Commentary on the
       'Terrible' Sonnets of Gerard Manley Hopkins." M.A.
       thesis, University of New Mexico, 1964.

3083 Trueblood, Charles K. "The Esthetics of Gerard Hopkins,"
       Poetry, 50 (August, 1937), 274-80.

3084 Turnell, George M. "Homage to Gerard Manley Hopkins."
       Review of New Verse, No. 14, April, 1935. Colosseum,
       2 (June, 1935), 156-58.

3085 _____ "Two Notes on Modern Poetry: I. Hopkins to W. H.
       Auden," Colosseum, 3 (June, 1936), 120-25.

3086 Turnell, Martin. "The Formation of Hopkins." Review of
       Gerard Manley Hopkins, Priest and Poet, by John Pick.
       Tablet (London), 180 (October 17, 1942), 192.

3087 _____ Modern Literature and Christian Faith. Westminster,
       Maryland: Newman Press, 1961.

3088 Turner, Edmond Glen. "A Study of Dialect in the Poetry of
       Gerard Manley Hopkins." M.A. thesis, University
       of Idaho, 1961.

3089 Turner, Brother H. Paul, F.S.C. "An Indexed Synthesis of the Critical Thought of Gerard Manley Hopkins." M.A. thesis, De Paul University, 1954.

3090 Turner, Luke, O.P. Review of Poems of Gerard Manley Hopkins, by W. H. Gardner. 3rd ed. Blackfriars, 30 (January, 1949), 40.

3091 Turner, Vincent, S.J. "An American Study of Gerard Manley Hopkins." Review of The Shaping Vision of Gerard Manley Hopkins, by Alan Heuser. Month, N.S. 21 (January, 1959), 54-5.

3092 _____ "An Essay in Inscape." Review of Gerard Manley Hopkins, by W. A. M. Peters, S.J. Tablet (London), 192 (July 3, 1948), 10.

3093 _____ "Gerard Manley Hopkins," Duckett's Register, No. 36 (September, 1948), 1-3.

3094 _____ "Gerard Manley Hopkins, 1844-1944," Dublin Review, 215 (October, 1944), 144-59.

3095 _____ "A Two-Dimensional Portrait." Review of Gerard Manley Hopkins: A Life, by Eleanor Ruggles. Tablet (London), 191 (January 24, 1948), 58.

3096 Turner, W. J. "Gerard Manley Hopkins (1844 to 1889)," Spectator, 173 (July 14, 1944), 32-3.

3097 _____ "Poet and Priest." Review of Gerard Manley Hopkins, Priest and Poet, by John Pick. Spectator, 168 (October 2, 1942), 318.

3098 _____ "Some Modern Poetry." Review of Poems of Gerard Manley Hopkins, edited by Robert Bridges. 2nd ed.; Ash Wednesday, by T. S. Eliot; The Collected Poems of Edith Sitwell, and Doctor Donne and Gargantua, by Sacheverell Sitwell. Nineteenth Century and After, 109 (February, 1931), 243-52.

3099 "20th Century Poets," Eastbourne Gazette, (December 22, 1948).

3100 Tyne, James L. Review of Gerard Manley Hopkins. A Study of Poetic Idiosyncrasy in Relation to Poetic Tradition, by W. H. Gardner. Thought, 24 (June, 1949), 351-52.

3101 Underhill, Evelyn. "Gerard Hopkins." Review of Gerard Manley Hopkins, by G. F. Lahey, S.J. Spectator, 145 (September 6, 1930), 318.

3102 _____ Mysticism: A Study in the Nature and Development of Man's Spiritual Consciousness. 16th ed. New York: E. P. Dutton and Company Inc., 1948, 254.

3103 United States Library of Congress. Division of Bibliog-
       raphy. Chief Bibliographer. Gerard Manley Hopkins,
       1844-1889. A Bibliographical List. Washington,
       D. C.: United States Library of Congress, 1940, 12 pp.

3104 Untermeyer, Louis. "Gerard Manley Hopkins." Lives of
       the Poets. New York: Simon & Schuster, 1959,
       590-600.

3105 _____ Makers of the Modern World. New York: Simon &
       Schuster, 1955, 137, 204-08, 521, 755-56.

3106 _____ Play in Poetry. New York: Harcourt Brace & Co.,
       1938, 40-8.

3107 _____, ed. The Book of Living Verse, Limited to the Chief
       Poets. New York: Harcourt, Brace and Company,
       1939, 473-75.

3108 _____, ed. A Concise Treasury of Great Poems. Garden
       City, New York: Permabooks, 1953, 376-79.

3109 _____, ed. A Critical Anthology. New York: Harcourt,
       Brace and Company, 1930, 15-7, 96-106, 506-07,
       520-22.

3110 _____, ed. Modern American Poetry; Modern British
       Poetry. combined ed. New York: Harcourt, Brace and
       Company, 1936, 15-7, 96-106, 506, 521.

3111 _____, ed. Modern British Poetry: A Critical Anthology.
       New York: Harcourt, Brace and Company, 1925, 36-9.
       [Pages 96-104 in 1936 edition; 45-54 in 1942 edition.]

3112 _____ and Carter Davidson. Poetry: Its Appreciation and
       Enjoyment. New York: Harcourt, Brace and Company,
       1934, 197, 304, 377.

3113 Unver, Leonard and William Van O'Connor. Poems for
       Study. New York: Rinehart & Company, 1953, 703.

3114 Unwin, Rayner. The Rural Muse: Studies in the Peasant
       Poetry of England. London: George Allen and Unwin
       Ltd., 1954, 15, 153-54, 159-61.

3115 Ure, Peter. Review of The Journals and Papers of Gerard
       Manley Hopkins, edited by Humphry House and The
       Sermons and Devotional Writings of Gerard Manley
       Hopkins, edited by Christopher Devlin, S.J. Review
       of English Studies, 11 (November, 1960), 445-47.

3116 _____ Review of Robert Bridges and Gerard Hopkins
       1863-1889. A Literary Friendship, by Jean-Georges
       Ritz. Review of English Studies, 12 (August, 1961),
       317-18.

3117 Vallette, Jacques. "Gerard Manley Hopkins." Review of
Note-Books and Papers of G. M. Hopkins, edited by
Humphry House; The Letters of G. M. Hopkins, edited
by Abbott; The Poems of G. M. Hopkins; G. M.
Hopkins, Priest and Poet, by John Pick; G. M. Hopkins,
A Critical Essay, by W. A. M. Peters; G. M. Hopkins,
A Life, by E. Ruggles and G. M. Hopkins, A Study, by
W. H. Gardner. Mercure de France (Paris), 307
(November, 1949), 529-32.

3118 _____ Review of The Journals and Papers of Gerard Manley
Hopkins, edited by Humphry House. Mercure de France
(Paris), 336 (June 1, 1959), 337.

3119 _____ Review of Reliquiae, par G. M. Hopkins, edited by
Pierre Leyris. Mercure de France (Paris), 331
(December, 1957), 696.

3120 Van Doren, Mark. Introduction to Poetry. New York:
William Sloane Associates, Inc., 1951, 426-28.

3121 _____ "The Plain Case of Gerard Manley Hopkins,"
Griffin, 2 (July, 1953), 23-6.

3122 _____, ed. An Anthology of World Poetry. New York:
Reynal & Hitchcock, 1936, 1256-57.

3123 Vann, Gerald, O.P. Review of The Mind and Poetry of
Gerard Manley Hopkins, S.J., by Bernard Kelly.
Colosseum, 2 (September, 1935), 233-34.

3124 Veech, T. "Notes." Review of A Hopkins Reader, edited
by John Pick. Australasian Catholic Record (Sydney),
30 (October, 1955), 335-38.

3125 Verdina, Renato. "Panorama della Lirica Inglese da Hardy
agli Apocalittici," l'Eco di Bergamo, (October 5, 1951).

3126 Versfeld, Marthinus. Mirror of Philosophers. London:
Sheed & Ward, 1960, 173-74.

3127 Vickers, Brian. "Hopkins and Newman" (Letter to the
Editor), Times Literary Supplement, (March 3, 1966),
178.

3128 Vines, Sherard. "Poetry from the Mid-Victorian Age." A
Hundred Years of English Literature. London: Gerald
Duckworth and Company, 1950, 33, 154-91.

3129 Vogelgesang, John. "Hopkins' Sonnet to R.B.,"
Philippine Studies (Manila), 6 (August, 1958), 315-24.

3130 W. D. A. "Lustgarten did his best, but . . . ," Derby
Evening Telegraph, (July 25, 1957).

3131 W. P. M. Review of Contemporary Irish Poetry, edited by
Robert Greacen and Valentin Iremonger and New Irish
Poets, edited by Devin A. Garrity. Dublin Magazine,
(July, 1949), 63-64.

3132 Wagner, Robert D. "Gerard Manley Hopkins: The
'Terrible Sonnets' and other Poems of Desolation."
M.A. thesis, Columbia University, 1948.

3133 Wain, John. "Discursive Critic." Anonymous Review of
Essays on Literature and Ideas. Times Literary Supplement, (October 11, 1963), 799.

3134 _____ "Gerard Manley Hopkins: An Idiom of Desperation."
Chatterton Lecture on an English Poet (Read 13 May
1959). Proceedings of the British Academy, 45 (1959),
173-197. [Reprinted in Venture, Karachi University
English Teachers Association, 2 (September-December,
1961), 147-73; also reprinted in Essays on Literature
and Ideas, by John Wain. London: Macmillan and Co.,
Ltd; New York: St. Martin's Press, 1963, 103-31;
also reprinted in Hopkins: A Collection of Critical
Essays, edited by Geoffrey H. Hartman. Englewood
Cliffs, New Jersey: Prentice-Hall, Inc., 1966, 57-70.]

3135 _____ "Hit and Miss." Anonymous Review of Preliminary
Essays. Times (London), (August 1, 1957).

3136 _____ "Prose Writings of a Great Poet-Priest whose Fame
Grows Steadily." Review of The Journals and Papers of
Gerard Manley Hopkins, edited by Humphry House.
New York Herald Tribune Weekly Book Review, (March
15, 1959), 8.

3137 _____ " 'A Stranger and Afraid': Notes on Four Victorian
Poets." Preliminary Essays. London: Macmillan and
Company, Ltd., 1957, 93-120.

3138 Waley, Arthur. "From the Chinese." Anonymous Review
of Ballads and Stories from the Tun-huang. Times
Literary Supplement (London), (March 3, 1961), 129.

3139 Walker, M. E. "Four Independent Men of Letters Within a
Tradition." Review of Four Independents, by Daniel
Sargent. New York Times Book Review, (July 7, 1935),
2.

3140 _____ "In the World of Gerard Manley Hopkins." Review
of The Note-Books and Papers of Gerard Manley
Hopkins, edited by Humphry House. New York Times
Book Review, (June 27, 1937), 6.

3141 _____ "Letters of Gerard Manley Hopkins." Review of
The Letters of Gerard Manley Hopkins to Robert Bridges
and The Correspondence of Gerard Manley Hopkins and
Richard Watson Dixon, edited by Claude Colleer Abbott.
New York Times Book Review, (March 10, 1935), 2.

3142 _____ "The Loneliness of the Priest." Review of Further
Letters of Gerard Manley Hopkins, edited by Claude
Colleer Abbott. New York Times Book Review, (July 10,
1938), 9.
3143 Walker, Ralph S. "An Introduction to the Poetry of Gerard
Manley Hopkins," Aberdeen University Review, 25
(July, 1938), 232-43.
3144 Wall, Sister Mary Aquin, C.S.J. "The Christian Synthesis
of Art and Prudence as Exemplified in Gerard Manley
Hopkins." M.A. thesis, Gonzaga University, 1950.
3145 Waller, Robert. "False or Inspired?" Review of A New
Romantic Anthology, edited by Stefan Schimanski;
Dylan Thomas, by Henry Treece and The Labyrinth, by
Edwin Muir. Time and Tide, 30 (October 29, 1949),
1082.
3146 Walsh, Thomas, ed. The Catholic Anthology. rev. ed.
New York: Macmillan Company, 1940, 292-96, 534-35.
3147 Walsh, William. "G. M. Hopkins and a Sense of the
Particular." The Use of Imagination: Educational
Thought and the Literary Mind. London: Chatto &
Windus, 1959, 121-36.
3148 Walsh, William Thomas. "Sabotage on Parnassus,"
America, 61 (May 6, 1939), 91-2.
3149 Walton, Eda Lou. "Portrait of a Poet." Review of The
Letters of Gerard Manley Hopkins to Robert Bridges, and
The Correspondence of Gerard Manley Hopkins and
Richard Watson Dixon, edited by Claude Colleer Abbott.
Nation, 141 (July 24, 1935), 109-11.
3150 _____ "A Study of the Poetry of Gerard Manley Hopkins."
Review of The Poetry of Gerard Manley Hopkins: A
Survey and Commentary, by E. E. Phare. New York
Times Book Review, (January 28, 1934), 2.
3151 Warburg, Jeremy. "Idiosyncratic Style," Review of English
Literature, 6 (April, 1965), 56-65.
3152 Ward, Adolphus William and A. R. Waller, eds. The
Cambridge History of English Literature. V. 13. New
York: Macmillan and Company, 1933, 230-31, 234.
3153 Ward, Dennis. "Gerard Manley Hopkins's 'Spelt from
Sibyl's Leaves'," Month, N.S. 8 (July, 1952), 40-51.
3154 _____ "G. M. Hopkins: 'The Windhover'." Interpretations:
Essays on Twelve English Poems, edited by John Wain.
London: Routledge and Kegan Paul, 1955, 138-52.
3155 Warrack, John. "Setting the Poets of Our Time," Daily
Telegraph (London), (July 7, 1956).

3156 Warren, Austin. "Gerard Manley Hopkins (1844-1889)."
Gerard Manley Hopkins, by the Kenyon Critics.
London: Dennis Dobson Ltd, 1949, 8-20.

3157 _____ "Instress of Inscape," Kenyon Review, 6 (Summer,
1944), 369-82. [Reprinted in Gerard Manley Hopkins,
by the Kenyon Critics, 1949, 74-89; in Victorian Literature: Modern Essays in Criticism, edited by Austin
Wright, 1961, 182-92; in Hopkins: A Collection of
Critical Essays, edited by Geoffrey H. Hartman, 1966,
168-77; and as "Gerard Manley Hopkins" in Rage for
Order: Essays in Criticism, by Austin Warren, 1948,
52-65 and 1959, 52-65.]

3158 _____ "Monument not Quite Needed." Review of Gerard
Manley Hopkins: A Life, by Eleanor Ruggles. Kenyon
Review, 6 (Autumn, 1944), 587-89.

3159 Warren, C. Henry. "Broadcast Poetry" (Letter to the
Editor), Listener, (September 18, 1958).

3160 _____ Review of The Letters of Gerard Manley Hopkins to
Robert Bridges and The Correspondence of Gerard Manley
Hopkins and Richard Watson Dixon, edited by Claude
Colleer Abbott. Fortnightly Review, 143 (April, 1935),
503-04.

3161 Wasmuth, Ewald. "G. M. Hopkins' Asthetik," Neue
Rundschau (Frankfurt/M.), 66 (Winter, 1955), 590-604.

3162 [Water, Charlotte Van de]. "Poems to Remember" ('The
Windhover'), Scholastic, 44 (March 13, 1944), 20.

3163 Waterhouse, John F. "Gerard Manley Hopkins and Music,"
Music and Letters, 18 (July, 1937), 227-35.

3164 Waters, J. Kevin, S.J. "Inversnaid" (Choral song with flute,
oboe, violas, harp, piano), words by Gerard Manley
Hopkins. Unpublished score, 1964. [Musical setting]

3165 Watson, George, ed. The Concise Cambridge Bibliography
of English Literature. Cambridge, England: University
Press, 1958, 145, 151, 172, 183, 204.

3166 _____ The Concise Cambridge Bibliography of English
Literature 600-1950. 2nd ed. Cambridge, England:
University Press, 1965, 180.

3167 Watson, Thomas L. "Hopkins' 'God's Grandeur',"
Explicator, 22 (February, 1964), 47.

3168 Watson, Youree, S.J. "The Loss of the Eurydice: A
Critical Analysis." Immortal Diamond, edited by
Norman Weyand, S.J. New York: Sheed & Ward,
1949, 307-32.

3169 Wayman, Dorothy G. "Mary and Two Poets," Cord: A
Franciscan Spiritual Review, 10 (April, 1960), 121-24.

3170 Weatherhead, A. Kingsley. "G. M. Hopkins: The Wind-
hover," Notes & Queries, N.S. 3 (August, 1956), 354.
3171 Webster, E. M. "Rubbra's 'Inscape' at Stroud Festival,"
Musical Opinion (London), (January, 1966).
3172 Wecker, John Clement. "A Survey of the Influence of a
Common Religion upon Four 19th-Century Catholic
Poets--Alice Meynell, Francis Thompson, Coventry
Patmore, and Gerard Manley Hopkins." M.A. thesis,
University of Southern California, 1948.
3173 Weiss, Theodore. "Gerard Manley Hopkins: A Study in
Romanticism." M.A. thesis, Columbia University,
1940.
3174 _____ "Gerard Manley Hopkins: Realist on Parnassus,"
Accent, 5 (Spring, 1945), 135-44. [Reprinted in Accent
Anthology, edited by Kerker Quinn and Charles Shattuck.
New York: Harcourt, Brace and Company, 1946,
664-77.
3175 _____ "On Seeing a Portrait of Gerard Manley Hopkins"
(Poem), Columbia University Quarterly, 32 (December,
1940), 332.
3176 Welby, Thomas Earle. A Popular History of English Poetry.
New York: Appleton, 1924, 271-72.
3177 Welch, Sister M. Charlotte, O.S.B. "The Unity of Gerard
Manley Hopkins' Achievement." M.A. thesis, Loyola
University, Chicago, 1942.
3178 Welland, D. S. R. "Half-Rhyme in Wilfred Owen: Its
Derivation and Use." Review of English Studies, N.S.
1 (July, 1950), 226-41.
3179 Wellek, Rene and Austin Warren. Theory of Literature.
New York: Harcourt Brace and Company, 1956.
3180 Wellesz, Egon. "The Leaden Echo and the Golden Echo"
(Cantata for high voice, violin, clarinet, violincello
and piano), words by Gerard Manley Hopkins. London:
Schott & Co. Ltd.; New York: Associated Music
Publishers, [1947]. [Musical setting]
3181 "Wellesz Setting of Hopkins: First Performance in London,"
Times (London), (February 24, 1959).
3182 Wells, Henry W. New Poets from Old: A Study in Literary
Genetics. New York: Russell & Russell, Inc., 1964,
35-43.
3183 West, Edward J. "Appleby Among the Earless People: Or,
Nightmares of the Ivory Tower," Shakespeare Quarterly,
1 (April, 1950), 84-8.

3184 Westerlinck, Albert. "Een Onsterfelijke Diamant: G. M. Hopkins," Dietsche Warande en Belfort (Antwerp), (August-September, 1950), 421-26.

3185 Westrup, Jack Allan. "A Great English Song-Writer," Listener, 30 (July 22, 1943), 109.

3186 _____ Review of The Journals and Papers of Gerard Manley Hopkins, edited by Humphry House. Music and Letters, 41 (January, 1960), 74-5.

3187 _____ Purcell. New York: Collier Books, 1962, 282.

3188 Westwater, Sister Agnes Martha, S.C.H. "Sea Imagery in Gerard Manley Hopkins' 'The Wreck of the Deutschland'." M.A. thesis, St. John's University, 1962.

3189 Weyand, Norman, S.J. The Catholic Renascence in a Disintegrating World. Chicago: Loyola University Press, 1951.

3190 _____ "A Chronological Hopkins Bibliography." Immortal Diamond, edited by Norman Weyand, S.J. New York: Sheed & Ward, 1949, 393-436.

3191 _____ "Gerard Manley Hopkins" (Letter to the Editor), Times Literary Supplement, (August 19, 1949), 403.

3192 _____ "The Historical Basis of 'The Wreck of the Deutschland' and 'The Loss of the Eurydice'." Immortal Diamond, edited by Norman Weyand, S.J. New York: Sheed & Ward, 1949, 353-92.

3193 _____ "Hopkins--Poet." Review of Gerard Manley Hopkins, Priest and Poet, by John Pick. Books on Trial, 2 (May-June, 1943), 273.

3194 _____ "Hopkins' Verse Forms" (Letter to the Editor), America, 79 (October 2, 1948), 608.

3195 _____ "Jesuit Scholar Lists Tributes to Famous Poet: American Author Writes Work on Gerard Hopkins." Review of Gerard Manley Hopkins, A Life, by Eleanor Ruggles. New World (Chicago), (September 15, 1944), 13.

3196 _____ "John Pick Writes of Great English Poet: Evaluates Work of Gerard Manley Hopkins." Review of Gerard Manley Hopkins, Priest and Poet, by John Pick. New World (Chicago), (July 9, 1943), 11.

3197 _____ (Letter to the Editor), Spirit, 2 (July, 1935), 90-1.

3198 _____ "Opening Some Doors." Review of Further Letters of Gerard Manley Hopkins, edited by Claude Colleer Abbott. 2nd ed., and Mastery and Mercy, by Philip M. Martin. Renascence, 11 (Fall, 1958), 53.

3199 _____ "Preface." Immortal Diamond. London: Sheed & Ward, 1948, ix-xiii.

3200 _____ "The Vision and the Writing." Review of The
Shaping Vision of Gerard Manley Hopkins, by Alan
Heuser; The Sermons and Devotional Writings of Gerard
Manley Hopkins, edited by Christopher Devlin, S.J.
and The Journals and Papers of Gerard Manley Hopkins,
edited by Humphry House. Renascence, 19 (Winter,
1962), 106-09.

3201 _____, ed. Anonymous Review of Immortal Diamond.
Harvester, 11 (1949), 110.

3202 _____, ed. Anonymous Review of Immortal Diamond.
Listener, 43 (March 9, 1950), 443-44.

3203 _____, ed. Anonymous Review of Immortal Diamond.
New Yorker, 25 (April 16, 1949), 107.

3204 _____, ed. "Poetry and Praise." Anonymous Review of
Immortal Diamond. Standard (Dublin), (January 27,
1950), 3.

3205 _____, ed. "Yeats and Hopkins." Anonymous Review of
Yeats: The Man and the Masks, by Richard Ellman and
Immortal Diamond, edited by Norman Weyand, S.J.
Scotsman (Edinburgh), (December 22, 1949).

3206 Weygandt, Cornelius. The Time of Yeats: English Poetry
of To-Day Against an American Background. New York:
D. Appleton-Century Company, 1937, 386-88, 398,
431, 435, 441.

3207 Whalley, George. Poetic Process. London: Routledge &
Kegan Paul Ltd, 1953.

3208 Wheeler, Charles B. The Design of Poetry. New York:
W. W. Norton & Company, Inc., 1966, 4, 57, 76, 114,
199, 227, 275.

3209 Whelan, Rosalie C. "The Critical Reception of the First
and Second Editions of the Poems of Gerard Manley
Hopkins." M.A. thesis, Marquette University, 1957.

3210 White, Antonia. "Revealing Dialogue." Review of Journal,
1939-49, by Paul Bloomfield. Public Opinion,
(December 15, 1950), 15.

3211 White, Eric Walter. "The Midsummer Marriage," Adelphi
(London), (2nd quarter, 1955), 263-72.

3212 White, Gertrude M. "Hopkins' 'God's Grandeur': A Poetic
Statement of Christian Doctrine," Victorian Poetry, 4
(Autumn, 1966), 284-87.

3213 White, Helen C. The Metaphysical Poets: A Study in
Religious Experience. New York: Macmillan Company,
1936, 19.

3214 White, John P. Review of The Disappearance of God, by
       J. Hillis Miller. Blackfriars, 45 (June, 1964), 279-82.
3215 White, Terence de Vere. "Gallimaufry or Hodgepodge."
       Review of Poets' Choice, compiled by Patric Dickinson
       and Sheila Shannon. Irish Times (Dublin), (August 5,
       1967).
3216 Whitehall, Harold. "From Linguistics to Poetry." Sound
       and Poetry. English Institute Essays 1956. New York:
       Columbia University Press, 1963, 138-39.
3217 _____ "Pararhyme in Three Poems," West African Journal
       of Education (Nigeria), 11 (June, 1967), 90-3.
       [Hopkins' "Moonrise"; Wilfred Owen's "Arms and the
       Boy"; Dylan Thomas' "Especially when the October
       Wind."]
3218 _____ "Sprung Rhythm," Kenyon Review, 6 (Summer,
       1944), 333-54. [Reprinted in Gerard Manley Hopkins,
       by the Kenyon Critics, 1949, 35-57.]
3219 Whitlock, Baird W. "Gerard Hopkins' 'Windhover',"
       Notes & Queries, N.S. 3 (April, 1956), 169-71.
3220 Whitridge, Arnold. "Gerard Manley Hopkins," University
       Review, 7 (June, 1941), 247-56.
3221 _____ "Poet's Workshop." Review of The Note-Books and
       Papers of Gerard Manley Hopkins, edited by Humphry
       House. Saturday Review, 16 (July 10, 1937), 20.
3222 Wickham, John F. "Mariology in G. M. Hopkins," Month,
       N.S. 12 (September, 1954), 151-72.
3223 Wiggin, Maurice. "A Buyer's Market," Sunday Times
       (London), (August 16, 1953).
3224 Wilcox, Stewart C. Review of The Unmediated Vision: An
       Interpretation of Wordsworth, Hopkins, Rilke and
       Valery, by Geoffrey H. Hartman. Books Abroad, 30
       (Autumn, 1956), 443.
3225 Wild, Freidrich. Sprache und Literatur." Review of The
       Letters of Gerard Manley Hopkins to Robert Bridges and
       The Correspondence of Gerard Manley Hopkins and
       Richard Watson Dixon, edited by Claude Colleer Abbott.
       Anglia, Beiblatt, 49 (1938), 78-82.
3226 Wilder, Amos Niven. "Gerard Manley Hopkins: The
       Priest as Poet." Modern Poetry and the Christian
       Tradition: A Study in the Relation of Christianity to
       Culture. New York: Charles Scribner's Sons, 1952,
       12, 73, 125, 148-75, 195, 250.
3227 _____ The Spiritual Aspects of the New Poetry. New
       York: Harper and Brothers, 1940, 9, 98, 198, 238.

3228 Willer, William Herman. "The Poetic Evolution of Gerard Manley Hopkins." M.A. thesis, University of Minnesota, 1937.

3229 Willey, Basil. Review of The Disappearance of God, by J. Hillis Miller. Modern Language Review, 59 (July, 1964), 467-68.

3230 Williams, Charles. "Gerard Hopkins." Review of Gerard Manley Hopkins: A Study of Poetic Idiosyncrasy in Relation to Poetic Tradition, by W. H. Gardner. Time and Tide, 26 (February 3, 1945), 102-03. [Reprinted in Image of the City and Other Essays, by Charles Williams. London: Oxford University Press, 1958, 48-51.

3231 _____ "Gerard Hopkins and Milton" (Letter to the Editor), Poetry Review, 30 (July-August, 1939), 307-08.

3232 _____ "Gerard Manley Hopkins" (Letter to the Editor), Times Literary Supplement, (January 1, 1931), 12.

3233 _____ The New Book of English Verse. London: Victor Gollancz Ltd., 1935, 16-8, 785-90, 809.

3234 Williams, Margaret. Word-Hoard. New York: Sheed & Ward, 1940, 19-20.

3235 Williams, Oscar, ed. Immortal Poems of the English Language: British and American Poetry from Chaucer's Time to the Present Day. New York: Pocket Books, Inc., 1952, 458-73.

3236 _____, ed. A Little Treasury of Modern Poetry, English and American. New York: Charles Scribner's Sons, 1946.

3237 Williams, Trevor. "Approfondi' gli Studi Sulle Vitamine: Giovinezza Solitaria di Hopkins Nobel Inglese per la Biochimica," Gazzetta del Sud (Messina), (August 23, 1961), 3.

3238 Williams, W. E. "Fireside Studies." Observer (London), (January 8, 1950).

3239 Williamson, Claude Charles H., O.S.C. "Gerard Manley Hopkins" (2 parts), Pax (Benedictines of Prinknash, Gloucester), 28 (July, August, 1938), 87-91, 107-10.

3240 Wills, Mary Suzanne. "An Analysis of the Influence of the Spiritual Exercises of St. Ignatius on the Poetry of Gerard Manley Hopkins." M.A. thesis, Indiana State College, 1963.

3241 Willy, Margaret. Review of Crisis in English Poetry, 1880-1940, by Vivian de Sola Pinto. English, 8 (Autumn, 1949), 290-91.

3242 _____ Review of Gerard Manley Hopkins, by W. H. Gardner. English, 5 (Spring, 1945), 126-27.

3243 _____ Review of Gerard Manley Hopkins: Priest and Poet, by John Pick. English, 4 (Spring, 1943), 131-32.

3244 Wilson, Carolyn. "Turntable," Records and Recording (London), (November, 1967), 20.

3245 Wilson, Conrad. "Dame Sybil Plays the Hostess," Scotsman (Edinburgh), (May 13, 1963).

3246 Wilson, Howard Aaron. "A Study of Gerard Manley Hopkins' Prosody." M.A. thesis, Washington State College, 1937.

3247 Wilson, Winefride. "Benedicite," Tablet (London), (March 2, 1957).

3248 Wimsatt, William Kurtz, Jr. The Verbal Icon: Studies in the Meaning of Poetry. New York: Noonday Press, 1958, 270-71.

3249 _____ and Cleanth Brooks. Literary Criticism: A Short History. New York: Knopf, 1957, 443, 547.

3250 _____ and Monroe C. Beardsley. "The Concept of Meter: An Exercise in Abstractions." Essays on the Language of Literature, edited by Seymour Chatman and Samuel R. Levin. Boston: Houghton Mifflin Company, 1967, 91-114. [Reprinted from PMLA, 74 (December, 1959), 585-98.]

3251 Winslow, Amy. "Marjorie Hill Allee," Horn Book, 22 (May, 1946), 194.

3252 Winstedt, Richard O. "Gerard Manley Hopkins," Guardian (London), (July 21, 1944), 251.

3253 _____ "Gerard Manley Hopkins" (Letter to the Editor), Guardian (London), (August 11, 1944), 276.

3254 Winter, J. L. "Notes on 'The Windhover'," Victorian Poetry, 4 (Summer, 1966), 212-13.

3255 Winters, Yvor. "The Audible Reading of Poetry," Hudson Review, 4 (Autumn, 1951), 433-47. [Reprinted in The Function of Criticism, by Yvor Winters. Denver: Alan Swallow, 1957, 81-100 and in The Structure of Verse: Modern Essays on Prosody, edited by Harvey Gross. Greenwich, Connecticut: Fawcett Publications, Inc., 1966, 131-49.]

3256 _____ Anonymous Review of The Function of Criticism. Times Literary Supplement, (March 30, 1962), 219.

3257 _____ "Gerard Manley Hopkins." Hopkins: A Collection
of Critical Essays, edited by Geoffrey H. Hartman.
Englewood Cliffs, New Jersey: Prentice-Hall, Inc.,
1966, 37-56. [Reprinted from "The Poetry of Gerard
Manley Hopkins" (Parts I and III) in The Function of
Criticism. Denver: Alan Swallow, 1957, 101-56.]

3258 _____ In Defense of Reason. New York: Swallow Press &
William Morrow and Company, 1947.

3259 _____ "The Poetry of Gerard Manley Hopkins" (Parts I and
II), Hudson Review, 1 (Winter, 1949); 2 (Spring, 1949),
455-76, 61-93. [Reprinted in The Function of Criticism
Denver: Alan Swallow, 1957, 101-56 and in On Modern
Poets. New York: Meridian Books, Inc., 1959,
144-91.]

3260 _____ "Robert Bridges and Elizabeth Daryush," American
Review, 8 (January, 1937), 353-67.

3261 Wintringham, Margaret. "To Understand Hopkins."
Review of The Selected Poems of Gerard Manley
Hopkins, edited by James Reeves and A Hopkins Reader,
edited by John Pick. Time and Tide, (September 5,
1953), 1153-54.

3262 Winwar, Frances. "Wilde and the Butterfly." Wilde and
the Yellow Nineties. New York: Harper Brothers,
1940, 145-47.

3263 Witherspoon, Alexander M. The College Survey of English
Literature. New York: Harcourt, Brace and Company,
1951.

3264 Wolfe, Ann F. "Impassioned Victorian Poet." Review of
Francis Thompson: In his Paths, by Terence L.
Connolly. Saturday Review, 28 (January 13, 1945), 26.

3265 Wolff, Lucien. Review of The Poetry of Gerard Manley
Hopkins, by E. E. Phare. Revue Anglo-Americaine
(Paris), 11 (August, 1934), 546-47.

3266 Wolking, Sister M. Teresa, O.S.B. "Hopkins' 'The
Blessed Virgin Compared to the Air we Breathe': A
Study in Unity." M.A. thesis, Catholic University of
America, 1952.

3267 Wollaston, Arthur. "Gerard Manley Hopkins: Catholic
and Poet." Review of Gerard Manley Hopkins, by
W. H. Gardner. Egyptian Gazette (Cairo), (December
12, 1949).

3268 Woodring, Carl R. "Once More 'The Windhover',"
Western Review, 15 (Autumn, 1950), 61-4.

3269 Woods, George Benjamin. Poetry of the Victorian Period.
Chicago: Scott, Foresman and Co., 1930, 776-78,1045.

3270 Woodyard, Vivian Welch. "A Study of the Vector in the Poetry of Gerard Manley Hopkins." B.A. thesis, University of California (Riverside), 1962.

3271 Wooton, Carl. "The Terrible Fire of Gerard Manley Hopkins," Texas Studies in Literature and Language, 4 (Autumn, 1962), 367-75.

3272 Wordsworth, Andrew. "The Dorset Poet." Review of William Barnes of Dorset, by Giles Dugdale. Time and Tide, (July 4, 1953).

3273 "Wordsworth and After," Yorkshire Evening Post (Leeds), (April 24, 1950).

3274 "The World of School." Anonymous Review of Pedagogues are Human. An Anthology of Pupils and Teachers, compiled by R. L. Megroz. Times Literary Supplement, (March 17, 1950).

3275 Worsley, T. C. "Parlour Games." Review of Fifty Works of Literature we could do Without, by Brigid Brophy, Michael Levey and Charles Osborne. Financial Times (London), (June 1, 1967).

3276 " 'Wreck of the Deutschland': Bath Doctor on Famous Poem," Bath and Wilts Chronicle (England), (January 22, 1949).

3277 Wright, Brooks. "Hopkins' 'God's Grandeur'," Explicator, 10 (October, 1951), 5.

3278 Wright, David. "American Poetry." Review of The Penguin Book of Modern American Verse, edited by Geoffrey Moore. Time and Tide, (March 20, 1954).

3279 Wright, J. B. "Sublimities Surveyed." Review of Immortal Diamond, edited by Norman Weyand, S.J. Poetry Review, 51 (July, 1950), 215-17.

3280 Wyatt, E. V. R. Review of Gerard Manley Hopkins, by the Kenyon Critics. Commonweal, 44 (April 19, 1946), 20-1.

3281 "Yale Graduate Student Discovers Unknown Hopkins 'Journals,' Poems," Yale News, 69 (December 16, 1947), 1.

3282 Yeats, William Butler, ed. The Oxford Book of Modern Verse 1892-1935. Oxford: Clarendon Press, 1937, xxxix-xl, xlvii, 17-23. [Also 1947 printing]

3283 Yetts, Walter Percival. "Memoir of the Translator." The Six Scripts or the Principles of Chinese Writing, by Tai T'ung, translated by L. C. Hopkins. Cambridge (England): University Press, 1954, vii-xviii.

3284 Yetzer, Bernard Edward. "The Victorianism of Gerard
Manley Hopkins." M.A. thesis, University of
Oklahoma, 1965.
3285 Yoggerst, Sister M. Hilary. "Gerard Manley Hopkins as
a Critic of Coventry Patmore's Poetry." M.A. thesis,
Marquette University, 1948.
3286 Young, B. A. (Letter to the Editor), G. K.'s Weekly, 22
(October 24, 1935), 70.
3287 _____ (Letter to the Editor), G. K.'s Weekly, 22
(November 21, 1935), 134.
3288 Young, George Malcolm. Daylight and Champaign:
Essays. London: Rupert Hart-David, 1948, 183-84,
188-91.
3289 _____ "Forty Years of Verse," London Mercury, 35
(December, 1936), 112-22.
3290 _____ "Tunes Ancient and Modern." Review of Aspects of
Modern Poetry, by Edith Sitwell and A Hope for Poetry,
by C. Day Lewis. Life and Letters, 11 (February,
1935), 544-54.
3291 _____ Victorian England: Portrait of an Age. 2nd ed.
New York: Oxford University Press, 1964.
3292 Young, Kenneth. "Ashamed to be a Poet." Review of The
Journals and Papers of Gerard Manley Hopkins, edited
by Humphry House and The Sermons and Devotional
Writings of Gerard Manley Hopkins, edited by
Christopher Devlin, S.J. Daily Telegraph (London),
(February 13, 1959).
3293 _____ "Mr. Auden Mellows." Review of Homage to Clio,
by W. H. Auden; Seeing is Believing: Poems, by Charles
Charles Tomlinson and Gerard Manley Hopkins; Edward
Thomas; Rupert Brooke; Laurie Lee (Vista Books). Daily
Telegraph (London), (July 8, 1960).
3294 Young, Lillian. "The 'Maker' and his Maker: A Study of
the Conflict Between the Devotion to Art and to God in
Michelangelo, Donne and Hopkins as a Background for
their Religious Sonnets." M.A. thesis, Cornell
University, 1959.
3295 Zabel, Morton Dauwen. "Gerard Manley Hopkins: Poetry
as Experiment and Unity," Poetry, 37 (December,
1930), 152-61.
3296 _____ "Hopkins in his Letters," Poetry, 46 (July, 1935),
210-19.

3297 _____ "The Palace and the House." Review of Further
    Letters of Gerard Manley Hopkins Including his
    Correspondence with Coventry Patmore, edited by
    Claude Colleer Abbott. New Republic, 97 (November
    30, 1938), 106.
3298 Zamboni, Armando. "Un Grande Poeta Inglese: Gerard
    Hopkins," Realta Politica (Rome), (December 5, 1959).
3299 _____ "La Poesia Inglese," Corriere Mercantile (Genoa),
    (December 20, 1950).
3300 _____ "Poeti Cattolici dell 'Inghilterra Moderna," Sicilia
    del Popolo (Palermo), (June 29, 1948).
3301 Zelocchi, Rosanna. "La 'Barbarica Bellezza' di Gerard
    Manley Hopkins," Convivium, 29 (July-August, 1961),
    461-71.

Index

1089
Boyle, Robert R., S.J., 1090-1105
Boyle, Robert R., S.J., review of, 1654, 1682, 1854, 1864, 1992, 2058, 2741, 2757, 2936, 3000
Bradbrook, Muriel Clara, 172, 1106-1108
Bradbury, Ernest, 1109
Bradley, Andrew Cecil, ed., 259, 446, 622
Bradley, Arthur Granville, 173
Bradley, Edward, 149
Bradley, Henry, 174-175, 193, 257-258
Braz, Joao, review of, 2888
Braybrooke, Neville, ed., 1110
Braye, Alfred, 176-178
Bregy, Katharine, 1111-1113
Bregy, Katharine, ed., 1211
Bremond, Andre, S.J., 1114-1116
Bremond, Henri, 179
Brennan, Joseph Xavier, 1117
Brennan, Norman Charles, 1118
Bretelle, Leon, 1119
Brewer, D. S., review of, 2943
Bridgeman, Cunningham, 313
Bridges (Elizabeth Daryush), see Daryush, Elizabeth
Bridges, John A., 181-183
Bridges, Monica, 274-275
Bridges, Robert Seymour, 158, 174-175, 184-262, 350, 378, 396, 435, 450, 501, 533, 644, 722, 740, 788-789, 804, 839-840, 871, 888, 893, 899, 1030, 1120-1122, 1275, 1282, 1484, 1632, 1708, 1763, 1871, 1936, 2201, 2230, 2447-2448, 2514, 2626, 2646, 2721, 2727, 2842, 2850,

2904, 2906, 2954, 3047, 3260
Bridges, Robert Seymour, bibliography of, 572, 799
Bridges, Robert Seymour, ed., 35, 49-54, 263, 382, 615, 1123-1137, 1264, 1323, 1491, 1579, 1749, 1785-1786, 2056, 2061, 2085, 2089, 2139, 2281, 2292, 2297, 2410, 2460, 2480, 2502, 2614, 2656, 2681, 2770, 2797, 2808, 3098
Brimley, George, 277
Brinkley, Maxine, 1138
Brinlee, Robert Washington, 1137
Brinnin, John Malcolm, ed., 1605
Brion, Marcel, 1140
Briscoe, John Fetherstonhaugh, 278
Bristol, England, 710
Britton, John, S.J., 1141
Broadbent, John Barclay, 1142
Brockington, Alfred Allen, 1143
Brooke, Jocelyn, 1144
Brooke, Rupert, 3293
Brooke-Rose, Christine, 1145-1146
Brooks, Cleanth, 1147-1150, 3249
Brooks, Cleanth, ed., 1151
Brooks, Edna Belle, 1152
Brooks, John Lee, ed., 1089
Brooks, Van Wyck, ed., 1242
Brophy, Brigid, 3275
Brophy, James, 1153
Brophy, James D., Jr., 1154
Brown, Alec, 1155
Brown, Edward K., 1156
Brown, Sister Margaret Eugene, C.S.J., 1157

Brown, Marie Patricia, 1158
Brown (Rosalie Moore), 2373–2375
Brown, Stephen, S.J., 1159–1160
Brown, Stuart Gerry, 3028
Brown, T. J., 1161
Brown, Thomas Edward, 280–281
Browne, Henry, S.J., 282
Browne, Wynyard, 1162
Browning, Robert, 2083, 2150
Brunini, John G., ed., 991, 1300, 1480, 1482–1483, 1569, 2162, 2284, 2789
Bryant, Arthur, 283
Bryce, James, 284
Brydges, Egerton, 602
Bryson, John, ed., review of, 3049
Buckler, William Earl, 285
Buckley, Jerome H., 1163–1166
Buckley, Vincent, 1167
Buckton, A., 286
Buffalo, University of, 712
Buggy, Sister James Marita, I.H.M., 1168
Bullen, Arthur Henry, 287–288
Bullough, Geoffrey, 1169, 1171, 1656
Bullough, Geoffrey, review of, 1170, 1656
Bungert, Hans, 1172
Burckhardt, Sigurd, 1173–1174
Burdett, Osbert, 289, 1175
Burgess, Anthony, 1176–1177
Burgum, Edwin Berry, 1178
Burke, Francis, S.J., 1179–1180
Burke, Kenneth, 1181–1182
Burke, Molly M., 1183
Burke, Sister Pauline, S.S.J., 1184

Burkhardt, Sigurd, see Burckhardt, Sigurd
Burne-Jones, Edward, 202, 290
Burne-Jones, Georgiana (MacDonald), 290
Burns, Chester A., S.J., 1185
Burns, George, S.J., 291
Burnshaw, Stanley, 1186
Burr, Carol, 1187
Burton, James Rector, 1188
Busby, Christopher, 1189
Bush, Douglas, 1190–1191
Bussey, George Moir, 292
Byles, Mary, 1192
Byrne, Virginia Carmel, 1193–1194

C. B., 1195
C. P., 293
C. T., 1196
Cabau, Jacques, 1197
Caine, T. Hall, 294–295, 1198, 2316
Cairns, Huntington, 1199
Caliri, Flavia M., 1200
Callahan, Virginia Woods, 1201
Calverley, Charles Stuart, 296
Camberwell, London, 121
Cambridge University, 297–299
Cameron, J. M., 300
Campbell, Lewis, ed., 530
Campbell, Sister M. Mary, S.C.M.M., 1203
Campbell, Roy, 301, 1202
Campbell, Vivian, ed., 1204
Campion, Edmund, S.J., (Blessed), 586, 783
Canon (music), 647
Canterbury, England, 764
Capellanus, 1205
Carey, Charles M., 1206
Carlingford, Chichester Samuel

Congreve, William, 2745
Conlay, Iris, 1296
Conley, John, 1297
Conlon, Sister M. Brendan, 1299
Conlon, Michael J., 1298
Connemara, Ireland, 451
Connolly, Cyril, 495
Connolly, Francis X., 1300-1302
Connolly, Terence L., 3264
Connor, Sister Juanita Marie, S.S.J., 1303
Conquest, Robert, 338-339
Consolata, Sister Mary, 1304
Contemporary Modes, 2987
Coogan, Marjorie D., 1305-1307
Cook, Albert, 1308-1309
Coombes, Henry, 1310-1311
Cooney, Mother Madeleine Sophie, 1312
Cooper, Charles W., 1313
Copland, Aaron, 3244
Copleston, Frederick C., 1314
Copyright, 742
Corcoran, Timothy, S.J., 340
Corke, Hilary, 1315-1316
Cornwall, England, 367
Corr, Gerard M., O.S.M., 1317
Corrado da Alatri, O.F.M., 1318
Cory, William, 573
Corvo, Frederick Baron (pseud.), see Rolfe, Frederick William
Cosmological Motion, 1875
Costello, William Thomas, S.J., 1319
Couldrey, Oswald, 1320
Counterpoint, 647, 2053, 2370
Coursen, Herbert R., Jr., 1321
Courtney, Janet Elizabeth

(Hogarth), 341
Courtney (Marjorie Quennell), 732
Courtney, Sister Therese, S.N.D., 1322
Courtney, W. L., 341
Cowley, Malcolm, 1323
Cox, Dorothy Scarborough, 1324
Cox, George Valentine, 342
Cox, R. G., 1325-1326
Crane, Hart, 944
Cranny, Titus, S. A., 1327
Crashaw, Richard, 2242
Crawford, John, 1328
Crawley, Richard, 343
Crehan, J. H., 1329-1330
Creighton, Louis (von Gehn) 344
Creighton, Mandell, Bishop of London, 344
Croce, Benedetto, 1332-1333
Crompton, Louis, 1334
Cronin, Anthony, 1335
Crosby Library, 2928
Crowley, Austin, 1336
Cruise, Edward, 1337
Crucifixion, 2366
Cruse, Amy, 1338
Culler, A. Dwight, 1339
Cumberland, England, 426
Cunningham, Margaret, 1340, 1396
Cunningham, Maureen Michaela, 1341
Curious Halo, 4
Curran, C. P., 346
Curran, John Patrick, 1342
Curran, Mary Doyle, see Doyle-Curran, Mary
Currier, Isabel, 1343
Curtis, John, S.J., 347
Cusack, Cyril, 69

1930, 1983, 2016-2017, 2032,
2145, 2299, 2387, 2424,
2486, 2549, 2563, 2606,
2744, 2781, 2900, 2940,
2959, 3017, 3115, 3200,
3292
Devon, England, 367
Dialect, 144, 3088
Dicey, Albert Vern, 368
Dickens, Charles, 526, 1588
Dickinson, Patric, 369
Dickinson, Patric, comp.,
review of, 3215
Dichotomies, 1008
Diction, 1763
Dicus, Sister Mary Vivian, 1431
Digges, Sister Mary Laurentia,
1435
Dilligan, Robert, 1434
Dilly Tante, see Kunitz,
Stanley J.
Dimnet, Ernest, 1436
Dinnage, Paul, 1437
Disher, Maurice Willson, 371
Disraeli, Benjamin (Earl of
Beaconsfield), 595
Ditchfield, Peter Hampson,
ed., 372
Dixon, Richard Watson, 2-3,
257-258, 373-379, 1814,
2021, 2556, 2793
Dobree, Bonamy, 1003, 1438-
1442
Dobree, Bonamy, ed., 1352,
2394
Dobson, Dennis, 1443
Dodgson, Charles Lutwidge,
381
Doherty, Francis, 1444
Doherty, Kevin F., S.J., 1445
Doherty, Paul C., 1446
Dohmann, Sister Ottilia,
S.C.C., 1447

Dolben, Digby Mackworth, 257-
258, 382, 706, 873, 1050,
1826, 1902
Dolman (Mary Helen Alicia
Stapleton), 808
Donne, John, 1271, 1448,
1490, 2167, 2384, 2958,
3294
Donner, H. W., ed., review
of, 2557
Donoghue, Denis, 1449-1451
Donovan, Mary, 1452
Donovan, Mother Mary Inez,
1453
Dore, Gustave, 383
Dorset, England, 3272
Doubleday, Neal Frank, 1454
Doughty, Charles, 1546, 2094
Dowden, Edward, 384
Downes, David Anthony, 1455-
1461
Downes, David Anthony,
review of, 1095, 1252, 1397,
1851, 1862, 2598, 2609
Downey, Harris, 1462-1465
Doyle, Francis G., S.J., 1466
Doyle, Louis F., S.J., 1467-
1469
Doyle, Richard, 385
Doyle-Curran, Mary, 1470
Drake, Robert, 1471
Drake, Walter, 1472
Drew, David, 1473
Drew, Elizabeth, 1474-1475
Driscoll, John Joseph, S.J.,
559
Driscoll, John P., S.J., 1476
Driskell, Leon V., 1477
Dryden, John, 27
Dublin, 133, 763
Dublin University, 386-388
Dublin Years, 2857
Duffy, John, C.SS.R., 1479-

1483

Dugdale, Giles, 389, 3272

Dumbleton, William Albert,
1484

Duncan-Jones, Mrs. Austin,
see Phare, Elsie Elizabeth

Durant, Albert A., O.S.A.,
1485

Durao, Paulo, 1486-1487

Durr, Robert A., 1488

Durrell, Lawrence, 1489

Durrwachter, Carol J., 1490

Duthie, G. J., ed., 2204

E. O., 1491

E. S. P., 1492

East Anglia, England, 739

Eberhardt, Richard, 1493-1495

Ecclesiastical Titles Act, 108

Edinburgh, Scotland, 391

Edlin, Herbert Leeson, 392

Edridge, Ray, 1498, 3276

Edwards, Hugh, 1499

Edwards, Philip, review of,
2943

Effects of Classical Study,
1893

Ehmann, Benedict, 1500-1502

Eisenbaum, Meredith Visnow,
1503

Ellrodt, Robert, 1514

Eleanor, Mother Mary,
S.H.C.J., 1504-1505

Eleanore, Sister M., ed., 1211

Eliot, George (Mary Ann Evans),
2902

Eliot, Thomas Stearns, 172,
944, 1167, 1222, 1506-1508,
1534, 1709, 1957, 1969, 1985,
2169, 2228, 2259, 2384, 2860

Eliot, Thomas Stearns, review
of, 3098

Elkins, Bill James, 1509

Ellart, Gerald, S.J., 1510

Elliot, Brian, 1511

Ellman, Richard, 1512-1513

Ellman, Richard, review of,
3205

Elton, Oliver, 396, 1515

Elliott-Binns, Leonard Elliott,
393

Ellis, Henry, 394-395

Elvin, Lionel, 1516

Emerson, Dorothy, 1517

Empson, William, 397, 1518-
1522

Engels, Friedrich, 398

Engle, Monroe, 1523

Engle, Paul, 1524

English Drawing, 1745

Enright, Dennis Joseph, 1526

Epstein, David, 1527

Erzgraber, Willi, ed., 2397

Essex, England, 125

Estelle, Sister M., O.P., see
Casalandra, Sister M., O.P.

Etman, Nol, 1528

Eton, England, 639

Evans, Benjamin Ifor, 1529-
1534

Evans, Benjamin Ifor, comp.,
1535

Evans, Illtud, 1536

Evans, Marjorie R., comp.,
1537

Evans, Richard X., 1538

Evarts, Prescott, Jr., 1539

Evelyn, Sister Mary, R.S.M.,
1541

Everett, Louella D., ed.,
993

Every, George, S.S.M., 1541

Experiment, 3295

Fabbretti, Nazareno, 1542

Fairbrother, Nan, 1543

Fairbrother, William Henry, 401

Fairchild, Hoxie Neale, 1544-1545

Fairley, Barker, 1546-1547

Farm Street, London, 147, 320-322

Farm Street Church, 402, 423, 746

Farrell, Fran, 1548

Farrell, Melvin Lloyd, 1549

Farren, Robert, 1550

Fausset, Hugh I'Anson, 1556-1561

Faverty, Frederic, ed., 1164, 2575

Feeney, Leonard, S.J., 1562-1569

Feeney, Thomas B., S.J., 1570

Fenelon, Francois, Archbishop of Cambray, 858

Ferguson, Samuel, 408

Fike, Francis George, Jr., 1571

Finlay, Ida, 1572

Fiore, Amadeus, O.F.M., 1573

Fire image, 1299

Fish, Helen Dean, 1574

Fisher, Phil J., 1575

Fitts, Dudley, 1576

Fitzgerald, Percy Hetherington, 410-411

Fitzgerald, R., 1577

Fitzpatrick, A. M., S.T.D., 1578

Flanner, Hildegarde, 1579-1580

Fleisher, Frederic, 1581

Fleming, Lenore Marie Moe, 1582

Fleming, Sandford, 442

Fletcher, Charles Robert Leslie, 412

Fletcher, John Gould, 1583

Flinn, Sean, O.F.M., 1584

Flower, Desmond, 1585

Football Barefoot, 9

Foote, Timothy Gilson, 1586-1587

Ford, Boris, ed., 1588, 2103

Forster, Leonard, 1589-1590

Forte, Felix, 1591

Fortescue, J. W., 859

Fortescue, Edward Bowles, Provost, 2329-2331, 2524

Fowlie, Wallace, 1592

Fowlie, Wallace, review of, 2917

Francis Xavier, St., 139

Frankenburg, Lloyd, 1593-1595

Franz, Louis Joseph, 1596

Fraser, George Sutherland, 1597-1599

Fraser, George Sutherland, trans., 547

Fraser, Maxwell, 413

Fraser, Ronald, 1600

Fraunces, John Manning, S.J., 1601

Frazier, Alexander, 1602

Freeman, Beatrice D., 1603

Freeman, James C., 1604

Friar, Kimon, ed., 1605

Friend-Pereira, F. J., 1606

Frith, William Powell, 414

Frontespizio, 2288

Frost, William, ed., 2199

Fry, Christopher, 1372

Fry, Katharine, 415

Fry, Northrup, 1607-1609

Fuger, Wilhelm, 1610

Fugue, 647

Fulweiler, Howard W., 1611-1612

Inspiration, 1114, 1200, 2378, 2595
Inspiration, Ignatian, 1033, 1423
Instress, 961, 1241, 1306, 1342, 3157
Intellectual Milieu, 2018
Ireland, 516, 645, 779
Iremonger, Valentin, ed., review of, 3131
Irish Catholic Directory, 517-519
Irish University Question, 867
Islington, London, 499

J. A., 1953
J. D. C., 1954
J. F. M., 1955
J. H. K., 1956
J. J. H., 1957
J. J. P., 1958
J. S. W., 1959
Jacks, Laurence Pearsall, 521
Jackson (Lucie Gertrude Raleigh), 734
Jacobson, Bernard, 1960
Jagger, J. H., 1961
Jakobson, Roman, 1962
James, Henry, 2305, 2312
James, Stanley B., 1963-1967
James, Trevor, 1968
Jankowsky, Kurt, 1969
Jannoud, Claude, 1970
Jarrett-Kerr, Martin, 1971
Jaworski, Sister M. Cunegundis, 1972
Jebb, Richard Claverhouse, 522, 795-797
Jefferies, Richard, 2320, 2548
Jennings, Elizabeth, 1973-1976
Jennings, Elizabeth, ed., 801
Jeremy, Sister Mary, 1977-1978
Jerrold, Blanchard, 383

Jesuits, 123, 340, 474, 523, 579, 611
Jesuits, Irish Province, 524-525
John of the Cross, St., 3064
Johnson, E. D. H., review of, 2213
Johnson, Edgar, 526
Johnson, Lionel, 527
Johnson, Ronald W., 1979
Johnson, Wendell Stacy, 1980
Johnston, J. J., 1981
Johnston, John Octavius, 528
Johnston, J. O., ed., 557, 729
Jones, David, 444, 529
Jones, Glyn, 1982
Jones, John, 1983
Jones, Phyllis M., ed., 2691
Joselyn, Sister M., O.S.B., 1984
Joshi, Barburao N., 1985
Jowett, Benjamin, 530-531, 786, 845
Joyce, James, 944, 1259, 1347, 1881, 2859, 2961
Julienne, Sister Mary, S.S.N.D., see Junkersfeld, Sister Mary Julienne, S.S.N.D.
Junkersfeld, Sister Mary Julienne, S.S.N.D., 1986

K. H., 1987
Kahler, Erich, 1988
Kaminsky, Marc, 1989
Kark, Austen, 1990
Karp, Georg, review of, 954
Kearney, Sister Mary Michael, 1991
Keating, John E., 1992-1993
Keating, John E., review of, 1105, 2108

Keating, Joseph Ignatius, S.J., 17, 1994-1999

Keats, John, 48, 532, 1434, 1527, 1664, 2717

Kelly, Bernard, 2000

Kelly, Bernard, review of, 1264, 2566, 2686, 3123

Kelly, Blanche Mary, 2006-2008

Kelly, Hugh, S.J., 2009-2014

Kelly, John C., S.J., 2015-2017

Kelly, Richard W., 2018

Kelshall, T. M., 533

Kelvingrove, Glasgow, 432

Kemp, Friedhelm, 2019

Kenmare, Dallas, 2020

Kenneally, John Daniel, 2021

Kennedy, J., 534

Kennedy, Leo, 2022-2023

Kennedy, R. Dingwall, 2024

Kenner, Hugh, 2025

Kent, Muriel, 2026

Kent, William, 535

Kenyon Critics, 2027, 2157, 2211, 2335, 2359, 3156-3157, 3218

Kenyon Critics, review of, 1414, 1422, 1443, 1479, 1714, 1816, 2028-2030, 2198, 2291, 2390, 2576, 2604, 2677, 2833, 3280

Kerr, Henry Schomberg, S.J., 591

Kermode, Frank, 2031-2032

Kernan, Sister Mary Noel, S.C., 2033

Kerr, Sister Marguerite M., R.S.C.J., 2034

Kersting, A. F., 305

Keunen, Jozef, 2035

Kezys, Algimantas, S.J., 1499, 2036

Kiely, Robert, 2037

Kilbracken, Arthur Godley, 536

Kilburn, Edmund E., 537-538

Kilby, Clyde S., ed., 2038

Kilcoyne, Francis P., 2039

Kildare, Ireland, 337

Kilmer, Joyce, 2040-2043

Kinerk, Robert, 2044

King, Anne R., 2045

King, David Ross, 2046

King, Donald R, 2047

King's College Chapel, Cambridge, 297-299

Kirschbaum, Leo, 2048

Kirwan, J. W., D.D., 853

Kissane, James, 2049

Kitchener, Lord Horatio Herbert, 210

Kite, Elizabeth S., 2050

Klapp, Brother Frank, S.M., 2051

Klein, Arthur Luce, 66

Kliger, Samuel, 2052

Klotz, Rose Mosen, 2053

Knight, Charles, ed., 539-540

Knight, William 541

Knox, Ronald, trans., 29

Koch, Edward, 542

Kopper, Edward A., 2054

Kornacki, Wanda Charlotte, 2055

Koszul, A., 2056

Kreuzer, James R., 2057-2058

Krieger, Murray, 2059

Kuan Hua Chih Nan, 491

Kunitz, Stanley, 2060-2063

Kurz, P. J., S.J., 2064

L. C., 2065
L. H., 2066-2067
La Salette, 631
La Tour du Pin, Patrice de, 547
Lackamp, John Jerome, S.J., 2068
LaDriere, J. Craig, 543, 2069-2070
Lahey, Gerald F., S.J., 2071, 2074-2079
Lahey, Gerald F., S.J., review of, 1264, 1323, 1491, 1579, 1759, 2026, 2060-2061, 2072-2073, 2089, 2292, 2459, 2614, 2665, 2681, 2805, 2820, 3101
Lamalle, Edmund, S.J., 544
Lamont, Corliss, 2080
Lancashire, England, 449, 461, 780
Lancaster, England, 880
Lancelot, John Bennett, 545
Lanctot, Sister Agnes, C.S.J., 2081
Landier, Germain, 2082
Landon, Letitia Elizabeth, 409
Langbaum, Robert W., 2083-2084
Lappin, Henry A., 2085
Lane, Edward William, trans., 126
Lang, Andrew, 249
Lark, 974
Larsson, Raymond, 2086
Lataste, Sister Marie, R.S.C.J., 546
Laube, Clifford J., 2087
Lawler, Donald L, 2088
Lawrence, D. H., 2947
Layard, Austen Henry, 550-551
Lea (Elizabeth Mary Wright), 894

Leahy, Maurice, 2089-2092
Leahy, Maurice, comp., 2125
Lear, Edward, 552
Leary, Jerome V., 2093
Leavis, Frank Raymond, 1167, 2094-2098
Leavis, Frank Raymond, review of, 1260, 2037
Lechmere, W. L., 2099
Lee, A. H. E., ed., 2425
Lee, Christopher, 2100
Lee, Frederick George, 553
Lee, Laurie, 3293
Lee, W. B., 2101
Lees, Francis Noel, 2102-2108
Lees, Francis Noel, review of, 2279
Leggett, Barbara Vaughan, 2109
Legouis, Emile, 2110
Lehmann, John, 2111-2112
Lehmann, John, ed., 357, 3075
Leicester Square, 825
Leighlin, Ireland, 337
Leishman, James Blair, 2113
Lenz, Sister Mary Baylon, O.S.F., 2114
Lenz, Mildred A., 2115
Leslie, Shane, 2116-2119
Leslie, Shane, ed., 2601
L'Estrange, H. K., S.J., 2120-2121
Leo XIII, Pope, 554
Levey, Michael, 3275
Levi, Peter, S.J., 2122-2123
Levin, Harry, review of, 2942
Levin, Samuel R., ed., 1962, 2333, 2489, 2716, 3250
Lewes, England, 293
Lewis, Arthur O., Jr., ed., 1794

Lewis, David, S. J. (Charles Baker), 2124
Lewis, Dominic Bevan Wyndham, 2124-2135
Lewis, Leslie Lisle, 936
Leyris, Pierre, trans., 30, 70, 2126-2128
Leyris, Pierre, trans., review of, 1140, 1197, 1221, 1970, 2241, 2276, 3018, 3119
Leys, Mary Dorothy Rose, 607
Liddell, Adolphus George Charles, 555
Liddon, Henry Parry, 528, 556-558
Lieder, Paul Robert, ed., 2129
Lienhardt, R. G., 2130-2131
Liljegran, Sten Bodvar, 2132
Lillie, Handley William Russell, S.J., 559
Lilly, Gweneth, 2133
Linane, Sister Francis Loretto, S.N.D., 2134
Lincoln, Eleanor, 2135
Lind, L. Roberto, 2136
Lindsay, Donald, 560
Linguistic Analysis, 1877, 1962, 2430
Linton, William James, 561
Lisca, Peter, 2137
Literary Form, 1181
Little, Arthur, S.J., 2138-2139
Little, Velma G., 562
Litzinger, Boyd, 2140-2149
Liverpool, England, 707, 709, 778
Lloyd's Register, 563
Lloyd-Jones, Richard, 2150
Lock, D. R., see Applejoy, Petronius
Lockhard, John Gilbert, 564

Loftie, William John, 565
London, 134-136, 154, 159-160, 383, 430, 499, 535, 539, 565-566, 582, 589, 629, 754, 770, 841, 843, 862, 864, 889-890, 898
Lougheed, W. C., 2151
Louise, Sister Mary, S.L., 2152
Louise, Sister Robert, O.P., 2153
Lorenz, Denis, comp., 956
Lovas, John Charles, 2154
Loveland, Kenneth, 2155
Lovett, Robert, 2367
Lowell, Robert, 927, 1765, 2156-2157
Lucas, Frederick, 359, 568
Lucas, Herbert W., S.J., 569
Ludwig, Hans-Werner, 2158
Ludwig, Hans-Werner, review of, 2132
Lukanitsch, Ruth Marion, 2159
Lynam, Thomas J., S.J., 2160
Lynch, John W., 2161
Lynch, William F., S.J., 2162
Lynd, Robert, 2163-2164

M. C. M., see Meagher, Margaret C.
M. D., 2165
M. M. C., 2166
M. M. W., 2167
M. R., see Roberts, Michael
M. R. R., 2168
M. T., see Michael Tierney
M. W., 2169
M. W. B., 2170
McBrien, William Augustine, 2171-2172
Maccaig, Norman, 2173

MacCallum, Hugh, 2174
McCarthy, Adrian J., S.M., 2177
McCarthy, Adrian James, 2176
MacCarthy, Desmond, 2178-2181
McCarron, Hugh, S.J., 2175
McChesney, Donald, 2182
MacColl, Dugald Sutherland, 2183
McCrossan, Sister Joseph Marie, I.H.M., 2184
McCrossan, Sister Virginia Elizabeth, 2185
McDonagh, Thomas, 2186
MacDonald (Georgiana Burne-Jones), 290
MacDonald, George, 1231
McDonald, Gerald D., 2187-2188
MacDonald, Isobel, review of, 1255
McDonald, Sister Mary Roy, O.S.F., 2189
McDonnell, Thomas P., 2190-2191
MacDougall, Allan Ross, 2336
McGaughran, Sister Ruth Marie, S.C.N., 2192
MacGillivray, Arthur, S.J., 2193-2194
McGowan, Madelon, 2195
McGuire, D. P., 2196
McH., R., 2197
Mack, Maynard, 2198-2199
Mackail, John William, 570-571
McKay, George Leslie, 572
Mackay, H. F. B., 278
McKay (Lucia Caroline Romberg Hart), 1823

MacKenzie, Faith Compton, 573
McKenzie, Gordon, 2200
McKenzie, Gordon, ed., 777
MacKenzie, Norman H., 2201-2206
MacKenzie, Norman H., ed., 62-63
MacKenzie, Norman H., ed., review of, 1177, 1750, 2122, 2173, 2518
McKinney, John F., 65 2207
Mackinnon, Alan Murray, 574
Mackworth, Cecily, 2208
McLaughlin, John, S.J., 2209-2210
McLuhan, Herbert Marshall, 2211-2214
MacLeod, J. G., S.J., ed., 7-8
MacManus, Francis, 2215-2218
McNamara, Peter L., 2219-2220
McNamee, Maurice B., S.J., 2221-2222
MacNeice, Louis, 575, 2223-2227
MacNeil, Stella Therese, 2228
McQueen, William A., 2229
Macqueen-Pope, W., 576
Macri, Clare Grace, 2230
MacS., J., 2231
Madeleva, Sister Mary, C.S.C., 2232-2234
Madge, Charles, 2235
Magdalen College, Oxford, 577
Magnus, Laurie, 577
Magny, Olivier de, 2236
Maguire, Alice Marie, 2237
Mais, Stuart Petre Brodie, 2238
Mallarme, Stephane, 1245, 2208

Mallock, William Hurrell, 578
Malloy, Margaret Gladys, 2240
Mambrino, Jean, 2241
Mambrino, Jean, trans., 42
Man, Isle of, 809
Manchester, England, 468, 708, 724-725
Mandelbaum, Allen, 2242
Mangan, Francis Joseph, S.J., 579
Mann, John S., 2243
Manning, Henry Edward, Cardinal, 580-581
Mansfield, Margery, 2244
Manuscripts of Hopkins, 1059, 2206, 2245, 2655
Marchant, James, 2246
Marcotte, Paul John, 2247-2248
Margoliouth, Herschel Maurice, 2249
Margrie, William, 582
Mariani, Paul Louis, 2250
Marie, Sister Joseph, I.H.M., see McCrossan, Sister Joseph Marie, I. H. M.
Mariology, 3222
Maritain, Jacques, 2251-2253
Markert, Marilyn Rose, 2254
Markby, A. Wilkinson, ed., 584
Marryat, Phillip, 2255
Marsden, M., 2256
Marsh, Derick, 2257
Martin, Philip Montague, 2259
Martin, Philip Montague, review of, 2013, 2258
Martin, Robert Grant, 2908
Martindale, Cyril Charles, S.J., 585-586

Martz, Louis Lohr, 2260
Marx, Carola Maxine, 2261
Masefield, John, 587
Mason, Colin, 2262
Mason, Frederick B., 588
Masson, David I., 2263-2266
Matchett, William H., 2267
Mateaux, Clara L., 589
Mather, Mary, 1525
Mathew, David, 2268-2269
Mathison, John K., 2270-2271
Matthai, A. P., 2272
Matthews, William R., 122
Matthiessen, Francis Otto, 2273
Maude, Mother Mary, C.S.M., 2274-2275
Mauriac, Claude, 2276
Mauriac, Francois, 2277-2278
Maxwell, Anna, 590
Maxwell, J. C., 2279
Maxwell-Scott, Mary Monica, 591
Mayhead, Robin, 2280
Maynard, Theodore, 2281-2287
Mazza, Sister Maria Serafina, S.C., 2288
Meagher, Edward F., 2289
Meagher, Margaret C., 2290-2295
Measure: Journal of the Gerard Manley Hopkins Poetry Society, 2296
Meath, Gerard, O.P., 2297-2301
Meditation, 2875
Mee, Arthur, 592
Meehan, Francis Joseph Gallagher, 2303
Megroz, Rodolphe Louis, 2304
Megroz, Rodolphe Louis, comp., review of, 3274

Melchiori, Giorgio, 2305-2308, 2310, 2312

Melchiori, Giorgio, review of, 2309, 2311, 2623

Melchner, Sister Mary Roberta, S.S.N.D., 2313

Mellers, Wilfrid, 2314

Mellown, Elgin W., 2315-2317

Melody, Sister M. Winifred, O.S.U., 2318

Melville, Herman, 2942

Mendel, Sydney, 2319

Menon, V. K. Narayana, review of, 2130

Mercer, W. C., 2320

Merchant Taylors' School, 593

Merchant, W. Moelwyn, 2321

Meredith, George, 1915

Merton, Thomas, 927, 972, 2228, 2322-2323

Mesterton, Erik, 2324

Metaphor, 1072, 1098, 1100, 1145, 1860, 2242, 2851, 2936

Metaphysical Poets, 3213

Metaphysics, 1271

Meter, 1918, 2679, 2946, 3042-3043, 3250

Methuen, Algernon, comp., 2325

Meuth, Georgeanna S., 2326

Meyer, Gerard Previn, 2327

Meyerstein, Edward Harry William, 2328

Meynell, Alice Christiana (Thompson), 594, 3172

Meynell, Wilfrid, 595

Meyrick, Frederick, 596

Michelangelo, 249, 3294

Micklewright, F. H. Amphlett, 2329-2331

Middleton, John Henry, 597-598

Middleton, Robert Dudley, 599

Miles, Alfred Henry, ed., 1120, 2332

Miles, Josephine, 2333-2335

Miles, Josephine, ed., 777

Milford, Sir Humphrey, 400

Mill, John Stuart, 600

Millais, Sir John Everett, 601

Millais, John Guille, 601

Millay, Edna St. Vincent, 2336, 2868

Miller, A. J., S.J., 2337

Miller, Betty, 2338

Miller, Bruce E., 2339

Miller, Joseph Hillis, 2341, 2343-2344, 2346-2347

Miller, Joseph Hillis, review of, 1334, 1339, 2140, 2319, 2342, 2345, 2473, 2530, 2865, 2997, 3214, 3229

Miller, Nancy Lou, 2348

Millspaugh, Clarence Arthur, 2349

Milton, John, 27, 213-217, 602, 842, 1520, 1586, 1709, 1778, 1850, 1868, 2489, 3231

Milton's "Lycidas," 1586

Milward, Peter, S.J., 2350-2352

Mims, Edwin, 2353

Minchin, Humphrey Cotton, 603

Minerof, Arthur F., 2354

Minot, Laurence, 606

Minten, Sister Grace Ellen, O.P., 2357

Mitchell, Donald, 2358

Noon, William T., S.J.,
review of, 2421, 2837
Noonan, James Joseph, 2440
Norris, Carolyn Brimley, 2441-
2443
Norfolk, Duke of, 627
North, Jessica N., 2444
Northcote, J. Spencer, 631
Northrup, Eileen, 2445
Novelli, Gino, 2446
Nowell Smith, Charles, see
Smith, Charles Nowell
Nowell-Smith, Simon, 2447-
2449
Nowell-Smith, Simon, ed.,
1437
Nowottny, Winifred, 2450
Noyce, Wilfred, comp.,
review of, 2407
Noyes, Alfred, 632, 2451
Noyes, Hugh, 633
Nute, Grace Lee, 634
Nye, Robert, 2452-2456

Obituary, 1553, 2457
O'Brien, A. P., 2458
O'Brien, Justin, 2459-2460
O'Brien, Kate, 2461
O'Brien, Robert David, S.J.,
2462-2463
Obscurity, 2477, 2991
Ochshorn, Myron Gustav,
2464-2465
O'Connor, Flannery, 1471
O'Connor, Sister M. Elizabeth
Therese, R.S.M., 2466
O'Connor, William Van, 2467,
3113
O'Dea, Richard J., 2468
O'Donnell, Margaret J., 2469
O Farachain, Roibeard, see
Farren, Robert

Ogden, Charles Kay, 2470
Ogilvie, John, 636-637
Ogilvie, Vivian, 638
O'Gorman, Ned, 2471
O'Hagan, John, trans., 794
Oldfield, Sybil, 2473
Oliphant, Margaret (Wilson),
640
Oliver, Edward James, 641
Olivero, Federico, 2474
Olney, James Leslie, 2475
O'London, John, 2476
Olson, Signe, 2477
O'Meara, Kathleen, 642
Omond, Thomas Stewart, 643,
2478
O'Neill, George, S.J., 2479-
2480
O'Neill, George, S.J., review
of, 2231
Onesta, P. A., 2481
Ong, Walter J., S.J., 2482-
2488
Onomatopoeia, 2175
Oppel, Horst, ed., 2398
Oras, Ants, 2489
Oratory, Birmingham, 854
Oratory, London, 704
Oratory, London, Church of,
538
Orchardson, William Quiller,
127
Oriel College, Oxford, 618
Originality, 2825, 3040
Orion, 2343
O'Riordan, Michael, 645
Ornsby, Robert, 482
Orr, Paul Anthony, 2490-2491
Orwell, George, see Blair,
Eric Arthur
Osborne, Charles, 3275
O'Shannon, Cathal, 2493

Otis, William Bradley, ed., 646

Ottilia, Sister, S.C.C., see Dohmann, Sister Ottilia, S.C.C.

Ouseley, Frederick Arthur Gore, 647

Owen, B. Evan, 2494-2497

Owen, Wilfred, 3178, 3217

Oxford City Council, 648

Oxford Libraries, 427

Oxford Movement, 325, 618

Oxford Tribute to Hopkins, 1432

Oxford Union, 610

Oxford University, 137, 324, 413, 458, 514-515, 558, 574, 586, 596, 599, 623, 648-649, 731, 735, 743, 761, 772, 781-782, 855, 2099, 2498-2499

Oxfordshire, England, 372, 592, 650, 808

Pace, George B., 2500

Paeonic Measures, 1679

Page, Frederick, 651, 2502

Page, Frederick, review of, 3044

Page, Frederick, ed., review of, 1255

Pagenstecher, G., 415, 652

Painting, 1215, 1224

Paley, F. A., ed., 115

Palgrave, Francis Turner, comp., 2503-2504

Palmer, Herbert, 2505

Panhuysen, Jos., 2506

Pantasaph Monastery, Holywell, Wales, 653

Paravicini, Frances de, 654

Park, A. J., 819

Park, B. A., 2507-2508

Parker, Dorothy Elizabeth Hagman, 2509

Parker, John Henry, 655

Parker, Mary, 2510

Parkhurst, C. A., 656

Parnassianism, 3081

Parnassus, 3148, 3174

Parrott, Thomas M., 2511

Parry, Thomas, 657

Parsons, Ian Macnaghten, ed., 2512

Pater, Walter, 156, 312, 658-664, 837, 896, 1460-1461, 2445, 2609, 3061

Paterson, Daniel, 665

Patmore, Coventry Kersey Dighton, 10-13, 289, 419-420, 641, 651, 666-695, 1111, 1325, 1629, 1705, 1711, 1909, 2055, 2119, 2183, 2271, 2514, 2558, 2788, 2954, 2965, 2988, 3044, 3068, 3172, 3285

Patmore, Coventry Kersey Dighton, review of, 1437

Patmore, Derek, 693-695, 2514

Patmore, Derek, review of, 1258, 2119, 2657, 2788

Paton, James, 432

Patricia, Sister Mary, C.S.J., 2515

Patterns, 1070, 2088, 2147, 2265-2266, 2534, 2803, 2900

Patterson, Jean Kenny, 2516

Paye, Sister Mary Paul, R.S.M., 2517

Payne, Mervyn, 2518

Payne, Michael, 2519

Peach, William W., 2520

Pears, David, ed., review of, 3066

Pearson, Norman Holmes,
2521-2522
Pearson, W. H., 2523-2524
Peasant Poetry, 3114
Peel, John Hugh Brignall, 2525
Pendergrass, Paula Belcher,
2526
Pendexter, Hugh, 2527
Pepler, Conrad, 2528
Pepper, Stephen Coburn, 2529
Perkins, Robert L., 2530
Perrine, Laurence, 2531
Perry, John Oliver, 2532
Peschmann, Hermann, 2533-
2535
Pessimism, 1035
Peters, Wilhelmus Antonius
Maria, S.J., 2536-2541,
2544, 2546
Peters, Wilhelmus Antonius
Maria, S.J., review of, 1040,
1106, 1201, 1257, 1297,
1411, 1558, 1589, 1760,
1803, 1957, 1987, 2069,
2179, 2381, 2404, 2542-
2543, 2545, 2550, 2577,
2594, 2599, 2671, 2980,
3020-3022, 3076, 3092,
3117
Petre, William, 701-702
Peyre, Henri, 703, 2547
Paul, Charles Kegan, 696
Payne, James, 697
Pearl, Cyril,°698
Perrin, Noel, 700
Phare, Elsie Elizabeth, 2548-
2551, 2556
Phare, Elsie Elizabeth, review
of, 962, 1162, 1259, 1274,
1408, 1464, 1547, 2168,
2295, 2552-2555, 2627,
2737, 2972, 3044, 3150,
3265

Philip Neri, Saint, 704
Phillips, Claude, 705
Phillips, Marjorie, 2557
Phillipson, Dom Wulstan,
O.S.B., 706, 2558-2567
Philomathic Society, 2568
Phonodiscs, 48, 65-66, 69,
1784
Piatier, Jacqueline, 2569
Pick, John, 2570-2586, 2590-
2609
Pick, John, ed., 18-20
Pick, John, review of, 906,
957, 973, 1036, 1196, 1206,
1296, 1412, 1492-1493, 1561,
1625, 1690, 1812, 1904,
2012, 2015, 2076, 2130,
2138, 2165, 2193, 2293,
2561, 2587-2589, 2880,
2960, 2966, 3086, 3097,
3193, 3196, 3243
Pick, John, ed., review of,
1107, 1261, 1530, 1532,
1559, 1581, 1597, 1650,
1718, 1734, 1777, 1808,
1837-1838, 2066, 2193,
2213-2214, 2301, 2363,
2535, 2571, 2610-2613,
2648, 2695, 2697, 2711,
2724, 2821, 2898, 2917,
2950, 2962, 3033, 3124,
3261
Pickman, Hester, 2614
Picton, James Allanson, 709
Pietrikiewicz, Jerzy, 2615
Piety, 2015
Pilate Pontius, 390
Pinto, Vivian de Sola, 2616-
2620
Pinto, Vivian de Sola, review
of, 3241
Piontek, Heinz, 2621
Pirie, Peter J., 2622

Prasad, Shreekrishna, 2640
Prayer, 1947
Praz, Mario, 2641
Prenderville, Brendan, 2642
Press, John, 2643-2645
Preston, Joseph Harold, 721
Preyer, Robert O., ed., 1241
Prezado, Sant'lago, review of, 2888
Price, Fanny, 2646
Price, J. B., 722
Price, R. G. G., 2647
Pridie, F. M., 2648
Proctor, Richard Wright, 724
Prometheus Myth, 1945
Prosen, Anthony J., S.J., 2650
Prosody, 926, 1340, 1602, 1765, 1892, 2026, 2171, 2183, 2954, 3246
Prudence, 3144
Pryce-Jones, Alan, 2651-2652
Przywara, Sister Benice, 2653
Psychic Life, 2640
Pugin, Augustus Welby Northmore, 726
Purcell, Henry, 226, 2992, 3185, 3187
Purcell, J. M., 2654
Purcell, William, 727
Purser, John Thibaut, ed., 1151
Pusey, Edward Bouverie, 557, 728-729, 758
Putnam, Sam, 2656
Putt, Samuel Gorley, 730
Pycroft, James, 731
Pythian, John Ernest, 708

Quennell, Charles Henry Bourne, 732
Quennell, Marjorie (Courtney), 732

Quennell, Peter, 733, 2657
Quennell, Peter, review of, 1255
Quiller-Couch, Sir Arthur, 281
Quiller-Couch, Sir Arthur, ed., 2658-2659
Quinn, Kerker, 2660, 3174
Quintana, Ricardo, ed., 2661
Quirk, Charles J., S.J., 2662

R. B. H., 2663
R. B. O'B., 2664
R. G., 2665
R. H., see Halsband, Robert
R. J. L., 2666
Rader, Louis, 2667-2669
Raine, Kathleen, 2670-2671
Ralegh, Sir Walter, 2943
Raleigh, Lucie Gertrude (Jackson), 734
Raleigh, Sir Walter Alexander, 734
Rambler (periodical), 726
Ramsay, Grace (pseud.), see O'Meara, Kathleen
Randall, Richard William, 278
Ransom, John Crowe, 2672
Ransom, John Crowe, review of, 1254
Rathmell, J. C. A., 2324, 2673
Ratliff, John D., 2674
Ray, Randolph, 2675
Raymond, William O., 2676
Read, Herbert, 1526, 2677-2689, 2691-2692, 2993
Read, Herbert, review of, 2534, 2690
Reality, view of, 2115
Recordings of poems of Hopkins, 48, 65-66, 69, 1784
Recordings, review of, 1401, 1846

St. Peter's Church, Dorchester, England, 584
St. Peter's Parish Church, Bournemouth, England, 132
St. Stanislaus' College, Beaumont, Windsor, England, 148
St. Thomas's Church, Canterbury, England, 764
St. Virginia, Sister Mary, B.V.M., 2789
St. Winefride's Church, St. Asaph, Wales, 569
Saintsbury, George Edward Bateman, 765-769, 2790-2791
Sala, George Augustus Henry, 770
Sale, William M., 2792
Salford Diocese, England, 771
Salter, Herbert Edward, 772
Sambrook, James, 2793
Sambrook, James, review of, 1267
Sampson, George, 2794
Sanders, Gerald DeWitt, 2795
Sansom, Clive, 773, 2796
Sapir, Edward, 2797
Sargent, Daniel, 2798-2801
Sargent, Daniel, review of, 3139
Sarma, G. V. L. N., 2802
Savant, John J., 2803
Sayce, Archibald Henry, 774
Sayre, Woodrow Wilson, 2407
Scape, 2248
Scarfe, Francis, 775, 2804
Schappes, Morris U., 2805
Schaumberg, Hans-Hubert, 2806
Scheetz, Sister M. Johannina, 2807
Scherer, Edmond Henri

Adolphe, 776
Scheve, Brother Adelbert, F.S.C., 2808
Schimanski, Stefan, ed., review of, 3145
Schlauch, Margaret, 2809
Schlegel, Desmond, O.S.B., 2810
Schmidt, Kenneth J., 2811
Schmitt, Franz, 604
Schneider, Elizabeth Wintersteen, 2812-2819
Schneider, Isidor, 2820
Schoder, Raymond V., S.J., 2821-2824
Schoeck, R. J., 2825-2826
Schoffler, Heinz, 2827
Schonauer, Franz, 2828
Schorer, Mark, 2829
Schorer, Mark, ed., 777
Schreiber, Annette Claire, 2830
Schrickx, Wim, 2831
Schulze, F. W., 2832
Schwartz, Delmore, 2833
Schwartz, Joseph Michael, 2834
Scott, Arthur Finlay, 2835
Scott, Dixon, 778
Scott, James Robert Hope, see Hope-Scott, James Robert
Scott, Michael M., S.J., 2836
Scott, Nathan A., Jr., 2837
Scott, R. A., review of, 2785
Scott, Rebecca Kathryn, 2838
Scott, W. T., 2839
Scott-James, Rolfe Arnold, 2840
Scott-Moncrieff, George, 2841
Scotus, Duns, 366, 923, 926, 1085, 1090, 1276, 1306, 1391, 1419, 1421, 1582,

1584, 1655, 1673, 1954, 2138, 2428, 2537
Scrope, Simon Thomas, 779
Scully, James, ed., 2842
Sebeok, Thomas A., ed., 1962
Seddon, Richard, 2843
Seelhammer, Ruth, 2844
Sehrt, Ernst Th., 2848
Self, 2340, 2361, 2481, 3078
Selion, 605
Sephton, John, 780
Seraphim, Sister Mary, O.S.F., 2846
Sergeant, Howard, 2847-2849
Sermons, 28, 38, 81-89, 2417, 2441-2443, 2890
Sewell, Brocard, O., Carm., 2850
Sewell, Elizabeth, 2851-2852
Seymour-Smith, Martin, 2853
Shadow-beams, 90
Shakespeare, 95-96, 209, 225, 438, 1811, 2059, 2351-2352
Shanks, Edward, 2854
Shannon, Sheila, comp., review of, 3215
Shapcott, Thomas W., 1250
Shapiro, Karl, 2855-2856
Shapiro, J. J., review of, 2891
Sharpe, Garold, 2857
Sharples, Sister Marian, I.H.M., 2858-2859
Sharrock, Roger, 2860
Shattuck, Charles, ed., 3174
Shaw, Brother William, S.J., 785
Shaw, James Gerard, 2861-2863
Shaw, Martin, 2864
Shaw, Priscilla W., 2865
Shea, Dennis Donald David, 2866
Shea, F. X., S.J., 2867
Sheean, Vincent, 2868

Sheed, Francis Joseph, comp., 2869
Sheffield, England, 616-617
Sherwood, H. C., 2870
Sherwood, William Edward, 781
Shewring, Walter, 2871-2872
Shields, Brother Daniel, S.J., 291
Shields, John, 2873
Shipley, Orby, ed., 2874
Shipwrecks, 445
Shkolnick, Sylvia, 2875
Shotover Papers, 782
Shuster, George Newman, 69, 2876-2884
Sichel, Edith, 334
Sidgwick, A., ed., 114
Sidney Psalter, 2673
Sieveking, Lancelot de Giberne, 2882
Significance of Christ, 1549
Silkin, Jon, 2885
Silverstein, Henry, 2886-2887
Simeon the Stileite, 92
Simoes, Joao Gaspar, 2888
Simons, John W., 2889-2890
Simpson, Richard, 783
Sinclair, John, 2891
Sino-British Club, 2170
Sitwell, Edith, 171, 2892-2894
Sitwell, Edith, ed., 2895
Sitwell, Edith, review of, 3290
Sitwell, Sacheverell, review of, 3098
Skelton, Robin, 784
Slater, John, 2896
Slattery, James J., 2897
Slevin, Gerard, 2898
Slocombe, George, 2899
Small, Christopher, 2900
Smalley, T., S.J., 785, 2901

264

Smidthus, Karlheinz, 1886
Smith, Arthur Lionel, 786
Smith, B. Webster, 889
Smith, Charles Nowell, 789, 2904
Smith (Elizabeth Rothenstein), 2764-2765
Smith, Grover, 2902
Smith, Helen, 2903
Smith, Horace, 787
Smith, J. C., 1739-1740
Smith, James, 787
Smith, Logan Pearsall, 788
Smith, R. L., 2905
Smith, Simon Nowell, see Nowell-Smith, Simon
Smith, William, ed., 790
Smullen, George J., 2906
Smyth, Herbert Weir, 791
Snavely, Robert Carl, 2907
Snow, Royall, 2956-2957
Snyder, Franklin Bliss, 2908
Society for Pure English, 792
Society of Jesus, 302, 307, 406, 476, 544, 583, 612-614, 1209, 1357-1358, 1698
Society of Friends, 568
Soderberg, Lasse, 2909
Song of Roland, 794
Sonnet form, 2254, 2906
Sonnet tradition, 2750
Sonnets, curtal, 2624
Sonnets, dark, 2526, 2667-2668
Sonnets of desolation, 1435
Sonnets, terrible, 1405, 1509, 1586, 1676, 2092, 2220, 2637-2638, 2722, 3082, 3132
Sonstroem, David, 2910
Sophocles, 795-797
Sotheby and Company, 798
Southwell's (Robert) hawk, 1505
Southworth, James Granville, 2911
Southworth, James Granville, review of, 1968
Spanos, William V., 2912
Spark, Muriel, 2913
Spark, Muriel, ed., 628
Spark, Muriel, review of, 1371
Sparrow, John Hanbury Angus, 799, 2914
Sparshott, F. E., 2915
Speaight, Robert, 66, 2916-2917
Spehar, Elizabeth Marie, 2918
Spellanzon, Giannina, 2919-2920
Spencer, Theodore, 2921
Spender, Stephen, 800-801, 2922-2927
Spenser, Edmund, 1763, 2489
Speyrer, Anna Elizabeth, 2928
Spheres (periodical), 2929
Spinkhill, England, 617
Spira, Theodor, 2397, 2930
Spiritual Life, 944-945
Spirituality, 2378
Sprigg, Christopher St. John, 803
Sprung Rhythm, 1005, 1680, 2483, 2485, 2488, 2817, 3218
Squier, Charles, 1018
Squire, John Collings, 804, 2931
Srinivasa Iyengar, Kodaganallur Ranaswami, 2932-2933
Srinivasa Iyengar, Kodaganallur Ranaswami, review of, 1041, 1297, 1637, 2403, 2579
Stadlen, Peter, 2934
Stageberg, Norman C., 2935
Stallknecht, Newton P., 2936
Stallman, Robert Wooster,

2937
Stallman, Robert Wooster, ed.,
1658
Stanek, Rose Marie, 2938
Stanford, C. V., 197
Stanford, Derek, 805-806,
2939-2943
Stanford, Derek, ed., 628
Stanford, Derek, review of,
3024
Stanford, William Bedell,
2944-2945
Stanier, R. S., 2946
Stanley, Arthur Penrhyn, 807
Stanzel, Franz, 2947
Stapleton, Mary Helen Alicia
(Dolman), 808
Stauffer, Donald A., 2949
Stauffer, Robert A., 2950
Stein, Karen F., 2951
Steiner, George, ed., 2952
Stempel, Daniel, 2953
Stenning, Ernest Henry, 809
Stenten, Cathryn David, 2954
Stenzel, H., S.J., 2955
Stephens, James, 2956-2957
Stephenson, A. A., S.J.,
2958-2959
Sterne, Laurence, 810-811
Sternfeld, Frederick W., 2961
Steuart, Robert Henry Joseph,
S.J., 812
Steuert, Dom Hilary, 2962
Stevens, Sister Mary Dominic,
O.P., 2963
Stevenson, Joseph, S.J., 715
Stillinger, Jack, 2964
Stobie, Margaret R., 2965
Stone, William Johnson, 217
Stonier, George Walter, 2966-
2973
Stonyhurst College, 411, 424,
473, 813-818

Storey, Graham, 2974-2976
Storey, Graham, ed., 23, 33
Storey, Graham, ed., review
of, 910, 1177, 2122, 2182
Storm, Melvin G., 2977
Strachan-Davidson, James
Leigh, 570
Strachey, Lytton, 2785
Strassmaier, John, S.J., 714
Strecto, James, 2978
Stress, 2173, 2711
Stroud Festival, 2979, 3171
Structure of poetry, 1799,
1876, 2243, 2432, 2458,
2466
Stuart, Charles Douglas, 819
Sturgeon, Mary C., 820
Stutterheim, Cornelius
Ferdinand Petrus, 2980
Style, 2114, 2716, 3151
Suffering, 2650
Sunsets, 71, 90
Superiors, 3012
Supernatural, the, 2221, 2440
Surtz, Edward L., 2981
Sussex, England, 293
Sutcliffe, Edmund Felix, 2982
Sutherland, Donald, 2983
Swallow, Alan, ed., 2984
Swanton, Ernest William
Brockton, ed., 821
Sweeney, John L., 1475
Sweeney, Maxwell, 2985
Sylvester, Howard E., 2986
Symbolism, 1146, 1245, 1286,
1539
Symes, Gordon, 2987
Symonds, John Addington, 822
Symonds, Julian, 2988
Syntax, 976, 1146
Szlosek, J. F., 2989

Warren, Austin, 3156-3158, 3179
Warren, Henry C., 3159
Warren, Herbert, 577
Warren, Robert Penn, 1150
Warren, Robert Penn, ed., 1151
Warren, Thomas Herbert, 871
Warwick Castle, 872
Washington, E. S., 560
Wasmuth, Ewald, 3161
Water, Charlotte Van de, 3162
Waterhouse, John F., 3163
Waters, J. Kevin, S.J., 3164
Watkin, Dom Aelred, 873
Watson, George, ed., 1639, 3165-3166
Watson, Thomas L, 3167
Watson, Youree, S.J., 3168
Wayman, Dorothy G., 3169
Weale, William Henry James, 874
Weatherhead, A. Kingsley, 3170
Weaver, J. R. H., 370
Webster, E. M., 3171
Wecker, John Clement, 3172
Weiss, Theodore, 79-80, 3173-3175
Weiss, Theodore, review of, 1816, 2337, 2390, 2605
Welby, Thomas Earle, 3176
Welch, Sister M. Charlotte, O.S.B., 3177
Weld, Alfred, S.J., 875
Weld, Charles, 418
Welland, D. S. R., 3178
Wellek, Rene, 3179
Wellesz, Egon, 2314, 3180-3181
Wells, Henry W., 1247
Wells, Henry W., 3182
Wells, England, 365

Welsh Alliteration, 2516
Welsh bardic meters, 3062
Welsh influence, 1742, 2133
Welsh language, 3010
Welsh literature, 657
Welsh poetry, 150, 886
Welsh prosody, 1084, 1377, 1681, 1982
West, Edward J., 3183
West Croydon, England, 345
Westerlinck, Albert, 3184
Westminster, England, 399, 877
Westminster Cathedral, Westminster, England, 876
Westrup, Jack Allan, 878, 3185-3187
Westwater, Sister Agnes Martha, S.C.H., 3188
Weyand, Norman, S.J., 3189-3200
Weyand, Norman, S.J., ed., 1079, 1104, 1185, 1209, 1485, 2194, 2221, 2439, 2488, 2822, 2824, 3168
Weyand, Norman, S. J., ed., review of, 1038, 1041, 1057, 1152, 1239, 1251, 1255, 1297, 1399-1400, 1426, 1512, 1541, 1620, 1634, 1696, 1715, 1762, 1807, 1847, 1857, 1953, 2039, 2069, 2087, 2197, 2217, 2429, 2528, 2594, 2599, 2754, 2768, 2839, 2863, 2879, 2925, 3022, 3201-3205, 3279
Weygandt, Cornelius, 3206
Whalley, England, 880
Whalley Abbey, 866
Whalley, George, 3207
Wheeler, Charles B., 3208
Wheelwright, Philip, 579
Wheelwright, Philip, review of,

3270
Wooldridge, H. Ellis, 271-273
Wooton, Carl, 3271
Wordsworth, Andrew, 3272
Wordsworth, William, 1832-
1833, 2505, 3273
Wordsworth Society, 541
Worsley, T. C., 3275
Wright, Austin, ed., 3157
Wright, Brooks, 3277
Wright, David, 3278
Wright, Elizabeth Cox, 893
Wright, Elizabeth Mary (Lea),
894
Wright, J. B., 3279
Wright, Joseph, 894
Wright, Thomas (1810-1877),
895
Wright, Thomas (1859-1936),
896
Wyatt, E. V. R., 3280
Wyatt, Thomas, 986
Wyatt-Edgell, Alfred, 897
Wydenbruck, Nora, review of,
1255
Wyndham-Lewis, D. B., see
Lewis, Dominic Bevan
Wyndham

Yates, Edmund Hodgson, 898

Yattendon Hymnal, 247, 262,
265-273
Yeats, William Butler, 986,
1222, 1512-1513, 1534,
1852, 1938, 2130, 2947,
3205-3206
Yeats, William Butler, ed.,
3282
Yetts, Walter Percival, 3283
Yetzer, Bernard Edward, 3284
Yoggerst, Sister M. Hilary,
3285
York, England, 880
Young, B. A., 3286-3287
Young, Francis Brett, 899
Young, George Malcolm, 3288-
3291
Young, Kenneth, 3292-3293
Young, Lillian, 3294

Zabel, Morton Dauwen, 3295-
3297
Zabel, Morton Dauwen, ed.,
963
Zabel, Morton Dauwen, review
of, 1331
Zamboni, Armando, 3298-3300
Zelocchi, Rosanna, 3301
Zulueta, Francis M. de, S.J.,
650, 900-901

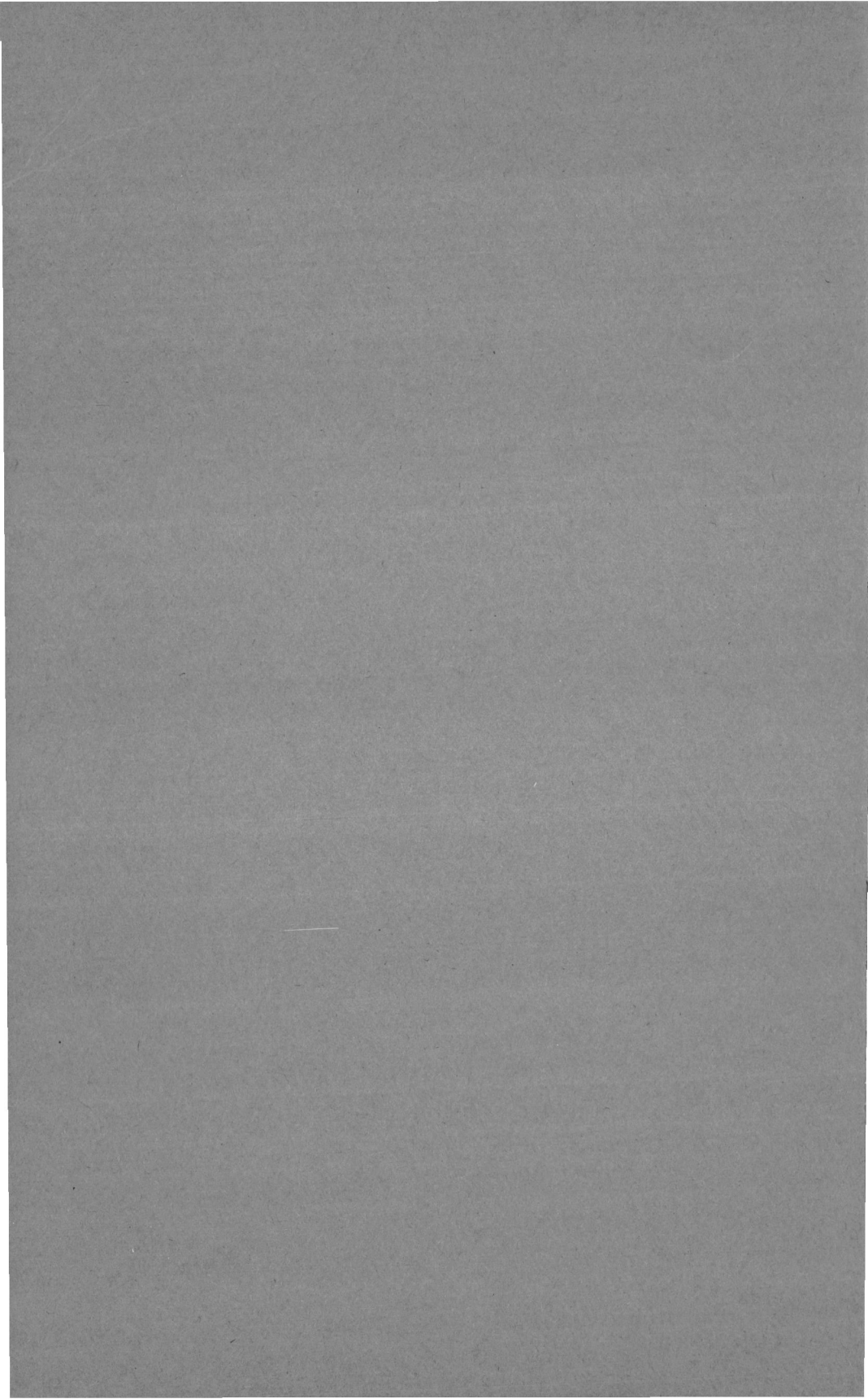